CAPITAL PUNISHMENT

Capital Punishment

A Hazard to a Sustainable Criminal Justice System?

Edited by

LILL SCHERDIN

University of Oslo, Norway

Routledge

Taylor & Francis Group

LONDON AND NEW YORK

First published 2014 by Ashgate Publishing

2 Park Square, Milton Park, Abingdon, Oxfordshire OX14 4RN
52 Vanderbilt Avenue, New York, NY 10017

Routledge is an imprint of the Taylor & Francis Group, an informa business

First issued in paperback 2020

British Library Cataloguing in Publication Data
A catalogue record for this book is available from the British Library

The Library of Congress has cataloged the printed edition as follows:
Scherdin, Lill.
Capital punishment : a hazard to a sustainable criminal justice system? / By Lill Scherdin
Ashgate.
pages cm
Includes bibliographical references and index.
ISBN 978-1-4094-5719-0 (hardback) 1. Capital punishment. I. Title.
K5104.S36 2014
364.66—dc23
2013033623

ISBN 978-1-4094-5719-0 (hbk)
ISBN 978-0-367-60083-9 (pbk)

Contents

List of Figures and Tables

Figures

Tables

List of Contributors

Mohammed Ayatt is currently Special Advisor to the Prosecutor of the International Criminal Court (ICC) on cooperation with the MENA Region (Middle East North Africa); Director of the Research Centre on International Criminal Justice based at Mohammed V University Rabat-Souissi School of Law; Full Professor of Law at the same university; member of the Moroccan National Council on Human Rights; and Attorney before the Moroccan Supreme Court, Rabat Bar Association. Mohammed Ayatt has also served in the United Nations for over 14 years, notably as senior legal advisor to the prosecutor of the International Criminal Tribunal for Rwanda, who is also Under Secretary General of the United Nations; he was his personal representative to the Rwandan Government and the diplomatic community accredited in Rwanda (1997–2012). He was elected member of the United Nations Human Rights Committee in 2008. He has twice held Fullbright scholarships at Rutgers University, USA, and before that held a fellowship as professor and legal researcher at Max Planck Institute, Freiburg, Germany. He is the author of several books, and of articles published in national and international specialist journals. The author is interested in international criminal justice, human rights, criminology and criminal law.

Sangmin Bae is Associate Professor in the Department of Political Science at Northeastern Illinois University (Chicago, IL). She was a visiting research scholar at the University of Tokyo's Human Security Program and at the Japan Institute of International Affairs (JIIA) in 2010. She teaches and does research in the areas of human rights, human security, the politics of capital punishment, international organizations, and East Asian politics. She is the author of *When the State No Longer Kills: International Human Rights Norms and Abolition of Capital Punishment* (SUNY Press, 2007). In this book she deals with the role of political leadership and domestic political institutions in explaining why countries respond differently to the international human rights norm that prohibits capital punishment. Now holding an Abe Fellowship awarded by the Social Science Research Council (SSRC) and the Japan Foundation Center for Global Partnership (CGP), she is currently working on a book project that explores the role and capacity of the state in handling critical human security issues. Seeking to 'bring the state back in', this book asks why sovereign states take on leadership roles to promote human security and implement it in concrete policies. In so doing, the book addresses state behaviour, preferences, and performance in the area of human security. Her work has appeared in various journals, including *Comparative Politics*, *International Journal of Human Rights*, *Asian Affairs*, *Pacific Affairs*,

International Politics, *Human Rights Review*, and *Zeitschrift Für Menschenrechte* (Journal for Human Rights).

Børge Bakken is Associate Professor at the Department of Sociology, Hong Kong University where he has also served as the director of the Master of Social Sciences programme in Criminology for more than four years. Dr Bakken has worked and lived in China and Hong Kong for nearly 15 years, and he has also worked at the Australian National University, Harvard University, Ludwig Maximilian University, Munich, Beijing University, and the Universities of Oslo and Copenhagen. He has written extensively on deviance, and crime and punishment in the People's Republic of China. Among his books are *The Exemplary Society. Human Improvement, Social Control and the Dangers of Modernity in China* (Oxford University Press, 2000), and *Crime, Policing and Punishment in China* (Rowman & Littlefield, 2007). He is currently working on a book with the working title *Crime and Control in the People's Republic of China* for Polity Press. He gave the 71st George E. Morrison Lecture at the Australian National University, Canberra, and the present article on the death penalty in China is based on that lecture.

Bikramjeet Batra is a policy adviser at Amnesty International. He is particularly interested in issues of criminal justice and human rights and is currently completing a monograph on the death penalty in India as a New India Foundation fellow. He studied law at the Universities of Pune and Warwick and previously worked as a lawyer–researcher in New Delhi.

John D. Bessler, twice a Minnesota Book Award finalist, is a law professor who has taught at the University of Minnesota Law School, The George Washington University Law School, the Georgetown University Law Center, and the University of Baltimore School of Law. He teaches contracts and civil procedure and has, since 1998, taught a capital punishment seminar. He clerked for US Magistrate Judge Jack Mason in the District of Minnesota, became an associate at the law firm of Faegre & Benson (now Faegre Baker Daniels), and practised law for many years as a partner at Kelly & Berens in Minneapolis, Minnesota. He has written four books on capital punishment, most recently *Cruel and Unusual: The American Death Penalty and the Founders' Eighth Amendment*, published by Northeastern University Press in January 2012. That book received a Silver designation in the 2012 *Independent Publisher* Book Awards in the US History category. Another of his books, *Writing for Life: The Craft of Writing for Everyday Living* (Minneapolis: Bottlecap Books 2007), won an *Independent Publisher* Book Award in the Writing/Publishing category and was a Midwest Book Awards finalist. His first book, *Death in the Dark: Midnight Executions in America* (Boston: Northeastern University Press 1997), also received an Honorable Mention for 'Outstanding Books' from the Gustavus Myers Program for the Study of Bigotry and Human Rights in North America. He has a BA in political science from the

University of Minnesota, a law degree from Indiana University in Bloomington, an MFA from Hamline University, and a master's degree in international human rights law from Oxford University. He is currently an Associate Professor at the University of Baltimore School of Law and an Adjunct Professor at the Georgetown University Law Center.

Nils Christie is Professor Emeritus at the Department of Criminology and Sociology of Law at the University of Oslo. Christie is well known for his longstanding criticism of drug prohibition, industrial society, school systems and prisons. He has written 15 books – most of which have been translated into several languages – and numerous articles. Christie has received honorary doctorates from the University of Copenhagen (Denmark), Stockholm University (Sweden), the University of Sheffield (United Kingdom) and the Academy of the Federal Penal Service (Ryazan Russia). He is a member of the Norwegian Academy of Science and Letters. Christie is a recipient of the Freedom of Expression Prize in Norway, the Sellin-Glueck Award from the American Society of Criminology, and the European Criminology Award from the European Society of Criminology.

David Garland is Arthur T. Vanderbilt Professor of Law and Professor of Sociology at New York University and a visiting professor at Edinburgh University. He graduated from the University of Edinburgh with an LLB and a PhD and from Sheffield University with a postgraduate MA in Criminology. From 1979 until 1997 he taught at the University of Edinburgh's Centre for Law and Society and held visiting positions at Leuven University, UC Berkeley, Princeton, and NYU's Global Law program. He is the author of *Punishment and Welfare* (1985), *Punishment and Modern Society* (1990), and *The Culture of Control* (2001), the founding editor of the journal *Punishment & Society* and the editor of *Mass Imprisonment: Social Causes and Consequences* (2001) and, with Richard Sparks, of *Criminology and Social Theory* (2000). His most recent books are *America's Death Penalty: Between Past and Present* (edited with R. McGowen and M. Meranze, 2010) and *Peculiar Institution: America's Death Penalty in an Age of Abolition* (Harvard, 2010). He is currently writing a short sociological introduction to the welfare state.

Mohammad Habash is a Syrian imam and an Islamic studies PhD. He was an imam in Syria, in Zahraa mosque in Damascus for 30 years, from 1981 to 2011. He was elected Chairman of the Islamic imams foundation in Syria (2004–2009) – there being only one official foundation for imams in Syria. He has written 52 books in the field of Islamic studies. Some of these books are still a part of the official curriculum in Dawa Islamic college in Syria. He has been a teacher of Islamic Fiqh in many Islamic universities, including Damascus University, Dawa College in Damascus, and Osool Aldeen University in Damascus. He is now associate professor of Islamic Fiqh in Abu Dhabi University and the supervisor of many MA and PhD degrees in Syrian and Jordanian universities. He was also a member of the board of trustees of Islam Abad University, Pakistan (2004–09) and a member of the board of trustees of Aljazeera University, Syria (2008–10). He was a member of the Arab Authors Union, Syria in 2009, and Director of the Islamic Studies Center in Damascus 1992–2008.

Vidar Halvorsen is Associate Professor at the Department of Criminology and Sociology of Law, University of Oslo. He has written on philosophy of science, philosophy of criminal law and punishment, and ethical issues in police work, including *Ethics, Force and Violence in Policing* (PhD thesis, 2001).

Roger Hood is Professor Emeritus of Criminology at the University of Oxford and Emeritus Fellow of All Souls College. He graduated in sociology at the London School of Economics, took his PhD at the Law Faculty of the University of Cambridge at the Institute of Criminology, and is a Doctor of Civil Law at the University of Oxford. From 1973 to 2003 he was Director of the Oxford Centre for Criminology. In 1986 he received the Sellin-Glueck Award of the American Society of Criminology for 'Distinguished International Contributions to Criminology'; in 2011 the Cesare Beccaria Medal from the International Society of Social Defence and Humane Criminal Policy; and in 2012 the ESC European Criminology Award 'for a lifetime contribution as a European criminologist'. As consultant to the United Nations, he prepared the Secretary-General's 5th, 6th and 7th Quinquennial reports on capital punishment. Among other works he is the author of *The Death Penalty: a Worldwide Perspective* (1st ed., 1989, 4th ed. with Carolyn Hoyle, 2008). Since retirement he has held visiting professorships at the University of Virginia, Hong Kong University and the City University of Hong Kong. He has published research on the mandatory death penalty in Trinidad and has recently completed a public opinion survey on the mandatory death penalty in Malaysia. He has been appointed CBE and Honorary Queen's Council, made a Fellow of the British Academy, received an Honorary Doctor of Laws from Birmingham and Edinburgh Napier Universities, and is a member of the UK Foreign Secretary's Death Penalty Expert Group.

David T. Johnson is Professor of Sociology at the University of Hawaii and Co-Editor-in-Chief of *Law & Society Review*. His books include *The Japanese Way of Justice: Prosecuting Crime in Japan* (Oxford University Press, 2002), which received awards from the American Sociological Association and the American Society of Criminology, *The Next Frontier: National Development, Political Change, and the Death Penalty in Asia* (Oxford University Press, 2009 with Franklin E. Zimring), and *Koritsu Suru Nihon no Shikei* (Japan's Isolated Death Penalty) (Gendai Jinbunsha, 2012 with Maiko Tagusari).

Fort Fu-Te Liao received his DPhil in Law from Oxford University, and is an associate research professor at the Institute of Law, Academia Sinica, Taiwan. His research interests include human rights law, European law, international law and constitutional law. He also teaches at the College of Law, National Taipei University, Taiwan and on the MA Degree in Human Rights at Soochow University, Taiwan. He has published several books on European human rights law, international human rights law and the national human rights commission.

Jody Lyneé Madeira, an Associate Professor of Law at the Indiana University Maurer School of Law, researches the intersection of law and emotion in criminal law, assisted reproductive technology, reproductive rights, and family law. Madeira's new book, *Killing McVeigh: The Death Penalty and the Myth of Closure*, applies collective memory to criminal prosecution and sentencing, exploring the ways in which victims' families and survivors came to comprehend and cope with the Oklahoma City bombing through membership in community groups as well as through attendance and participation in Timothy McVeigh's prosecution and execution. Additionally, she has investigated the effects of legal proceedings, verdicts, and sentences upon victims' families; the role of empathy in personal injury litigation; and the impact of recent developments in capital victims' services upon the relationship between victims' families and the criminal justice system.

Lill Scherdin is senior researcher at the Department of Criminology and Sociology of Law, University of Oslo. She received her doctorate degree in 2004 for the thesis 'Control Cultures and Ethics Pinpointed' at the Department of Criminology and Sociology of Law, The Faculty of Law, University of Oslo. Her research interests encompass: punishment and social structure, comparative studies of crime and control, human rights and the death penalty, Holocaust and genocide studies, processes of exclusion and criminalization. She has also focused on the study of caste and the position of the Burakumin in Japanese society together with black people in the American South. She was granted a Mombusho (Japanese State Scholarship), and also a Fullbright scholarship, and gave the honorary Fullbright lecture at Sam Houston University, Crime and Justice Center, Huntsville, Texas, USA. She has been a guest researcher at Chuo University, Graduate School of Law in Hachioji (Tokyo), Japan – and at Tulane University in New Orleans, Louisiana, USA. She has been an expert advisor for the Norwegian Ministry of Foreign Affairs in five annual Human Rights Dialogues between Norway and Vietnam (2005–10). She has been the initiator and organizer of a series of conferences and symposiums on punishment and the death penalty. Scherdin sits on the international committee that created the thematic guidelines for the World Congress on the abolition of the death penalty, Madrid, 2013.

Knut Storberget is a Norwegian lawyer and Norwegian Labour Party politician. From 1992 to 2002 he worked as an attorney-at-law, participating in several high-profile cases, including as a defence attorney at the supreme court. At the local level he was a member of Elverum municipal council for the Labour party from 1991 to 1999. He was first elected to the Norwegian Parliament from Hedmark in 2001, and has twice been re-elected. He had previously served as a deputy representative during the terms 1993–97 and 1997–2001. Storberget became Minister of Justice and the Police serving in the second Stoltenberg cabinet from 2005. He resigned as minister on 11 November 2011.

Foreword

Punishment in a Time of National Tragedy

For many, it would perhaps seem natural that the question of death penalty would come to the fore when on 22 July 2011, Norway experienced its worst criminal act since World War II. Norway was the victim of terror that day.

Seventy seven people lost their lives in the atrocities that took place between twenty five past three and half past six that afternoon. A Norwegian man parked a car containing a huge bomb outside the 17-storey government block that houses the Prime Minister's Office and the Ministry of Justice. I was the Minister of Justice at the time. The whole of our building, including my office, was totally destroyed. Eight people lost their lives, four of whom were members of my staff in the Ministry of Justice.

Immediately afterwards the perpetrator of this crime, disguised as a police officer, drove to the island of Utøya, the venue for the Labour Party Youth League's traditional summer camp, where over 600 people were gathered together. Here he shot and killed 69 young people, some as young as 14. He was apprehended and arrested by the police on Utøya, taken into custody, and he was tried the following year in Oslo and convicted.

Prior to the attack, this man published a manifesto via the Internet; this explained the supposed motives for his actions. By and large his arguments are based on an extreme right-wing anti-multiculturalism, anti-Muslim and anti-immigration ideology.

In this man's view, the Labour Party and Government are responsible for a situation in which Norway is being destroyed by the arrival of people with a different nationality and cultural background.

He has caused such huge destruction. Take Bendik, a 17-year-old youth politician. He was so very proud to have got a summer job in my ministry. I met him. He also wanted to be Minister of Justice. I believe he could have achieved his ambition.

He was only going to have two days off last summer. Not to go on holiday with his mother and father, but to take part in the summer camp on Utøya. His mother was so relieved when she understood that Bendik wasn't at work when the explosion destroyed his office. Because Bendik was on Utøya. Just hours later she received the news that he had been shot and brutally killed. On Utøya.

These actions shook a terror-stricken Norway. People all over the country united in their compassion and concern for the victims, their families and their friends. Alongside the great publicity surrounding the victims, the offender and his background, and, of course, our collective ability to prevent and prepare for such actions, Norwegian society now stands closer together than ever before.

I visited Viljar Hansen, a seriously injured 18-year-old, at Ullevål Hospital a few days after the atrocity on Utøya. He had been shot in the head, stomach and arm. He had only just survived. The first words he said to me were: 'There are so many good people out there, Knut'. This was his message. It was a thoughtful Minister of Justice who left the hospital that day.

Since then, I have followed Viljar. Like many others, he believes that feelings of revenge, hatred and retribution would destroy his life. That's just not him. In this, he's a fairly typical victim. We've learnt a huge amount from these young people during the past year.

We've been witness to a fantastic popular mobilization. Thousands of Norwegians have gathered in churches and squares. They have carried roses and taken part in rose processions: For solidarity, for peace, and out of compassion for the victims. On the evening of 22 July, Prime Minister Stoltenberg said that such atrocities could only be met with more democracy and openness; but not naivety.

During the trial 40,000 children and adults demonstrated with roses while they sang the Norwegian version of the popular song 'My Rainbow Race'.

Everyone in Norway feels in some way connected to the events of 22 July. That includes me as Minister of Justice, right from the tragic day itself to the day in November 2011 when I stepped down from the Government. Many of us have lost people we knew well. We have been bombed out of our offices. Many people are without their nearest and dearest. Many others have been brutally injured. Over 600 young people have found themselves in the middle of a massacre. This has caused fear and terror, but also warmth and compassion. These young people return again and again to the same thing: confidence in our justice system. The courts must pass sentence. Punishment can't undo what has already been done. We don't change the rules as we go along.

The approach we have had to the debate involving minimum and maximum sentences, the serving of such sentences, and different forms of punishment – all this has been characterized as much as anything else by not changing the rules in the aftermath of such an attack. Laws in Norway are not retrospective. We must behave with dignity in the court proceedings. And those concerned are acting with dignity. With great dignity.

There has been little debate about whether or not penalties are too lenient or if they don't work. Rather, the debate has centred on how we could have prevented such an act in the first place. What went wrong in the offender's early life, and later on?

Some excitable bloggers and commentators have said that he should be executed. But this view has not been espoused by politicians, the police or the public prosecutors, and is held by only a small minority of people.

At this point, I would like to point out that an important aspect of the Norwegian justice system is that ordinary people are picked out from among the population as lay judges in criminal cases. When the prosecution of the offender started, it was revealed that on 23 July 2011, one of the lay judges had posted on Facebook that he thought the perpetrator of these acts should be put to death. For this reason, he was relieved of his responsibilities. His comments weren't representative of the Norwegian population, and he himself later regretted them; they had been made in the heat of the moment, just a day after the atrocities had happened.

The Norwegian justice system is based on the principles of hearing both sides of a case, the rule of law and humanitarian principles. Our maximum prison sentence is 21 years; for terrorism, 30 years. The second of these is a recent addition to the penal code, which was actually passed *before* the fatal events of last July, but which hasn't yet come into force. What this means is that the man responsible could only be sentenced to the maximum 21 years in prison. If the court fears that the person might be a repeat offender, it can impose a sentence of preventive detention well beyond the 21 years; for life, even, if the case is frequently reviewed in court. If he is deemed to be not criminally responsible, he can't be sentenced to prison, but must have compulsory psychiatric care.

The offender had four publicly-funded defence counsels. Several psychiatric experts have assessed his soundness of mind, and there is still disagreement here. It was to be the court's job to make the final decision on this question. They found him responsible for his actions.

I would also like to add that there is considerable investment in improving prison standards in Norway. While in prison, inmates receive education, work training, substance abuse treatment and have contact with their families. For those convicted of less serious crimes, we have introduced such initiatives as mediation boards, community service, non-custodial sentences for young offenders, home detention with electronic tagging, and detention in treatment institutions. There are currently around 3,500 people in prison out of a population of five million. The majority of these are serving sentences of fewer than 90 days. One of our greatest challenges remains how best to help these people when they come out.

I believe this shows the sustainability of our system. We have no need for the death penalty; nor do we want it. No political party in Norway has asked for it. What, then, explains the sustainability of these reactions and this attitude towards the death penalty?

Firstly, it's based on the great faith our population has in both the system and the penal code. Changes are never made overnight; we look for consensus over and above the parliamentary majority necessary for changing the law.

Because such a sanction as the death penalty is irreversible, any wrong decision or allegation made in such cases would rapidly diminish the confidence we are so dependent on. Penal sanctions are most effective when people have genuine confidence in them.

We believe that by and large our sanctions work. In recent years, we have seen that the number of re-offenders has decreased. Furthermore, the rate of recidivism is lowest amongst those sentenced to the alternative types of sanction previously mentioned; as low as 20 per cent in many instances. Much of this can be linked to an improvement in welfare services, a largely uniform standard of living, small disparities between people, and a genuine sense of community among the population.

Thirdly, the total level of crime hasn't risen. We have seen a considerable fall in the number of reported crimes in recent years, despite the fact that certain types of crime – violent crime, drugs offences and financial crime – have risen. This may have as much to do with greater internationalization and a higher risk of detection as with anything else.

With the obvious exception of last year, the rate of homicide in Norway is low; approximately 30 per year. The average number of homicides in Norway during the last 20 years has been halved from 60 to 30 per year.

The fact that the debate in Norway has concentrated more on prevention and rehabilitation than the ultimate penalty sanctions, means that everyone has to take their share of responsibility. The death penalty could end up as a pretext for doing nothing in some cases. This, again, would lead to less investment in preventive measures. The paradox is that we would then see a rise in crime.

It is interesting that countries with much stricter penalties, less humane prison conditions and a higher prison population per capita, such as the USA, also have far more crime. Could it be that investment in brutal penalties has led these countries to forget the importance of prevention and rehabilitation? Do these penalties give a sense of false security?

We have a rational system. When the Government published its white paper on the correctional services, it called it 'Punishment that works'. We want our work to be effective. We want offenders to stop breaking the law, and there to be fewer victims of crime. Our approach is not characterized by irrational feelings of revenge and retribution, even though justice considerations of a more general nature are of course important; some sort of closure is necessary.

There is a strong school of thought that, as far as possible, sanctions must seek to repair damage, foster reconciliation, and lay the ground for a future life in the community.

To a large degree, our system contributes to order in society. There are few acts of revenge and vindictiveness. Even after 22 July, there was no sign of mob mentality. By and large the accused has been able to sit unmolested in court, even though he has been shouted at by a bereaved relative, and there was an attempt to throw a shoe at him. The court has dealt with these episodes in an exemplary fashion.

Mistakes can be made. And mistakes *are* made in Norwegian courts. This is why we have established several safety mechanisms in order to prevent and reverse wrongful convictions. One of the most important of these mechanisms is the Criminal Cases Review Commission. Fortunately, our system gives us the opportunity to right the damage done by a wrongful conviction. This would never be an option if we had the death penalty.

Our system is based on a humanitarian perspective which views human life as inviolable. There is no need for such a form of punishment as taking a life. This would only create a more brutal society, since a society's attitudes and values are a mirror image of the Establishment's potential means of coercion over its population.

There is also an important ethical dimension to the majority of Norwegians' overwhelming opposition to capital punishment. Whatever the situation, the taking of human life is unacceptable. Life is inviolable. End of story. The state's acceptance of the taking of a life would be a signal to individuals wanting to take the law into their own hands, and paradoxically lead to more serious violence. Some would ask themselves the question: If the state can do this kind of thing to people, why can't I?

As Minister of Justice, I could never have played a part in implementing capital punishment. As much as anything else this is a matter of conscience. I can be part of carrying out policies put together by political bodies I disagree with. But the death penalty goes way beyond my personal limits.

I make no bones about the importance of abolishing the death penalty. Uniting the world in saying no to capital punishment would reinforce the global community's efforts to combat serious crime.

In conclusion: We lost a lot of people the summer of 2011. One girl worked for me in the Ministry of Justice. She was working late Friday in the middle of the school holidays. She gave everything. She was killed by the terrorist's bomb. She was trying to finish a report for me about the use of mediation to reduce conflict and come up with alternative solutions and reconciliation in both civil and criminal cases. That very day she'd posted the following quotation by Mahatma Gandhi on her Facebook page: 'An eye for an eye *makes* the whole world blind'.

Her closest family used this quotation at her funeral: 'An eye for an eye *keeps* the whole world blind'. That really says it all.

Knut Storberget

Acknowledgements

This anthology grew out of two symposia at the Department of Criminology and Sociology of Law at the University of Oslo – 'The First International Oslo Symposium on the Death penalty in Asia' held in the spring of 2010, and 'The Second International Oslo Symposium on the Death Penalty' held in December 2012. Special thanks therefore go to the Department of Criminology and Sociology of Law, the Faculty of Law and the University of Oslo. I also sincerely thank the Vietnam Project at the Norwegian Centre for Human Rights at the University of Oslo, for their cooperation in connection with the first symposium.

In addition, one symposium: 'The Death Penalty: Part of a Sustainable Criminal Justice Development?' was held in Tokyo as a result of cooperation between Aoyama Gakuin University, the Norwegian Embassy in Tokyo and the Fafo Institute for Applied International Studies (Fafo AIS). This symposium took place in June 2012 in remembrance of the murder of more than 77 people in Norway on 22 July 2011, and in remembrance of those killed or hurt in the sarin gas attack in 1995 on the Tokyo underground. The Tokyo symposium addressed national reactions in Norway and Japan to these unfathomable tragedies.

I thank the Fafo Institute for Applied International Studies (Fafo AIS), the Aoyama Gakuin University and the Norwegian Embassy in Tokyo for their help. I also want to send special thanks to the Criminal Justice Research Centre and Law School at Ryukoku University in Kyoto and to the Centre for Prisoners' Rights in Tokyo.

All these symposia were generously funded by the Royal Ministry of Foreign Affairs in Norway. Without the Norwegian Foreign Service's clear and focused engagement in the long term fight against the death penalty, these symposia, with all their direct and indirect consequences, would not have taken place. I therefore thank the Ministry of Foreign Affairs.

I also thank the Norwegian Research Council for a post-doctoral grant for death penalty research, and 'Lovsamlingsfondet' at the Faculty of Law for contributing to the two Oslo symposia.

Turning from institutions to individuals: I thank all the contributors to this book; more information about them can be found in the list of contributors. I would, however, like first to especially mention and sincerely thank Nils Christie, whose many groundbreaking works have been the most important inspiration throughout, and whose support has been invaluable to me.

I sincerely thank David Garland for framing the book in the best scholarly way, and I thank Roger Hood for rounding off and looking forward. I hereby thank all of the contributors: Mohammed Ayatt, Nils Christie, Sangmin Bae, Børge

Bakken, Bikramjeet Batra, John Bessler, David Garland, Mohammad Habash, Vidar Halvorsen, Roger Hood, David Johnson, Fort Fu-Te Liao, Jody Madeira and Knut Storberget.

I also thank all those that have spoken at these different symposia and thus contributed to everyone's understanding of the death penalty both in the past and in the present, and of its possible abolition in the future.

I especially thank David Johnson whose monumental work written with Franklin Zimring on death penalty in Asia was the primary inspiration for the first symposium. He and Koichi Hamai have in recent years contributed with several lectures, sometimes at short notice. I also thank Roger Hood who kindly and brilliantly summarized the first and second Oslo symposia.

I would like to thank the Rector of the University of Oslo, Ole Petter Ottersen for his inspiring opening words at 'The Second International Oslo Symposium Against Death Penalty' and his continued keen interest and cooperation in the campaign against the death penalty. I would also like to thank the Vice-Rector of the University, Ragnild Hennum for her support and the Director of the Department of Criminology and Sociology of Law, Kristian Andenæs, for his unfailing support and his interesting opening words at the first and second Oslo symposia.

Among the people at the Department of Criminology and Sociology of Law at the University of Oslo, some have been absolutely central to the completion of this book. I sincerely thank Per Jørgen Ystehede who has given outstanding support, both technical and content-wise far beyond the usual, sometimes working far into the night. He contributed substantially to the Introduction and several other chapters. A very special thanks goes to Turid Eikvam who has organized with clear and kind aforethought such that all possible support should be available until the completion of the book. I also thank Julie E. Stuestøl, Jenny Maria Lundgaard and Kristin Hobson for technical help with different parts of the manuscript. I thank Vibeke Lagem for years of excellent library help and library research. I thank Frode Røed for help with copying and various tasks necessary to the preparation of the manuscript. I also thank Daphne Day for excellent and efficient proofreading at untimely hours and for indexing.

Many more have taken part in the discussions of themes that are part of the book. I am grateful for inspiring discussions with present and former colleagues: Jane Dullum, Kjersti Ericsson, Liv Finstad, Hedda Giertsen, Ragnar Hauge, Nicolay B. Johansen, Per Ole Johansen, Kjersti Lohne, Ida Nafstad, Sverre Flaaten, Cecilie Høigård, Guri Larsen, Monika Lindbekk, Thomas Mathiesen, Leif Petter Olaussen, Knut Papendorf, Thomas Ugelvik, Lasse Walberg and Per Jørgen Ystehede. Katja Franko Aas has been especially ready to engage in exchanges on criminological theory, in particular as regards the death penalty in relation to transnational and international phenomena and 'cosmopolitanism from above and below'. A very special thanks goes to Jane Dullum, Hedda Giertsen and Vidar Halvorsen, all so professionally inspiring and supportive at different times when the going was rough.

At Fafo Institute for Applied International Studies (Fafo AIS) I thank May-Len Skilbrei sincerely for invaluable support and criminological inspiration, and for a never-ending series of conversations and interesting discussions. May-Len Skilbrei has been essential in making many things possible, notably the Tokyo Symposium on the death penalty in cooperation with Aoyama University and the Norwegian Embassy. I also thank Eli Eriksen Sveen at FAFO AIS for friendly and efficient administration.

I would also like to thank the State Secretary in the Ministry of Foreign Affairs, Gry Larsen for a wide-ranging and poignant opening speech at the Second Oslo Symposium on the Death Penalty.

At the Ministry of Foreign Affairs I must first and foremost thank Lene Richter Strand for her engagement with the death penalty in the world, for her informed support, and also for her very necessary and highly efficient help in making the symposium a success, with as many interesting speakers as possible. I also want to sincerely thank Hege Røttingen for excellent cooperation, and for the initial support for the research on the death penalty in Asia, which prepared the way for 'The First International Oslo Symposium on the Death penalty in Asia'.

I want to thank everyone at the Vietnam Programme for the vital role they played from the outset, especially Kristin Høgdahl, Fredrik Steen, Marte Hamren and Camilla F. Wedul, and later Gisle Kvanvig, as well as Teis Daniel Kjelling on NCHR for administrative and budget tasks. I want to thank the directors of the NCHR Nils Butenschøn and Geir Ulfstein.

Turning to Japan, I want first to take this opportunity to thank those that were instrumental in initially making possible my more than 30-year engagement with criminal justice and the death penalty in Japan. I want to thank Toyo Atsumi, at that time professor in criminal law and criminal procedure at Chuo University, for accepting me as a Mombusho student and for years of serious conversations about what Japanese culture and criminal justice is, and should or could be. I want to thank Takayuku Shiibashi, Yoshinori Nakanome, Kazumichu Tsutsumi and Ryo Ogiso for welcoming me and subsequently inviting me to return. I especially thank Yoshinori Nakanome for all the research help I received during my guest research period at Chuo University, and for our many friendly encounters since then.

In the area of criminology, it was Tetsuya Fujimoto, professor at Chuo University Graduate School of Law, who took care of me time and time again during my Mombusho years and my many subsequent returns to Japan to continue researching. He offered encouragement and scholarly discussion and put me in contact with people of crucial importance for my research, people from all levels of Japanese society. He gave me the opportunity to visit prisons when it was rare for women to do so. He kept his door open at all times, and I will always be more grateful to him than can be expressed. He has an impressive and unusually large number of publications. His prized doctorate in what we now might call the crimmigration area, is truly pioneering. I thank him for accepting my invitation to Oslo, and for giving two excellent lectures at the Department of Criminology and Sociology of Law at the University of Oslo.

As for the Symposium in Tokyo in 2012, I thank the Norwegian Embassy in Tokyo, and the Ambassador Arne Walther for his support and excellent opening words. Special thanks go to Arne Follerås who with true diplomacy carried the task through and Hanna Slaatta Leinebø who systematically carried so much of the task out. I also thank Ami Semba, Yoko Nakatsukasa and Snøfrid Emterud Byrløkken for their kind help with the symposium.

The Aoyama Gakuin University was essential in making this symposium a reality. I sincerely thank the President of Aoyama University Ken-ichi Senba for entering into partnership with the Norwegian Embassy in Tokyo, for his support, and for the wonderful new conference room that was a splendid setting for such an event, and for his opening words.

I especially thank Setsuo Miyazawa and Osamu Niikura for joining forces with me to make this happen and for working very hard indeed for several months.

Special thanks go to the three former Ministers of Justice, Hideo Hiraoka, Seiken Sugiura and Knut Storberget, as well as to former Governor Bill Richardson for sharing their views, and to the International Commission Against the Death Penalty for their support. I thank the judges Akira Kitani and Iver Huitfeldt and the experts on police interrogations and judicial mistakes, Makoto Ibusuki and Asbjørn Rachlev, for the lectures they gave.

I thank the World Coalition Against the Death penalty and Amnesty International Japan with its former and present directors Makoto Teranaka and Hideki Wakabayashi, and Amnesty International Norway, especially Helle Biørnstad. I am grateful for the support of the Defence Lawyers group at the Federation of Bar Associations in Japan, and from Ryukoku University, and I especially thank Shinichi Ishizuka, now Dean of the Law School.

Without the unfailing help, the clear mind, the warm heart and the moral resolve of Maiko Tagusari, the symposium, as well as many other important human rights initiatives in Japan, might not have been realized. I thank her sincerely for this and for her lecture.

I would also like to thank my colleague and good friend Won-Kyu Park, professor at the Law Faculty at Kitakyushu University. Without his company both in countless interviews of former prisoners in Japan, and later in life, I would have understood far less.

In connection with my research in Louisiana I would like to thank Raymond and Alfreda Diamond, Wilbert Rideau, Richard Bourke, Ben Cohen and Nick Trenticosta.

A special thanks goes to a supremely inspirational being no longer here with us: Vibeke Lund.

I want to thank those that have shared my family life: Hans-Ingar, Siri, Øyvind, Ove, Inge, Serdar, Ashraf and Badshah.

Last, but most importantly, I thank my children Mira and Marcus, and my husband Ronald Craig to whom I dedicate this book, without whom …

Lill Scherdin,
Oslo

Introduction

Lill Scherdin

The death penalty was for centuries an ordinary and largely uncontested tool for the exercise of government power (see Garland in Chapter 3). How is it then that Europe has turned its back on this punishment, and how is it that the Norwegian government and its people, in the face of such an atrocity as the one described by former Minister of Justice Knut Storberget rejected any call for the death penalty? Does this mean that a moderate criminal justice system without the death penalty is sustainable? Some central questions must be: What are the historical, economic, political and cultural conditions making governance without the death penalty possible? Furthermore, what are the necessary conditions for a criminal justice system without the death penalty to be sustainable over time? Or should the question be whether a criminal justice system *with* the death penalty can be sustainable in the world today – in its global, international and transnational complexity? Can the death penalty itself be a hazard to a sustainable criminal justice system? These are some of the questions in the forefront in the explorations in this book.

Over the last forty years there has been an extraordinary development: in 1970 a large majority of states carried out executions and only 21 countries had abolished the death penalty, while in 2012 only 21 countries carried out executions and a majority of states have abolished it. This development is described in depth and detail by Roger Hood in Chapter 15. By September 2013, 106 of 197 nations in the world had abolished the death penalty. Only 39 countries have carried out an execution since 2003. The remaining 52 countries are classified by the United Nations as 'abolitionist *de facto*' because they have not carried out an execution in the last ten years. They do, however, still have the death penalty in the law and many still sentence people to death. What is it that characterizes these retentionist countries seen as nations, seen as parts of regions and seen as parts of a web of transnational and international relationships? What characteristics might help explain why they maintain the death penalty as a form of punishment and a strategy of governance? The conclusions drawn by some authors are that the types of national governance and the types and intensity of death penalty practices are intimately related. The most authoritarian governments with the least attention to human rights are also those who execute the most – indeed they are responsible for an increasing proportion of executions worldwide. The least authoritarian retentionist countries execute correspondingly much less. The situation is put in perspective, when only seven countries have carried out more than ten executions every year over these last ten years. These countries are: China, North Korea, Iran, Iraq, Saudi Arabia, Yemen and the USA.

In some countries a dominant group of retentionists might still see the death penalty as essential for their national, political or religious identity. For example, Iran hangs large numbers of people from the tallest cranes and bridges for everyone to see, and encourages the ordinary population and victims' families to actively take part in the executions. However, there is considerable ambivalence in most, if not all, retentionist countries. Indeed, most of them execute sparingly, if at all. On the other hand many states, among them Norway, are now seeing their core identity defined by the very act of stepping back from harbouring an institution for state killing, or from aiding others in this.

This book invites an exploration of the unique situation in some important countries that still have the death penalty, including the ambivalence found in most of these countries. This entails a focus on theories about the relationships between governing through the death penalty and governance more generally, and with an eye more specifically on what Johnson and Zimring calls 'leadership from the front'. We explore what specifically furthers or hinders the development of a moderate, balanced and sustainable criminal justice system, and what makes a criminal justice system swell out of proportion, so that it constantly increases the pain or death it delivers. We ask how the practice of the death penalty and of other punishments also expresses the relations of governance between the leaders and their people, between different status groups, classes, castes, nationalities, ethnicities and gender, between the transnationally mobile and the immobile. Examining how international, transnational and regional forces intersect with national and local ambivalence towards the death penalty, different chapters sketch dynamic scenarios of the past, the present and the possible futures of the death penalty within their jurisdictions.

Part I: Governance and the Death Penalty

Chapters 1–3 concern general ways of understanding the close relationships between state governance and governing through the death penalty, through history and across national and global space. Lill Scherdin's Chapter 1 stands firmly on the shoulders of the fundamental insights found in Chapter 2 by Nils Christie and Chapter 3 by David Garland. It is thus natural to start with a description of these chapters.

Nils Christie takes us to the heart of the matter in *Chapter 2: Death as Punishment*. In his early studies of the Holocaust he pioneered the central sociological tradition that takes as its starting point the fact that most of those committing atrocities were ordinary people who found themselves enmeshed in extraordinary or abnormal social situations. The main trend just after the war, however, was to seek explanations for the terrible things done in the concentration camps in special characteristics of the Germans or the German Third Reich, i.e., in characteristics of 'the monstrous other'. However, when it became known that Norwegian guards had actively taken part in the death and destruction in these camps, blaming 'Norwegianness' as such did not seem so natural an option. It then seemed one should study the monstrosity of these individual Norwegian guards. But as Nils Christie points out in Chapter 2, he found no such monstrosity. Instead he found the guards to be ordinary people caught in an extraordinary stressful and extreme situation. This situation opened the way for, and even encouraged, violent abuse at the same time as it blocked empathy. In a variety of ways it prevented the guards from seeing the prisoners as fellow human beings. Nils Christie went on to explore social conditions in modern societies that stop us seeing others as people like ourselves, thus creating the conditions for extreme forms of punishment and the use of the death penalty. Nils Christie insists in his chapter that to understand the opposite is of equal importance: to identify what characteristics of social life bring us closer in a way that enhances understanding and trust, and therefore reduces the perceived need to define troublesome acts as crimes and to punish severely. In his chapter Nils Christie alerts us to new dangers ahead, to new aspects of our society that might threaten the hitherto seemingly moderate criminal justice of Norway. What new rifts between people are in the making, what common arenas are we about to lose? His chapter also challenges the limited focus on criminal justice. He envisions a more sustainable society, with minimal systems of criminal justice combined with alternative ways of conflict resolution. In such societies most 'crimes' or 'troublesome acts' would be handled through restorative justice based on meetings between victims and perpetrators, using their conflicts as resources to understand and bridge the social divides that hinder empathy and lead to greater pain delivery.

The basic proposition of David Garland in *Chapter 3: Why the Death Penalty is Disappearing* is that the death penalty is everywhere an exercise of state power. Because the nature and environment of the state has changed in different nations over time, so too has capital punishment. He eloquently describes the emergence of sovereign states as fundamentally altering former practices of the death penalty. It then became a vehicle in despotic states' efforts to secure their rule by monopolizing legitimate violence and prohibiting private vendetta and acts of revenge. Later the death penalty was made unessential by the formation of secure bureaucratic states supported by criminal justice systems of police, courts and prisons. Still later it was 'made problematic' by the development of liberal-democratic and welfare state institutions, and by an associated culture of civilized refinement and humanism, all of which worked to limit state violence and surround it with prohibitions and taboos. As the death penalty became less essential to state security, the door was also opened for the launch of the abolitionist movement. Across time and space, increased democratization seemed to coincide with the increased force of the abolitionist movement. With the onset of human rights regimes at the international level, the nature and environment of states would change once again: the abolition of the death penalty became elevated to the status of an international human rights norm.

Indeed with the elevation of the abolition of death penalty to the status of an international human rights norm (although contested), the amazing turnaround that David Garland has described was completed. The death penalty had gone from being a natural tool of state governance for centuries to being widely seen as a breach of international human rights norms.

In *Chapter 1: The Death Penalty: A Hazard to a Sustainable Development of Criminal Justice?*, Lill Scherdin explores how relationships between states' socioeconomic mode of governance and their governance through punishment (penal governance) can frame a dynamic understanding of why differently governed states tend to deliver more or less pain – abolish or retain the death penalty. This understanding underpins her step-by-step exploration of the conditions for the sustainability of criminal justice systems and the role played by the death penalty.

She departs from the differences found between more coordinated capitalist democracies and less coordinated liberal democracies, where more coordinated states, like Norway, with consensual politics, strong labour unions, high equality and high levels of trust, governed less by way of punishment, compared to less equal, less coordinated liberal states.

To understand why, she explores how perceptions of harms and risks as well as the birth and orbits of mobilization movements against these harms, tend to fare differently in differently governed societies. Following Stanley Cohen, she draws attention to how such harms or risks (including serious crimes) can be ignored or denied, assessed and proportionately reacted to, or they can be exaggerated way out of proportion, fuelling mobilization movements that run wild, causing much collateral damage. The form and fate of mobilization movements depend on the deliberative processes, veto points or institutional hindrances they meet on their way through politics, legislation or the criminal justice system. These also tend to be different in differently governed states.

According to Scherdin, sustainable governance, whether through electoral politics, legislative processes or the criminal justice system, seeks to give form and set limits to mobilization movements to make them controllable. This should allow for assessment of the character of the harm and the proportionality of the reaction, as well as the collateral damage involved for all possible stakeholders. A sustainable criminal justice system as part of a sustainable society seeks to meet the needs (to address harms) of today without compromising the needs of future generations. The USA's massive use of incarceration, with its colossal collateral damage for individuals, families and society, and its accompanying failure to adhere to its own core principles of justice, must be the star example of such unsustainability. It creates more social insecurities, more inequality, more othering – thus eroding the very moral soil from which legitimacy, trust and empathy grow. Correspondingly, when states with the death penalty assess the proportionality of the reaction, this would also mean assessing the range of serious collateral damage that has gradually come to light: the many innocents sentenced to death, the arbitrary and disproportionate application of the death penalty with respect to race, religion, minority, gender, class and citizenship, the adverse effects on victims' families (including children) and on defendants' families (including children), and the harm to all involved in state killings, from judges to prison wardens and executioners.

Furthermore Scherdin suggests that the death penalty, in and of itself, plays a unique role in making such mobilization movements stronger and less controllable. It should therefore be seen as an independent hazard to the sustainable development of criminal justice systems. Scherdin suggests that the death penalty's unique mesmerizing force also weakens a society's ability to focus politically on evaluating other harms and threats as well as the different measures that should be taken against them. Inspired by Garland, she asks whether the huge collateral damage arising from the massive restructuring of society caused by the disproportionate rise of incarceration, could have happened in the same way and been kept out of main-stream discussion for so long *without* the reoccurring dramas of the death penalty.

Scherdin warns that one should never underestimate the power of mobilization when dominant groups in society feel fundamentally threatened – even in countries that have abolished the death penalty. The temptations to seek larger-than-life dramatic measures reoccur in times of crisis. As Ulysses binds himself to the mast to resist the temptations of the sirens, binding oneself constitutionally against the reinstating of the death penalty makes for less dramatic mobilizations and thus further secures sustainability. So does ratifying the human rights treaties abolishing the death penalty.

Part II: The USA

The development in the USA seems crucial to the success of the abolition movement worldwide. Many countries that retain the death penalty point to its continued use in the USA. Not only does the majority of US states (32) retain the death penalty, the USA also maintains that the retention of the death penalty shall not be seen as an international human rights issue.

However, six US states have recently abolished the death penalty, making a total of 18 non-death penalty states. Several other states seem to be moving in the same direction. Only nine of the 51 jurisdictions actually executed anyone in 2012. Executions seem to be limited to fewer and fewer states. Only ten states have executed at least one person each year since 1976 (see Hood's Chapter 15).

The development of the United States Supreme Court's interpretations of what is 'cruel and unusual punishment' in the light of 'evolving standards of decency', can be seen as an embodiment of evolving forces of democracy, civilized refinement and humanism as depicted by Garland. In this vein John Bessler recounts the death penalty history of the USA.

In John Bessler's *Chapter 4: The American Enlightenment: Eliminating Capital Punishment in the United States*, he revisits the founding fathers of the US Constitution in the era of the enlightenment and sees this as the moment of birth of the abolition movement. He also follows the rulings of the US Supreme Court, rulings that gradually curb and transform the death penalty in the light of the Eighth, the Fourteenth and the Fifth Amendments. This transformation takes place in the womb of the changing state and the court rulings also contribute to this change. In contrast to what is often assumed – that America's founders were passionate death penalty supporters – Bessler found important founders highly ambivalent to the death penalty. Although they chose to retain death penalty laws for certain offences, especially murder and treason, they nonetheless despised 'cruel and unusual punishments', which they saw as products of oppressive aristocratic states – as unnecessary punishment signifying tyranny. Many at this time were inspired by Cesare Beccaria's book 'On Crimes and Punishments'. Dr Benjamin Rush, a signatory of the Declaration of Independence, together with John Quincy Adams and Thomas Payne totally opposed the death penalty, while Benjamin Franklin and Thomas Jefferson opposed it for lower offences and theft. Towards the end of his life, Thomas Jefferson regretted that the general ideas of the USA had not yet advanced to the point of accepting hard labour as a substitute for capital punishment. Thus many founders also believed that times and conditions would change and the death penalty with them. This was at least a notion Thomas Jefferson explicitly embraced. Against this background Bessler takes issue with the originalists currently in the US Supreme Court and concludes that the US Constitution, properly viewed, and taking into account the intentions of the founding fathers, does not in any way bar the US Supreme Court from declaring the death penalty to be unconstitutional.

In Jody Lyneé Madeira's *Chapter 5: Clear and Ever-Present Dangers?: Redefining 'Closure' in a Post 9–11 World*, the needs of victims are a central theme. These needs are also perceived differently at different times in history. A fairly new way of expressing what victims need is the term 'closure', which at certain times and in certain states seems to have acquired the status of an inalienable right for the victim, with little clarity about what it is and whether it is attainable through killing the perpetrator. Madeira raises a series of important questions regarding the elusive concept of 'closure' for the victims and other actors in and outside the criminal justice system. She focuses on the state's complicity in structuring the choice of punishment – death penalty or life in prison, and the punishment rituals – according to state actors' conception of closure, and how the various victims accept or furiously reject this. A key question is, in the wake of terrorist attacks, how do victims regard 'closure', what associated needs do they have, and how are these needs affected by other factors such as the perpetrator's behaviour, criminal justice proceedings, and mass media coverage? The chapter compares how closure was constructed following two devastating American attacks – the 1995 Oklahoma City bombing and the infamous 11 September 2001 attacks and explores what it has come to mean. It discusses core closure themes present in the Oklahoma City victims' remarks on Timothy McVeigh's 2001 execution and the key patterns in media coverage of Osama bin Laden's 2011 death in a US special forces raid. The chapter then discusses how the social construction of closure following both attacks expands 'justice stakeholder' status beyond family members and survivors, demonstrates the depth of governmental commitment to fulfilling what they construct as closure needs, and illustrates how execution methods impact these needs. Capital punishment and mass media can, in Jody Madeira's words, brew a series of 'perfect storms' that also creates and intensifies closure needs, that prolong victims' involvement with criminal justice processes and thus with the perpetrators. There is evidence that non-capital sentences such as life without parole (given to Nichols, the co-defendant of McVeigh) may to a larger degree fulfil such 'closure' needs.

Part III: Asia

Asia is home to at least 90 per cent of the world's executions; thus Asia is of central importance. It seems natural to start with Japan since Japan and the USA are now the only two developed democracies that not only retain the death penalty, but still carry out executions regularly. In 2012 the USA executed 43 and Japan executed seven. According to David Johnson, Japan's homicide rate is so low that if one compares the number of executions per potential capital case, Japan's execution rate is in some years even higher than the execution rate of Texas. As in the USA, the wave of support for a seemingly inalienable right of victims to something similar to closure through 'the ultimate punishment' has become a more dominant part of the Japanese death penalty discourse. David Johnson discusses the influence of such a discourse at the end of his elegantly shaped chapter.

In *Chapter 6: Why Does Japan Retain the Death Penalty? Nine Hypotheses*, David Johnson steps back, armed with his comprehensive knowledge of the death penalty in Japan and Asia, and looks at the possibilities for abolition by constructing nine hypotheses about why Japan has retained the death penalty. These are organized around three themes. The first entails explanations that focus on history: he questions whether there was a missed opportunity for death penalty abolition during the postwar occupation period, and whether the almost continuous rule by the (conservative) Liberal Democratic Party reduced any impetus to change the traditional governance through punishment. He considers whether this is partly because Japan became geopolitically strong, economically independent, democratically stable and legally self-sufficient. The second theme entails explanations that emphasize facts and forces external to Japan. He highlights how America's retention of capital punishment provides 'cover' for Japan's (and other countries') retention, given America's power and portrayal of itself as the archetypical guardian of democracy and human rights. In the same way that he questions what Japan would do if the USA abolished the death penalty, he also questions what Japan would do if South Korea (the closest other developed democracy) were to abolish it. He also points out that, unlike those in other parts of the world, regional organizations such as ASEAN and APEC put less pressure on their member states to abolish the death penalty and promote human rights. The discussion of the first two themes shows clearly the importance of internal forces at the national level, which is the third theme of the chapter. Johnson considers whether Japan's retention of the death penalty is a result of democracy at work, given the high public support for it in opinion polls. Johnson, however, points out that the public seems to know very little about the actual death penalty practices in Japan and that Japanese leaders are not particularly responsive to public opinion in other areas. He therefore goes on to explore two other hypotheses. The first of these is the Japanese cultural belief that death is the appropriate way to atone for heinous crimes: Johnson sums up the reasons used by the Minister of Justice Kunio Hatoyama for escalating the practice of the death penalty in Japan: '[I]n order for an offender to make amends and in order to satisfy society's sense of justice, the offender must give up his or her life: it is a matter of moral proportion and symbolic purification'. This is what Hatoyama presumes that victims raised in the Japanese culture will invariably feel. In relation to this Johnson notes the claim that the Japanese are more averse to the universalistic and absolutist claims of human rights. This would also be in accordance with Hatoyama's further claim that there are lasting 'civilizational differences' between Japan and the west. Secondly, Johnson explores the role of penal populism, the perceived needs of victims and 'leadership from the front' in the retention of the death penalty. He notes that the recent surge in executions might be related to the last decade's rise in penal populism and the victims' movements. However, he also notes that there have been moratoriums or abolition in other Asian countries despite moral panics, penal populism and victims' movements. The key proximate cause of change, he finds, is leadership from the front, often in the face of resistance from citizens and criminal justice officials. Such leadership has played a decisive role for the moratorium in South Korea.

South Korea has had a moratorium on all executions since 1997, as described by Sangmin Bae in *Chapter 7: Death Penalty Moratorium in South Korea: Norms, Institutions and Leadership*. Although retaining the death penalty for ordinary crimes, it now has a *de facto* abolitionist status since it has not executed anyone during the last ten years. South Korea's experience is notable because of the declared political intention of two recent governments to abolish the death penalty, and because the normative discussion surrounding the death penalty (in contrast with that in Japan as described by David Johnson), has mostly been associated with the discourses of democratic values and human rights. Despite the declared intentions of these two governments, and a parliamentary majority supporting abolition bills in 2001 and 2004, they never became law. The constitutionality of the death penalty has also been tried several times before the Constitutional Court – most recently in 2010 – when a 5–4 majority found the death penalty to be constitutional.

Bae focuses on political, legal and grassroots actors to explore the driving force behind South Korea's abolitionist developments and its implication for the rest of Asia. She points out that, contrary to traditional modernization theory, which assumes a positive correlation between economic development and democracy, modernization and economic growth in South Korea was not accompanied by political liberalization or respect for human rights. Until the transition to democracy in 1987 the death penalty was frequently imposed on political dissidents, often in the name of social stability. However it actually seemed to undermine this stability because the denial of basic civil rights provoked political discontent and opposition among the people. Bae describes how different actors contributed to the moratorium after the transition to democracy, and points out the importance of the facts that the moratorium was voluntary, without peer group pressure from neighbouring countries, that it prevails in the face of public opposition, and – that therefore it is and will continue to be highly dependent upon leadership from the front.

This brings our attention to Taiwan which, like South Korea, has had considerable economic and social development, has tried to limit inequality, has had a clear change from totalitarian to democratic rule and a general turn towards an acceptance of human rights norms. Like South Korea, Taiwan for a time had a moratorium in place. What happened? That is the theme of the next chapter.

In *Chapter 8: Why Taiwan's* de facto *Moratorium Was Established and Lost*, Fort Fu-Te Liao describes how, after a long period under marshal law, Taiwan began moving towards democracy in 1986. Although democratization did not automatically mean it became an abolitionist state, the number of executions per year did diminish as it became more democratic. As in the case of South Korea, the change in death penalty practice in Taiwan seems to have been related to a more general acceptance of human rights norms. However, unlike South Korea, after a moratorium from 2006 to 2010 Taiwan began executing again.

In order to explain how the moratorium came about and its demise, Liao examines the views and actions of different actors in the judicial, legislative and executive branches of government. He explains the changes in law and procedure, together with the unique, behind-the-scenes political manoeuvres that resulted in an absence of executions in 2006. He also depicts the dramatic exchanges in the struggle of Minister of Justice Wang Ching-Feng to continue the moratorium and the formidable forces that led to her resignation.

Unlike the preceding governments, the KMT, now in power, has never expressed any firm policy on abolition; it has pragmatically stated that, 'when the crime rate is high the time is not right for abolition'. Liao notes that during the 2008 presidential election campaign, the KMT president candidate Ma Ying-jeou did adopt a softer tone, saying that when conditions became mature and with public acceptance, they hoped to move toward this goal. However, the rule of law demanded executions should continue in the meantime.

The executive government is limited by the decisions of the Council of Grand Justices (CGJ, Constitutional Court). The CGJ had played a crucial role in facilitating political transitions and constitutional reforms, most notably as a guardian of human rights with special emphasis on the rule of law. Nonetheless, both before and after Taiwan's democratization, the CGJ has consistently ruled that the death penalty is constitutional. Liao concludes that under these circumstances, there are no firm barriers to executions, and there is an absence of political will and judicial leadership as regards abolition.

The views of the KMT are closer to the official views in China than those of previous governments, and this death penalty narrative is also close to that of mainland China. Regional influences on Taiwan might be sizeable. On this note we turn to China.

In *Chapter 9: The Norms of Death: On Attitudes to Capital Punishment in China*, Børge Bakken takes issue with the retentionist argument that 5000 years of the death penalty is evidence of a culture of punitive norms as deeply ingrained as the native language itself. Bakken takes us far back in history, and into today's world of Chinese intellectuals and legal philosophers, and into a broad range of opinion polls. Everywhere he takes us, he finds – as did Bessler in the history of the founders of the USA – ambivalence and multiple normative tendencies rather than one ingrained cultural pattern. Which of the multiple normative tendencies is given most weight at any one time varies according to the political system.

Thus Bakken finds that death penalty practice is clearly political and malleable rather than set in stone, as many proponents of the death penalty would have us believe. Such proponents resemble the Japanese Justice Minister Hatoyama, quoted in David Johnson's chapter, who speaks of an eternally different Japanese culture of harmony that would always demand the death penalty in a Japan true to itself.

Bakken points to years without the death penalty in the past, before the imperial Chinese state. He also points to mercy and alternative punishments present in the imperial state, side by side with fluctuating levels of execution. Today the authorities often claim that it is the Chinese people, the masses, rather than the elites that demand the death penalty. Bakken however, finds from the opinion polls that part of the elite is considerably more in favour of the death penalty than the ordinary people, the peasants or the urban poor. He also finds a growing awareness that the criminal justice system has executed innocent people, and that the death penalty is used considerably more often on the poor than on the rich or the governing elite.

He describes a China where 'leadership from the front' is limited to the goal of containing and keeping the death penalty intact, albeit in a moderate and centrally controlled form, evading accelerated moral panics or securitization movements towards ever more executions, such as was seen from 1997 to 2001.

Bakken notes that Chinese scholars are more and more aware of the dangers of moral panics and securitization movements, after seeing execution numbers probably close to 15,000 per year during the peak period, when local criminal justice discretion was not shaped and limited by the rule of law. Both Lu and Chen touch on the very important theme of the escalating character of revenge-based principles and hatred, and their warnings are well founded. As Bakken points out, scholars in the field of revenge and retribution have found that revenge seems always to tend towards excess and 'escalating cycles of violence', where the state is 'likely to lose control'; that the appetite for blood is hard to stop when such principles are set in motion.

As to abolition, Bakken notes 'leadership from the front' is not taking place. Instead the leaders are the ones holding the people back from death penalty changes.

Departing from an image of one core population group of death penalty proponents, one group in the vanguard for abolition, and a larger group of the ambivalent, he poses interesting questions for the future. From theories of a smaller critical mass and its dynamic possibilities to change the attitudes of a far bigger population, he gives us a glimpse of the potentially changeable nature of attitudes to the death penalty in China today.

Turning towards the other most populous country with the death penalty in Asia: India, one should bear in mind that approximately half of Asian jurisdictions are without the death penalty, in law or in practice. Furthermore, when it comes to those that do have it, there is 'a tale of two *kinds* of retentionist nations'. Many seldom execute, while some execute extensively.

The difference between India and China, the world's most populous countries, is illustrative, as described by David Johnson. China's execution rate is at least 50,000 times that of India's. Such a difference in degree is also a difference in kind (Johnson 2010: 7) (see Chapter 1 for reference).

In *Chapter 10: A Knotty Tale: Understanding the Death Penalty in India*, Bikramjeet Batra draws the long lines from death penalty laws and practice in the colonial period and charts the dramatic decline in capital sentences over recent decades in the world's most populous capitalist democracy. His chapter examines the political, legal and institutional framework within which capital punishment operates, the limit to the worst of the worst, and in particular the role played by the office of the President of India in the clemency process.

India's death penalty as described in detail by Batra, is full of contradictions and complexities. The chapter is an intriguing story with a puzzling end as to which leadership is doing what – on which front. Batra points out that, although Indian courts sentence over a hundred people to death every year, few executions have actually been carried out. There was only one between 1997 and 2012. This is due in part to the large number of overturned sentences, and in part to a gridlock in the treatment of mercy petitions, where three Presidents have stretched, but not overstepped, the boundaries of their limited powers. In the light of this, Batra asks whether the 'capital gridlock' during these years is a result of political choices or 'a freak occurrence resulting from a series of unconnected individual actions'. At any rate, very few of those sentenced in the first instance actually get executed.

Moreover, although there are moral panics and securitization movements concerned with the death penalty, there does not seem to be any unanimous or long lasting outcry about this absence of executions, either among citizens or the leaders of the different parties. Ironically, when in power, the parties most opposed to the death penalty in principle ended up executing more people than the parties explicitly supporting it. It is unclear if there will be a continuous political thrust to dramatically increase the number of executions. No party, however, is strongly committed to the struggle for abolition. Batra notes that, although most civil liberties groups and many human rights organizations oppose the death penalty, the opposition 'in principle' has rarely transformed itself into active mobilization or campaigns against the death penalty. Given India's return to executions, Batra highlights the ambivalence and discomfort with the death penalty in practice that seems to coexist with support for it in principle. He concludes by discussing whether we can expect a continuation of moderate or nil executions, or if we are about to witness another twist in the tale of the death penalty in India.

Part IV: Countries with Majority Muslim Populations

When we turn our attention to Muslim majority countries, we find that there is a relatively small group that executes extensively: Iran, Saudi Arabia, Yemen and Iraq. On the other hand, we find several secular states with large Muslim majorities that have joined the abolitionist movement: Albania, Azerbaijan, Bosnia-Herzegovina, Kyrgyzstan, Turkey, Turkmenistan and Senegal (see Hood, Chapter 15). We also find several with a low execution rate, or a *de facto* moratorium. The next section will explore such non-execution or ambivalence in the light of varying interpretations of Islam, the relationship between Islamic and secular law, as well as different types of leadership from the front.

In Mohammad Habash's *Chapter 11: Islamic Visions for the Abolition of the Death Penalty*, he claims that through traditional Islamic jurisprudence (*Fiqh*) Islam can be harmonized with the main UN conventions on human rights. He shows more specifically how it is possible to work within the tradition of Islam to avoid and even abolish the death penalty. Even though retribution is mentioned in the verses of the Holy Quran, retribution is not synonymous with execution. The Court has the right to avoid using the death penalty in any individual case, and even to stop the use of this form of punishment altogether.

Habash demonstrates, among other things, that there are 14 ways in Islam to avoid imposing the death penalty. These are important in and of themselves. They show in detail why retribution does not necessarily mean execution in Islam. Most importantly, they are also manifestations of an overarching and overriding intent to create a form of justice that limits the harshness of sanctions and strives towards finding possibilities for justice through leniency and mercy.

For example, Habash points out how Islamic law requires full consensus among Islamic scholars in order to permit the use of the death penalty in general. He suggests that the ratification of international treaties against the death penalty could be interpreted as meaning that the necessary consensus is absent. Furthermore, in the individual criminal case there must also be a full consensus among the judiciary. One judge who does not want to pass the death penalty is enough to open the way for alternative sanctions. Quoting the Prophet Mohammad, Habash writes: 'The Imam who mistakenly pardons is better than one who mistakenly punishes'. According to Habash, these conditions demanding consensus of scholars in general and judicial consensus in individual cases, have prompted some Islamic countries to abolish the death penalty altogether.

Habash argues that a correct interpretation of Islamic law is contrary to how it is applied by revolutionary armed militias and Islamist states which use the death penalty in the name of Islam. His vision is one of many different Islamic justifications for the abolition of corporal punishments and the death penalty today.

The vision of Habash is especially interesting and far reaching in that it insists that abolishing the death penalty is in full accordance with the overriding intentions of Islam. Other influential critics of the practice of the death penalty in Muslim majority countries claim that Islam demands the death penalty, but it does so only under certain very strict conditions – conditions that are so far from being present in these countries today, that an indefinite moratorium on the use of death penalty should be put in place. Some critics might go further and claim that we now know that all systems of state killing are fallible, and thus the conditions of Islam can never be fulfilled – an indirect support for abolition.

In *Chapter 12: An Overview of the Ongoing Debate on the Death Penalty in Morocco*, Mohammed Ayatt points out that Morocco has been a *de facto* abolitionist country for the last two decades, but still has 111 individuals on death row. He describes how the death penalty situation in Morocco is both contradictory and complex. On the one hand there is a new constitution providing the right to life as a primary right of every human being. There has also been a clear recommendation by the Equity and Reconciliation Commission to abolish the death penalty, and both public officials and previous members of government have supported such a position. The practice of non-execution started during the reign of the previous monarch and the present monarch has never signed an execution decree.

On the other hand the current penal code as well as a new draft penal code both retain the death penalty. The current Minister of Justice (who belongs to a moderate Islamist political wing) has not taken a stand for abolition, but instead wants to limit the death penalty to 'serious crimes'. Thus there seems to be a lack of leadership from the front for the moment. Addressing Islamist arguments that abolition of the death penalty is forbidden, Ayatt discusses the relationship between the Moroccan penal code and Islamic Law.

Ayatt describes how different countries have moved towards abolition in different ways by drawing our attention to the difference between England and France. Some countries make a clear break from the full practice of death penalty to total abolition, while others take a step-by-step gradual approach. Contemplating possible trajectories for abolition in Morocco, he points out that traditions of consensual decision-making could suggest that Morocco might move forward in a gradual step-by-step manner. He draws interesting parallels to the complex compromises that had to be made in the process of creating the International Criminal Court for the most serious crimes, without the penalty of death.

The case of Morocco, as shown in Ayatt's chapter, is a good example of how vulnerable the fight against the death penalty is to changes in political leadership, and in the face of terrible terrorist acts.

Part V: Reflection and Outlook

In Vidar Halvorsen's *Chapter 13: Criminal Justice, Sustainability and the Death Penalty*, his point of departure is the Brundtland Commission's famous and influential definition of sustainability as '[development that] meets the needs of the present without compromising the ability of future generations to meet their own needs' (WCED1987: 8, see Chapter 13 for reference). Halvorsen argues that this notion of sustainability might be fruitfully applied not only to problems of environmental justice, but also to problems of retributive justice. A sustainable criminal justice system must accommodate both non-consequentialist and consequentialist moral intuitions of citizens. The stability and legitimacy of the system is crucially dependent on these intuitions being either reconcilable within an overall justificatory theory of punishment or at least able to function as coherent normative elements within what John Rawls has called an overlapping consensus.

Halvorsen suggests that the most promising attempt to develop such an overlapping consensus for a sustainable criminal justice system has been provided by Andrew von Hirsch in *Censure and Sanctions* (Hirsch 1993, see Chapter 13 for reference). Furthermore, von Hirsch's description of free and rational, yet morally fallible, persons, exposed to the temptation of crime and other forms of harmful conduct, is compatible with the basic idea of constitutionalism. Like Ulysses in Homer's epic poem, citizens of nation-states hope to be able to navigate their societies through political temptations by binding themselves to a constitution, an overlapping consensus of pre-commitments that can only be changed by more demanding procedures. Ulysses' story illustrates, moreover, a basic virtue of constitutional self-binding. By restricting their power by self-imposed constraints, citizens are able to expand it in the sense that they can now achieve by indirect means objectives they would be unable to achieve in a direct manner. In short, their system becomes more sustainable.

By institutionalizing an overlapping consensus about which pre-political moral principles should be 'constitutionalized' as internal, normative standards for punitive practices, a criminal justice system enhances its sustainability. Nevertheless, the predicament of fallibility applies to the meta-level of constitutional constraints as well. Constitutions, as devices of Ulyssean pre-commitments, might include provisions that eventually fail to redeem their moral ambitions. Or courts might interpret and apply constitutional provisions in a way that likewise fails to do so. For example, the Eighth Amendment's prohibition against 'cruel and unusual punishment' in the US Constitution has consistently been interpreted by the Supreme Court as compatible with the death penalty, albeit with some significant modifications that might indicate a trend towards an alternative, more sustainable 'overlapping consensus'.

In Roger Hood's *Chapter 14: Staying Optimistic*, Hood draws the long lines of abolitionist history from World War II up to the present and uses this as a platform from which to look into possible future scenarios of the death penalty. He recounts the pulsations of and alternations between doubts and hopes – doubts that further abolition will be possible and hopes for universal abolition. Just when one thought that the movement had ground to a halt, suddenly there arrives some impetus propelling new advances.

Going region by region and sometimes country by country, Hood combines depth and detail to elucidate the growth towards a critical mass of abolitionist countries and the possible tipping of the balance towards worldwide abolition. He shows how this movement towards a critical mass changes the very context of classical arguments against the death penalty and the resonance that can be expected in the light of this new context.

Hood gives an overview of the remaining retentionist countries and analyses the depth of opposition to abolition in these countries. He selects certain dominant retentionist countries (for example China) and goes deeply into the national ambivalence towards the death penalty over time and thereby demonstrates the changed resonance for different types of arguments for or against the death penalty.

One of the most significant changes in resonance has been caused by the de-coupling of the death penalty from being seen as a purely sovereign issue of crime control, to being at least partly accepted as a legitimate concern of international human rights. Hood describes how an international counter-movement has attempted to stigmatize this de-coupling as a form of cultural imperialism attempting to invade countries' sovereign space. Hood points out that this is a false antithesis in that the argument implies that the issue of death penalty cannot be both an international and a national concern. Abolition has in fact been embraced across the globe by so many countries with different political systems, religious creeds and cultures that any attempt to characterize abolition as cultural imperialism can no longer be credible. Hood concludes by claiming that the abolition of capital punishment and its replacement by a humane system of imprisonment should not only be seen as a clear human rights concern, but is in many ways becoming the very litmus test for the respect for human rights.

PART I
Governance and the Death Penalty

Chapter 1
The Death Penalty: A Hazard to a Sustainable Development of Criminal Justice?

Lill Scherdin[1]

The terrorist attack on Norway in 2011 struck at the very core of the Norwegian governing power as well as at our young and vulnerable. The gruesome details are described in the Foreword by Knut Storberget, the Minister of Justice at the time, and in Chapter 2 by Nils Christie. The first part of the attack destroyed the offices of the prime minister and several other central ministries: eight people died. The second part of the attack targeted the ruling party's youth league – killing 69 children and adults (some as young as 14 years old). The assassin's explicit intention was to eradicate the seeds of Norway's social democratic political future, to radically change the democratic form of government in Norway and to replace it with totalitarian rule. It was not just the most gruesome crime; it was a *crimen majestatis*, i.e., a crime against the heads of government or the state itself. The prime minister came to no harm, but if ever there was the ultimate test of a criminal justice system without the death penalty, this was it. Yet there were no demands for the death penalty by any professional or citizen group, by any political party or by the government itself.

This is in stark contrast with the role the death penalty played in the aftermath of Timothy McVeigh's bombing in Oklahoma, after the sarin gas attacks in the Tokyo underground, and most comparably, in the aftermath of the attacks of 9/11 in the USA.

It is also in stark contrast with the way that *crimen majestatis,* and particularly dreadful murders, have been punished throughout most of world history, including in the Norwegian past. Governing without the death penalty has a short history – even in the west.

The death penalty was for centuries an ordinary and largely uncontested tool for the exercise of government power (Garland 2014). How then is it that Europe has turned its back on this punishment, and how is it that the Norwegian government and its people, in the face of such an atrocity, rejected any call for

1 I want to thank Ronald Craig, Jane Dullum, Vidar Halvorsen, May-Len Skilbrei, Per Jørgen Ystehede and Katja Franko Aas for generously reading and commenting on this chapter.

the death penalty? What characterizes the sustainability of a moderate criminal justice system with no death penalty, in the face of events that in many societies would lead to moral outrage immediately crystallizing into a cry for the death penalty? How is it that states move from having such pride in the spectacle of the death penalty as an expression of their identity and might, to a pride in not having it? Indeed, many states are seeing their core identity defined by the very act of stepping back from it. They express something central about their state when recoiling both from taking the life of a human being who is already pacified and under state control, and from asking or ordering other citizens – human beings – to kill someone already under state control.

The *sustainability perspective* tentatively explored in this chapter is inspired by, and combines knowledge from, three different but interrelated fields of comparative research. Although largely developed in the west, I suggest that the findings of these research traditions might also be highly relevant for understanding differences in governance through punishment – including the death penalty – in Asia and in countries with Muslim majority populations. This book invites further exploration along such lines. The first of these research traditions arises out of studies of holocaust and genocides, the second from historical and sociological studies of the interrelationships between political economic governance and governance through punishment, and the third tradition from studies of how different types of harms or risks are seen and tackled in differently governed societies.

This chapter will be a step-by-step exploration of such a sustainability perspective.

The Backdrop: Conditions for Empathy

An important backdrop to exploring the sustainability perspective is understanding the situational conditions in which people are willing to inflict pain on others, for example in the form of severe punishments, including the death penalty. Much of this research has its origin in genocide and holocaust research and in social-psychological experiments inspired by these (Christie 1952, Milgram 1974, Zimbardo 2007). One initial finding was that if social situations were construed in certain ways, normal people could be led to deliver limitless and deadly amounts of pain to others. Another main finding was that it becomes more difficult to inflict pain or punishment on others the more you are able to see them as people like yourself. When this happens, everyday norms of behaviour towards others kick in and might reduce or prevent extreme pain infliction. Thus the formation of social situations, indeed of whole societies, where there are great distances between people – between different classes, castes, ethnicities, religions, genders, etc. – might also generate societies where people are more likely to perceive others as fundamentally different from themselves, both rationally and morally. This leads to less empathy with their situation, and therefore fewer reservations about meting out severe pain to them (ibid.). From this it can for example be hypothesized that there is likely to be more pain infliction in societies characterized by inequality and distance, provided that institutionally there are few obstacles between the dominant groups' inclination to define new troublesome acts as punishable crimes, or old crimes as deserving more severe punishment, and the enactment of new penal laws (Christie 1981, 1985, 1993). This leads us to the research that explores whether this might indeed be so in 'the real world' of today.

Understanding Why States Differ in Governance Through Punishment

The quest to understand why states differ in governance through punishment, including the death penalty, has been spurred by the sudden and fast-widening gap between the criminal justice practices of Europe and those of the USA from the start of the 1980s. States in the USA increased their use of the death penalty, while European countries totally eradicated its use. The use of prisons in the USA soon increased to a level five to ten times higher than in Europe. This rise in incarceration was accompanied by a rise in capital penalty sentences that did not peak until 1996 with 315, and a rise in executions (especially in the southern states) that did not peak until 1999 with 98 (DPIC 2013). This gigantic and all too real 'incarceration experiment' and the sharp rise in state killings, have both had dramatic consequences – some intended, but frighteningly many unintended. The massive suffering, the individual, social, cultural and structural 'collateral damage' of these decades of US governance through punishment, gradually comes into view. Because of it, comparative criminology has acquired essential insights into the relationships between state governance, crime, and punishment.

The dramatic 'in-your-face' differences within the west between the two sides of the Atlantic reduced the appeal of facile essentialist, orientalist or occidental 'comparative' approaches. More nuanced, complicated approaches were needed, leading to sociological models of increasing complexity for comparison. It was necessary to keep open ways to understand the uniqueness of each state or locality as it had developed historically, and not to lose sight of how international or transnational forces might intersect with local ones.

Theorizing about relationships between state governance, crime and punishment is classic in sociology. Various versions of critical criminology in particular have kept this tradition very much alive. However, it was not until the dramatic split between Europe and the USA in the politics and practices of punishment that a wave of comparative research with this focus gained sustained attention in mainstream criminology. The seminal works of Nils Christie, David Garland, David Nelken and Piers Beirne (Christie 1993, 2004, Garland 1990, 2001, Beirne and Nelken 1997) framed this comparative field and gave urgency and meaning to the development of the more concrete quantitative studies related below.

To understand the immense increase in incarceration Beckett and Western (2001) did an early study using data from 32 states in the USA for the years 1975, 1985 and 1995. Later, Downes and Hansen (2007) did basically the same study with data from 18 'capitalistic democracies', most of them in Europe. Tapio Lappi-Seppälä (2008) used a large compilation of data from a series of international surveys, including data on crime (victimization and official statistics on crime and incarceration), data from social, economic and political indicators, and data on public sentiments from the European Social Surveys and World Values Surveys. He included East-European states, and has subsequently incorporated many countries from outside the west. Cavadino and Dignan (2006) did an in-depth study of 12 capitalist democracies, including Japan. Many others have followed: too many to address. I depart from these in order to introduce central perspectives and findings.

No Systematic Relationship between Incarceration, Death Penalty and Crime

Surprisingly for many in mainstream criminology, all these studies showed the same results. They found no clear, systematic relationship between crime and punishment in the form of incarceration numbers. For the most part, the ups and downs of incarceration did not vary systematically with the ups and downs of crime, when controlled for relevant factors. Indeed, comparison of states in the USA showed that those with the most incarceration saw the smallest fall in crime. As to the case of New York (well known for its large decreases in crime), one fact is clear: such decreases were not due to an overall increase of incarceration, nor to the use of capital punishment (Jacobson 2005, Zimring 2007). In general increased incarceration had no systematic effect on crime.[2] This does not mean that a further decrease from the lowest levels of punishment studied, e.g., in the Scandinavian countries and Japan, to a level of no punishment at all, would render the same result. But it does mean that those in favour of punishment levels considerably above the penal regimes with the lowest punishments, have no scientific grounds for believing that increasing prison expenditure, prison terms or the pain inflicted will lead to less crime.

As for the death penalty, a wealth of deterrence research studies has been conducted over the last decades. These studies have subsequently been incorporated into grand meta-studies of ever more complexity. In 2012 these were re-evaluated by the National Research Council of the National Academies (NRCNA). They found no scientific basis for claiming anything about the effects of death penalty, so there was no support for the claim that the death penalty had greater deterrent effect than long-term imprisonment (NRCNA 2012).

The lack of deterrent effect of the death penalty as against long prison terms for homicide is not limited to the sphere of western civilization, as some non-western

2 These research results should not be considered inconsistent with the fact that there are certain situations where punishment threshold levels might be significant for certain crimes, nor do they imply that police work and clearance rates have no effect.

death penalty retentionist governments insist. David Greenberg and Valerie West found in a worldwide study of 193 countries that there was no systematic relationship between having, or using the death penalty and trends in homicide. Although there were exceptions, they also found a positive statistical relationship between incarceration and the death penalty. For states that had the death penalty, those that proportionately imprisoned more of their citizens were also likely to kill more of them (Greenberg and West 2008).

To further explore the death penalty's possible deterrent effect in Asia, Franklin Zimring, Jeffrey Fagan and David Johnson did a comparative study of Singapore and Hong Kong in 2009: *Executions, Deterrence and Homicide: A Tale of Two Cities*. The tale they told was that these two jurisdictions were as similar as is possible in a 'natural experiment'. They were similar in scale, density, geography, demographics, literacy, culture, historical and economic development, and in recent growth in population (Hong Kong is a bit larger and 95 per cent Chinese, compared with 75 per cent Chinese in Singapore). When it came to the death penalty, however, they were totally different. Hong Kong had not had an execution for a generation and abolished the death penalty in 1993, thus having no executions throughout the 35 years period of comparison. Singapore, on the other hand, had an execution rate close to one per million per year until there was an explosive twentyfold increase in the middle of the nineties (1994–96), escalating to a level of execution that was probably the highest per capita in the world. It was higher than that of the county with most executions in the most-executing state in the USA at the time: Harris County in Texas. It was probably higher than in China, which was in the middle of its most violent 'hard strike' campaigns. Then over the next 11 years Singapore's executions fell back by almost 95 per cent. Singapore had mandatory death for murder, and a short time between conviction and execution. Thus high predictability and certainty gave ideal conditions for measuring deterrent effect (ibid.).

So what happened to the homicide rates in the two cities? They were remarkably similar, following each other, sloping downwards, albeit with ups and downs. Despite all Singapore's killings, there was a remarkable lack of effect on the homicide curve.

In conclusion, one found no greater deterrent effect of the death penalty *vis-à-vis* long-term imprisonment, when comparing states with and without the death penalty in the USA. No such effect was found in quantitative studies worldwide, and no such effect was found in the clear-cut, dramatic 'Tale of Two Cities' in Asia (ibid.). At least when focusing on deterrence of homicides, one can claim that this research sets us free to choose a moderate criminal justice system with no death penalty without fear: such a system can be sustainable.

This is what many criminologists, with Nils Christie in Scandinavia in the lead, claimed years ago, with considerable impact on penal moderation in the Nordic countries (Christie 1981, 1993, 2004). The new quantitative and qualitative studies support them.

Different Political-Economic Governance, Different Prison and Death Penalty Policies

If they are not related to crime, how can one understand extreme increases in imprisonment and the death penalty, e.g. in the USA? And how can we understand the opposite: What has made a moderate criminal justice system with no death penalty sustainable in other states in the same period? To understand the conditions for the sustainability of a moderate criminal justice system both in a balanced relationship to other part of the state, and over time, we shall explore: What differences in how states are governed generally, *make a difference* for the sustainability of criminal justice systems with or without the death penalty?

For most of the capitalist economies in the west the last decades of the twentieth century were times of global economic changes, beginning with the 1970s recession. They saw the contraction or collapse of manufacturing industries, with serious increases in unemployment, and the flight of investment overseas. This is referred to as the end of the Fordist era of western capitalism. These were brutal societal changes. Business elites still made money from increased salaries and investments abroad, creative financial products and global financial trade, but local and smaller businesses suffered, and public employees and blue-collar workers lost their jobs or had their salaries cut. Many states saw increases in inequality, albeit to different degrees (Lacey 2008, Wilkinson and Pickett 2011).

With this in mind we return to the comparisons between states in the USA and also between capitalist democracies more broadly from 1975 to the turn of the century. At any particular time throughout the period, all the comparative research studies found that the greater the inequality, and the higher the percentage of poverty and minorities, the more people there were in prison. They found that the larger the percentage of GNP states allocated to social welfare, the lower the incarceration rate in the state (Beckett and Western 2001, Cavadino and Dignan 2006, Downes and Hansen 2007, Lappi-Seppälä 2008). Beckett and Western found that these relationships got stronger over time and were strongest in 1995 (Beckett and Western 2001).

A primary finding of Wilkinson and Pickett 2011 is that the greater the inequality, the more incarceration there is, and the greater the likelihood that the state will use the death penalty. They point out that there are different ways to bring about less inequality. Most states that do well as to equality have comparatively higher social and welfare expenditures. However, the state of New Hampshire (USA) is cited as a state that achieves a great degree of equality through more equality in market income (income before taxes) though with low social, health and welfare expenditures (Wilkinson and Pickett 2011: 241).

One may question whether equality based on market income, with minimal redistribution schemes, is as sustainable in times of fluctuating international markets, when more people suffer hardship and can no longer rely on the market to survive. In other words, the question is whether sustainable equality *over time* in any state must rely on some *decommodification* measures, i.e., redistributive measures that allow people to be not entirely dependent on markets; when they are too young, too old, too sick, or for some other reason unable to find work. Similarly, when one is unable to find work combinable with care giving, or when one lacks the re-education to fit a changing market.

Other important and often underestimated forms of decommodification, which are less typical of western democratic capitalist societies, can characterize more collective and traditional societies. Today, the sheer size of transnational remittances from workers in the diaspora to families in developing countries is vastly important as a form of decommodification. I will, however, continue to focus on substantive inequality and access to affordable health care, education and social welfare as central forms of decommodification, and turn to their relationship to governance through punishment in the different states being compared.

Striving to understand the connection between governing through punishment, and different forms of political economic governance generally, Cavadino and Dignan (2006) adopted Esping-Andersen's typology of 'families of states' (Esping-Andersen 1990). In his research on social welfare, Esping-Andersen had grouped capitalist democratic states into three 'families of states' characterized by their main socioeconomic governing structure: the neo-liberal family, the conservative corporative family and the social democratic corporative family. Cavadino and Dignan used this typology on their 12 capitalist democracies and fused it with research on differences in incarceration rates. They found that different 'families of states' were consistently different as to incarceration rates. The 'neo-liberal' states consistently had less of their GNP going to welfare and higher incarceration numbers. Next came *all* the 'conservative corporative states' and then *all* the 'social democratic corporative states'. Notwithstanding possible discrepancies and discussions that might modify and muddle the picture, the overall trends were supported by other studies. Cavadino and Dignan added Japan as an 'oriental corporative' type. Japan alone had the highly atypical profile of, on the one hand, allocating a relatively low percentage of GDP to social welfare and on the other hand, having exceptionally low incarceration rates (Cavadino and Dignan 2006). Wilkinson and Pickett (2011) explain *some part of this anomaly* by the fact that Japan has a higher degree of equality of income before taxes, like New Hampshire, and take the view that the important relationship is the one between equality and punishment.

Cavadino and Dignan found that although the countries in the different families were undergoing continuous change during this time period, the relative differences in incarceration rates and allocations to welfare (or other decommodification measures) seemed relatively robust.[3]

---

3 These seemed at that moment robust, notwithstanding the strong impact of different forces of globalization, e.g. the fluctuations of world trade and finance, the movement of people and goods across borders, the developing nodes of commerce within and across nations, the growing communities of migrants or refugees that to varying degrees are integrated into the societies or detained in other types of prison-like institutions. I will

As Nicola Lacey says, Cavadino and Dignan's analysis sharpens our sense of relevant state differences. But then the question arises: Why do these family resemblances hold together over time and how do different political-economic and institutional variables combine to produce these sustained different patterns of punishment? (Lacey 2008). In *The Prisoner's Dilemma*, Lacey adopts a distinction made by Peter Hall and David Soskice (2001), between 'liberal' families on the one hand and the more 'coordinated' or corporate market economies on the other (ibid.). She argues that different political and economic forces at the macro level in different market economies are mediated not only by cultural filters, but by the economic, political and social institutions of each of these states (ibid.).

In the most 'liberal democracies' there is *very limited coordination*, with a greater freedom for capital and business to act. Great Britain, Australia, New Zealand and the USA are examples. By contrast, in the most coordinated market economies like the Nordic states, the institutionalized tripartite processes of bargaining between labour unions, employer organizations and government stabilizes societies in a number of ways. The bargaining is oriented toward dividing productivity gains created in the economy more fairly among social partners and in return gaining wage restraints from workers in recessionary or inflationary periods.

In the most coordinated market economies the workers or employees are more unionized and more strongly present with their demands and priorities than in other countries. The employers are also more united as a coordinated negotiating party and the state is a third party, responsible for overseeing the process, with power to enforce arbitration under certain circumstances. Such coordination gives structure to the sequences of negotiations, periods of peace and periods of conflict – and thus predictability. Predictability increases the willingness to compromise in the light of planned priorities over time. This works as an incentive for moderation for both employers and employees. Predictability, long-term planning and moderation have increased equality in pay, and led to other protective labour laws e.g. protection against being fired or injured in the work place. This creates common interests for employers and employees e.g. to improve public education and strengthen rights

return to problematize this point later in the chapter. Other forces influencing the politics of the state were supranational institutions and treaties regulating communications technically and commercially, together with global and regional human rights treaties, their control and oversight regimes and many different NGO's and interest group actors. It seems that although all of these forces influenced the different capitalist democracies in question in different ways, they did not bring about changes fundamental enough to distort relations between or inside the 'families'. Indeed, this is just a moment of history, whether this will still be the case in five or ten years, is hard to say, especially with the European economic difficulties that are now being widely felt. Possibly at a certain point we will see quantitative changes in inequality suddenly result in qualitative leaps, bringing fundamental changes. However, our business here is not to insist on typological maps for capturing different social landscapes forever; we are rather seeking models that help us understand how less incarceration, and life without the death penalty became sustainable for many states at this point in time, and how this might be possible for more states today.

to (re)education that will help them adapt to changing markets, and to strengthen support for state-sponsored training and research development. Strong workers' unions in a state strongly correlate with less inequality, less poverty, more welfare, and less people in prison (Wilkinson and Pickett 2011). The question is why?

Different degrees and forms of coordination seem to exist in a nondeterministic, though mutually reinforcing, relationship with political institutions, e.g. the electoral systems, which again seems to influence how and to what extent a state governs through welfare, and how and to what extent one governs through punishment.

The Cooperative Socioeconomic Systems

The cooperative socioeconomic systems are often characterized by ruling coalitions of large and small parties that have negotiated broad platforms from their ideologically different political programmes. Successful negotiation of complex agreements on the economic level seems to increase trust and bring about broader cooperation on the political level. This supports consensus-based politics, where a variety of interests are taken into account (Lappi-Seppälä 2008).

Welfare generosity and trust in government, trust in politicians as well as trust in other citizens, appear to thrive more in consensual and corporatist societies – where there is more stability over time, more long-term policy deliberation, and where the politicians are voted in on broader party platforms. This is also so because policy making and law drafting processes (including those of penal laws) tend to include a wider variety of interest groups, both as members of drafting committees, and as 'experts' called in to inform the drafting committees. Comprehensive white papers setting out draft legislation are vetted in broad public consultative hearings, and the feedback given is not infrequently taken into account. In parliament, public parliamentary hearings give affected groups the possibility to voice their opinions once again (Lappi-Seppälä 2008: 109).

The importance of the broader compromises and negotiations in both the economic and political spheres motivates the media to inform and compete at a somewhat deeper level of nuance and complexity, despite the attraction to personalized, dramatized black and white, conflict-oriented stories as found in the media of less consensual societies. There tends also to be greater equality in the media's structuring of the electoral process, e.g. with all political party leaders ritually engaged together with the same allotted time in a series of TV debates covering broad areas of politics, with criminal justice being just one of these.

When we try to understand differences in politics and in the media, too little attention might be paid to what I would call *the facts on the ground.* In these relatively economically stable welfare states, there already exists a strong bureaucratic state, relatively secure within its boundaries. Norway is an example: to a large degree it practices redistributive health with institutions and bureaucracies that exist throughout the country. *This state is peppered with institutions doing 'health, social and welfare things'.* These institutions provide employment to a large part of the population. Thus more people in coordinated economies are actively and practically engaged in the daily business of planning and providing welfare: doing such 'health, social and welfare things'.

These are the facts on the ground. Neither politicians nor the media can ignore great numbers of people working in complexly interrelated care systems, nor the perspectives and practices they develop when seeking solutions inside a system that (notwithstanding its many failings) has an all-encompassing aspiration to provide welfare. Nor can they ignore all the people that over time actually receive affordable health and welfare services.

Politically, the fact that the state and local bureaucracies *are there* makes repressive policies less necessary in welfare states; politically one can strengthen welfare in different parts of an already existing system without the creation of new institutions. It provides the institutional alternatives to exclusion, police and prison. At times of small or large crises, when people commit problematic acts, social services and welfare institutions exist as practical and political alternatives, albeit never enough, and far from perfect – indeed generating economic, social and ethical problems of their own. (e.g., Barker 2013 and Johansen, Ugelvik and Aas 2013).

Thus, in relatively economically stable welfare states, proportionately fewer people than in liberal societies might be marginalized and more people treated more equally and not excluded. Broad public sharing of the costs might also more directly imply that people are somewhat more willing to see society and individuals as sharing responsibility when things go wrong, and thus more willing to share the responsibility of setting things right, e.g. sharing costs and responsibility for the consequences for victims e.g. through state-sponsored compensation schemes for victims of violent crime, which are not dependent on the resources of the defendant. Indeed guilt does not even have to be clearly established. People living in these societies will be somewhat less willing to dispose of 'people problems' by imposing heavy penalties on 'problem people'. It is, of course, far from remarkable that proportionally more people might actually show trust and empathy in a more stable society of relative equals. Indeed the research on trust show this.

There is also a tendency for less privatization in the more coordinated economies with more consensus-based democracies, especially in the core areas of health and criminal justice. They have less (if any) penal institutions owned or run by private for-profit corporations with an interest in economic growth, that does not necessarily coincide with the public interest in preserving a sustainable criminal justice system with the least possible collateral damage for individuals and for society (Cavadino and Dignan 2006).

Liberal, Less Coordinated Economies

The liberal, less coordinated economies with weaker workers' unions and more inequality, have an affinity with more *majoritarian electoral politics* where the will of the majority often dictates political and penal choices. From 1975 to the turn of the century, majoritarian democracies tended to increase economic inequality considerably more than the more coordinated capitalist democracies (Lappi-Seppälä 2008, Wilkinson and Pickett 2010: 308).

In Great Britain and the USA, income inequality between the richest and poorest ten per cent of population, increased by 40 per cent from 1975 to 2004 (Wilkinson and Pickett 2010: 308–9). This inequality is higher than it has been for generations. Paul Krugman, Nobel Prize winner in economy, has studied the causes for this dramatic increase in inequality. Krugman claims that it was largely a question of political choices, not national and international market competition. Reagan and Thatcher no longer felt pressure from the socialist left and at the very time of economic crisis they chose to use this chance to conquer the trade unions, and force through the politics of economic liberalism. They repealed formal treaties or more informal deals for sharing product gains; they reduced progressive taxation, social benefits and welfare support, and refused systems for regulation of decent minimum wages (Wilkinson and Picket 2010: 311–12).

The political battle took place through majoritarian electoral politics. The majority principle in politics means single seat electoral districts where the winner takes all (Lappi-Seppälä 2008, Lacey 2008). Majority-driven politics are more often based on two parties in fierce competition. This sharpens a contrast in views and also leads to confrontational decision making. The civil servant bureaucracies tend over time to be less comprehensively involved, and more politicized at the top, with the new ruling party bringing in their own advisers to draft future policies, instead of using the somewhat more neutral civil servants. Each party tends to describe the politics of the other party in crisis terms, insisting that if the other party gets into power, harmful change will inevitably occur. Politics are more personalized, and more leader-oriented, so that politicians, once elected, are less bound by party platforms, platforms that are anyway less complex and less worked out than those of more coordinated and consensual democracies. Thus the voters must to a much greater extent 'read into' the party programme what they think a good man (like the one they are about to elect) would do, and more often than in consensual democracies, they feel betrayed. Consultations and compromises are only sought when necessary in confrontational majoritarian decision making: they are all about acquiring the necessary votes. Thus one sees voters caught in a vicious cycle of needs and hopes, disappointment, and growing inequality and distrust – all feeding into the sharpening of political strife, which translates into talk of crises (Lappi-Seppälä 2008, Lacey 2008).

This in turn plays into the structure and culture of the media in the majoritarian democracies that seem to foster more confrontational, sensational and crisis-maximizing stories, than do the media in the more consensual democracies (Lappi-Seppälä 2008).

Since there is less party loyalty and less clear party platforms, there tends to be a larger number of what Lacey and others call *floating medium voters*. They float between the parties at election time. This provides room for single-issue interest groups such as, the interest groups of crime victims, to make large differences. Votes might change because of single issues of emotional relevance, and all candidates will compete viciously to be 'best' on these. Such are the main battlefields of the cultural wars. For long periods at a time, whether crime goes up or down, in non-coordinated capitalist economies with majoritarian democratic systems, crime control tends to return again and again to the centre of electoral attention as a prime emotionally relevant issue. Three points of elaboration follow.

First, greater inequality, less unions, less resources for welfare and other forms of decommodification, all seem to have a clear relationship with increased fear of becoming victims of crime. Hummelsheim, Hirtenlehner, Jackson and Oberwittler took the 'families of states' as a starting point in a study called: 'Social Insecurities and Fear of Crime: A Cross-National Study on the Impact of Welfare State Policies on Crime-Related Anxieties' (Hummelsheim et al. 2010). This was a multilevel analysis of respondents in 23 European countries sampled in the 2004/2005 European Social Survey. They found that public insecurity about crime was associated, again, not with the level of crime in a country, but rather with the degree of social security provided through its various welfare state provisions. In other words, they found strong relationships between insecurity about crime and low national levels of social expenditure on decommodification, i.e., setting people free from market forces. They also found that some protective social welfare measures were more strongly inversely related to fear of crime than others. These were measures – resources made available – that strengthened the individual's capacity to cope with their problems on their own. Having these available to them enabled them to get back control over their lives, and thereby reduce unpredictability and powerlessness. In more unequal capitalist economies, where these welfare measures were less available, social and economic anxieties crystallized to a greater degree around fear of crime (Hummelsheim et al. 2010). Hummelsheim et al. find that the data supported the idea that public anxiety about crime should be understood as part of a mix of broader social anxieties linked to the fundamental social and political conditions of the society (Hummelsheim et al. 2010).

Secondly, crime control is an issue where electoral candidates in this period seldom had to make explicit economic promises. Promises such as the criminalization of new acts, the increase of punishments, and the withdrawal of welfare from felons, did not seem to incur costs for institutions, cities or the state. The underlying claim was often that increased punishment and exclusion will somehow reduce crime – so over time money will be saved.

Thirdly, elected officials and electoral candidates can be depicted as locked into a competitive 'prisoner's dilemma' with no alternative but to continue to up the stakes – to up their promise for less welfare and more exclusion and more criminalization and more punishment (Lacey 2008). Years later the situation on the ground as to incarceration is such that none of these political candidates would have voted for it or described it as the goal of their political choices. While each candidate demonstrates superiority in accountability and attentiveness to the needs and rights of the public, together they create a more polarized and exclusive society and a less sustainable criminal justice system. With crisis-maximizing media profiting from all electoral strife, this process is further exacerbated (ibid).

This all seems to result in greater inequality: less decommodification. Over time the data shows less trust in government, less trust in politicians and less trust in other citizens, more fear of crime *and* more people in prison (Hummelsheim et al. 2010, Lappi-Seppälä 2008). And where the death penalty exists, there is more use of it.

The USA – Immense Incarceration – the Last Western Nation with the Death Penalty

While the non-coordinated and majoritarian democracy Great Britain has seen a formidable increase in pain delivery, it is nowhere near the increase in punishment seen in the USA, which is off the charts with five to ten times more people in prison, depending on the region of comparison. Is the explanation for this simply that the USA liberal democracy has *more of everything*, as is typical of the majoritarian system? As Lacey asks, does the USA simply have: An even weaker system of party discipline? A more politicized bureaucracy? An economy marked by particularly low levels of unionization and employment protection and industry/union/government coordination? A more dramatic collapse of Fordist industry? A particularly ungenerous welfare system? And an especially high level of social inequality and polarization, most vividly around the characteristic of race? (Lacey 2008).

The US certainly has all of the above, but the relative impact of these might not be sufficient to explain the extreme differences between the USA and other non-coordinated and majoritarian democracies. A further suggestion is that the USA has a local populist democracy that has more 'winner take all' elections on federal, state, city and county levels and in particular, has numerous direct elections of criminal justice actors: police chiefs, sheriffs, prosecutors and judges – something not found in other majoritarian democracies.

More elections at all level of politics, with a larger number of floating medium voters with crime control as the vital issue from 1980s to the end of the century, would indeed mean a steady flow of competitive electoral combats, locking both Democrats and Republicans (at both federal and state levels) into a race to the sky on pain delivery and a race to the bottom on social welfare. This dynamic is further strengthened by the federal-state structure, as Garland points out, which makes it difficult to establish political agreement on any social welfare enhancement, while at the same time giving great room to states to increase pain delivery (Garland 2013).

I think President Clinton's legal initiatives in the middle of the 1990s, say it all. As to the race to the bottom on social welfare, Clinton not only ended welfare as we know it with time-limited workfare; he also cut almost all social services for ex-prisoners, taking exclusion to wholly new extremes. As Loïc Wacquant puts it:

> Prisoners are systematically excluded from social redistribution and public aid in an age when work insecurity makes access to such programs more vital than ever for those dwelling in the lower regions of social space. Laws deny welfare payments, veterans benefits and food stamps to anyone in detention for more than 60 days. The Work Opportunity and Personal Responsibility Act of 1996 further banishes most ex-convicts from Medicaid, public housing, Section 8 vouchers and related forms of assistance. In … 1998, President Clinton denounced as intolerable 'fraud and abuse' perpetrated against 'working families' who 'play by the rules', the fact that some prisoners (or their households) continued to get public payments due to lax bureaucratic enforcement … . (Wacquant 2001: 106)

In some places these practices are taken so far that if mother, father, spouse or children receive social benefits, or live in publicly funded housing, the former inmate cannot move home without jeopardizing their situation. By their very presence, the family risks being accused of fraudulent abuse of social services, and can be evicted. Landlords who do not report the presence of ex-prisoners lose their right to participate in the programme (Ericson 2007). Not only does the state now exclude the ex-criminal from all public support, it also intrudes into the family, separating ex-criminals from the only people that might be able to give help and impetus to change. Instead the state makes all contact potentially toxic.

Regarding the race to the sky on pain delivery and the death penalty, Jonathan Simon has documented this period convincingly in his book *Governing through Crime* (2008). Both Democrats and Republicans competed at all political levels to be the toughest on crime and most pro-death penalty. Governors held big press conferences when rejecting petitions for mercy from death-penalty inmates. The politicians positioned themselves consistently through new death-penalty legislation that honoured new victim groups with special death-penalty protection. They proposed limiting appeal possibilities and weakening rule of law and due process protection. Police chiefs, prosecutors and judges won elections all over the USA by demonstrating their will to demand the death penalty, however young, psychologically ill or mentally retarded the accused was. Bill Clinton infamously broke off his election campaign to be present at the execution of a mentally retarded inmate (ibid.).

Most pertinently, after 38 years of a *de facto* death-penalty moratorium at the federal level, President Clinton, in 1994 and 1996, re-initiated executions, and extended death penalty laws to new areas of crime, e.g. drug kingpins. Timothy McVeigh's execution, so eloquently described in Madeira's chapter, was the first federal execution to take place after Bill Clinton blew new life into federal death (Hood and Hoyle 2008: 113–14).

Even if the 'prisoner's dilemma' of overbidding by political candidates partly explains how they walked backwards into a dystopian punishment future, this does not fully explain how this penal empire was built with real money in space and time, or what *fuels* the move to ever higher incarceration and more use of the death penalty in the US.

Due to the states' autonomy in the area of criminal justice Congress cannot require states to build more prisons, but it can earmark funds to states for prison building, if they demonstrate in various stipulated ways that they are serious about crime control. From the 1980s and throughout the 1990s less money was earmarked for social services, education and rehabilitation both inside and outside of prisons, and more money was made available for the joint financing of e.g. new prison buildings. This funded a large expansion of state, federal and local prisons. Additionally, these large sums of money for prison building and prison administration also attracted competitive private corporations.[4]

Although the infamous history of private prisons and convict leasing systems had been terminated by early 1980, by 1990 they were once more a force to be reckoned with, there being 67 for-profit facilities (ACLU 2011). From 1990 to 2009 the number of prisoners held in private prisons increased by about 1600 per cent, from approximately 7,000 to 129,000 inmates. This increase was far steeper than the increase of prisoners held in federal and state-run prisons. By 2010 private prisons were responsible for 6 per cent of state prisoners, 16 per cent of federal prisoners and 49 per cent of immigrant detainees – and the curve continues to go up (ibid.). As the American Civil Liberty Union states in its report on for-profit prisons:

> … as mass incarceration led to disastrous effects for the nation as a whole, one special interest group … emerged as a clear winner. A massive transfer of taxpayer dollars to the private prison industry accompanied the unprecedented increase in incarceration. (ACLU 2011: 13)

These promising profits (at a time when many other businesses fared much worse) were used to create an image of crisis in the media, to lobby intensely at all levels, to contribute handsomely to the election campaigns of politicians, as well as those of sheriffs, police chiefs, prosecutors and judges. An excellent description can be found in *Crime Control as Industry: Towards Gulags, Western Style*, the seminal work of Nils Christie, where the glossy information material describing the danger we are all in, and the for-profit-prison-products that are presented as the solution, are analysed (Christie 1993).

The for-profit private prison industry has, since the 1990s, dominated and subsidized the American Legislative Exchange Council, an influential organization of state legislators that produced streams of model legislation for harsher punishment, 'three strikes and you are out' and 'truth in sentencing' laws. '[C]ompanies get to sit around a table and write "model bills" with the state legislators, who take them home …' (ACLU 2011: 14).

Recall the candidates locked in the 'prisoner's dilemma'. Add to this the fact that the candidates have received handsome contributions to their election or

4 As found by Cavadino and Dignan (2006) prison privatization was more prominent in liberal non-coordinated capitalist majoritarian democracies, and especially so in the USA.

re-election funds from the prison industry, and possibly from police unions and prison workers' unions too. Recall the floating medium voters focusing on single issues – often crime control. This can lead some candidates to think: When in doubt and facing unclear risks, take a tough stance on more incarceration and more death penalty. It might be best for everyone. But large-scale privatization for profit adds a motivation and a force independent of (and sometimes in stark opposition to) a society in balance with a sustainable criminal justice system.

The South is Different, a Tale of Two Nations, the Peculiar Institution of the Death Penalty

All this still cannot explain the extreme differences *within* the USA from the 1980s to the end of the century. The prison industry had lobbied nationwide with few exceptions, yet the highest rates of incarceration were in the states that sentence people to death, and especially those that executed the most. As Steiker and Steiker have shown – focusing on states with the death penalty in the law – it is really *a tale of two nations*: Those that have the death penalty and rarely use it, and those that have made heavy use of it throughout this period (Steiker and Steiker 2006:1869). *Those that incarcerate and execute the most are those with the most extensive histories of involvement with the peculiar institution of slavery.*

Garland describes how the history of death penalty use across the USA in many ways resembled the historic development in Europe, at least up to the end of the sixties.

> [S]everal American states abolished capital punishment long before the European nations, and one of them – Michigan – has been continuously abolitionist since 1846, making it a world leader in the abolitionist cause. Indeed, for the 200 years between the 1770s and the 1970s, America was in lockstep with the other Western nations as they gradually withdrew from the scaffold and disavowed the executioner. (Garland 2010: 11)

In step with growing democracy, stronger labour unions, a rise of decommodification measures like social security and President Roosevelt's New Deal, there were less death sentences and less executions in the 1950s and 1960s before the Supreme Court decision in *Furman vs. Georgia* in 1972, a decision that in effect repealed all death penalty laws in all death penalty states, finding the death penalty *as practised* unconstitutional (Garland 2010).

The Southern states reacted furiously to the Supreme Court's decision in *Furman vs. Georgia*. In their view this decision was the latest in a series of examples of the federal government's attacks on southern society's mores and practices of governance. Indeed the only order that this society had ever known was the deeply segregated and authoritarian order presided over exclusively by whites. Forced integration of schools, housing and public places had been followed up by federal laws giving black people civil rights in 1964 and voting rights in 1965 (Obama 2006: 97–8, Fairclough 2008). When these laws were not implemented, or were circumvented or ignored, the federal government sent military forces to the south to enforce compliance. Thus local white government officials were 'stripped' of authority and security. Their identity as political leaders representing states, that should be autonomous in the area of criminal justice, was at stake. The same could be said of their identity as leaders within the southern states and in local governance. Their life had already been invaded, that daily life which previously had been secure in its segregated containment, whose borders white men and women oversaw, defined and controlled.

With the Furman decision, the Federal Supreme Court was (in their eyes) crowning this fundamental humiliation by taking from them their constitutional right to 'protection' by means of the death penalty. It did not help that the NAACP (National Association for the Advancement of Coloured People) and other black civil rights movements were in the forefront in the movement against the death penalty, pressing for a moratorium on it until the Supreme Court had decided its constitutionality (Hood and Hoyle 2008: 113).

Despite the fact that the death penalty was not found to be unconstitutional *per se*, southern emotional reactions were intense – visceral. Until new laws were passed, infamous convicted murderers would have to be transferred to life in prison, rather than suffer the death penalty. Many southern officials swore that the Supreme Court would not have the last word, and they joined forces to neutralize the Supreme Court by proposing an amendment to the Constitution. The Lieutenant Governor of Georgia called the Supreme Court decision a licence for anarchy, rape and murder (Acker, Bohm and Lanier 2003: 7). 'Proportionality' became a code word for 'liberal, politically correct, federal infringement'. This is not unlike the way, later on in the south of the USA and in many Asian and Muslim majority countries, the term 'human rights' became, for those who had previously ruled without restrictions, code words for politically correct, international 'moral imperialism'.

In the heat of this furor after Furman, a passionate movement arose in the US south and spread to other states, a movement towards regaining the death penalty, towards more punishment, and ever more extensive control over 'problem populations' and 'dangerous others', who were largely seen as poor and out-of-control blacks. Although riots, student protests and antiwar struggles were happening all over the USA, out-of-control blacks were a more salient threat in the southern states, and white leaders felt the struggle for regaining the death penalty and the quest for containment of 'problem people' by means of crime control, was also a fight to 'regain autonomy' from all 'rule of law' mechanisms which slowed down the criminal justice process from arrest to conviction and execution.

I think it is essential to note that at this time the southern states, in comparison with the other states, did have: a weaker system of party discipline; a higher degree of politicization of bureaucracies; lower levels of unionization, employment protection and industry/union/government coordination; a higher rate of poverty, a more ungenerous welfare system; higher levels of social inequality and polarization, and more ferocious local election processes characterized by candidates locked into their competitive dynamics for ever higher punishments: elections that were also fuelled by the federal money and the interests of the private prison industry. All this was true of the southern states, but also and most importantly, at the time of *Furman vs Georgia*, they were not even functioning democracies in the most elementary form. These states were still *de facto race-based deeply authoritarian caste societies*. Thus *neither blacks nor whites* lived in states of democracy.

The fact that the Civil Rights Act of 1964 abolished segregation in law, and that the 1965 Voting Rights Act secured the right to vote for all, and made illegal the poll taxes, special literacy tests and registration processes adversely affecting the ability of some groups to vote, does not mean that the black vote had any power at the time of *Furman vs Georgia*. Democratization did not come first, followed subsequently by mass incarceration and the increase of the use of the death penalty. Rather, the reality of democratic rights for blacks only came slowly and partially into being in a lengthy, thorny and twisted process in lockstep with the immense incarceration buildup and the new ways of containment. The new residential, geographical, educational and racialized class separation even increased *de facto* segregation in some areas (although in slightly new forms and with other local legal regulatory means) (Fairclough 2008). With the immense incarceration buildup there also came a variety of disenfranchisement laws that caused disproportionate numbers of blacks to lose the right to vote for the rest of their lives, or while in prison or on parole. They required complex reinstatement and registration processes to regain voting rights (ibid.). At the time of *Furman vs. Georgia* in 1972, seven years after the Voting Rights Act, the black vote was not of a size that could make a difference. The dominant political leaders in the south during the eighties and early nineties were still from a generation of white people, raised during segregation in law or in practice. At the time of Furman only two blacks had been elected to Congress from the entire South since reconstruction: Barbara Jordan and Andrew Young (www.aclu.org/timeline-history-voting-rights-act last visited 30/4/2013).

Might it be the case that the southern dynamic of emerging democratization in lockstep with accelerated incarceration, greater use of the death penalty and new ways of containment, had propelled the southern states *in certain ways* to bypass a clear stage of 'a democratic welfare state'? Did this dynamic take the south directly from an authoritarian caste order to a particular type of 'culture of control' – a peculiar kind of security state?

The Facts on the Ground: When Does Difference in Scale of Imprisonment Become Difference in Kind – a Peculiar Kind of Capitalist Security State 'Authoritarisnism'?

In these polarized and unequal states with little welfare or other decommodification measures a large security and criminal justice sector has firmly established itself since the 1990s, with a massive workforce. If you add those incarcerated to this workforce, the criminal justice system comprises almost a tenth of all inhabitants of several of the southern states. Indeed, even a low execution state like California was by the mid-1990s spending more on prisons than on higher education, with prison expenditure rising from 2 per cent to nearly 10 per cent of the state budget from 1980 to 1995 (Lacey 2008: 172).

It is not remarkable that, when so many people are connected to people 'doing security and police and prison guard things', these people and their perspectives cannot be ignored by politicians or the media. Their perspectives will permeate the society to a considerable degree, and other institutions will tend to 'govern through crime' (Simon 2008) in addition to the direct group interests at play in political processes. For example over the years the powerful union of California prison guards (California Correctional Peace Officers Association) has backed all tough-on-crime candidates, and supported the model legislation for 'three strikes and you are out' and the death penalty. At the time of small or large crises, when people commit problematic acts, more inclusionary services are by and large simply not available. Thus, returning people to the systems of control and incarceration, although these are fraught with problems and unintended consequences, still remains the practical and political option at hand. This will also influence the perception of the problem. If all you have is a hammer, all problems tend to look like nails.

All states are different, but let us look at Louisiana as an example: an oil and seafood state with roughly the same population as Norway (another oil and seafood state). Louisiana has slightly fewer people: 4,601,893 inhabitants, while Norway has 5,003,367.

Louisiana has the greatest inequality in the USA; it is also the second poorest state in the USA: 18 per cent of the population was below the poverty line in 2002; 30 per cent of the population are minorities (mostly blacks). Louisiana has the highest level of health and social problems in the USA except for Mississippi (Wilkinson and Pickett 2010: 228, Jacobson 2005) and its welfare measures (percentage-wise) are the lowest in the US, except for New Mexico (Jacobson 2005). With the highest inequality and the lowest decommodification, what would we expect Louisiana's per capita imprisonment to be?

Louisiana has 71,576 incarcerated: 39,709 in prisons (2011 statistics) and 31,867 in local jails (2010 statistics). In comparison, in 2012 Norway's prison population was 3,575. Louisiana's imprisonment rate was approximately 1,569 per 100,000, while Norway had an imprisonment rate of 71 per 100,000 inhabitants. Thus, Louisiana's imprisonment rate is 22 times Norway's (www. Sentencingproject. org, 2 May 2013). In 2007, 8.7 per cent of Louisiana's population was either under the control of the criminal justice system or working in this system in some capacity. Today it would be closer to 10 per cent.

As for the death penalty, measured by number of executions, Fairclough sums it up in this way: 'Since the resumption of executions in 1976, … Louisiana has executed more prisoners than any other state except Florida and Texas; in proportion to its population, it is America's leading executioner' (Fairclough 2008: 471). Louisiana's incarceration rate is at least five times Iran's, possibly 13 times China's and 20 times Germany's, according to the *Times-Picayune* online newspaper of 13 May 2012.

Extreme incarceration in Louisiana is not mainly due to large private prison corporations as described above; although 50 per cent of the inmates are housed in for-profit facilities. In a uniquely Louisianan twist, most of the prison entrepreneurs are rural sheriffs, who organize things in such a way that much of Louisiana's law enforcement or regular police work is financed with dollars legally skimmed off the top of prison operations (ibid.). Even though the state only pays 24.39 dollars a day for every inmate, which is by far the least money allocated per inmate of any state (ibid.), the very size of the industry makes it profitable. But this industry must be supplied with a constant influx of human beings, or a 182 million dollar industry would have to be seriously downsized (ibid.).

In Louisiana a two-time car burglar can get 24 years without parole. Three drug convictions can result in life imprisonment. Murderers automatically receive life without parole (LWOP), and Louisiana has the highest percentage of LWOP-inmates (The *Times-Picayune* online, May 13, 2012). Angola, the largest state prison, 'is the home of scores of old men who cannot get out of bed' (The *Times-Picayune* online newspaper of May 13, 2012). Even for the least serious non-violent drug and theft offences, former inmates must adhere to a set of extra rules lest they be guilty of 'technical violations' and sent back to prison with additional prison time. In this too Louisiana is the strictest state: 19 months' extra prison time for technical violations. In 2001, violators of parole or probation were 63 per cent of those entering prisons (Jacobson, 2005). In this way, large waves of mostly young black males migrate between poor neighbourhoods and prisons – a perfect illustration of Wacqaunt's seminal: *Deadly Symbiosis: When Ghetto and Prison Meet and Mesh* (2001).

The sheer size of the criminal justice system must be fully understood. If one looks at a map of prison institutions, *this small state is peppered with prisons*. This has resulted in a disproportionate system where the police, and the prison system with its massive numbers of employees, is now so large a part of local institutional life and the income structure of local communities throughout Louisiana (an otherwise poor state of only 4.6 million people) that the sheer weight of this sector and all its ties with other parts of society, could seriously *skew the balance of the now more established democratic process itself.* There is so much money involved, and so many people with vested interests in the maintenance of the system as it is. So much money is at stake in the election of police chiefs, sheriffs, judges, officials, politicians at all levels, that it seems to block any movement towards the reduction of the number of prisons and the use of punishment, so as to free up resources for other sectors such as schools, health and social services or welfare. With these facts on the ground, and the weight against change that they constitute, there is a grave danger that in the democratic process, any movements for change, e.g. to alleviate suffering in other areas will tend to be ignored or suppressed.

Has *a peculiar kind of capitalist security state with authoritarian tendencies* been produced? Such a claim may be supported by the combination of large-scale incarceration, strong support for the death penalty, and a thoroughly ingrained practice of ignoring poor people's suffering. The latter is evidenced by a *de facto*, long-standing acceptance of an extreme market ideology that supports only the most minimal decommodification, and *embodies an ultra-liberal willingness to let die.*

Relationships between Governance Generally, and Governance through High Incarceration and the Death Penalty in the Rest of the World

The correlations between relative lack of democracy, greater inequality, more incarceration and greater use of the death penalty (where it exists) are not limited to states in the west and a few other particular capitalist democracies. Garland depicted such a general tendency in his arc of history (Garland 2014). Greenberg and West found in their study of 193 countries that there seemed to be a positive relationship between democracy and death penalty abolition. However, the more inequality there is and the more authoritarian governments are, the more incarceration there is, and the greater the use of the death penalty. For the states that had the death penalty as a legal option, those with more of their citizens in prison were also likely to execute more of them (Greenberg and West 2008).

The Tale of Two Nations by Steiker and Steiker, has its parallel in David Johnson and Franklin Zimring's description of differences in Asia in their seminal work *The Next Frontier. National Development, Political Change, and the Death Penalty in Asia* (2009).

Approximately half of Asian jurisdictions are without the death penalty, in law or in practice, but when it comes to those that do have the death penalty, there too it is 'a tale of two *kinds* of retentionist nations'. Many seldom execute, while some execute extensively.

The difference between India and China is illustrative, as described by David Johnson:

> Compare China and India, the world's two most populous countries … . India executed one person in the twelve years between 1998 and 2009, for an annual rate per million persons that is 1/3000th that for the United States over the same period of time. If the rest of the world shared India's low rate, there would be, worldwide less than one execution per year. China's execution rate, by contrast, is at least 50,000 times that of India. A difference of degree this vast is also a difference in kind that is not captured by the usual death penalty categories. (Johnson 2010: 7)

The countries that execute the most in East Asia are China, Vietnam, possibly North Korea, and Singapore (until 2002), and these are also countries that are more authoritarian although in different ways, and that have proportionately the largest per capita incarceration. In principle China, North Korea and Vietnam are non-changeable and therefore authoritarian one-party communist states with great inequality in power between the leaders and the majority of the people. Singapore has had its own brand of on-the-right authoritarianism (Johnson and Zimring 2009). None of these high-use states provide decent death penalty data, which goes along with their general non-transparent authoritarianism in governance. China probably executed 15,000 persons per year between 1998 and 2001. Until Singapore's execution rate started to decline in 2002 (described earlier), this city state was considered by many the world's execution capital (ibid.).

> In Singapore and PRC, and in North Korea and Vietnam as well, the key determinant of high execution levels is the preference of strong governments with pervasive authority over executive and judicial actions. ... In these settings, leadership comes from the front on almost all matters, and it frequently contradicts public opinion. ... Whatever the governmental system, the key proximate cause of substantive change in death penalty policy is the leadership of political elites. (Johnson 2011, quoted from paper version: 12)

The same pattern (the tale of two kinds of retentionist nations) applies to the Muslim majority countries. Some seldom or never execute, and a smaller group executes extensively: Iran, Saudi Arabia, Pakistan, Iraq and Yemen (Hood and Hoyle 2009: 42). Development towards secure political stability, less economic and status inequality and more democracy for all different classes, castes, religions and genders, can make possible and legitimate ways of governing through punishment that do not involve the death penalty.

> As regards the largest group – the countries with majority Muslim populations – the prospects for abolition will depend on whether political stability can be achieved and whether governments remain politically and legally dominated by fundamentalist interpretations of Islam or whether they move toward secular democratic government, which allows for a more modern, 'scientific', and less authoritarian interpretation of Islam (Hood and Hoyle 2009: 41).

In principle both Iran and Saudi Arabia have non-changeable and therefore authoritarian Islamist rulers. Once more we see that frequent use of the death penalty goes along with large-scale incarceration, and with non-democratic societies with a great deal of poverty, little welfare or other decommodification measures for the poor, and great inequality. Protest or movements for change from below are ignored or neutralized. The combination of military, police and religious guards responsible for the containment of vice and dissent, are formidable forces. In these countries movements for change come mainly from above, with 'hard strikes' or 'fundamentalist religious purification'. They selectively hit the poor, foreigners, minorities and those questioning the unchangeability of the governing regimes.

As Garland shows in his chapter of this book (Why the Death Penalty is Disappearing), the death penalty is inversely related to democracy. Johnson and Zimring claim the same to be true in Asia and elsewhere, as Asia shares with the rest of the world two related nondeterministic causes of death penalty decline. The first is the fall of authoritarian regimes. Maybe a milder version of this is to be seen in the second common pattern – the decline of capital punishment after a left-liberal party, meaning a party in favour of less inequality and broader democracy, takes control of government (as happened for example in France, when Mitterand came to power). This, according to David Johnson and Franklin Zimring, helps to explain the cessation of executions in South Korea immediately after Kim Dae Jung became president in 1998 (Johnson and Zimring 2009).

How States Mobilize against Harms and Risks – Collateral Damage

Stanley Cohen pointed out in *States of Denial: Knowing about Atrocities and Suffering* (2001) that there is a broad spectrum of ways governments define and react to harms, risks and serious crimes. They can be ignored or denied, assessed and proportionately reacted to, or they can be exaggerated out of proportion, leading to rash and dramatic reactions with large amounts of collateral damage.

Most governments ignore harms to the lower classes and minorities more readily than harms to others. All societies are in constant change resulting in new and unforeseen harms and risks for different sectors and groups. Mobilization against such harms takes place in the policy-formation of the executive, legislative and judicial branches. While resourceful actors are able to voice, lobby and counteract such harms and risks through regulation or criminalization of them, the growth of harms to less resourceful groups are left unrecognized and unencumbered.

Also, depending on their types of governance, societies often systematically ignore various types of harms and risks. For example, the USA seems to a large extent to ignore inequality, poverty and the suffering typically caused by the market economy as well as the collateral damage of the control deemed necessary to uphold it. Iran and Saudi Arabia ignore the harms and risks caused by the lack of political and religious freedom and the collateral damage of the control necessary to suppress these freedoms, while communist countries ignore the harms caused by the lack of economic and political freedom and the collateral damage of the control necessary to suppress these.

All too often mobilization against very serious, widespread and well-known risks and harms fails to take off. It fails to muster the necessary support, and does not achieve any of the protective measures that are sorely needed. The harms are there, mobilization starts over and over again, but it runs into all the kinds of institutional and political obstacles described earlier in this chapter. Without institutional empowerment of less resourceful groups or support from powerful allies, the mobilization runs to a halt. Important powerful groups or key actors fail to give it consistent support. Sometimes this is because change would simply affect prevailing ways of life too much, and powerful ruling groups perceive that they might lose when others gain. Openly recognizing the harms as serious but remediable might change 'a whole way of life'. The facts on the ground and vested interests outweigh the voices of those who suffer (Cohen 2001, Christie and Bruun 1985).

At the other extreme, societies can sometimes exaggerate or even construct the harms or risks they face, and launch into disproportionate defence or securitization movements or *moral panics*, often with extensive collateral damage (Cohen 1980, 2001).

These moral panics or securitization movements tend to strike very selectively, and further increase inequalities, thus generating conditions for more *othering* – i.e., perceiving others as rationally and morally different. As pointed out earlier, some societies (with their institutions) are already characterized by greater social insecurity, less trust of others and fewer institutional hindrances to block the move from reasonable mobilization to moral panics. The research on moral panics describes how different actors in the institutions of politics, media and criminal justice, contribute to the mobilization frenzy (Kassman 1998, Scherdin 2003) In this process actors distinguish themselves and enhance their position together with that of their newspaper, their institution, their part of the criminal justice system or their political party. They directly or indirectly cast themselves as spokespersons for their caste, race, class, religious belief or gender. The research on moral panics emphasizes how such movements may become similar to crusades that the entire society gets caught up in (ibid.). Often such mobilization movements are intensely averse to any reflection. Loyalty to the cause is expected, critical questions shunned. Sweeping changes are demanded, and whatever collateral damage arises is to be ignored.

Thus the first victim of a moral panic is the truth (Christie and Bruun 1985). Some types of mobilization movements, even those arising from very real harms, seem to be clouded by collective misunderstandings as to the nature and cause of the harms and risks in question. When movements run wildly towards highly disproportionate, irrational and immoral measures, they often have little beneficial impact on the harms or risks that they claim to be concerned with. The *Kennedy vs. Louisiana* case below shows how the wish to protect the valuable and vulnerable, e.g. children, from terrible crimes becomes so intense that people do not stop to consider the central facts about these terrible crimes, and based on such facts whether the punishments suggested, might hurt more that they help.

A whole range of collateral damage connected with the use of the death penalty had been known for a long time, or been documented by research throughout the 1980s and 1990s. But this knowledge was curiously absent from mainstream discussion. For example, the execution of innocent people and the inequality in the application of the death penalty, although given significant weight in *Furman vs. Georgia* in 1972, were given little or no weight in the dominant mobilizations for more punishment and more use of the death penalty during the 80s and 90s. In this period it seemed morally despicable or traitorous to talk about the financial costs of the death penalty. Justice could not be weighed in money.

When moral panics subside it becomes once more possible to discuss a wider range of collateral damage. In the midst of the moral panic in the USA, if you were not for the death penalty, you were not truly hard on crime, or in favour of justice for victims. Death penalty was the very symbol of your broader commitment. When the moral panic subsides, people can again decouple these issues from each other and evaluate them separately.

For example in 2012 the California union of prison guards (California Correctional Peace Officers Association) for the first time stepped back from taking a position in the California referendum on the abolition of the death penalty. They *decoupled* the question of the death penalty from other criminal justice issues such as long-term imprisonment. A politician would thus be able to assume that he or she could be against the death penalty without necessarily losing the financial support of the union or the private prison industry.

It appears that the moral panic in the USA might finally be subsiding to some extent. The immense collateral damage is at last impossible to ignore: the financial costs of the death penalty, the fallibility of the public institution of the death penalty, the shocking exoneration of 142 innocent people previously on death row, and the enormously disproportionate and arbitrary application of the death penalty with respect to race, class and geography – all these seemed to have entered into mainstream discussion again (Bessler 2014). Indeed, in Louisiana there has been found to be 98 per cent more chance that the convicted person will get the death penalty if the victim is white (ibid).

There is a growing understanding that most death penalty cases end without a final death penalty sentence, and only a very small per cent of death sentences actually end in an execution many years later (Garland 2010). The geographic disparities are enormous. Law professor Robert Smith recently stated that the vast majority of counties in death penalty states do not use the death penalty at all. Only ten per cent of counties nationally returned a death sentence in the 2004 to 2009 period. Less than one per cent of counties sentenced anyone to death who was actually executed in that time frame (Smith 2012).

These dismal facts prompt one to question whether it is *not only* grossly unjust in the individual case, but also belies the principles of justice fundamental to the entire criminal justice system. The very small execution rate relative to all cases that seek death penalty at the initial trial, also negates any reality in the proclaimed 'absolute necessity of *retribution in kind*' or in the proclaimed 'rights' of victims to so-called closure.

The collateral damage of the death penalty on the victims' families (including children) has come more to the forefront, revealing a multitude of experiences that contradict the stereotype of a unified demand by victims' families for the death penalty in the interest of 'closure' (Madeira 2014). The very fact that victims' families can give their opinion on the choice of death penalty can split families just when they need each other most. Fewer victims' families are asking for the death penalty in the light of a whole range of negative consequences connected with enduring a prolonged and torturous engagement with the criminal justice system, the cases in court and the appeals. This engagement, which can last for decades, often overshadows and damages the family's ability to come to their own terms with their loss and find their own way (ibid). Children are particularly vulnerable to this in that the family's preoccupation with the criminal justice system can end up structuring all the child's formative years and their lives far into adulthood. Victims' families are becoming more aware that only a small part of death sentences actually end in execution, prompting the question whether this is really hurting more than helping. In the light of such statistics, families who asked for the death penalty often end up feeling slighted or undervalued or 'set up to fail' (Madeira 2012, Bohm 2012).

There is also more recognition that there are parallel sufferings in defendants' families (including the children), who are often engaged in a perpetual fight to keep the defendant from being executed, which exhausts material resources and psychological strength, and inhibits their ability to author their own lives. They have no influence on the choice of the death penalty. They carry a burden of shame that often overshadows the children's lives far into adulthood, through school, work and marriage. This is relived at each step of the criminal judicial process, with its accompanying media attention.

It is now starting to be realized that those who contribute in some capacity to the institution of state killing suffer serious after-effects from this. Many have testified to the adverse consequences for them in capital cases: increased stress, anxiety, flashbacks and life-long feelings of moral responsibility. Such people include the police, prosecutors, defence attorneys, judges, capital jurors, prison guards, executioners, wardens, and government officials with the power to pardon (especially governors) (Bohm 2012). Those taking part in the execution or the decision to execute feel this the strongest.

California Governor Pat Brown confessed in his memoirs:

> The longer I live, the larger loom those fifty-nine decisions about justice and mercy that I had to make as governor … It was an awesome, ultimate power over the lives of others that no person or government should have, or crave. And looking back over their names and files now, despite the horrible crimes and the catalog of human weaknesses they comprise, I realize that each decision took something out of me that nothing – not family or work or hope for the future – has ever been able to replace. (Bohm 2012: 262)

Prison warden Ron McAndrew described the impact of carrying out repeated executions:

> Each new execution brought me closer to the hearth in terms of disgust … Following Medina's execution I began to feel dirty [because I] associated myself with the act. Moreover, I began to feel as a pawn for the filthy chest pounding

> politicians who had asked me to do this dirty work. I began [to] question why anyone would hide out in the governor's office with a speaker phone waiting to hear that the killing they'd ordered had been carried out. [Following his execution] [t]here was a serious psychological emptiness in my stomach. I began to go home, shower for a long time, change clothing, and try to send the guilt down the drain. (Bohm 2012: 215)

A member of an execution team in Texas, who participated in 120 executions, described his trauma in the following way: 'I was just working in the shop and all of a sudden something just triggered in me and I started shaking … And tears – uncontrollable tears – was coming out of my eyes' (ibid. at 234). Three years later he could still see the eyes of the men he tied down:

> I don't know [it] … probably would be classified more as a traumatic stress, similar to what individuals in war had. You know, they'd come back from war, it might be three months, it might be two years, it might be five years, all of a sudden they relive it again, and all that has to come out. (ibid.)

These voices raise fundamental questions about the state's right to ask people to kill.

These are questions troubling many, not only in the west. Sangmin Bae cites a dissenting judge in the Constitutional Court of South Korea. The Court found the death penalty to be constitutional, however, Justice Kim Jin-woo dissents in part because 'capital punishment is inhuman in the sense that it infringes on the freedom of conscience and dignity of the judges who have to pass sentence in capital punishment cases, and of the people in charge of actual executions' (Constitutional Court of South Korea 95 Hun Ba 1: 538 in Bae 2014).

Whether such voices and other kinds of collateral damage enter into the mainstream discourse or are ignored, clearly varies with the fluctuation of mobilization movements' opening and closing of space for assessment and reflection.

We find these same dynamics in all societies as they mobilize against harms, risks and terrible crimes. Even in authoritarian societies (with limited freedom of expression), we see, for example, shifts between permitted 'hard strike' campaigns in China's provinces, involving enormous increases in the death penalty, and subsequent periods of greater deliberation inside the Communist Party, which has led to Supreme Court oversight and control of all death penalty decisions (Johnson and Zimring 2009).

The image of these fluctuations in most countries, between the closing of discoursive space for discussion, and periods more open to reflection, also gives us a wider understanding of the role that outside forces might play in the death penalty question. The human rights conventions and their enforcement mechanisms, the international NGOs and the many bilateral human rights dialogues can serve to puncture the periodic closure of discoursive space. They can also contribute to inform, intensify and nuance the deliberations when the space for reflection opens again. In addition, large transnational movements of professionals, academics and people in general, on levels below the political, allow the gaze and perspective from the outside to seep in. The silence around the death penalty becomes recognized as being a silence and gets lifted out of doxic space – the space of the unsaid. Although influence from the outside can ignite a national backlash, *total silence gets more difficult to uphold.* The possibility inside a country to build up a 'critical mass', not necessarily a majority, in favour of openness and reflection increases. For example, professionals who are involved in the death penalty meet other professionals who do not have to kill – professionals who view being asked to kill as an extreme, morally inappropriate demand. Viewing the death penalty only as a natural part of criminal justice, and totally unrelated to human rights thus becomes more difficult. To *decouple* the death penalty from the sphere of national criminal justice and treat it instead as a question of human rights, now exists as a possibility. Proponents of the death penalty cannot escape back to entirely uncontested peace (Hood and Hoyle 2009). Although the national space is where the mobilizing and battling take place, and where the death penalty decision is taken.

The case of Louisiana (USA) illustrates such mobilization movements and their paths. A Louisiana law of 1995, designed to dramatically increase the use of the death penalty, shows the damaging potential of such movements when they run wild with few institutional hindrances.

The Kennedy Case, a Quest for a Radical Expansion of the Death Penalty

It was not surprising that a law bringing the most radical expansion of the death penalty would be enacted in Louisiana. The state has already been described as the US state with the greatest inequality and thus likely to have the highest level of social insecurity and few institutional hindrances for the mobilization movements on their way through the political process, and with many to help them on their way. Since the 1980s Louisiana's politicians have enthusiastically joined large numbers of securitization movements and moral panics, including those targeting sexual offences against children (Janus 2006). Wacquant describes Louisiana's adoption of a series of laws about the registration of sexual offenders as extreme:

> In Louisiana, for instance, the (ex-) sex offender himself must notify in writing his landlord, neighbors, and the director of the local school and municipal parks of his penal status; he must also post warnings of his presence in a community newspaper within thirty days of his arrival. The law further authorizes 'all forms of public notification', including posters, handbills, and bumper stickers – a judge can even request that the offender wear 'a distinctive garb' that will readily identify him as a sex offender … in the manner of the yellow star or hat donned by Jews in the principalities of Medieval Europe and Hitler's Germany. (Wacquant 1999: 76–7)

In 1995 Louisiana took the lead in mobilizing to extend the death penalty to the rape of children under 12, i.e., to perpetrators who had not themselves killed. In a state that at the time did not allocate any funds to protect and assist victims of sexual offences and abuse, it was decided to go beyond 'a life for a life' and give these children 'the ultimate protection'. Prior to enactment there was virtually no documentation containing problem description and analysis of consequences in the legislative committee that prepared the draft legislation. The audio tape of the deliberations in the committee was less than five minutes long. There was no problematization of the fact that the vast majority of such offences are within families, which is closely connected to the low level of reported offences. There was also no discussion of the immense problems of proof when a minor victim is the only witness. Nor did anyone raise the point that, with the same ultimate punishment for rape and murder, the temptation to kill the rape victim to avoid being found out is considerable. Nor did anyone take up the range of adverse consequences for such minors who had to participate for years in the extended criminal justice process typical for death penalty cases.

There was no mention of the fresh wave of death penalty cases that would flood the overburdened criminal justice system, and the potentially dramatic increase in executions that this would result in. The draft legislation passed the committee with three dissents. The three representatives who voted against the law were not re-elected, while all those in the committee in favour of the law were (Interview of rep. McCain, Justice Committee 2007).

Like a hurricane gathering strength from the heated waters off the coast, unencumbered by terrain, the winds of Louisiana's mobilization movement grew, unhindered by institutional procedures in the overheated landscape of social anxieties, and brought a cry for the death penalty for the rape of minors. The winds were strong enough to draw five other states into the same preventive fury before a test case (*Kennedy vs Louisiana*, 128 S.Ct. 2641, 2008) came before the US Supreme Court in 2008. Several other states considered such laws and wrote amicus briefs to the Supreme Court to support the law's constitutionality. The winds were almost strong enough to sway the Supreme Court.

The US Supreme Court found Louisiana's child rape statute unconstitutional in a 5–4 decision. It was found to be a cruel and unusual punishment in violation of the 8th and 14th Amendments. All of the above mentioned considerations *not* taken into account in the Louisiana legislative and political process of drafting the law, became part of the grounds for the Supreme Court's finding of unconstitutionality. In particular, the Court mentioned the adverse consequences of such a law for the child victim:

> Society's desire to inflict death for child rape by enlisting the child victim to assist it over the course of years in asking for capital punishment forces a moral choice on the child, who is not of mature age to make that choice '… [B]y in effect making the punishment for child rape and murder equivalent, a

> State may remove a strong incentive for the rapist not to kill his victim.' (128 S.Ct. 2641, 2663)

The Supreme Court calculated that such a law would almost triple the number of potential death penalty sentences with 5702 registered vaginal, anal or oral rapes of children under 12 years old, compared to 3405 death penalty eligible murders (ibid. 2660). The consequences and potential collateral damage of this would have been immense.

If these considerations had been given weight in lengthy deliberations in the initial legislative and political process in Louisiana in 1995, the winds of mobilization for extending the death penalty beyond a 'life for a life' would never have acquired such strength. Indeed, the winds of mobilization were pervasive; both presidential candidates at the time, McCain and Obama, publicly criticized the decision of the Supreme Court. The reactions in Louisiana and the south seemed almost as furious as after the *Furman* decision, but they died down faster. The south in 2008 was, after all, different than in 1972 (the year of *Furman*) and 1995 (the year of the Louisiana rape law). The winds of mobilization had died down. The broader range of collateral damage was no longer excluded from mainstream discussions. Innocents on death row had been exonerated in Louisiana. Several states had at that time abolished the death penalty or had proposals to abolish it pending.

Is the Death Penalty in and of Itself a Hazard to a Sustainable Criminal Justice System?

The Louisiana illustration prompts one to question whether the death penalty has an independent effect in feeding the winds of mobilization towards protective rage. Is the death penalty in and of itself a hazard to the sustainable development of criminal justice?

The death penalty is different: it is a proclaimed and staged death. It is the supreme moment that draws full attention. Such a moment is attractive to all actors contributing to the dynamics of moral panics, and increases the emotional charge of each step in the heightened mobilization. Painting with broad strokes, Garland captures this eloquently:

> The dramatic relation between these paired killings – the murder and the execution – draws the audience in, ensuring popular interest, emotional involvement, and continuing engagement with the story. As the sociologist Emile Durkheim long ago observed, news of atrocious crimes provokes passionate outrage, generates collective excitement, and produces powerful narratives that concentrate public sentiment and give it force and focus. Capital cases – cases in which the death penalty is invoked – double this dramatic effect. The story of the initial killing is intensified by the promise of another, more righteous killing

> that will settle accounts, express collective anger, and move the public audience cathartically from outrage to relief. That the terrifying mystery of death lies at the heart of these dramas serves only to deepen their emotional impact and extend their metaphoric appeal. (Garland 2010: 6)

This hypnotic quality of the death penalty should be treated as a potential independent hazard to sustainability. As the goal for mobilization movements, the death penalty lures with the promise of a catharsis. Each step of the movement of death penalty cases through the system, gives rise to the possibility for political and media attention of a special intensity. All actors strive to share in this larger-than-life limelight, where one can demonstrate protective resolve. Each step in the mobilization gives a new opportunity to recall the horror of the original crime, doubling the emotional impact. It thus produces greater collateral damage by intensifying the moral panic and its protective outrage. As Garland points out, it moves the threshold of punishment, everything else seems less serious (ibid). Of utmost importance might be that the preoccupation with the death penalty sidetracks mobilization against important harms, and the dazzle of the repetitive drama serves to blind us to the collateral damage of mobilization run wild in other areas.

Could it be, for example, that the connection between sharp rises in incarceration and the death penalty is more complex than is usually assumed? It is often assumed that the same dynamic processes led both to the rise of the death penalty and the rise of the prison population. In the USA these processes took a different turn from that in Europe. Up to the time of the Furman decision, there were similar trends away from the death penalty – both in Europe and the USA. All of the above-mentioned differences acknowledged, could it also be that having the death penalty *in and of itself* contributed substantially to the different developments? Without the dramatics of the death penalty, would the enormous increase in incarceration have taken place? Or been so unobtrusively accomplished? Would the prison sentences of 300 and 400 years, so out of proportion with the normal human life span, have been perceived differently? Would proportionality in punishment in relation to less serious crimes have been so ignored? Was it the dramatic fights over the death penalty that also contributed so that the huge collateral damage (caused by the rise of incarceration) could be kept out of mainstream political discussion for so long? Garland points to the endless talk about the death penalty, and the comparative silence as to mass incarceration:

> [C]ompare the endless talk about capital punishment with the relative silence with which American public discourse (and Supreme Court case law) passes over extraordinarily severe prison sentences and the mass imprisonment they produce, even though incarceration affects tens of millions of individuals and families in the United States while death sentences are imposed on fewer than 120 offenders each year. (Garland 2010: 10)

If unsustainable mass incarceration is seen as a *weapon of mass destruction* destroying the ability of future generations of poor and minorities to live normal lives, the mesmerizing drama of the death penalty might be *a weapon of mass distraction* from these very facts.

Conclusion: The Death Penalty, Constitutionalism, Human Rights and a Sustainability Perspective

I have described the Norwegian reaction to the atrocities of 2011, a reaction that surprised many people all over the world because there were no cries for the death penalty. I have used a great part of this chapter to suggest a sociological frame for understanding such different reactions to terrible crimes. This conclusion will recapitulate some main points in order to suggest how they relate to the sustainability perspective tentatively explored here.

This sociological frame focuses to a large degree on the relationships between socioeconomic governance and governance through punishment. These relationships became central to understanding why states had the death penalty, when research overwhelmingly showed that the death penalty had no greater deterrence on homicide than long-term imprisonment (NRCNA 2012, Greenberg and West 2008). This frame is also supported by historical studies showing that when states become stable, well-developed bureaucracies, secure in their monopoly of territorial power, and more democratic, they tend to abolish the death penalty (Garland 2014). Moreover, research shows that the states that use the death penalty the most in their governance through punishment, also tend to incarcerate extensively and be more authoritarian (Greenberg and West 2008).

Although this research has largely been developed in the west, I suggest that this sociological frame might also be highly relevant to understanding differences in the use of the death penalty as a part of governance through punishment in Asia and in countries with Muslim majority populations. This book invites further exploration along such lines.

I have described systematic differences in governance through punishment between more coordinated democratic capitalist democracies and less coordinated liberal democracies following Nicola Lacey (2008) and Tappio Lappi-Seppälä (2008). More coordinated democratic states, like Norway, with consensual politics, strong labour unions and high equality, govern systematically less by way of punishment, compared to less coordinated liberal democracies with majoritarian politics.

To understand why, I explored how perceptions of harms and risks (including serious crime) and the birth, orbit and culmination of mobilization movements against these harms, tended to fare differently in such differently governed societies. Such harms can be ignored or denied, assessed and proportionately reacted to, or they can be exaggerated way out of proportion, producing mobilization movements that run wild, turning into moral panics, and often causing much collateral damage. This threatens the sustainability of the criminal justice system as well as the sustainability of governance in society at large.

Sustainable governance, whether through executive or legislative politics or through the criminal justice system, seeks to give a form to mobilization movements that make them controllable. This should allow for assessment of the character of the harm and the proportionality of the reaction, as well as the collateral damage involved. The sociological frame indicates that control of the mobilization movements matters for the sustainability of criminal justice.

Mobilization movements tend to be influenced by factors such as the degree of public insecurities, inequalities, cleavages and distances in societies, which in turn factors into the potential for and likelihood of *othering*: the willingness to mete out severe pain including punishments, and the willingness to ignore the suffering that results. Research indicates that the level of public insecurities and inequalities in a state is inversely related to the level of trust and the amount allocated to decommodification – redistributive measures that allow people not to be totally dependent upon the market. In this way the level of decommodification can influence the level at which a state governs through punishment. The fate of mobilization movements also depends on the institutional hindrances they meet.

More coordinated societies such as those with the tripartite coordination of workers' unions, employer organizations and the government, as in the Nordic model, tend also to have more deliberative political institutions and practices of negotiating broad political platforms (characteristic of consensus-based societies). These tend to generate greater equality. They typically offer more welfare and other decommodification measures. Thus they also generate more trust and less social insecurities that could crystallize into fear of crime and fuel repeated, heated mobilization. Moreover, such mobilization movements meet more hindrances in the deliberative political processes. More stakeholders' voices are invited into the institutional process, sustaining equality. Such societies deal comparably more with 'people problems' by way of the available systems of health and social services, than by their moderate-sized criminal justice systems: these are the facts on the ground.

On the other hand, less coordinated and more unequal societies characterized by majoritarian politics, with less resources allocated for decommodification, tend to generate less trust and more social insecurities, which more often crystallize into fear of crime, fuelling more mobilization movements for higher punishment and greater securitization. These movements meet fewer institutional hindrances, are rather helped along by confrontational electoral processes and media focused on crisis and strife, and more often turned into moral panics with drastic measures and much collateral damage. The synergetic dynamics of electoral politics (including elected judges, prosecutors, sheriffs etc.), media and actors connected to the institutions of criminal justice, appear to keep returning crime control to the centre of electoral and media attention – regardless of whether crime goes up or down. In such a setting politicians and others running for election, appear in periods to be locked into a race to the sky on pain delivery and a race to the bottom on social welfare. There are few institutional hindrances to prevent reasonable mobilization from turning into moral panic. Instead it is spurred on by the overbidding of politicians appealing to floating medium voters. Here also, the existence of institutions actually available for dealing with 'people problems' – the facts on the ground – are central to the control of mobilization movements and a sustainable criminal justice system. Societies dominated by institutions of prison and police will naturally address people problems through the available institutions.

Seen this way, it is not surprising to find that Norway has a lower tendency to govern through punishment, since Norway has a highly coordinated economy, a consensus-based political system with a consultative legislative process, an affluent welfare system with a high degree of equality, and a lower level of social insecurities and fear of crime.

This is not the whole story. Even when states become relatively secure, with well-developed bureaucracies and democratic governments, they do not necessarily have an impetus or immediate reason to abolish the death penalty. In Europe as well as in Asia, the last decisive political momentum for abolishing the death penalty was often achieved through what has been called 'leadership from the front' (Johnson and Zimring 2009). Leaders can step into an open space where resonance of arguments to keep the death penalty cohabits with resonance of arguments to abolish it. At this juncture a majority of the public might still be skeptical about abolition, as they were in France and England. Leadership from the front has often made the difference (ibid.). The public most often accepts life without the death penalty relatively quickly. Such an acceptance confirms that criminal justice without the death penalty has been morally and politically sustainable.

However, one should never underestimate the power of mobilization *anywhere* when dominant groups in society feel fundamentally threatened. An attack on the head of government and a horrendous slaughter of children would always 'stop time' and prompt exceptional attention. It would prompt the question whether exceptional measures should be taken. At such times there is room for sovereign leaders to choose extraordinary actions. Some will claim that as long as the sovereign capacity to decide the exception exists, the death penalty can only be suspended and not completely abolished (Bailliet and Aas 2011).

As we saw after the atrocities in Norway, the political leadership stepped into the situation of stunned silence with a message of continued support for its moderate criminal justice system and demonstrated its commitment to political openness and democracy.

One can, however, ask whether different circumstances surrounding the atrocities, or if Norway had not been a party to the European Convention on Human Rights, could have led to different responses from the leadership as well as from the public. Would one have seen dramatic mobilization movements for exceptional measures if an Islamist extremist had been responsible and it was suspected that there were more terrorists ready to strike on Norwegian soil? What if a considerably larger minority could have been construed or feared to silently applaud such an attack? What if Norway, or other European nations, had an even higher disproportionate number of minorities in prisons and an increasing number of detention institutions contained asylum-seekers and non-documented immigrants? And what if this coincided with the deterioration of decommodification measures for the population at large and greater social insecurities? And what if waves of mobilization, demanding harsher punishments and exceptional measures, grew in strength and frequency? Many claim that some European countries are already far along this road (Wacquant 2009, Aas 2013). They claim that the containment of 'potentially dangerous others' goes hand in hand with the curtailment of civil rights and the freedom of movement (Aas 2013 and Johansen, Ugelvik and Aas 2013). A reconstruction of citizenship and the state takes place partly also through movements for securitization in a twisted lockstep with forces for human rights and cosmopolitanism, somewhat parallel to the story of the American south told before. I shall not answer the questions above. I will note that Norway and the European countries are parties to the European Convention on Human Rights, which gives room for state discretion in many human rights areas, but bans the use of the death penalty under all circumstances.

The forms and practices of penal institutions today are also the living tales that long histories matter, either of equality in the case of Norway, Sweden and Finland (Pratt and Eriksson 2013), or of cruel suppression, violence and exclusionary containment in the case of the USA. Commenting on the retention of the death penalty in the American South, Garland writes:

> That [death penalty] has been so widely retained is a consequence, at base, of group relations and their political expression. Stark inequalities and enmities between groups, limited solidarity and fear of crime and violence – these are what allow this punishment to persist. The degradations of capital punishments are not the result of an American disregard for status and dignity, as some have claimed, but a consequence of a deep-rooted inequality of status and respect that shapes race relations and permits the dehumanization of offenders at the bottom of the social hierarchy. For hundreds of years ... America's democracy enslaved, segregated and excluded African Americans ... that has had major consequences for the course of capital punishment's history. (Garland 2001: 310)

The differential handling of bodies, rights and identities in many European countries, in the use of partial exclusion from social and health services, penal incarceration, administrative detention, and different types of containment, is the history of the present – creating lasting relations of status inequality and disrespect. A sustainable criminal justice system as part of a sustainable society, seeks (like all sustainable systems) to meet the needs (of addressing harms) of today without compromising the needs of future generations. The USA's mass incarceration with its colossal collateral damage for individuals, families and society and its accompanying failure to adhere to its own core principles of justice, must be the star example of such unsustainability. It is creating more social insecurities, more inequality, more othering – thus eroding the very moral soil from which legitimacy and trust grow. Sustainability will be compromised if a criminal justice system is not kept moderate and in some balance with practices of restorative justice and core decommodification measures.

The sustainability of a criminal justice system depends on controlling mobilization movements in a way that makes it possible to assess the character of the threat, and the intended and unintended consequences of the reaction. When it comes to states that have the death penalty, this means taking seriously the whole range of serious collateral damage that has gradually come to light: the innocent people sentenced to death, the arbitrary and disproportionate application of the death penalty with respect to race, religion, minority, gender and class, the adverse effects on victims' families (including children) and on defendants' families (including children), and the serious effects on those who contribute to the institution of state killing (police, prosecutors, defense attorneys, judges, capital jurors, prison guards, executioners, wardens and government officials with the power to pardon). Many responsible for executions have experienced traumas similar to those suffered in war.

In addition, I suggest that the death penalty, in and of itself, plays a unique role in making such mobilization movements stronger and less controllable. It should therefore be treated as a potential independent hazard to the sustainable development of a criminal justice system. I have indicated how the death penalty tends to become the ultimate goal of such mobilization movements with its promise of a righteous catharsis. Following Garland (2010) I have suggested how the death penalty increases the intensity of such movements. Each step in the movement of death penalty cases through the system gives rise to the possibility for political and media attention of a special intensity. All the different actors strive to share in this larger-than-life limelight, where one can demonstrate protective fury, as well as sincerity and resolve. Each step in the mobilization gives a new opportunity for recalling the horror of the original crime, thus doubling the emotional effect. Following from Garland's observation that the death penalty constantly captured the attention, while the huge restructuring of the US society through disproportionate mass incarceration disappeared into the background, I have suggested that the death penalty's unique mesmerizing force weakens a society's ability to focus politically on evaluating harms and threats as well as the different measures that could be taken against them. I questioned whether the huge collateral damage arising from the immense, disproportionate rise of incarceration could have happened in the same way and been kept out of mainstream discussion for so long *without* the reoccurring dramas of the death penalty.

I suggest that we use the compelling image of Ulysses binding himself to the mast. Vidar Halvorsen invokes this image in Chapter 14 in an elegant way to capture the essence of constitutionalism in the language of moral and political philosophy.

I invoke, however, this image in a broader sociological sense, where the sustainability of a criminal justice system implies acting on the knowledge of the inevitable temptations ahead and how one must be institutionally prepared to counteract them, politically and in the criminal justice system. Ulysses binds himself to the mast as he prepares to navigate his ship through the dangerous waters ahead, in a sea of temptations to stray from the safest course.

'Binding oneself to the mast constitutionally' by abolishing the death penalty would save society both from its very special and dangerous seduction and the wide range of collateral damage that unavoidably follows any institution of state killing. Abolishing the death penalty also in the constitution of the state, can be an essential part of building and securing a moderate sustainable criminal justice system for the future.

The case of Michigan (USA) may be illustrative in this regard. Michigan was the first state in the western world to abolish the death penalty for murder. It has been continuously abolitionist since 1846. At its 1962 Constitutional Convention, Michigan adopted a resolution proposed by Eugene G. Wanger to prohibit the death penalty in the state constitution (Wanger 2013). In an interview Wanger described how his proposed resolution came into being. In the face of a flurry of Democratic proposals to the constitutional convention, the young Republican Wanger felt a great pressure to produce something from the Republican side. He decided to propose prohibition of the death penalty in the constitution, and it met with little opposition. A decade later, after the *Furman vs. Georgia* decision, there was the first of many mobilization movements to reinstate death penalty in the state of Michigan. Eugene Wanger, who made it his life's project to keep Michigan abolitionist, claims that without the constitutional protection, abolitionists would very likely have lost the fight, since fewer votes would have been necessary for its reinstatement (personal interview with Wanger 2010).

Another way of binding yourself to the mast is to ratify international human rights treaties. The human rights regimes created under the auspices of the United Nations and certain regional institutions have had great significance as regards the use of the death penalty (Hood and Hoyle 2009). Some treaties specifically address the death penalty and prohibit its use outright: one such is the European Convention on Human Rights, another the Second Optional Protocol of the International Covenant on Civil and Political Rights (ICCPR). Others, the ICCPR art 6, aims at its abolition, however, accept the progressive limitation of its use to only the most serious crimes. After much negotiation (Ayatt 2014) the International Criminal Court (ICC) ended up not having death penalty as a penal option.

This sends an important message. Even in crimes of war and genocide, death penalty is not applicable. Indeed, all the conventions and their mechanisms of enforcement invoke and strengthen the view that the death penalty is to be *decoupled* from the national autonomous sphere of criminal justice, and be treated as a legitimate international human rights concern.

Importantly, all human rights treaties embody norms that set limits to state powers and obligate states to adopt laws and institutions that safeguard the fundamental rights of their citizens. Acceptance of them, combined with the implemented practice of such human rights norms can thus over time also lead to the cessation of executions or abolition of the death penalty (Bae 2007). For example, the actual implementation of such norms in the work of the police and the courts increases understanding of the necessity for limits to state power, and instills habits of and pride in the rule of law, and thus might also contribute to the acceptance of and even pride in the relinquishing of the death penalty.

On the other hand, the human rights situation in a state develops at different times in different areas, depending on political events as well as on the efforts of individuals. The implementation of these norms is often discriminatory, uneven and unpredictable. Thus, implementing human rights practices in the criminal justice field generally does not necessarily bring about the abolition of the death penalty. And the death penalty has been abolished in states that have not implemented human rights norms extensively in all parts of their criminal justice systems, and in states that are not in fact exceedingly democratic.

No human right is more important than the right to life. The death penalty is, however, often portrayed by many serious proponents as the ultimate protector of life. This, in my opinion, distorts our most fundamental values. Taking the life of a human being already pacified and under state control, is deeply contrary to the right to life and human dignity. Building an intrinsically fallible institution for state killing, and asking citizens to kill someone already under state control, are deep infringements upon the life and dignity of those who are asked to kill. States should proudly and explicitly step back from doing so. This would in and of itself make criminal justice systems more sustainable.

References

Aas, K. 2013. *Globalization & Crime*. London: Sage Publications.

Acker, J.R., Bohm R.M. and Lanier, C.S. (eds) 2003. *America's Experiment with Capital Punishment*. 'Introduction'. Durham: Durham Academy Press.

ACLU. 2011. *Banking on Bondage: Private Prisons and Mass Incarceration*. American Civil Liberties Union (Report). New York.

Ayatt, M. 2014. *An Overview of the Ongoing Debate on the Death Penalty in Morocco* (in this book).

Bae, S. 2007. *When the State No Longer Kills: Internation Human Rights Norms and Abolition of Capital Punishment*. Albany: State University of New York Press.

Bae, S. 2014. Death Penalty Moratorium in South Korea: Norms, Institutions and Leadership (in this book).

Bailliet, C. and Aas, K. (eds) 2011. *Cosmopolitan Justice and its Discontents*. Abingdon: Routledge.

Barker, V. 2013. Nordic Exceptionalism Revisited: Explaining the Paradox of a Janus-Faced Penal Regime. *Theoretical Criminology* 17: 5–25.

Beckett, K. and Western, B. 2001. Governing Social Marginality. D. Garland ed. *Mass Imprisonment: Social Causes and Consequences*. London: Sage Publications.

Beirne, P. and Nelken, D. 1997. *Issues in Comparative Criminology*. Aldershot: Dartmouth.

Bessler, J.D. 2014. The American Enlightenment: Eliminating Capital Punishment in the United States (in this book).

Bohm, R. 2012. *Capital Punishment's Collateral Damage*. Durham: Carolina Academic Press.

Cavadino, M. and Dignan, J. 2006. *Penal Systems: A Comparative Approach*. London: Sage Publications.

Christie, N. 1952. *Fangevoktere i konsentrasjonsleire: en sosiologisk undersøkelse*. Oslo: University of Oslo.

Christie, N. 1981. *Limits to Pain*. Oslo: Universitetsforlaget.

Christie, N. 1993. *Crime Control as Industry: Towards Gulags, Western Style?* London: Routledge.

Christie, N. 2004. *A Suitable Amount of Crime*. London: Routledge.

Christie, N. and Bruun, K. 1985. *Den Gode Fiende: Narkotikapolitikk i Norden*. Oslo: Universitetsforlaget.

Cohen, S. 1980. *Folk Devils and Moral Panics: The Creation of the Mods and Rockers*. London: Routledge.

Cohen, S. 2001. *States of Denial, Knowing about Atrocities and Suffering*. Cambridge: Polity.

Downes, Rock, Chinkin and Gearty (eds). 2007. *Crime, Social Control and Human Rights: From Moral Panics to States of Denial. Essays in Honor of Stanley Cohen*. Collumpton, Devon: William Publishing.

Ericson, R. 2007. *Crime in an Insecure World*. Cambridge: Polity Press.

Esping-Andersen, G. 1990. *The Three Worlds of Welfare Capitalism*. Cambridge: Polity Press.

Fairclough, A. 2008. *Race & Democracy: The Civil Rights Struggle in Louisiana, 1915–1972*. Athens: The University of Georgia Press.

Furman vs. Georgia 408 US 238 (1972).

Garland, D. 1985. *Punishment and Welfare: A History of Penal Strategies*. Heinemann/Gower.

Garland, D. 1990. *Punishment in Modern Society: A Study in Social Theory*. Chicago: University of Chicago Press.

Garland, D. 2001. *The Culture of Control. Crime and Social Order in Contemporary Society*. Chicago: University of Chicago Press.

Garland, D. 2010. *Peculiar Institution: America's Death Penalty in an Age of Abolition*. Cambridge: Harvard University Press.

Garland, D. 2013. The 2012 Sutherland Address: Penality and the Penal State. *Criminology* 51: 475–517.

Garland, D. 2014. Why the Death Penalty is Disappearing (in this book).

Greenberg, D. and West, V. 2008. Siting the Death Penalty Internationally. *Law & Social Inquiry* 33: 295–343.

Hall, P. and Soskice, D. 2001. An Introduction to the Varieties of Capitalism, in Hall, P. and Soskice, D. (eds), *Varieties of Capitalism*. Oxford: Oxford University Press.

Hood, R. and Hoyle, C. 2008. *The Death Penalty: A Worldwide Perspective*. Oxford: Oxford University Press.

Hood, R. and Hoyle, C. 2009. Abolishing the Death Penalty Worldwide: The Impact of a 'New Dynamic'. *Crime and Justice* 38: 1–63.

Hummelsheim et al. 2010. Social Insecurities and Fear of Crime: A Cross-National Study on the Impact of Welfare State Policies on Crime-Related Anxieties. *European Sociological Review* 27: 327–45.

Jacobson, M. 2005. *Downsizing Prisons. How to Reduce Crime and End Mass Incarceration*. New York: New York University Press.

Janus, E. 2006. *Failure to Protect: America's Sexual Predator Laws and the Rise of the Preventive State*. Ithaca: Cornell University Press.

Johansen, N., Ugelvik, T. and Aas, K. 2013. *Krimmigrasjon? Den Nye Kontrollen av De Fremmede*. Oslo: Universitetsforlaget.

Johnson, D. 2011. Death Penalty Lessons from Asia: Asian and European Consistencies. *Quarterly Criminal Defense* 68.

Johnson, D. and Zimring, F.E. 2009. *The Next Frontier: National Development, Political Change and the Death Penalty in Asia*. New York: Oxford University Press.

Kassman, A 1998. *Polisen och narkotikaproblemet*. Stockholm: Almquist & Wiksell International.

Kennedy vs. Louisiana, 128 S.Ct. 2641 (2008).

Lacey, N. 2008. *The Prisoners' Dilemma*. Cambridge: Cambridge University Press.

Lappi-Seppälä, T. 2008. Explaining National Differences in the Use of Imprisonment. *Japanese Journal of Sociological Criminology* 33: 93–121.

Madeira, J.L. 2012. *Killing McVeigh: the Death Penalty and the Myth of Closure*. New York: New York University Press.

Madeira, J.L. 2014. *Clear and Ever-Present Dangers?: Redefining 'Closure' in a Post 9–11 World* (in this book).

Milgram, S. 1974. *Obedience to Authority: An Experimental View*. London: Tavistock Publications.

National Research Council of the National Academies (NRCNA). 2012. *Deterrence and the Death Penalty*. Nagin, D. and Pepper, J., eds. Washington, DC: The National Academies Press.

Obama, B. 2006. *The Audacity of Hope: Thoughts on Reclaiming the American Dream*. New York: Crown.

Pratt, J. and Eriksson, A. 2013. *Contrasts in Punishment: An Explanation of Anglophone Excess and Nordic Exceptionalism*. London: Routledge.

Scherdin, L. 2003. *Kontrollkulturer og Etikk Satt på Spissen* (translation: *Control Culture and Ethics Pinpointed*) (Doctoral thesis). Institute for Criminology and Sociology of Law, University of Oslo.

Simon, J. 2008. *Governing through Crime. How the War in Crime Transformed American Democracy and Created a Culture of Fear*. Oxford: Oxford University Press.

Smith, R.J. 2012. The Geography of the Death Penalty and Its Ramifications. *Boston University Law Review* 92: 227–89.

Steiker, C. and Steiker, J. 2006. A Tale of Two Nations: Implementation of the Death Penalty in 'Executing' versus 'Symbolic' States in the United States. *Texas Law Review* 84: 1869–928.

The *Times-Picayune* (online newspaper). 13 May 2012. http://www.nola.com/crime/index.ssf/2012/05/louisiana_is_the_worlds_prison.html.

Wacquant, L. 1999. *Prisons of Poverty*.

Wacquant, L. 2001. Deadly Symbiosis: When Ghetto and Prison Meet and Mesh, in Garland, D. (ed.), *Mass Imprisonment: Social Causes and Consequences*. London: Sage Publications.

Wacquant, L. 2009. *Punishing the Poor: Neoliberal Government of Social Insecurity*. Durham, N.C.: Duke University Press.

Wanger, E. (ed.). 2013. *Legislative Testimony against Capital Punishment by Eugene G. Wanger, 1962–2005*. Michigan Committee Against Capital Punishment. Death Penalty Information Center (DPIC).

Wilkinson R. and Pickett K. 2011. *Ulikhetens pris: Hvorfor likere fordeling er bedre for alle*. Oslo: Res Publica. [Original title: *The Spirit Level: Why Equality is Better for Everyone* 2010].

Zimbardo, P. 2007. *The Lucifer Effect: Understanding How Good People Turn Evil*. New York: Random House.

Zimring, F.E. 2007. *The Great American Crime Decline*. Oxford: Oxford University Press.

Zimring, F.E., Fagan, J. and Johnson, D. 2009. *Executions, Deterrence and Homicide: Tale of Two Cities*. Paper Number 09-206. Columbia Law School (Public Law & Legal Theory Working Paper Group).

Chapter 2
Death as Punishment

Nils Christie[1]

When the Atrocities Hit Norway

At midday, 22 July 2011, when the clock passed 15.26, Norway became another country. A huge bomb exploded in the core government building. The area looked as if after war. Seven persons were immediately killed, more were in hospital, badly hurt. Hundreds of lives were probably spared because it happened in the middle of the summer vacation, and some minutes after official office hours.

Terrorism had reached Norway. A search for explanations followed immediately: Maybe it was Muslim revenge for our participation in wars in Iraq, Afghanistan and Libya? Or for reprinting those caricatures of Mohammed? If so, bad times would be ahead for our immigrant population.

But then, as night drew closer, other alarming news: There were shootings at a summer camp for politically active young people from the Labour Party – the dominant Party in government. This took place at a tiny island in a lake an hour from Oslo. A tall man walking back and forth, systematically killing everyone he could find – young people in their teens. Without mercy, just killing anybody he saw. He saw many.

The horror, despair, and sorrow that spread through the country needs an artist's hand to describe. I refrain, but point to one piece of news during the long night that brought some sort of relief to many among us: The offender was not an immigrant. He was a Norwegian, a very Norwegian-minded Norwegian. His acts were directed against our political establishment that accepts immigrants and refugees with a Muslim background. His was a one-man war from the extreme right.

Thereafter we got the news that the Prime Minister was alive. Soon he was on radio and television. His statements expressed sorrow and despair, solidarity with the victims, but then, central to his words that night, and in the days and nights that followed; 'we will not meet these acts with vengeance and terror, but preserve our ideals for a democratic society'. Or, as one of the young survivors from the island expressed it a few days later: 'We will meet terror with roses'.

With my wife I attended a memorial meeting outside the City Hall of Oslo three days after the atrocities took place. Oslo has 600,000 inhabitants. Estimates suggest that 200,000 of us were there. The Crown Prince spoke, the prime minister

1 An earlier version of parts of this chapter was printed in the *Japanese Journal of Sociological Criminology* 2011(36), 11–27.

spoke, the mayor of Oslo spoke, survivors spoke. I did not hear one sentence about revenge. Only roses in words and in reality. Nearly everyone had flowers in hands and later left them at a number of memorial points. The public transportation system had to be rearranged, so as not to destroy the monuments of flowers in the centre of town. Similar memorial ceremonies took place all over the country. And it continued. The import tax on roses was temporarily removed to get a sufficient supply to the country.

Norwegians came closer to each other during these days. But then a central question arises: Will it be possible to preserve this spirit?

On Being Close

I grew up during the German military occupation of Norway. It was World War II. From when I was 12 to 17 German soldiers were a common sight in the streets of Oslo. In these five years I never had a conversation with a German soldier. Nor did I ever talk with a member of the Nazi party, the one led by Vidkun Quisling, perceived as the super-traitor. Except, of course, there was Asbjørn. He was my classmate, seated just behind me at school. He was physically handicapped with cerebral palsy. He was kind and nice and helpful. The children were once given the task of creating a historical play about how Norway got its constitution in 1814. Without hesitation we let Asbjørn have the major patriotic role of the person writing the draft of the constitution. The teacher disliked this strongly. A Nazi in that role! To us it was Asbjørn, not a Nazi monster, who got the role, one we knew from thousands of encounters. But with Quisling, the super-traitor, the case was clear. He was immediately imprisoned when the occupation ended, and later executed. So were 21 other Norwegians and 16 Germans. Only a tiny minority of the population protested against the re-introduction of capital punishment at that time. To the majority, those seen as monsters deserved nothing more than death.

One of the problems that remained after the end of war and occupation was the horrors of the German concentration camps: Buchenwald, Auschwitz, horrors without end from a country once close to us. But then, posing a serious threat to our Norwegian self-image, it turned out that there had been concentration camps in Norway, with hundreds of Norwegian guards actively participating in the killing and maltreatment. These were extermination camps for Yugoslavian partisans, some of the camps with death rates equal to the worst in Germany.

As a young student after the war, I was asked to find out what sort of Norwegian monsters had operated in these camps. I talked with a great number of guards who were sentenced for killing and maltreating the camp inmates – I found most of these guards in various prisons. I also talked with a similar number of guards who had not been sentenced for killing and maltreatment. I did not ask them why they behaved as they did, but asked them to describe their prisoners. The essence of my findings was that the killers never came so close to the prisoners that they saw them as human beings. They saw dirty, stinking, dangerous animals from the

Balkans, exactly as the Germans described them. The non-killers had come closer. They talked with some of their prisoners, were shown photos of life with wife and kids back home in Yugoslavia. They began to see their suffering and to understand the prisoners' despair. The prisoners became human beings.

In situations of severe stress, or when not seeing the others as human beings, trapped in places we do not control, many among us might be capable of committing gruesome acts, as was later shown by both Milgram (1974) and Zimbardo (2007). To the prison guards, the prisoners appeared as monsters, just as these Norwegian guards appeared to us after the war. Through my conversation with the Norwegian guards I was struck by the thought that, if I had been recruited as a guard at the age of 16, and with a similar background to theirs, I might have become one of them.

And my findings, that these killers were not monsters, but relatively ordinary Norwegians like most of us? How were these findings received in Norway?

They were buried in a sea of hatred. Germans, the enemies, the occupiers, they could do such horrible things. Not proper Norwegians. My findings blurred the division between black and white and was a highly unwelcome message in Norway. There was hardly any public interest in my findings. It took 20 years before my manuscript was published in the form of a book (Christie 1972). Additionally 40 years later the book was re-published. This time it was elevated to the status of a canon of Norwegian sociological literature (Christie 2010a). It takes time to splinter monster images.

Ordinary People in Non-ordinary Situations

My thesis is: The Norwegian prison guards in the Norwegian concentration camps were not monsters. They were ordinary people in a non-ordinary situation.

But how could all this happen in the Europe of that time? Germany was the centre of culture in Europe; how can we explain these atrocities, the extermination of the unwanted?

The fate of the Jews is still the most illustrative example.

Part of the explanation here was the long, long process of creating a picture of the Jews as completely de-humanized. All the caricatures of the evil looking Jews, bent over their piles of money, the money that brought other people bottomless debts. The Crystal Night in Germany and Austria, 1,000 synagogues burning, Jews killed and losing everything they had, and together with this the bonfires of books in the streets, books by Jewish authors and those deemed somehow different, degenerate and inferior. Then the ideology of the Aryans as the best of all races, born to rule. Later we have of course seen that Germany was not alone in holding such views. For all sorts of colonizers a picture of 'the primitive man' has been a comforting one.

After this systematic degradation, firstly of Jews, later of Eastern Europeans and others, these people were excluded from being seen as normal human beings. In Bauman's terminology (1989), they were seen as weeds to be removed from society – garden states – build on functional rationality. To weed out the dehumanized was not to kill in the ordinary meaning of that word.

There was, in addition, another unpleasant element: Education was no guarantee against participating in appalling acts. The final solution to what was called 'the Jewish question' was decided at a famous meeting in Germany. As Michael Wildt (2003) writes of the Wannsee-conference in 1942, 'rarely had a meeting been convened with so many members with doctorate degrees'. Similarly, when the trains with prisoners arrived in the camps, there was always a medical doctor on the platform, to sort out those who were to be sent directly to the gas chambers, and those who would be permitted to work for a period before they met their death. If not a doctor, a dentist might prove to be sufficient.

The killings in the extermination camps were also prepared in another way, again a medical one. Doctors were given the mandate to decide over persons in mental and other institutions. Was this patient a person with a 'life worth living'? Perhaps some persons were not to be categorized as humans at all? If so, it would be better to let them die so that food and resources could be used for more useful purposes. Handicapped people, and a gradually ever-widening circle of people with deviant life styles or attitudes, were seen as sick elements, a sort of cancer on what we could call the 'folk-body'. It was a medical task to heal that body. Executions became a political and medical tool.

This brings me to the core of what has been both my personal and scientific interest throughout much of my life: The question of the conditions for, and consequences of coming close to others.

It has to do with coming so close to the other, through life or art, that it becomes possible to recognize elements of common humanity in all sorts of people. *The man behind the horrors in Norway on 22 July seems to have been an extraordinarily lonely person, one standing outside social life, a man forcing himself to remain an outsider, not seeing the others. A man blinded by his mission. The challenge ahead will be to see him as one of us. Once he was a child, maybe he is fond of birds.*

In all simplicity, it is my supposition that the more we are brought into positions that enable us to see each other as fellow human beings, the more we are under the control of that knowledge. We are then controlled by the whole set of norms ingrained in us throughout life on how to behave towards people of all sorts, from babies to old people. To see the other is to be captured in the web of norms that makes us human. The closer we come in this way to another person, the more inhibitions are created against handling that person in ways usually seen as unacceptable within the culture we belong to.

Language is often a most useful barrier against seeing the other. Therefore some words on this.

Words as Walls

Words can create bridges between people – beautiful and useful bridges which carry ideas, emotions and understanding back and forth. But words can also function as barriers to understanding.

Some words are so big that they contain everything, and therefore nothing. We do not understand more when such concepts are used – we understand less and thus give room for manoeuvre to all sorts of authorities.

'Crime' is one of these words. We do not understand more by using this concept. Is crime in Norway increasing? It is a question without meaning. When I was a young man, homosexuality was called a crime, and severely punished. Nowadays in Norway, gay couples marry in city halls. Back in time abortion was a crime, now abortion pills can be bought in drugstores. But new dangers have emerged. The war against drugs is the most productive creator of 'criminals' in my country these days.

Instead of joining the chorus of voices claiming that crime is on the rise, standing still, or going down, I believe it is more fruitful to say: Crime does not exist! We can not use one loaded word for so many acts. Acts are not, they *become*.

For all acts, including those seen by most people as criminal, there are dozens of possible alternative understandings; bad, mad, evil, misplaced honour, youth bravado or political heroism. The 'same' acts can thus be understood within several parallel social systems such as the judicial, psychiatric, pedagogical, theological – or simply by meanings valid among family and friends.

Social and/or physical distance is of particular importance when giving meaning to acts. Persons close to me are mostly not seen as criminals, I see them too well; understand the reasons for their acts. But family life is only one of several examples of social conditions of a sort that create resistance against perceiving acts as crimes and persons as criminals.

'Crime' and 'criminals' are strong terms with a considerable ability to stick to people. They obscure other understandings of the acts and the humans behind these labels. I have never met a person – who, when I come close – is just a criminal. They are, like most of us, a mixture of good and bad. Some, maybe all, are walking mysteries.

But some might have committed and have been sentenced for something terrible, and then all other aspects are overshadowed by that act or the personality type he or she is found to be.

Destructive words will often proliferate among the many professionals so central in defining how humans are to be understood and governed: The psychopath, the paedophile, the manic-depressive, the ADHD-child – the diagnostic manuals are filled to the brim.

And how would I like the supposed behavioural expert to describe those they diagnose?

I want them to be described as whole persons, in old-fashioned, pre-professional terms. Described so thoroughly that they will become unsuited for categorization.

I want to know something concrete about what occurred, and about the people. Small words put together in small stories are particularly well suited to give us such knowledge. The big words from the toolbox of the professionals will often close both for insight into what happened and for informed social participation.

But without their language, would experts lose authority?

Yes.

Neighbours

One of my earlier books (Christie 1975) had a title difficult to translate from Norwegian into English. It was 'Hvor tett et samfunn?' Maybe 'How tightly knit a society?' might be adequate, or 'How close to one another?' How close do we dare to come to one another in households, neighbourhoods, states, or globally?

But are we able to choose any more? We are distanced from one another by modernity, by ideas of growth and material progress and the belief that the grass is greener and more tasty on the other side of the fence. And then, as we know so well, modernity and mobility are closely related.

Increasingly, we move between districts and between countries. Gone are the times when we grew up, lived, and continued to live close to the house were we were born. At a farm close to Oslo, there are descendants of a family that has lived and worked there for 13 generations. Rather heavy to be born in such a place, with the expectations of continuation, but fine seen from the point of social control. People knew each other in such neighbourhoods. As a teacher from one of the valleys once told me – he had been born there and was now back home working as a teacher – 'I don't need to ask the first-graders on their first day in school where they come from. I can see it from "*ganglaget*" – the way they walk'. But those days are gone. The teacher was an exception to the trends of modernity by not having moved away from the valley and his old neighbourhood. The normal consequence of education is ignorance – ignorance about the local neighbourhood and local neighbours. Local knowledge dwindles while abstract knowledge increases.

'Kitchen academies', places where knowledge about local matters is shared, are replaced by all sorts of people from scientific academies. And then, inevitably, when neighbourhood spirit, local knowledge and local control moves out, police and behaviour experts move in with power and supposed knowledge. Neighbours are incapacitated in their functions as neighbours. The surroundings become invisible, maybe even dangerous. Thus is the ground prepared for external authority as the major agency of social control.

On Punishment

Back in the 1950s, some 30,000 cases were officially handled as 'crimes' in Norway. Now it is more than 260,000 (Statistics Norway 2010). This does not necessarily mean that the amount of unwanted acts has increased in this period. But it means that we now live under social conditions where most of us have lost close contact with the acts and actors, and thereby also lost the possibility to create our own interpretations of what happened. In such a situation, the message of the necessity of law and order gets more interpretative power.

So also does the demand for punishment.

But here, again, there is a need for clarification of the words we use.

Punishment, what do I mean? Let me explain by describing a trip to a small island in the Oslo-fjord.

It was a beautiful day in May. Some birds had just come back from the South to spend the summer with us up in the North. A group of workers rested on the ground, enjoying the warm sun shining down on them and the farmland. I recognized one of them. Some years ago he had been sentenced for several very serious offences.

The island was an open prison called Bastøy. Once upon a time it was a place for naughty boys. In my youth, boys were told they would have to go to Bastøy if they did not behave. Today it is considered one of the most lenient prisons, both in Norway and elsewhere. There have been journalists here from all over the world, describing the virtues of the place; no locked doors, life like that on an ordinary farm, good meals, sun bathing and swimming in the fjord.

I was there to give a lecture to the prisoners and the staff. I have forgotten the topic, but not the last part of the session. I asked the prisoners: 'Having been here now, in this summer paradise, a place most Norwegians would find perfect for a summer holiday, how would you respond to an offer from the authorities to stay on here for some weeks after your prison time was over – just stay for a holiday?' A low rumble started in the crowd, then, loudly, from several voices came: 'never, ever!!'

There are huge differences in the material standards and physical and mental suffering produced by different prisons. But they have one major feature in common; they are all places where suffering is the reason for your being there. Society, represented by a judge, has decided that you have acted in ways that makes it right to let you receive a quota of pain. Even paradise converts to a place for suffering and shame when the penal courts order you to go there. So, there is no danger in prison reform. A prison is a prison.

But prisons are also a mirror of society. The Scandinavian countries are affluent, with ideals of equality and welfare for all. How far below usual standards can we let prisoners fall without damaging our identity as belonging to societies that have created welfare for all? Not far, I hope.

My preferred definition of punishment is that it is pain, intended as pain. Penal law ought to be called pain law. The learned professors of penal law ought to be called professors of pain law. This clarifies the central element in the activity.

What then about my own views on punishment and on penal courts?

Penal Courts, a Necessary Anomaly

Some would say: 'In these welfare states of yours, why not abolish punishment and penal courts altogether? Can't you control what ought to be controlled in other, more civil ways?'

I agree, and disagree. It is an important ideal to create social forms where we do not need formal penal courts and the accompanying delivery of punishment; pain intended as pain. My social ideal is to work for a reduction in the amount of formal punishment used in my country. I have the good luck to live in a state with a relatively small prison population. Norway has 71 prisoners per 100,000 inhabitants (International Centre for Prison Studies, London). That is the normal level in Scandinavia. The USA has 716 prisoners per 100,000. That high figure is not a North American destiny, since Canada has 'only' 117 prisoners per 100,000. Prison figures reflect social organization.

I am a minimalist, not an abolitionist. I saw no reason to change that position after the atrocities of 22 July. And I am not alone in my caution regarding punishment in situations like this. Newspapers and TV were filled with statements from survivors, in funerals and in public meetings. They had two common themes. One was deep sorrow, the other the need for defence of the basic arrangements and values of our society. To change these basic features of the country as a result of such acts would have been to give victory to the offender.

We have no death penalty in Norway. The maximum for murder is 21 years of imprisonment, but persons seen as particularly dangerous might get a sentence called preventive detention. In extraordinary cases, and they are not many, the stay in prison can be extended to more than the 21 years, each time in periods of five years. Each such extension would have to be decided by ordinary judges in ordinary court hearings.

But is this not too kind? Should we not imprison for life? Or, to be certain, and with future madmen in mind, sentence to life imprisonment without parole? Or we might go all the way and reintroduce the death penalty.

I hope none of this will happen. Instead, as formulated by a central spokeswoman for the victims, outside the City Hall: 'Let us answer with roses, not with vengeance'. Or, from one of the others: '*If one man can cause so much by hatred, imagine how much we can create through love*'. The mayor of Oslo put it like this: '*Together we will punish the killer. Our punishment will be more openness, more tolerance and more democracy*'.

These days of horror also illustrate an essential feature of Penal Courts: They are cool places. Emotions are kept to a minimum. Participants are not allowed to present themselves as full human beings, but as characters in a well-directed play. Training in law is to a large extent a trained incapacity, it is an education in what is not allowed to be brought before the judge. A penal judge has to decide on facts: did the accused do what she or he is accused of doing? And secondly, if pain is to be decided on, it is designed to balance interests. Equal cases are to be met with equal amounts of pain. But humans are not equal, not even twins when they have lived for some time. People before the judge are made equal by limiting the amount of information admitted to the court.

Penal courts are beautiful and valuable constructions when seen as instruments for clarification of what happened, and when the task is to decide what, according to penal law traditions, is the just amount of pain to be delivered in a case. I know of no better system for that purpose. And then there is a particular reason for preserving the penal courts: Without penal courts, other, less suitable social bodies might be tempted, or forced, in a hidden way, to deliver some sort of pain, but then a pain uncontrolled by considerations of justice.

This danger is accentuated by the present growth and strength of the many victim movements in modern society. Victims deserve to be listened to. And much has been accomplished, particularly with more information to victims from police, from courts and from prisons. There is also now more room in some courts for victims to tell their whole story, unrestrained by legal conventions regarding relevance. Victim movements are to be honoured for bringing victims' rights forward and for combatting professional monopolies.

But there are also needs for limits. Victim movements might, through their present strength and insistence on rights for victims, damage valuable instruments available in traditional penal law and courts. Penal law might lose balance. If so, we lose penal law. The prosecutor gets the upper hand and the road is open towards a more punitive society. In this situation, it is important to see that there is another road open to the victim movements. This is a road towards elevated status for the victim in direct communication with the person, or system, that might have hurt her or him (Kirchhoff 1991, Christie 2010b).

On Restorative Justice

Restorative justice is nothing new. Where humans live together, conflicts follow. When states are weak or kings far away, local solutions are found; some with more authority than others come together, or the whole community becomes involved. Sometimes they fail, and whole communities are endangered by blood feuds, vendettas and continued conflicts.

Modern practices, now called restorative justice, are based on this simple principle: some people come together, listen to the case, and try to find a solution. No mystery.

But this ancient solution contains two fundamental differences from what we find in modern penal courts of today. They were not based on an easily mobilized authority. If parties agreed, fine. If not, the threat of violence might loom. And they did not always have the power to punish. To a large extent they were there to calm conflicts and create some sort of peace. This oversimplification of history might drive historians to insanity, but I do not need more from the past to be able to say that, as a minimalist, one that wants to reduce the delivery of pain in my society, I see restorative justice, or boards for conflict resolution as we call it in Norway, as the major avenue to approach solutions more in accordance with important values common to most of us.

Here also are my reasons for not being a total abolitionist, but only a pale minimalist when it comes to punishment: To be able to care for justice in meting out pain, penal courts are restricted in the information they can receive. Boards for restorative justice have no such restrictions. On the contrary, the more they know, the more the parties are able to present themselves as full human beings in life situations which are possible to recognize and understand. The more they know, the greater are the possibilities for finding peaceful solutions to the conflicts. But if these boards, as the only alternative in a conflict, are also given the task, often hidden, to deliver pain, they are highly unsuited to this task. Parties will keep back information not to expose facts that might increase the punishment. Restoration will be hampered. It will be like a copy of a penal court, but a bad one.

The strength of meetings for restorative justice is that the parties in the conflicts are back to the position of being the central actors. It is their stories, the full stories, which count. Here is an example: some young people had forced their way into the apartment of an old couple. They were looking for brandy; the couple thought they were there to kill them. Both sides told their stories. Slowly the meaning of the misdeeds, and the actors, changed. The old ones started to seem like grandparents and the youngsters, grandchildren. They hurried to be together in the same lift after the session.

Returning to Punishment – Capital Style

Basic values must come first when we discuss crime and punishment. It is no problem preventing thieves from continuing to steal – just brand a warning on their foreheads! We did this in some periods. Or for kids that misbehave a bloody dose of flogging in public places could do the trick. Or those that forensic psychiatry say are dangerous – put them away for life.

We do not, we can not. The penal system of a country creates a mirror of that society. It tells us who we are. Certain images become unacceptable basic values among most of us. One such is capital punishment and having a state which kills.

The last ordinary execution in Norway took place in 1876.

The last extraordinary one, after World War II, took place in 1948. More were sentenced to die, but soldiers in the Kings Guard who had to carry out the job by shooting them gradually became so unhappy with this task that the executions came to a halt. I have this story directly from the man who conveyed the soldiers' views to the political authorities. In 1950 the death penalty was again formally abolished, and from 1979 it was also abolished from our military penal law.

The reactions of the men in the Kings Guard could be understood in the light of the difference between the killers and the non-killers in the Norwegian concentration camps. In the immediate aftermath of the war those executed were seen only as Nazis, but as time went by, they 'reappeared' as human beings.

But it was not just the soldiers who were troubled by the killings. The judges were also troubled. I described a case in my book 'A suitable amount of crime' (Christie 2004) and repeat it here, because it is so typical of what happens. It was a serious case. A man had received the death penalty in the lower courts, and now that decision was to be tried in the Supreme Court. The man had collaborated with the German occupiers at the very top level. He had joined the Nazi cabinet created by Quisling and functioned as Minister of Cultural Affairs during the occupation. The accused does not usually appear in the Supreme Court in person. But the accused *may* insist on attending, and this man did. Day after day he was escorted to the courtroom. He was the prototype of a civil servant of his day. Tired, pale, with a sad face, a worn suit like those his judges also once used to wear, with a polite voice, respectful manners and vocabulary. As a lawyer by education, he could have been one of them, if not for a fatal belief in a different political system. For this man the Supreme Court changed the death sentence to one of life imprisonment. A participant in the process told me many years later that in his opinion it was the former minister's daily appearance in the Supreme Court that saved his life. There was no doubt that his acts were criminal according to the interpretation of the law seen as valid at the time, but this man came too close to his judges to be considered a criminal unworthy to live.

Executions in Modernity

Today, the use of death as punishment has come to an end in all European states. It is the price European states have to pay to be members of the Council of Europe.[2] It is just a pity the US is not under the same pressure.

In 2010 they executed 46, in 2011 43, and the same number in 2012. The total number of executions in the US since 1976 is 1,321. More than 3,000 are on death row, waiting for execution. They have to wait a long time – generally it takes more than ten years from receiving the death sentence to being killed, if this happens at all (Death Penalty Information Centre 2013).

Seen from a Western European perspective it is difficult to understand the US on this point. It is something peculiar in the US, something important to understand also outside the US. It was a landing place for immigrants behaving as if they had come to an empty land. This led to actions close to genocide of the native populations. Later it became a slave state. Slaves, and later black people, were the major targets for the executioners. David Garland (2006) describes one of the old executions in a recent paper: Thousands of white people thronged around the black man to be killed, fought to come close, fought to get possession of a bit of his clothes, fought to get the best photo – as a souvenir for the mantelpiece. Bloody Europeans, Norwegians certainly among them, were 'heroically' confronting the 'wild animals' from Africa, animals not knowing their place in the new world.

2 Belarus is the only exception.

But Garland is not trapped in the simple idea that the continued use of the death penalty in the US is a historical relic – a continuation of slavery traditions. Instead he finds an explanation by looking at the US as a land of fundamental cleavages. The founding fathers created a weak federal government, one where each of the states were given autonomy over their criminal justice system. And here keeping the death penalty came to be a symbol of independence from a centralized federal power. '*... the collective killing of hated criminals (or merely the assertion of the right to do so) remains one of the ways in which groups of people express their autonomy, invoke traditional values, and assert their local identity*'. (Garland 2006: 23).

But there is ambivalence, counterforces are also in action. Several states in the US have abolished the use of the death penalty and Federal authorities regulate the *forms* of executions. It has to be a death without pain; deaths by poison, but not until those who are to die are heavily tranquillized. But before death they wait – for years.

I was in Utah, the Mormon state on the west coast of the US, when I came up against the gravity of this problem. A very courageous British PhD student was deeply involved in understanding life among those waiting for execution on death row.[3] She came so close to them that the next in line for execution asked her to attend, to be there when he was killed. So she did.

Why was this man killed, poisoned to death?

He could not stand it any more. He could not stand waiting for death, among all the others also waiting. So he cancelled all appeals. The state was forced to kill him. The authorities did not like it. He broke the main rule. *They* were to decide on his death, not he. He empowered himself by declaring an end to the charade. He was very popular among those on that death row. They begged him to go on living by further appeals. He refused and died with a feeling that he had once again become a man.

Death – or Life as a Death

For me, this drama in Utah brings us straight into a most unpleasant dilemma: I am a strong opponent of the use of capital punishment. The practice must come to an end, be abolished. As long as there is life, there is hope. Until the moment of execution new facts might appear, or new attitudes among those who govern. And fundamental to an abolitional stand is the ethical command: Thou shall not kill.

But then there are the embarrassing similarities between death and a life resembling death. If the alternative to death is imprisonment for natural life, is this an obvious improvement? Or even more complicated: If countries that abolish the use of death thereby feel both obliged, or more free, to increase the

3 Sandra McGunigall-Smith. See her preliminary report in Robert Johnson and Sandra McGunigall-Smith (2008).

use of imprisonment, is it then obvious that this brings us closer to fundamental values? Self-confident authorities can sit back and say 'We are not like our brutal neighbours across the border. We don't kill. We only keep them – and an extra quota similar to them – imprisoned until they die a natural death. Or we take their lives away for periods of these lives'.

We are forced to look at the unpleasant similarities between death and imprisonment.

What is the essence of imprisonment? It is to remove human beings from ordinary life. It is to take ordinary parts of life away from individuals, forever, or for important periods of their lives.

We ought not to exaggerate the difference between these two types of punishments; death and imprisonment. This is clearly seen if we go back to the situation in the state of Utah with the prisoner who made the choice to die rather than spending the rest of his life in prison not knowing when and how his life would end. Would tomorrow be the day of his execution? Or maybe that would not happen at all – and he would die a natural death. He knew it was life in a box, every day, every month, every year – a whole life – growing old and feeble there, and then a 'natural death'. And all the time closely watched to prevent something terrible happening, such as the prisoner escaping by jumping the wall, or committing suicide. What a defeat for the system if that happened!

What to Expect in the Future?

In my evaluation, the European ban on death by killing is far from safely established. I do not wholly share the optimism expressed in several recent articles by Roger Hood (2009, 2010), but hope his views will prove to be the right ones. In particular, I think the ban on killing is far from safely established in some states in Eastern Europe. With a political split, particularly if states were no longer interested in membership of the Council of Europe, forces in favour of reintroducing death as punishment might gain increased strength. I also fear what might happen if social cleavages as well as economic troubles increase.

But is the situation stable in Scandinavia?

Yes, and no.

Yes, if we think of physical death. If we escape extreme social conflict, war or natural catastrophe, I can't imagine that physical death will be reintroduced as a type of punishment in our Northern societies, but in times of turmoil, reinstating the death penalty will always tempt the powers that be.

The Danger of Affluence

But then there is the other form of death: imprisonment, living death. Here I think the Scandinavian situation is a vulnerable one. Taking away parts of life in the form of imprisonment, that form of death I fear will expand in the Nordic societies, – maybe particularly in Norway.

Why?

Because we have become so rich! Most of us have increased our standard of living immensely. And at the same time, the rich have increased their material wealth even more. In old-fashioned language: class differences have increased. And the wealth of the upper classes is made visible to an extent earlier unknown. Rich people in Scandinavia in earlier centuries had a certain inhibition against displaying their affluence. That trend is gone. This means a society with increased social distance – the perfect breeding ground for social conflicts of a type preventing parties from seeing those on the other side as valuable human beings.

Two types of mobility work in the same direction. First upward social mobility; you leave your less successful friends or relatives behind. Secondly geographical mobility. In this process, old-fashioned villages, or stable and long-established quarters within cities disappear. These were places where inhabitants saw each other, knew each other, and were also able to some extent both to help and to control each other. When they disappear, deviance is converted into crime and social control becomes a task for officials. The ground is fertile for increased trouble of a type the state is ready to meet with the police force and imprisonment.

And what to do in such a situation?

I have no more space left for a discussion of this. Only one sentence: For a country like Norway, it is not obvious that the answers for our future are to be found in that future. They might be found in our past.

References

Bauman, Z. 1989. *Modernity and the Holocaust.* Cambridge: Polity Press.

Christie, N. 1952, 1972, 2010a. *Fangevoktere i konsentrasjonsleire.* (Guards in Concentration Camps). Oslo: Universitetsforlaget.

Christie, N. 1975. *Hvor tett et samfunn?* (How tightly knit a society?). Oslo: Universitetsforlaget.

Christie, N. 2004. *A Suitable Amount of Crime*. London: Routledge.

Christie, N. 2010b. Victim movements at a crossroad. *Punishment and Society*, 12(2), 115–22.

Death Penalty Information Centre 2013. Available at: http://www.deathpenaltyinfo.org.

Garland, D. 2006. *Death, Denial, Discourse: On the Forms and Functions of American Capital Punishment.* [Unpublished Manuscript.]

Hood, R. 2009. Abolition of the Death Penalty: China in World Perspective. *City University of Hong Kong Law Review*, 1(1), 1–21.

Hood, R. 2010. *Towards Global Abolition of the Death Penalty: Progress and Prospects.* [Manuscript.]

International Centre for Prison Studies. Available at: www.prisonstudies.org.

Johnson, R. and McGunigall-Smith, S. 2008. Life Without Parole, America's Other Death Penalty. Notes on Life under Sentence of Death by Incarceration. *The Prison Journal*, 88(2): 328–46.

Kirchhoff, G.F. 1991. The Unholy Alliance between Victim Representation and Conservatism and the Task of Victimology, in *Victims and Criminal Justice*, edited by Kaiser, Kury and Albrecht. Freiburg, 838–55.

Milgram, S. 1974. *Obedience to Authority: An Experimental View.* New York: Harper and Row.

Statistics Norway 2010. Available at: http://www.ssb.no/english/subjects/03/05/.

Wildt, M. 2003. *Generations des Unbedingten. Das Führungskorps des Reichssicherheitshauptamtes.* Hamburg: Hamburger Edition. HIS Verlages.

Zimbardo, P. 2007. *The Lucifer Effect. Understanding How Good People Turn Evil.* New York: Random House.

Chapter 3
Why the Death Penalty is Disappearing*

David Garland

> (1) Auto da fe (2) Beating with clubs (3) Beheading: Decapitation (4) Blowing from cannon (5) Boiling (6) Breaking on the wheel (7) Burning (8) Burying alive (9) Crucifixion (10) Decimation (11) Dichotomy (12) Dismemberment (13) Drowning (14) Exposure to wild beasts etc. (15) Flaying alive (16) Flogging: Knout (17) Garrote (18) Guillotine (19) Hanging (20) Hari kari (21) Impalement (22) Iron Maiden (23) Peine Forte et Dure (24) Poisoning (25) Pounding in mortar (26) Precipitation (27) Pressing to death (28) Rack (29) Running the gauntlet (30) Shooting (31) Stabbing (32) Stoning (33) Strangling (34) Suffocation.[1]

This is a list of execution methods compiled by a New York State Commission in 1888. The Commission had been charged with investigating the most humane and practical methods of carrying into effect the sentence of death. The Commission, and the state of New York, would eventually introduce a new item into the historical record: the electric chair – first used in Auburn Prison on 6 August 1890 (Banner 2003).

There is a reason this list is so long. Capital punishment has been practised in most known societies over the course of human history. One might say that, until quite recently, it was the historical norm, a cultural universal. But in modern liberal democracies – in societies like Norway – the death penalty no longer exists.

We rarely think of it, but this transformation is remarkable. The death penalty once formed an elementary particle of governmental power in every nation state. Today the practice is widely regarded as a shameful violation of human rights and is prohibited throughout most of the western world. What happened?

This answer is by no means simple. There are exceptions to the Western trend – the USA being the most notable – and outside the Western world the death penalty is still alive and well, especially in the Middle East and Asia. Even in the West, the direction of historical change is not always the same. But we can roughly

---

* Lecture held at Oslo Symposium on Death Penalty, December 2012. This lecture draws upon David Garland (2010), *Peculiar Institution: America's Death Penalty in an Age of Abolition.*

1 *New York State Commission to Investigate and Report the Most Humane and Practical Methods of Carrying into Effect the Sentence of Death*, 1888.

sketch the overall arc of change and trace the social causes that brought about this remarkable development.

In the early modern period – between about 1400 and 1700 – newly-emergent state authorities took up the death penalty and accorded it a central role in the project of state building. Elaborate public ceremonies, horrifying execution techniques, and ritual proclamations were so many means to this end, with the most atrocious punishments being reserved for crimes of *lese majesty* and challenges to the state (Sharpe 1990, van Dulmen 1990, Merback 1999).

A crucial element of state-formation was the effort of nascent political authorities to exert a monopoly of power over territory they now claimed as their own. This historic struggle to impose sovereign rule gave a new prominence and intensity to capital punishment. Prior to the emergence of the state, the death penalty appears to have been carried out without elaborate ceremony. Discussing the late medieval evidence from Germany, Evans says 'Illustrations of executions in the fourteenth and fifteenth centuries show them as casual and unceremonial affairs, with a handful of people standing informally around while the hangman does his work'. Referring to England, Sharpe writes that there 'is little evidence that any elaborate ceremonial attended the execution of felons in the later middle ages'. Otterbein's ethnographic survey also suggests that pre-state societies mostly executed in secret or without fanfare (Evans 1996: 50, Sharpe 1990: 31, Otterbein 1988).

The emergence of sovereign states altered these older practices in several respects. The punishment of death became the prerogative of state authorities who asserted their monopoly over legitimate violence and prohibited traditional practices of private vendetta and vengeance. Death penalties came to be imposed and administered under the auspices of the royal courts, imparting a greater degree of rule-governed formality and legal rationality. And the execution of these penalties became more public, more elaborately ceremonial and more violent, as the new states sought to use shock-and-awe tactics to impress the populace and strike fear in the hearts of enemies (Royer 2003: 323). Though we sometimes describe cruel punishments as 'medieval', it was in fact the emergence of despotic states in the late medieval and early modern period that transformed these events into elaborate spectacles of suffering. It was not Europe's medieval lords but the absolutist rulers who replaced them that gave capital punishment its greatest cruelty, intensity, and display.

By the mid-nineteenth century, in a context of increasingly well-established and rationalized states, capital punishment's main purpose had altered, so that what had once been an instrument of rule, essential to state security, became an instrument of penal policy, focused on the narrower goals of doing justice and controlling crime (Evans 1996).

As its functions changed, so too did its forms. The death penalty came to be formatted as a penal sanction rather than a political spectacle. Its focus came to centre on criminal rather than political offences. Its executions came to be more swiftly administered, not in the political space of the town square but in the penal space of the jail yard. It sought to minimize bodily pain rather than maximize it, as before (Garland 2010: ch. 3).

By the late twentieth century, in the very different context of the modern liberal democratic welfare state, capital punishment had ceased to be a vital instrument of crime control and had become increasingly rare and controversial. By the century's end, it had been abolished by all the developed western nations other than America, and by several non-western nations besides (Banner 2003, Hood and Hoyle 2008).

The widespread use of the death penalty – in earlier centuries in the West, and in much of the world still today – should hardly surprise us. If we set aside contemporary moral qualms and political objections to its use, it is easy to see why capital punishment has been so important. As a political weapon and a penal instrument, the death penalty has an irresistible power. Putting political enemies, serious wrongdoers, and dangerous individuals to death is an obvious, effective, and efficient way for authorities to eliminate the threat such individuals represent. Imposing a death penalty on law-breakers permits authorities to proclaim their power, impress onlookers, exact revenge, undo pollution, restore social order and send a warning to would-be offenders.

Nor has this self-evident efficacy diminished in the contemporary period. If swiftly applied, frequently utilized, and imposed with the requisite amount of pain and publicity – as it still is in places such as China, Iran, Saudi Arabia and Singapore – the death penalty retains much of its power as a penal and political instrument.[2]

The Character and Capacity of States

How should we explain the rise and fall of capital punishment in the modern West? The explanation is to be found in a series of social transformations that altered *the character of the state* in western society, its strategic interests, and the social fields in which it operates.

The death penalty is always and everywhere an exercise of state power. Capital punishment's use and character are – and have always been – shaped by the structure of state institutions and the decisions of state officials, acting in accordance with their perception of governmental interests. State actors strive to maintain control and deploy power in the interests of their institutions, their allies and their constituents. The death penalty is one more tool to be deployed – or not – in the furtherance of these ends.

As the nature and operational environment of the state have changed in different nations over time, so too has capital punishment (see Garland 2010: chs 3–5).

In the wake of the *ancien régime*, a series of political and cultural forces altered the state in western societies in ways that had major consequences for capital

2 On the death penalty in Asia today, see Johnson and Zimring (2009).

punishment. Processes of state-building enlarged the institutional capacities of government and the ability of state actors to exert social and penal control. The struggles of liberal and democratic forces transformed state institutions, forged new power balances, and imposed legal constraints on state policy. The emergence of cultural practices embodying civilized and humanitarian sensibilities softened state power, establishing new criteria of legitimacy and imposing new limits on the use of violence (Spierenburg 1984, Starr 2007, Hunt 2007).

The coming of mass democracy, universal citizenship, and the welfare state transformed the government's relation to the individual citizen/voter and placed his or her welfare at the centre of political calculation.

Over the long run, the social fields in which the state deploys its powers have been continuously transformed. Throughout the West, societies have become more pacified, more orderly, more market-dominated, and more individuated. All these processes impacted capital punishment (Tilly 1992).

Relations *between* states have also affected death penalty practice, especially in the context of war, imperial conquest, and decolonization. (Several South American nations repealed their death penalty laws to mark their new-found independence. Other nations, including several postcolonial Caribbean ones, insist on retaining capital punishment as a mark of their sovereign autonomy.) From the end of the twentieth century onwards, pressure for abolition has been exerted by the Council of Europe, the European Union and the United Nations (Hood and Hoyle 2008).

The state's control imperatives have shaped the death penalty at every turn. But the nature of these imperatives has changed over time: from the brutal assertion of violent power in the formative phase, to a more restrained use once state power was well established, to an attenuated, ambivalent deployment when the death penalty became embroiled in problems of legitimacy and efficacy.

The penalty of death was made inessential by the formation of a stable bureaucratic state, secure in its monopoly of violence, supported by a criminal justice apparatus of police and prisons, and relatively effective in its control of interpersonal violence. It was made problematic by the development of liberal-democratic and welfare state institutions, and by an associated culture of civilized refinement and humanism, all of which worked to limit state violence and surround it with prohibitions and taboos (Garland 2010).

That capital punishment was long considered an indispensable tool of state-craft meant that it was spared critical attacks: an essential practice could hardly be abolished. But once capital punishment became inessential to state maintenance, the politics of the death penalty were fundamentally transformed. We can date from that moment in the eighteenth century the emergence of a powerful anti-gallows critique and the modern anti-death penalty movement. And right from the beginning, that critique had practical as well as ideological dimensions (Hunt 2007).

Early modern authorities used executions to project state power. But these public events brought dangers for officials, since they put the state's power and authority on the line. The great ritual of state could be spoiled by an executioner's incompetence, a condemned man's recalcitrance, or by a disruptive, unruly crowd.

Instead of affirming state sovereignty the execution could undermine it. An execution's meaning was inherently unstable, always vulnerable to resistance and re-appropriation.

State officials have always been motivated to increase their control over these difficult events – to minimize opportunities for disruption, to limit the impact of other actors, to develop protocols that can be carried through without fail. And a large part of capital punishment history can be understood in these terms. Consider, for example the changing pattern of public access to executions. At a certain point in the nineteenth century, the benefits of public executions came to be outweighed by their attendant costs, and state authorities began to move scaffolds behind prison walls. (Public executions were first abolished in the northeastern states of America – several decades before the UK and the Netherlands followed suit, and a whole century before France gave them up (Garland 2010, Banner 2003, McGowen 1987 and Gatrell 1994).)

This process of 'privatizing' the execution, of reducing its visibility and the extent of public involvement is best understood not as a result of more refined sensibilities, or a reaction to unruly urban crowds, though both of these played a role. It is best viewed as the ongoing effort of government officials to exert ever-tighter control over a fraught undertaking and to manage the meanings that it put into circulation. Time after time, from the seventeenth century onwards, officials moved to reduce the extent of the ritual, the size of its audience, the performative role of the condemned, the time taken to die, and the opportunities for viewing and communicating about what was seen. Official concern to avoid spoiled public rituals eventually ended both ritual and publicity (Smith 2008). This same process continues today in places as far apart as China and Iran, where authorities recently declared an end to public executions and in the USA, where executions are increasingly contained and concealed.

Political Processes of Reform

State institutions and state interests dictate the character and use of the death penalty. But these institutions and interests are shaped, in their turn, by political and cultural forces. The most important of these forces have been liberalism, democracy, civilized manners and humanitarian sentiment (Garland 2010: ch. 5).

Most western nations today are liberal democracies of one kind or another and modern liberal thought has become infused with democratic ideals. But liberalism and democracy, for all their modern overlap, are *distinct* political traditions with different histories, values and priorities. And we need to stress this distinction because, when it comes to the death penalty, liberalism and democracy have sometimes pressed in different directions (Starr 2007).

At the core of classical liberalism are two essential commitments: a conception of social order that values individual freedom and autonomy; and a commitment to limiting governmental power by means of the rule of law. Liberal institutions aim to restrain the coercive power of the state and uphold the rights and freedoms of individuals. Little wonder, then, that liberals have always been among the death penalty's chief critics (Holmes 1995).

The growing power of liberal ideas and social forces impacted the death penalty from the eighteenth century onwards. In early modern Europe, punishments would sometimes be collective, as when in 1757 the relatives of the regicide Robert Damiens were deprived of their family name and banished from France (McManners 1981). Against this, liberals insisted that crimes were an individual responsibility and only the offender ought to be subject to official punishment. Reacting against the arbitrariness of personalistic rule, liberal opponents of absolutism demanded procedural protections for those accused of crimes and the establishment of legal rules and principles that would limit the reach of state power (Beccaria 1995 [1764]).

As early as the thirteenth century, English nobles pressed for *habeas corpus* and trial by jury and by the seventeenth century these 'rule of law' principles – together with rights to counsel and to public indictment – had become central to liberalism's agenda.[3] Liberal demands for procedural propriety and due process remain a mainstay of death penalty opposition in America today.

The rise of liberalism also changed how capital punishment was justified. The early modern death penalty had been phrased in the language of tradition, of religion, and of the Divine Right of Kings, none of which invited criticism or argument. From the eighteenth century onwards liberals applied tests of utility and reason to the ancient institution and argued that if it could not be justified in these terms it ought not to exist at all.

The age of liberal revolutions (roughly from 1774 to 1848) coincided with the first abolitions – most often in small states and principalities such as Tuscany, San Marino and Prussia. This earliest age of reform forged an association between liberal states and abolitionism that has persisted up to the present day (Garland 2010: ch. 4).

Anti-liberalism forged the opposite association. Wherever authoritarian governments emerged, the turn against liberalism brought with it a return to capital punishment. Twentieth-century Fascism revived the deployment of death as an instrument of state policy. And the criminal justice system of Nazi Germany made massive use of executions (Evans 1996). But the dominant tendency of the modern West has been to institutionalize liberal forms of law and government and to extend these protections to all social groups. And as the rule of law, procedural protections, and civil rights spread over the course of the nineteenth century, so too did death penalty reforms. By the late twentieth century, death penalty abolition

3 These rights were embodied in the English Bill of Rights of 1689 and the Treason Trials Act of 1696. Later they featured in most of the new constitutions of the late eighteenth and nineteenth centuries.

had become a tenet of modern liberalism, and a principle of the international movement for human rights (Hood and Hoyle 2008).[4]

Democratic rule means the 'government of the people by the people for the people' (to quote Abraham Lincoln). But democracy is understood in different ways and implemented through different arrangements. In America, democracy is institutionalized in a radically localist and populist form, which is one reason why the death penalty survives there today. Elsewhere, democracy is offset by other values and institutions that set limits on majority rule and permit counter-majoritarian reforms.

Democratic writers and theorists of democracy have mostly been unenthusiastic about capital punishment, seeing it as a degrading practice emblematic of absolutist power and repressive rule. Like the lash, capital punishment suggests a kind of tyranny, an utter subordination of the punished by the punisher (Garland 2010).

The development of modern democracy closely parallels that of death penalty abolition, with the nations of northern Europe and Scandinavia (and parts of the USA) being in the lead in both respects. In many respects, democracy did not fully come of age until the late twentieth century, the period in which abolition became normative across the western nations.[5]

Although a few abolitions occurred during the nineteenth and early twentieth centuries, the majority took place in the decades after World War II, with the abolitionist trend accelerating in the 1990s. The temporal pattern of death penalty reform matches the temporal pattern of democratization. The end of Fascism in the 1940s prompted constitutional abolition in Italy, Germany and Austria. The Iberian transition from authoritarian corporatism to democracy in the 1970s led to abolition in Spain and prompted Portugal to repeal all its residual capital offences. And the Soviet Union's collapse in the late 1980s led to abolition in East Germany (GDR), Romania, Hungary and the Czech and Slovak Republics, and later in countries such as Poland, Serbia, Croatia, Macedonia, Slovenia (though this last group was also motivated by a desire for European Union membership). The same pattern is visible outside Europe: South Africa and the Philippines both marked the commencement of democracy by ending capital punishment (Hood and Hoyle 2008).

At the level of values and ideals, then, there is an affinity between democracy and death penalty abolition. But the link is by no means straightforward. A nation such as France, which led the European continent in its march towards democracy, was the last European nation to give up its death penalty (the French authorities were still decapitating offenders as late as 1977). And no one denies that the USA is a democratic nation – and *fully* democratic since the 1960s and the end

4 Protocols 6 and 13 of the European Convention on Human Rights (1983 and 2002) prohibit the death penalty, as does the United Nations' 2nd Optional Protocol to the International Covenant on Civil and Political Rights (ICCPR), which was passed in 1989.

5 A time-series study by Neumayer finds that capital punishment abolition coincided with the rise of democracy and that the widespread abolition after World War II was a fundamentally political process (Neumayer 2006).

of Jim Crow – but its commitment to capital punishment continues. Indeed, that commitment is nowadays justified in the name of democracy and the 'will of the people' (Garland 2010).

The fact is that death penalty abolition did not occur because the newly enfranchised masses demanded it. Rather, their parliamentary representatives – whose background, education and culture were generally more elite than those of their constituents – felt an elective affinity between democracy and death penalty reform and were able to act upon it, with or without popular support.

Cultural Processes of Reform

The decline of capital punishment is commonly viewed as an effect of cultural change. If we no longer hang, draw and quarter offenders, or execute them in the public square it is because our society has become more civilized and our sensibilities more refined.[6]

Nor is this understanding a recent one. For more than two centuries now the standard reform narrative has been a story of how cultural change – more refined manners, less tolerance for violence, more sensitivity to the pain of others – has led to changes in capital punishment.

From Beccaria onwards, critics of capital punishment have viewed themselves as aligned with 'the cause of humanity' – expressed in both religious and secular terms – and viewed each reform as a progressive step in the advance of civilization. And from the Enlightenment to the present, the language of civilization and humanitarianism has framed the reform effort, with each step towards abolition being viewed as the result of our 'evolving standards of decency'.

Historians agree about the civilization idiom and humanistic understandings in which death penalty reform has been articulated, but there is no consensus about the causal weight to be given to this language and the cultural currents to which it refers. When we turn from describing normative debates to developing historical explanations, the status of 'culture' becomes more problematic. The question becomes how to assess the causal role of cultural currents such as humanism and the refinement of sensibility. Should we regard culture as a real cause of action or merely a glossy surface that overlays more basic causal processes? Are civilizing and humanizing sentiments distinctive engines of historical change or merely the incidental music that accompanies the real action?[7]

6 On the rise of humanitarian sensibilities, see Haskell (1992), Bender (1989), Halttunen (1998), Evans (1996), Elias (2000) and Spierenburg (1984).

7 Spierenburg (1984) argues the former position, Foucault (1977) the latter. The 'civilizing process' account has been taken up by Pratt (2002) and Garland (1990). Smith (2008) makes a strong case for a 'culturalist' account of punishment and penal change. The sceptical view of humanitarian sentiment can be found in Georg Rusche and Otto Kirchheimer (1968) and, in a more sophisticated form, in Gatrell (1994).

In my view, the conventional wisdom is largely correct: cultural change did indeed prompt death penalty reform. But a closer look adds some nuance to this standard account: (i) The cultural shifts that mattered affected social elites and not the mass of the people; (ii) Processes of reform operated on and through state actors, so cultural preferences had to be aligned with political realities; (iii) Different strands of enlightened culture had quite different implications for capital punishment reform.

The emergence of modern bourgeois culture, which became increasingly widespread during the eighteenth and nineteenth centuries in both secular and religious forms, had important consequences for the place of physical violence in social life – consequences made all the more forceful because they reinforced the state's efforts to subdue the old warrior classes and their aristocratic culture (Spierenburg 1984, Elias 2000).

Private feuding and dueling declined, as did the routine use of violence to chastise wives, children, and servants. Torture was prohibited. Corporal punishments such as maiming, branding, flogging and whipping were used less widely. Punishments involving bodily exposure or suffering – the stocks, the pillory, flogging, birching and branding – were mostly abandoned. The death penalty grew less frequent and less violent, so that from the eighteenth century onwards, execution practices that disfigured, dismembered or displayed the condemned's body became much less common and the suffering of the condemned on the scaffold was greatly reduced. By the middle of the nineteenth century, long after scaffold tortures had been abolished, middle-class commentators complained that the sight of a person being put to death was too disturbing to watch and criticized the callous vulgarity of those who continued to attend public hangings (Banner 2003, Spierenburg 1984).

From the late eighteenth century onwards, western elites denounced public executions in the name of civilization, criticizing state officials for staging such 'barbaric' displays and providing occasions for 'vulgar' despicable conduct. By the mid-nineteenth century, a practice once supported by ruling groups everywhere was now being criticized by them (McGowen 2003).

But if a civilized aesthetic of refinement helped form the sensibility of the anti-gallows movement, it was not its only cultural foundation. An equally important strand in the movement's make-up has always been humanitarianism: a moral – and often religious – sensibility that regards human life as sacred, presses for an end to cruelty and aims to extend compassion to all fellow creatures. This sensibility has been a constant theme of penal reformers: from Beccaria and his 'cause of humanity' in the eighteenth century, to Norval Morris (1996) and his 'decency, empathy' and concern for 'human suffering' in the twentieth.[8]

8 The 'motive force of penal reform' is, according to Morris (1996: 627), 'Decency, empathy, the ability to feel at least to a degree the lash on another's back, the removal occasionally of our customary blinkers to human suffering, a respect for each individual springing from religious or humanitarian beliefs'.

Humanitarianism has many sources – the Enlightenment writings of Montesquieu and Voltaire, the moral individualism of liberalism, the credos of eighteenth-century Quakers and nineteenth-century Evangelicals, the Romantic Movement in fiction and poetry. Its characteristic sentiments of empathy and identification with others were acquired and transmitted through cultural practices such as reading novels, keeping diaries, and putting oneself in the position of others. But its central principle is the simple moral imperative that human life is sacred and ought not to be violated – and this imperative has emerged most fully as an organizing principle of governance and social life in modern liberal democracies and as the central value in the reform discourse of human rights (Hunt 2007).

Humanitarianism has at its core a fundamental respect for individuals and for personhood. Such values may seem obvious and unavoidable today, but their emergence marked a new phase in western history: an epochal revaluation of morals in which the claims of kin, tribe, sect, and state were downgraded and those of autonomous individual persons made paramount. In its implacable opposition to killing and violence, humanitarianism is a decidedly anti-military sensibility, grounded in peaceable forms of life and commercial social relations. In contrast to the warrior ethos of the preceding era – with its history of blood and cruelty, its idea of honourable violence, and its enjoyment of killing and blood sports – humanitarianism regards human suffering as unconscionable and utterly deplores violence. Its horror of cruelties even extends to those perpetrated by God: it is the New Testament doctrine of compassionate forgiveness that appeals to the humanitarian, not the fire and brimstone vengeance of the Old (Holmes 1995).

With the decline of traditional honour codes and the spread of humanitarian ideals, physical violence became the new taboo of liberal democratic societies – the more peaceful and stable the society, the more problematic the violence. The rise of humanitarian sensibilities had clear and direct consequences for capital punishment. Humanitarianism generated a new sympathy for the scaffold's victims and their suffering. Members of the governing classes who once regarded the sacrifice of felons as a necessary tonic for social order began to consider the suffering of the man facing death. Their moral horizons were extended, and with them, their moral imagination and ability to empathize. Humanitarian concerns helped put an end to torture and afflictive executions and prompted the search to develop a painless execution technique. Humanitarian sentiments changed the attitudes of legislators, judge and juries, encouraging them to recognize the defendant as a fellow human being where they had once seen only a lower class felon (Garland 2010).

By the second half of the nineteenth century, the humanitarian sensibility was so widespread that even supporters of capital punishment were phrasing their arguments in these terms. But if 'sanctity of life' arguments could be made for *and* against the death penalty for murderers, the sacred place now accorded to human life discredited the use of capital punishment for lesser offences. Capital codes narrowed accordingly. By the twentieth century, the opposition between humanitarian sentiment and capital punishment was being expressed in a new and more powerful form by a human rights movement that viewed the death penalty as a violation of the most fundamental right of man (Hunt 2007, Hood and Hoyle 2008).

From the eighteenth century to the present, death penalty debates have been framed in the language of civilization *and* humanity. Civilized sensibilities might best be understood as an aesthetic of refinement, delicacy and self-restraint, combined with social norms designed to minimize unpleasant encounters with vulgar and disturbing behaviour. Humanitarian sensibilities, in contrast, are feelings of human sympathy and compassionate identification with others, and the moral imperatives that flow from such identification. These two sensibilities may run alongside one another, and draw on the same language of refined feeling, but at a certain point their effects diverge. One is concerned to reduce the aesthetic affront involved in putting a person to death while the other fundamentally objects to human suffering. One aims to reduce the sight of pain, the other aims to reduce its infliction. One is primarily about manners and appearances, the other about underlying moral substance (Garland 2010: ch. 5).

Like liberalism and democracy, civilizing sentiments and humanizing sentiments are often run together. But they are not the same thing. Civilized sensibilities push to reduce the aesthetic affront involved in putting a person to death, humanitarian ones object to the unnecessary human suffering that capital punishment involves. One aims to reduce the sight of pain, the other aims to reduce its infliction. One is primarily about manners and appearances, the other about underlying moral substance. We could say that death by lethal injection is highly civilized in form, but it is not exactly humanitarian.

Conclusion

The movement of western states towards the complete abolition of capital punishment began, haltingly, in a few small jurisdictions in the late eighteenth century. It spread to a handful of larger nation-states in the course of the nineteenth and early twentieth centuries, often producing complete abolitions only for 'ordinary' crimes (not 'extraordinary' or political ones) with many of these abolitionist developments subsequently being reversed. Then, in the last third of the twentieth century, the movement greatly expanded until it encompassed all of the western nations, each of which – with the exception of the USA – had abolished the death penalty entirely by the end of the century.

The restriction of the death penalty was a process that unfolded over an entire region and over a long period of time. In the great majority of cases, where sustained and comprehensive abolition occurred, it emerged as the final phase in a reform process that had already restricted, restrained, and refined the practice and greatly reduced its frequency. Except in a very few instances, complete and sustained abolition has been a late twentieth-century development that capped a much longer process of transformation.

The majority of western European abolitions occurred in the second half of the twentieth century, either in the years immediately after World War II or else in the 1960s and 70s. Italy, Germany and Austria included abolitionist provisions in the new liberal constitutions they enacted following the end of the war and the collapse of fascism. After the Second World War, nations such as Britain, Spain, France, Ireland, Australia, New Zealand and Canada experienced a decline in the frequency of executions though legislative attempts failed to bring about complete abolition for decades thereafter. In several nations where capital punishment had long been abolished for 'ordinary' crimes, the death penalty remained on the books for political offences against the state – a reminder of capital punishment's historic role in the maintenance of state power. In the relative stability of western Europe in the post-war years, these 'extraordinary' penalties were never invoked, and they too were eventually abolished: by Portugal in 1976, Denmark in 1978, Luxemburg and Norway in 1979, the Netherlands in 1982, Ireland in 1990, Italy in 1994, Spain in 1995, Belgium in 1996, and the UK in 1998 (Hood and Hoyle 2008, Garland 2010).

Between the 1980s and the present, anti-death penalty provisions have increasingly been embodied in human rights conventions, transnational treaties and international law. Protocols 6 and 13 of the European Convention on Human Rights (1983 and 2002) prohibit the death penalty, as does the United Nations' 2nd Optional Protocol to the International Covenant on Civil and Political Rights (ICCPR), which was passed in 1989 and also the American Convention on Human Rights Protocol to Abolish the Death Penalty adopted in 1990 by the General Assembly of the Organization of American States.

The emergence of these international legal norms has changed the nature of the death penalty as a political issue. Their existence exerts abolitionist pressure on other states and in some cases provides states with political and economic incentives to abandon the death penalty. They have internationalized death penalty politics, transforming a domestic matter into an issue that has a bearing on international relations. They 'lock in' death penalty abolition in those nations that are signatories to the ICCPR, or members of the European Union and the Council of Europe, making continued abolition an international obligation rather than merely a domestic policy choice. As a result, capital punishment has tended to fade from political debate in these nations and popular opinion in some countries has begun to loosen its attachment to the death penalty. The new reform movement has succeeded in elevating death penalty abolition to the status of an international human rights principle.

The long-term history of the death penalty in the West thus approaches its absolute antithesis: what was once an unproblematic institution, universally embraced, is fast becoming a violation of human rights, universally prohibited. Except, of course, in the United States, where capital punishment remains constitutionally permissible and executions continue to be carried out.

References

Banner, S. 2003. *The Death Penalty: An American History.* Cambridge: Harvard University Press.

Beccaria, C. 1995. *On Crimes and Punishments and other Writings*, edited by R. Bellamy. New York: Cambridge University Press [first published in 1764].

Bender, J. 1989. *Imagining the Penitentiary: Fiction and the Architecture of Mind in 18th Century England.* Chicago: University of Chicago Press.

Elias, N. 2000. *The Civilizing Process: Sociogenetic and Psychogenetic Explorations.* London: Blackwell.

Evans, R. 1996. *Rituals of Retribution: Capital Punishment in Germany 1600–1987.* Oxford: Oxford University Press.

Foucault, M. 1977. *Discipline and Punish: The Birth of the Prison.* London: Allen Lane.

Garland, D. 1990. *Punishment and Modern Society: A Study in Social Theory.* Chicago: University of Chicago Press.

Garland, D. 2010. *Peculiar Institution: America's Death Penalty in an Age of Abolition.* Oxford: Oxford University Press.

Gatrell, V.A.C. 1994. *The Hanging Tree: Executions and the English People 1770–1868.* Oxford: Oxford University Press.

Halttunen, K. 1998. *Murder Most Foul: The Killer and the American Gothic Imagination.* Cambridge: Harvard University Press.

Haskell T. 1992. Capitalism and the Origins of Humanitarian Sensibility, in *The Antislavery Debate: Capitalism and Abolitionism as a Problem in Historical Interpretation*, edited by T. Bender. Berkeley: University of California Press.

Holmes, S. 1995. *Passions and Constraints: On the Theory of Liberal Democracy.* Chicago: University of Chicago Press.

Hood, R. and Hoyle, C. 2008. *The Death Penalty: A Worldwide Perspective.* Oxford: Oxford University Press.

Hunt, L. 2007. *Inventing Human Rights: A History.* New York: Norton.

Johnson, D. and Zimring, F. 2009. *The Next Frontier: National Development, Political Change and the Death Penalty in Asia.* New York: Oxford University Press.

McGowen, R. 1987. The Body and Punishment in the Eighteenth Century. *Journal of Modern History* 59: 651–79.

McGowen, R. 2003. History, Culture and the Death Penalty: The British Debates, 1840–70. *Historical Reflections/Réflexions Historiques* 29: 229–49.

McManners, J. 1981. *Death and the Enlightenment: Changing Attitudes to Death among Christians and Unbelievers in Eighteenth Century France.* New York: Oxford University Press.

Merback, M. 1999. *The Thief, the Cross and the Wheel: Pain and the Spectacle of Punishment in Medieval and Renaissance Europe.* Chicago: University of Chicago Press.

Morris, N. 1966. Impediments to Penal Reform. *University of Chicago Law Review* 33: 627.

Neumayer, E. 2006. *Death Penalty: The Political Foundations of the Global Trend Toward Abolition* [Unpublished manuscript].

Otterbein, K.F. 1988. The Ultimate Coercive Sanction: A Cross-Cultural Study of Capital Punishment. *American Ethnologist* 15(4): 818–19.

Pratt, J. 2002. *Punishment and Civilization: Penal Tolerance and Intolerance in Modern Society.* London: SAGE.

Royer, K. 2003. The Body in Parts: Reading the Execution in Late Medieval England. *Historical Reflections/Réflexions Historiques* 29: 323.

Rusche, G. and O. Kirchheimer 1968. *Punishment and Social Structure.* New York: Russell and Russell.

Sharpe, J. 1990. *Judicial Punishment in England.* London: Faber and Faber.

Smith, P. 2008. *Punishment and Culture.* Chicago: University of Chicago Press.

Spierenburg, P. 1984. *The Spectacle of Suffering: Executions and the Evolution of Repression.* Cambridge: Cambridge University Press.

Starr, P. 2007. *Freedom's Power: The True Force of Liberalism.* New York: Basic Books.

Tilly, C. 1992. *Coercion, Capital and European States, AD 990–1992.* Cambridge: Blackwell.

van Dulmen, R. 1990. *Theatre of Horror: Crime and Punishment in Early Modern Germany.* Oxford: Polity.

PART II
The USA

Chapter 4
The American Enlightenment: Eliminating Capital Punishment in the United States

John D. Bessler

The State of the State

The American death penalty is in decline. The number of US executions fell from 98 in 1999 to 43 in 2012, leading one set of scholars to characterize America's death penalty as 'on a downhill slope' (Koch et al. 2012). The number of American death sentences also fell from more than 300 per year in 1995 and 1996 to 80 in 2011. And the executions that do occur are increasingly concentrated in just one region, the American South, with just three states – Texas, Virginia, and Oklahoma – accounting for more than half of all American executions since 1976 (DPIC 2013). Indeed, in terms of capital prosecutions, just a small fraction of US counties account for the executions that have taken place in the modern era. As law professor Robert Smith recently wrote in the *Boston University Law Review*: 'The vast majority of counties do not use the death penalty at all'. Smith's study found that just ten per cent of counties nationally returned a death sentence in the 2004 to 2009 period, and that less than one per cent of counties sentenced anyone to death who was actually executed in that time frame (Smith 2012). A recent report by the Texas Coalition to Abolish the Death Penalty notes that even in the Lone Star State – America's execution capital – death sentences have dropped more than 75 per cent since 2002 (TCADP 2012). The only statistic that keeps going up is the number of death-row exonerations, now up to 143 since 1973 according to the Washington, D.C.-based Death Penalty Information Center (DPIC 2013).

The death penalty's slow demise in the United States – as well as its continued persistence in a few locales – is attributable to multiple factors. First, America's system of federalism, with power split between federal, state and local actors, means that laws and practices vary widely by jurisdiction. Regional differences are reflected in state laws, and the preferred punishment – death or imprisonment – is a product of local customs and traditions (Garland 2010). Second, Western conceptions of cruelty and human rights have changed substantially over time, especially since World War II, with the Universal Declaration of Human Rights adopted in 1948. Though geographic variations within the US still exist, the death penalty – despite attempts to sanitize it through lethal injection – has not fared well in light of evolving norms and changes in societal attitudes (Koch et al. 2012). Third, individual prosecutors – cloaked with broad discretion as they perform their duties – are the ones who ultimately decide whether capital charges will be brought. While some prosecutors continue to pursue capital prosecutions, many district attorneys have put the brakes on capital punishment (Garland 2010). For example, Craig Watkins, the district attorney for Dallas, Texas, has expressed major reservations, calling for fairer, more race-neutral administration of the law and revealing in 2012 that his great-grandfather had been executed (Goldstein 2013). Also, American juries – even 'death-qualified' ones stripped of all death penalty opponents – have been more hesitant lately to impose death sentences. From 2004 to 2009 in California, 64 per cent of counties did not sentence anyone to death, and 90 per cent of counties returned no more than one death sentence. Just three counties – Los Angeles, Riverside and Orange – were responsible for more than half of all death sentences in the state during that time period (Smith 2012).

And the number of death penalty states is shrinking, too. While the US Government, the US military, and 32 American states still retain capital punishment, 18 American states no longer authorize executions (DPIC 2013). More significantly, the death penalty is largely dormant in most death penalty states, with few if any executions taking place. For instance, California now has 731 death-row inmates and Kansas has ten, but no executions have taken place in those states for many years now (DPIC 2013). The last executions in the State of Kansas took place in 1965 (Evans 2010), and the state's current Republican governor, Sam Brownback, has called for 'a culture of life', saying, 'I have difficulty with the death penalty'. In 2007, at a forum in Baltimore, Brownback – a Catholic – expressed his sentiments this way: 'I think we should limit the death penalty to cases only where we cannot protect society from the individual, such as when Osama bin Laden is caught' (Koch et al. 2012). In the last ten years alone, Illinois, Maryland, New Jersey, New Mexico and Connecticut all abolished the death penalty, with New York's death penalty law declared unconstitutional in 2004 (Udoma 2012). In fact, as statistics reveal, death sentences are down nationwide as local prosecutors and juries in retentionist states increasingly opt for life-without-parole sentences in lieu of the death penalty (DPIC 2013).

Apart from recent legislative activity and local decisions resulting in the curtailment of death sentences, the US Supreme Court – as a matter of constitutional law – has also restricted the categories of death-eligible offenders. The Court imposed such restrictions in a series of cases beginning in the 1970s based on the US Constitution's Cruel and Unusual Punishments Clause – a provision that has been applied to the states via the Constitution's Fourteenth Amendment (Bessler 2012a). The Eighth Amendment unequivocally prohibits 'cruel and unusual punishments', while the Fourteenth Amendment guarantees 'due process' and 'equal protection'. In *Coker v. Georgia*, 433 US 584 (1977), the Supreme Court held that the Eighth Amendment forbade the death penalty for a non-homicidal rape of an adult woman – a prohibition extended to non-homicidal child rape in *Kennedy v. Louisiana*, 554 US 407 (2008). The Court also held that the death penalty is disproportionate for robbery where the victim is not killed, and for kidnapping and rape where no murder took place (Hooks v. Georgia, 433 US 917

(1977); Eberheart v. Georgia, 433 US 917 (1977)). In *Enmund v. Florida*, 458 US 782 (1982), the Court likewise set aside the death penalty for a defendant who neither took nor intended or attempted to take a life. In other rulings, the Court has read the Eighth Amendment to bar the execution of the insane, the mentally retarded and juvenile offenders. Those decisions – *Ford v. Wainwright*, 477 US 399 (1986), *Atkins v. Virginia*, 536 US 304 (2002), and *Roper v. Simmons*, 543 US 551 (2005) – further restricted the death penalty's use. More than three decades ago, in *Woodson v. North Carolina*, 428 US 280 (1976) and *Roberts v. Louisiana*, 428 US 325 (1976), the Court had already declared that mandatory death sentences, though once America's norm, are unconstitutional. The Court emphasized that 'the practice of sentencing to death all persons convicted of a particular offense has been rejected as unduly harsh and unworkably rigid'.

The US Supreme Court has actually ruled both ways on the death penalty's constitutionality, with Justices Thurgood Marshall and William Brennan – during their time on the Court – finding executions unconstitutional *per se* (Mello 1996). In *Furman v. Georgia*, 408 US 238 (1972), the Court first ruled that American death penalty laws were unconstitutional. In concurring opinions, the five Justices who issued that landmark decision worried about the 'uncontrolled discretion of judges or juries'; the 'selective and irregular use of penalties'; discrimination; 'wholly arbitrary' punishments; and the 'rarity', 'infrequency', and 'totally capricious selection of criminals for the punishment of death' (Bessler 2012a). But just four years later, the Court – yielding to legislative pressure – reversed course and upheld death penalty laws in three companion cases: *Gregg v. Georgia*, 428 US 153 (1976), *Proffitt v. Florida*, 428 US 242 (1976), and *Jurek v. Texas*, 428 US 262 (1976). The Court's reversal came after 35 American states reenacted death penalty laws in *Furman*'s wake (Bessler 2012a). In cases reviewed since 1976, America's bicentennial, the Supreme Court – in interpreting its Eighth Amendment 'evolving standards of decency' test, first articulated in *Trop v. Dulles*, 356 US 86 (1958) – has consistently upheld the death penalty's constitutionality while rejecting systemic challenges to US death penalty laws. For example, in *McCleskey v. Kemp*, 481 US 279 (1987), the Court rejected a challenge to Georgia's death penalty in spite of unrebutted statistical proof that the state's death penalty was administered in a racially discriminatory fashion. Likewise, in *Baze v. Rees*, 553 US 35 (2008), the Court rejected a legal challenge to Kentucky's three-drug lethal injection protocol.

The Enlightenment and the Founding Era

The conventional wisdom is that America's founders and framers – those responsible for approving the Declaration of Independence (1776) and the US Constitution and its Bill of Rights, ratified in 1788 and 1791, respectively – were avid death penalty supporters. Indeed, US Supreme Court Justice Antonin Scalia, in upholding death sentences, has frequently emphasized that the Founding Fathers authorized executions in their time. In particular, he points out that the US

Congress made crimes punishable by death before the US Bill of Rights was put in place and that language in the US Constitution's Fifth and Fourteenth Amendments contemplates the death penalty's use (Bessler 2012a). The Fifth Amendment, ratified when mandatory death sentences were still in use, provides in part: 'No person shall be held to answer for a capital, or otherwise infamous crime, unless on a presentment or indictment of a Grand Jury'; 'nor shall any person be subject for the same offence to be twice put in jeopardy of life or limb', 'nor be deprived of life, liberty, or property, without due process of law'. The Fourteenth Amendment, ratified in 1868 after Abraham Lincoln and the Civil War brought an end to slavery, further reads: 'nor shall any State deprive any person of life, liberty, or property, without due process of law; nor deny to any person within its jurisdiction the equal protection of the laws'. Early American executions were a fact of life in places such as Boston, Philadelphia and Charleston (Gottlieb 2006). But America's founders were, in fact, highly ambivalent about executions. Not only did many Founding Fathers reject the severity of English laws and question the efficacy of state-sanctioned killing, but it was in the founding era that lawmakers began to develop a penitentiary system to alleviate the need for executions (Bessler 2012a).

The United States of America, which declared its independence from Great Britain in 1776, inherited its legal system and traditions from England – a country that frequently inflicted death sentences. English judges also utilized 'transportation' – or exile – to punish offenders, but English executioners had plenty of work. In London, countless hangings took place at the Tyburn gallows until they were moved to the exterior of Newgate prison in 1783, and executions – as is well documented – were a routine part of English life (Gatrell 1994). Although America's Founding Fathers chose to retain death penalty laws for certain offences, especially murder and treason, the founders nonetheless despised 'cruel and unusual punishments' and 'sanguinary laws', viewing such punishments and laws as products of an oppressive monarchical system. In Virginia's Declaration of Rights (1776), drafted by George Mason, Virginians included a specific prohibition against 'cruel and unusual punishments' – a legal protection lifted from the English Declaration of Rights of 1688. In 1776, Maryland delegates also approved a declaration of rights that contained two clauses addressing cruel acts. Clause 14 read: 'Sanguinary laws ought to be avoided, as far as is consistent with the safety of the State: and no law, to inflict cruel and unusual pains and penalties, ought to be made in any case, or at any time hereafter'. And Clause 22 provided: 'Excessive bail ought not to be required, nor excessive fines imposed, nor cruel or unusual punishments inflicted, by the courts of law'. In Pennsylvania's Revolutionary War-era 1776 constitution, that state's founders also included this provision: 'The penal laws as heretofore used shall be reformed by the legislature of this state, as soon as may be, and punishments made in some cases less sanguinary, and in general more proportionate to the crimes' (Bessler 2012a).

The First Congress of the United States, in 1790, authorized the federal death penalty, making a handful of crimes punishable by death. It did so, however, for far fewer crimes than the English 'Bloody Code', which once made more than 200 crimes capital offences (Bessler 2012a). 'The Bloody Code', as one historian has said of the laws of America's mother country, 'is the name traditionally given to the English system of criminal law during the period 1688–1815'. In 1688, approximately 50 English felonies were punishable by death, with that number climbing to roughly 160 in 1765 and to more than 220 by the end of the Napoleonic wars (McLynn 1989). America's founders – men such as Thomas Jefferson, James Madison and James Wilson – flatly rejected that draconian approach, working to change American law to make punishments less severe. 'Let the punishment be proportioned – let it be analogous – to the crime', James Wilson told a grand jury in 1791, expressing with pride the difference between English and American attitudes on penal codes: 'How few are the crimes – how few are the capital crimes, known to the laws of the United States, compared with those known to the laws of England!' In fact, the criminal code passed by the First Congress drastically curtailed the list of capital crimes, making only the following offences capital in nature: treason, piracy, murder within federal enclaves, rescuing any person from the gallows, forgery, and counterfeiting. In a reflection of the times, much different than our own, the First Congress also authorized as punishments standing in 'the pillory for one hour' and public whipping not to exceed 'thirty-nine stripes'. For offences made capital under federal law, the death penalty was mandatory, with Congress dictating that offenders 'shall suffer death'. The method of execution specified by Congress: 'hanging the person convicted by the neck until dead' (Bessler 2012a).

The eighteenth-century – the period of America's birth and the country's parting of ways with King George III – was a time of violent revolutions as well as that of the Enlightenment (Beales 2005). In the aftermath of the Glorious Revolution of 1688 and as part of an intellectual awakening in Europe, Montesquieu, a French jurist, published *The Spirit of the Laws* in 1748; Jean-Jacques Rousseau published *The Social Contract* in 1762, opening his book by writing 'Man is born free; and everywhere he is in chains'; and Cesare Beccaria – a young Italian nobleman who joined a Milanese salon calling itself the Academy of Fists – published *On Crimes and Punishments* in 1764. The latter book, translated into English in 1767, was the first Enlightenment text that, in addition to opposing torture, made a comprehensive case for abolishing capital punishment. Before its publication, very little penal reform had taken place anywhere. Prussia's king, Frederick II, had done away with torture in 1752, but it was not until 1772 that Sweden outlawed torture for all crimes. It was also not until 1776 – the year America declared its independence – that Austria's Holy Roman Empress Maria Theresa, inspired in part by Beccaria's ideas and the writings of like-minded thinkers, abolished torture. After the publication of Beccaria's bestselling treatise, monarchs and European and American intellectuals alike were moved by Beccaria's words and humanistic sentiments. In 1786, when America's Articles of Confederation, ratified in 1781, were still in place, Grand Duke Leopold of Tuscany made history by adopting a Tuscan penal code that totally eliminated capital punishment. And in 1787, the year the US Constitution was signed by delegates to the Constitutional Convention in Philadelphia, Holy Roman Emperor Joseph II (Leopold's brother) followed suit, abolishing Austria's death penalty save for crimes of revolt against the state. In America, these developments did not go unnoticed, with American political leaders later hailing the Tuscan example in their anti-death penalty advocacy (Bessler 2012a).

The material influence of Beccaria's treatise on American law can be gleaned from a 1786 letter that William Bradford, Jr., then Pennsylvania's attorney general, sent to an Italian botanist, Count Luigi Castiglioni, while Castiglioni was touring the United States in the mid-1780s. Castiglioni – the nephew of Pietro and Alessandro Verri, brothers from Milan in the Academy of Fists who had inspired Beccaria to write *On Crimes and Punishments* – had come to America in 1785 aboard the 250-ton American vessel *Neptune*. In his letter, Bradford – a close friend of James Madison from their days together at the College of New Jersey, now Princeton – heaped praise upon Beccaria's treatise, with Bradford giving Castiglioni a newly printed American edition of *On Crimes and Punishments*. In presenting that new edition of Beccaria's book to Castiglioni, Bradford – who believed Castiglioni to be Beccaria's nephew – wrote: 'It is a new proof of the veneration my countrymen harbor for the opinions of your famous relative. I should like it to be known by the author of this book, so well received in the Old World, that his efforts to extend the domain of humanity have been crowned in the New World with the happiest success'. 'Long before the recent Revolution', Bradford explained in his letter, 'this book was common among lettered persons of Pennsylvania, who admired its principles without daring to hope that they could be adopted in legislation, since we copied the laws of England, to whose laws we were subject'. 'However', Bradford continued, 'as soon as we were free of political bonds, this humanitarian system, long admired in secret, was publicly adopted and incorporated by the Constitution of the State, which, spurred by the influence of this benign spirit, ordered the legislative bodies to render penalties less bloody and, in general, more proportionate to the crimes' (Pace 1983).

In his letter, Bradford took note of the fact that a plan had already been drafted – and was just awaiting final legislative approval – to reform Pennsylvania's penal laws. That plan eliminated 'the lash, branding, mutilation, and death', replacing them – as Bradford noted – with 'strenuous and continuous labor for variable periods of time'. '[I]nstead of one hundred sixty capital crimes in the country from which we have recently separated', Bradford wrote, 'there will be only four in Pennsylvania'. As Bradford's letter, crediting Beccaria's *On Crimes and Punishments*, emphasized: 'One must attribute mainly to this excellent book the honor of this revolution in our penal code. The name of Beccaria has become familiar in Pennsylvania, his authority has become great, and his principles have spread among all classes of persons and impressed themselves deeply in the hearts of our citizens'. 'You yourself must have noticed the influence of these precepts in the other American states', Bradford wrote to Castiglioni, who travelled to all 13 states during his trip to America from 1785 to 1787. Of Beccaria's influence, Bradford's 1786 letter concluded: 'The tyranny of prejudice and injustice has fallen, the voice of a philosopher has stilled the outcries of the masses, and although a bloody system may still survive in the laws of many of our states, nevertheless the beneficent spirit sown by Beccaria works secretly in behalf of the accused, moderating the rigor of the laws and tempering justice with compassion' (Pace 1983). Dr Benjamin Rush – a signer of the Declaration of Independence and a fellow Pennsylvanian – would himself vigorously advocate the total abolition of capital punishment in the United States (Bessler 2012a).

Count Castiglioni, who befriended Benjamin Franklin, mostly made observations about trees, plants and social customs during his trip. But in the course of his travels, he met with a wide array of early American political leaders and took special note of US penal reforms in his *Viaggio*, his later published travelogue. Written decades before Alexis de Tocqueville, the French writer of *Democracy in America* fame, came to America in the 1830s to study the US penal system, Castiglioni's *Viaggio* was published in Italy in 1790 after he interacted with a veritable who's who of American law and politics. Not only did Castiglioni hobnob with the likes of Dr Benjamin Rush, but he stayed with George Washington at Mount Vernon for four days and paid a visit to Thomas Jefferson's Monticello, though Jefferson wasn't there at the time (Pace 1983). After delegates at the Constitutional Convention met in Philadelphia to hammer out the language of the US Constitution, Benjamin Franklin felt such kinship with 'Count Castiglione' – as Dr Franklin later recorded – that he wrote him a letter from Philadelphia on 14 October 1787, shortly after the Constitutional Convention had completed its work. 'Supposing that a Gentleman who had so much Curiosity respecting the natural Productions of our Country, may have some respecting its political Productions, I send you enclos'd a Copy of the new federal Constitution propos'd by the Convention of all the States lately held in this City. It is a singular Thing in the History of Mankind, that a great People have had the Opportunity of forming a Government for themselves. This Plan is now to be submitted to the Consideration of separate State Conventions, and probably will be adopted by most if not all of them'. 'I hope that after all your Peregrinations you got safe home to your Country', Franklin wrote, 'and that this will find you well and happy in your own Habitation'.

On Crimes and Punishments, in which Beccaria argued for proportion between crimes and punishments, proved to be extremely influential on both sides of the Atlantic. It was serialized in newspapers, and in his *Commentaries on the Laws of England*, Sir William Blackstone – a much-respected figure – cited Beccaria's work. 'It is a kind of quackery in government, and argues a want of skill, to apply the same universal remedy, the *ultimum supplicium*, to every case of difficulty', Blackstone concluded in his legal commentary, which was widely read by aspiring lawyers and the colonists who, through revolution, became Americans. 'It is, it must be owned, much easier to extirpate than to amend mankind: yet that magistrate must be esteemed both a weak and a cruel surgeon, who cuts off every limb, which through ignorance or indolence he will not attempt to cure', Blackstone advised. Thomas Jefferson and George Washington bought copies of

Beccaria's treatise, likely in 1769, and other leading revolutionaries, including Massachusetts natives John Adams and John Hancock, read Beccaria's book too. Indeed, Adams passionately quoted Beccaria in 1770 in defending the British soldiers accused of murder after the Boston Massacre. 'I am for the prisoners at the bar', Adams said in an opening line, 'and shall apologize for it only in the words of the Marquis Beccaria: "If by supporting the rights of mankind, and of invincible truth, I shall contribute to save from the agonies of death one unfortunate victim of tyranny, or ignorance, equally fatal, his blessings and years of transport shall be sufficient consolation to me for the contempt of all mankind"'. John Adams's son, John Quincy Adams, who became the sixth US President and who came to oppose the death penalty, would himself remark on the 'electric effect' Beccaria's words – as spoken by his father – had on jurors (Bessler 2012a).

Dr Benjamin Rush, William Bradford, James Wilson and Benjamin Franklin – all of Pennsylvania – were four of Beccaria's biggest disciples. Dr Rush – a devout Christian and a Philadelphia physician – invoked Beccaria's name at a reading he gave at Benjamin Franklin's house in March 1787. 'I consider the death penalty an improper punishment for any crime', Rush explained, citing the death penalty's abolition in Tuscany. Dr Rush's friend, William Bradford, also wrote an influential legislative report in 1793 titled *An Enquiry How Far the Punishment of Death is Necessary in Pennsylvania*. In that report, Bradford echoed many of Beccaria's arguments and advocated for the death penalty's abolition for all offences except premeditated murder. And even for murderers, Bradford was willing to entertain the prospect that future evidence might show that executions were unnecessary. James Wilson, one of just six signers of both the Declaration of Independence and the US Constitution, also frequently referred to Beccaria's treatise. The College of Philadelphia's first law professor and an early Associate Justice of the US Supreme Court, Wilson called the English practice of not affording counsel to those accused of capital crimes 'unreasonable and severe'. In charging a Virginia grand jury in 1791, Wilson specifically invoked Beccaria, saying, '[l]et the punishment be proportioned … to the crime'. In the same era in which Americans outlawed 'cruel and unusual punishments', Wilson labelled 'cruel' punishments 'dastardly and contemptible'. Benjamin Franklin himself opposed the execution of thieves and lower-level offenders (Bessler 2012a).

That America's founders were highly ambivalent about executions is made clear by their actions and their writings. The nation's first commander-in-chief, George Washington, though viewing death sentences as necessary to maintain order and discipline, often showed leniency to condemned men. And General Washington, like his aide Alexander Hamilton, felt that executions were far too frequently employed. In 1778, even in the midst of the bloodshed of the Revolutionary War, Washington wrote to the Continental Congress: 'One thing, we have suffered much from, is the want of a proper gradation of punishments: the interval between a hundred lashes and death is too great and requires to be filled by some intermediate stages'. 'To inflict capital punishment upon every deserter or other heinous offender', Washington wrote, 'would incur the imputation of cruelty, and by the familiarity of the example, destroy its efficacy' (Bessler 2012a). Charles Lee – another military man – also wrote this of Beccaria: 'The Marquis of Beccaria, in his incomparable treatise on Crimes and Punishments, is of opinion, that a community ought to punish with death such criminals only whose existence is absolutely pernicious to the community; if his reasoning is just, a criminal king is almost the only criminal on whom death ought to be inflicted, as his existence, (if not always absolutely destructive,) is undoubtedly highly dangerous to society' (Bunbury 1874). Thomas Paine, often called the Father of the American Revolution because of his authorship of the pro-independence, runaway bestseller *Common Sense*, was – like Dr Rush – an ardent abolitionist who, in France, even stood up to vocally oppose Louis XVI's execution (Bessler 2012a).

In the Commonwealth of Virginia, Thomas Jefferson – later the third President of the United States – was especially intrigued by Beccaria's ideas. Between 1774 and 1776, Jefferson copied 26 different passages from Beccaria's text into his commonplace book. Jefferson also drafted proposals for Virginia's constitution that would have severely curtailed the death penalty's use, and the Declaration of Independence he famously penned speaks of the 'inalienable' right to life. In addition, Jefferson laboriously drafted a bill for Virginia's legislature calling for proportionate punishments, allowing the death penalty only for treason and murder. While Jefferson was abroad in France, his friend and political ally James Madison – who later succeeded Jefferson as America's President – tirelessly advocated for that bill's passage. After the bill failed to pass by a single vote, Madison – who attributed a rage against horse thieves with dooming the bill – lamented to Jefferson that 'our old bloody code is by this event fully restored'. In 1823, Madison – a firm believer in penal reform even into his later years – wrote a veteran in Kentucky to say this: 'I should not regret a fair and full trial of the entire abolition of capital punishments, by any State willing to make it'. In correspondence, Jefferson – Madison's mentor, and a political leader who advised aspiring lawyers on what to read to prepare for the bar – specifically singled out Beccaria's *On Crimes and Punishments* in 1807 as one of only a handful of books he recommended on the principles of government. Toward the end of his life, in the 1820s, Jefferson also wrote a lengthy autobiographical statement, lauding Beccaria as follows: 'Beccaria and other writers on crimes and punishment had satisfied the reasonable world of the unrightfulness and inefficacy of the punishment of crimes by death'. Noting that 'hard labour' had been suggested as a substitute for capital punishment, Jefferson regretted that 'the general idea of our country had not yet advanced to that point' (Bessler 2012a).

Back to the Future: The Path to Abolition

Executions in the US are heavily concentrated in the South, with studies showing that the odds of receiving a death sentence increase dramatically for African Americans who kill whites (Gross 2012). Of the 1,355 executions since 1976, 1,108 took place in the South – with 617 of them taking place in either Texas or Virginia. In contrast, since 1976, America's Midwest region has seen 159 executions, its Western region 84 executions, and its Northeast region four executions. The statistics for persons executed in the US for interracial murders in recent years illustrates the race-of-the-victim discrimination that is so pervasive in America's legal system: whereas 20 white defendants were executed for killing black victims, 263 black defendants were executed for killing white victims (DPIC 2013). Meanwhile, despite the fact that its author, Justice Lewis Powell, renounced the Supreme Court's decision in *McCleskey v. Kemp*, 481 US 279 (1987) after retiring from the bench, that decision – effectively requiring defendants to prove intentional racial discrimination through means other than statistical proof – remains the law of the land. '*McCleskey*', writes University of Michigan Law School professor Samuel Gross, 'remains one of the most controversial decisions in the history of the Supreme Court'. 'It is often compared', he notes, 'to other notorious cases in which the Court endorsed discrimination by race: *Dred Scott v. Sandford*, *Plessy v. Ferguson*, and *Korematsu v. United States*'. Not only did Powell tell his biographer that he would have changed his vote in *McCleskey*, but Powell said that he would have voted the other way in any capital case. 'I have come to think that capital punishment should be abolished', Powell noted (Gross 2012).

Just as executions have become heavily clustered in the same geographic region that once spawned Jim Crow laws and frequent lynchings (Brundage 1997, Tischauser 2012), US death sentences are now on the decline (DPIC 2013). This latter trend, no doubt, is largely attributable to the public's growing ambivalence toward executions, the public's awareness of their arbitrariness, well-publicized mistaken convictions, and the passage of life-without-parole statutes in all death penalty states (DPIC 2011, DPIC 2007). There were more than 300 death sentences in 1995 and 1996 – 312 and 315 to be exact. But DNA exonerations of multiple death-row inmates, coupled with an error-laden system and questions about the efficacy of executions, has caused many Americans to rethink their views and reject death sentences (NRCNA 2012, Lytle 2008, Liebman et al. 2000). Since 2004, less than 150 American death sentences have been imposed per year, with the annual number of death sentences dropping dramatically since 1999. In 2010, 109 death sentences were handed out nationwide, but in 2011, that number dropped to 80, the first time the number has fallen below one hundred in recent times (DPIC 2013). For those who are sentenced to die, the factor of race often continues to play a decisive role, as a judge found in 2012 in *North Carolina v. Robinson*, a North Carolina Racial Justice Act case. In Louisiana, the chances of receiving a death sentence were found to be 97 per cent higher for those whose victim was white than for those whose victim was black (DPIC 2013). 'The main reason that race is a powerful issue in debates about the death penalty', writes Samuel Gross, 'is that everyone who cares *knows* that race plays a major role in determining who gets sentenced to death' (Gross 2012).

Ever since US executions resumed in 1977 with Utah's firing squad death of Gary Gilmore (Gilmore 1994), America's Eighth Amendment jurisprudence – normally read *to protect* prisoners from harm – has been mired in the thicket of, and thus marred by, the practice of state-sponsored killing. In cases such as *Hudson v. McMillian*, 503 US 1 (1992), the US Constitution's Cruel and Unusual Punishments Clause has been regularly read to bar the excessive use of force and the mistreatment of inmates. That Eighth Amendment provision has likewise been routinely interpreted to prohibit the neglect of the serious medical needs of inmates. For example, in *DeShaney v. Winnebago County Department of Social Services*, 489 US 189 (1989), the Supreme Court held that the Eighth Amendment requires that the government provide for a prisoner's 'basic human needs – *e.g.*, food, clothing, shelter, medical care, and reasonable safety'. Likewise, in *Helling v. McKinney*, 509 US 25 (1993), the Court held that exposure to harmful amounts of second-hand cigarette smoke might also violate an inmate's Eighth Amendment rights. In still another case, *Hope v. Pelzer*, 536 US 730 (2002), the Court took up the case of an Alabama inmate who had been shackled to a hitching post for several hours in the hot sun without water, resulting in dehydration and sunburn. In that case, the Supreme Court described the inmate's mistreatment as an 'obvious' Eighth Amendment violation. While non-lethal corporal punishments, such as whipping and ear cropping, have long been abandoned in America's prison system, the use of executions, ironically, has continued (Bessler 2013). Although the Supreme Court calls 'human dignity' an Eighth Amendment touchstone, the Court still permits executions, even of severely mentally ill inmates who have, in some instances, spent more than three decades on death row (Bessler 2012b). The Supreme Court has let executions go forward despite the fact that executions inflict a much harsher punishment – death – than lesser corporal punishments that judges themselves no longer tolerate (Bessler 2012b, Bosworth 2002, Miller 2012).

In Europe, meanwhile, both corporal and capital punishments have come to be seen as human rights violations (Hodgkinson and Schabas 2004, Oette 2011, Tonry and Frase 2001). As far as the death penalty is concerned, specific European treaties have been put in place to ensure its eradication. Protocol No. 6 to the Convention for the Protection of Human Rights and Fundamental Freedoms, promulgated in 1983, abolished capital punishment in peacetime for all signatories. That protocol provides: 'The death penalty shall be abolished. No one shall be condemned to such penalty or executed'. Protocol No. 6's only exception: 'A State may make provision in its law for the death penalty in respect of acts committed in time of war or of imminent threat of war…' But even those narrow exceptions have now gone away with the adoption of Protocol No. 13 to the Convention for the Protection of Human Rights and Fundamental Freedoms. The text of Protocol No. 13 specifically bars the death penalty's use under all circumstances, including in time of war or during imminent threat of war. Indeed, the signatories to Protocol No. 13 described 'everyone's right to life' as 'a basic value in a democratic society' and also emphasized that 'the abolition of the death penalty is essential for the protection of this right and for the full recognition of the inherent dignity of all human beings'. Today, Europe is a death-penalty-free zone, with all of the member states of the Council of Europe having either abolished capital punishment or instituted a moratorium on executions (Hood and Hoyle 2008, Mowbray 2012, Schabas 2002).

Over time, America's death penalty has morphed into a much different animal than what it resembled two hundred plus years ago. The anti-death penalty movement has ebbed and flowed, with death penalty laws passing through various stages as societal attitudes have evolved. In the Founding Fathers' era, death sentences were mandatory for eligible offences. 'Mandatory death penalty statutes existed in all of the original 13 colonies prior to the Revolutionary War', explains one scholar (Palmer 1998). Because of the harshness of mandatory death sentences, however, American states moved to discretionary sentences as more and more juries simply refused to convict (Erastus-Obilo 2009). '[A]t least since the Revolution', the US Supreme Court itself once noted, 'American juries have, with some regularity, disregarded their oaths and refused to convict defendants where a death sentence was the automatic consequence of a guilty verdict' (Abramson 2001). This change in mores ultimately led to a revision of death penalty laws, with judges or jurors given unbridled discretion to decide whether convicted felons should live or die. But that approach, initially approved by the US Supreme Court in *McGautha v. California*, 402 US 183 (1971), allowed juror biases, including instances of racial prejudice, to continue to infect capital sentencing decisions. Only in the post-*Furman* period did death penalty statutes really attempt to guide juror discretion, with many laws asking jurors to weigh 'aggravating' versus 'mitigating' factors (Hall 2008). But even then, the death penalty continued to be administered in an arbitrary and racially discriminatory fashion, as shown by the Baldus study presented in *McCleskey v. Kemp*, 481 US 279 (1987) (Davis 2007). Ultimately, the history of capital punishment – from both a legislative and judicial perspective – is one of successive restrictions on its use (Banner 2002, Bessler 2012a).

Already, many sitting or retired US Supreme Court Justices have questioned the efficacy of executions or described them as unconstitutional. Aside from Justice Powell, who regretted having upheld death sentences after leaving the Court, Justices William Brennan and Thurgood Marshall both asserted that executions violate the Eighth and Fourteenth Amendments. In a dissent in *Gregg v. Georgia*, 428 US 153 (1976), Justice Brennan emphasized that 'the State, even as it punishes, must treat its citizens in a manner consistent with their intrinsic worth as human beings – a punishment must not be so severe as to be degrading to human dignity'. '[W]e should declare', Brennan wrote, 'that the punishment of death, like punishments on the rack, the screw, and the wheel, is no longer morally tolerable in our civilized society'. In that case, Justice Marshall also dissented, concluding that the American people, if fully informed as to the death penalty's liabilities, would 'reject it as morally unacceptable'. Seeing no way of eliminating arbitrariness and discrimination without jeopardizing the requirement of individualized sentencing (*Woodson v. North Carolina*, 428 US 280 (1976);

Lockett v. Ohio, 438 US 586 (1978)), Justice Harry Blackmun also came to reject executions. In his famous dissent in *Callins v. Collins*, 510 US 1141 (1994), Justice Blackmun bluntly concluded that death penalty laws could not be administered in a manner consistent with constitutional demands. 'From this day forward', he announced, 'I no longer shall tinker with the machinery of death'. Other Justices have also called into question the propriety of executions (Bessler 2012a). For example, Justice John Paul Stevens, shortly before his retirement, concluded in his separate opinion in *Baze v. Rees*, 553 US 35 (2008) that death sentences are unnecessary.

Since its earliest days, the death penalty's long, gruesome arc – stretching back as far as recorded human history – has cast a dark shadow on American law. In early America, the country's founders – though proponents of the nation's nascent penitentiary system – did not do away with capital punishment entirely. However, they substantially restricted its scope and they actively advocated for penal reform (Bessler 2009). They set up societies to remedy inhumane prison conditions; they experimented with hard labour and solitary confinement as alternatives to death sentences; and they regularly read Enlightenment writers, including Montesquieu and Beccaria (Bessler 2012a). 'Every punishment, which does not arise from absolute necessity', Beccaria wrote, quoting Montesquieu, 'is tyrannical' (Jones and Johnstone 2012). And for many lawmakers, such as the American patriot John Adams, that motto became a personal mantra, a maxim to follow. 'Every Act of Authority, of one Man over another for which there is not an absolute Necessity, is tyrannical', Adams recorded in his diary, translating Beccaria's Italian words into English (Caso 1995). Indeed, the state-by-state development of a penitentiary system, begun first in Philadelphia with the opening of the Walnut Street Prison in 1790, finally provided authorities with a viable alternative to death sentences: life imprisonment (Lewis 1922). Although the Founding Fathers did not live to see the completion of a fully developed, nationwide penitentiary system, they welcomed the building of secure prisons in their respective states. New York passed legislation in 1796 providing for the construction of the Newgate state prison in Greenwich Village; New Jersey completed its state penitentiary in 1797; and penitentiaries in Virginia and Kentucky opened in 1800, the same year Massachusetts appropriated money for a prison at Charlestown (Morris 1995). The new facilities were a far cry from the primitive dungeon – a former copper mine – that Connecticut adapted for use as a colonial prison in 1773 (Keve 1995, Lewis 1965).

Prisons in the twenty-first century, built to securely house offenders, include Supermax facilities that bear little resemblance to late eighteenth-century penal institutions. Today, the ready availability of maximum-security prisons – structures built with concrete and iron to incarcerate inmates for their natural lives if necessary – make executions anachronistic and obsolete. Just as ear cropping and the pillory are vestiges of a bygone era, capital punishment – a penalty that originated in ancient societies when legal codes such as Greece's Draconian code made *every* crime punishable by death – is simply no longer necessary (Kronenwetter 2001).

Indeed, if the Eighth Amendment is read in a fair-minded way, executions must be classified as 'cruel and unusual punishments' in this day and age. Rapists are not sentenced to be raped, nor should civilized societies kill killers. Not only is it cruel to inject another human being with lethal chemicals, but from a factual standpoint, life-without-parole sentences now far outstrip death sentences in terms of their popularity. Right now, more than 49,000 people are serving life-without-parole sentences in the United States (Sentencing Project 2013), making that a much-used sentencing option (Ogletree and Sarat 2012). That number dwarfs the number of men and women – less than 3,200 – currently on death row in America (DPIC 2013). This means that life-without-parole sentences are now the norm or the 'usual' punishment for first-degree murderers. In contrast, death sentences – in the United States, as well as in most other countries – have become extraordinarily rare, making them 'unusual' in the extreme. As Ohio Supreme Court Justice William O'Neill dissented in 2013 in *State v. Wogenstahl*: 'It is clear that the death penalty is becoming increasingly rare both around the world and in America. By definition it is unusual'.

Because only a handful of American states execute inmates with any regularity, America's death penalty is more arbitrary and unusual than ever. Geography or the quality of defence counsel, not the nature of the crime, often determines an inmate's fate. When those realities are combined with an appellate system that so frequently overturns sentences, the legal process more closely resembles a state-run lottery than a rational system of criminal justice. Meanwhile, more Americans – along with the broader community of nations – are gradually turning away from capital punishment altogether. A 2010 poll by Lake Research Partners found that 61 per cent of Americans would choose a punishment other than the death penalty for murder. The most preferred alternative: life without parole plus restitution (38 per cent), followed by life without parole (13 per cent) and life with parole (9 per cent) (DPIC 2013). According to Amnesty International, the United States was the only country in the G8 to have carried out executions in 2011. And just three countries in the G20 – China, Saudi Arabia, and the US – did so. In total 175 of the 193 member states of the United Nations carried out no executions in 2011. This means that the United States now finds itself uncomfortably in the company of largely autocratic or totalitarian regimes – like Iran, Iraq and Yemen – when it conducts executions. In 2011, only a small number of countries – among them, China, Iran, Iraq and Saudi Arabia – are known to have carried out more executions than the United States (Amnesty 2012).

Predictions are hard to make, especially on an issue as emotionally charged as capital punishment. The American death penalty, however, seems destined to go the way of the stocks, the pillory and whipping post. When that day will come is unknowable, but when it does arrive, it is likely to happen through a combination of grassroots, executive, judicial and legislative efforts. At the local level, where activism begins and where politicians take the pulse of their constituents, as support for executions wanes, fewer prosecutors are likely to seek – and fewer juries are likely to impose – capital sentences. At the state level, more legislatures are already poised to do away with executions and more governors may grow uneasy with state-sanctioned killing. In the first month of 2013, one state's governor, Mike Beebe of Arkansas, already acknowledged that signing a death warrant had changed his thinking on capital punishment. Once a death penalty supporter, Beebe told a reporter: 'The awesome burden of being the last person to have to sign one of those things sobers you differently than talking about it in the abstract'. 'Everybody can claim they're for it until you're actually the person who's got to sign it', Beebe said (Stratford 2013). Abolition efforts are already underway in American states such as Kansas and New Hampshire, and the battle to abolish California's death penalty will no doubt continue apace (Wagner 2012, Koch et al. 2012). Indeed, in November 2012, California voters – by a 52 to 48 margin – just narrowly defeated a referendum to abolish that state's death penalty in its entirety (Barabak 2013). The close vote was particularly significant because in 1978, when California voters put the death penalty on the books, 70 per cent of voters supported the death penalty (Mintz 2012).

Times have changed, and the law must change with the times – a notion Thomas Jefferson embraced when he wrote that 'laws and institutions must go hand in hand with the progress of the human mind'. In speaking of the development of human progress, Jefferson wrote in the age of the American Enlightenment: 'As that becomes more developed, more enlightened, as new discoveries are made, new truths discovered and manners and opinions change, with the change of circumstances, institutions must advance also to keep pace with the times'. As Jefferson emphasized: 'We might as well require a man to wear still the coat which fitted him when a boy as civilized society to remain ever under the regimen of their barbarous ancestors' (Bessler 2012a). The American death penalty has already undergone a series of changes since Jefferson's time. The death penalty is no longer a mandatory punishment; it is now imposed in a discretionary, if capricious, fashion. And the way in which executions are conducted has changed, too. Gone are the days of midday executions in the public square. Instead, from the 1830s to the 1930s, state legislatures voted to move executions into prisons or enclosures adjoining them. Beginning in the 1880s, some American states also began requiring that executions take place in the dead of night to further reduce publicity surrounding executions (Bessler 1997). Such laws – like lethal injection protocols – were an effort to sanitize state-sanctioned killing.

The Eighth Amendment – the focal point of so much capital litigation – contains just 16 words, reading: 'Excessive bail shall not be required, nor excessive fines imposed, nor cruel and unusual punishments inflicted'. In the days of colonial and early America, Beccaria and others, including multiple US political leaders, described executions as cruel. Dr Benjamin Rush characterized them as such, and James Madison himself spoke of substituting 'penitentiary discipline' for 'the cruel inflictions so disgraceful to penal codes' (Bessler 2012a). In the founding era, however, the death penalty – as a factual matter – could not fairly be described as 'unusual'. After all, death sentences were then the mandatory, or usual, punishment for certain crimes. But today, executions are rare – and when they do occur, they are arbitrarily and discriminatorily imposed. That capricious and prejudicial system, which makes modern-day executions akin to being freakishly struck by lightning, contravenes basic principles of American law – in particular, the Fourteenth Amendment's 'due process' and 'equal protection' guarantees. The Constitution does contain language that assumes the death penalty's use. Those provisions, however, were intended *to protect* the rights of the accused at a time when, upon conviction, executions were mandatory. As drafted, the Constitution contemplates 'capital' charges subject to a grand jury's approval and the deprivation of 'life' so long as 'due process' is met. The Constitution's Double Jeopardy Clause, which prohibits being 'twice put in jeopardy of life or limb', also contemplates the deprivation of 'life' or 'limb', though judges today readily concede that courts would no longer tolerate the lopping off of an inmate's limbs (Bessler 2009). Non-lethal corporal punishments, in fact, are already a thing of the past in American penal institutions. Even Justice Scalia – a vocal proponent of 'originalism' – has called himself a 'faint-hearted originalist' because he would no longer allow such gruesome corporal punishments (Bessler 2012a).

The Eighth Amendment, unlike the Fifth and Fourteenth Amendments, specifically prohibits 'cruel and unusual punishments' in absolutist terms. That general language, put in place in 1791, allows living judges – in their own time – to decide what so qualifies. While the meaning of 'cruel' and 'unusual' have not changed much from the eighteenth century to the twenty-first century, societal views of cruelty – as well as our understanding of human rights – have evolved a great deal. For example, unlike in the founders' time, slavery is now outlawed as a matter of national and international law. And the US Supreme Court, which heralds its judicial independence, no longer considers itself bound by eighteenth-century practices in issuing its rulings. Indeed, in its prior decisions, the Court has already rejected a purely historical view of the Eighth Amendment – one which, if centred on 1791 practices, would render the 'cruel and unusual punishments' language little more than a toothless phrase. Instead, the Court follows what has been described as a 'living constitution' approach and interprets the Cruel and Unusual Punishments Clause under its 'evolving standards of decency' test. In its analysis, the Court regularly tallies states that permit or prohibit a particular practice and gauges whether a 'national consensus' exists and what the 'trends' or the 'consistency of the direction of change' look like. Essentially, the Supreme Court looks at legislative acts, jury verdicts, and the frequency of a punishment's infliction to determine a penalty's constitutionality, though the Court specifically reserves its right to 'independently' gauge what is impermissible (Bessler 2012a). Ultimately, though, the Court's Eighth Amendment legal analysis should be more straightforward: if a punishment is 'cruel' and 'unusual', it is unconstitutional. If executions qualify as such, and the evidence indicates they do, they – like other horrific, non-lethal corporal punishments – should be struck down.

It seems likely that the US Supreme Court will one day declare death penalty laws unconstitutional. Executions are cruel and they have become unusual. Though Justice Antonin Scalia sees the text of the US Constitution as a barrier to such a ruling, a constitutional amendment is not necessary for the Court to rule that death sentences and executions are unconstitutional. The Constitution did not establish a permanent penal code, and it nowhere states that the death penalty is deemed constitutional, let alone for all time. The Cruel and Unusual Punishments Clause certainly nowhere exempts the death penalty from its scope. Indeed, when the First Congress debated the US Bill of Rights, one legislator, Samuel Livermore, specifically contemplated that American judges might one day read the Cruel and Unusual Punishments Clause to bar punishments that were then thought to be acceptable. As Livermore, a New Hampshire lawmaker, worried aloud: 'The clause seems to express a great deal of humanity, on which account I have no objection to it; but as it seems to have no meaning in it, I do not think it necessary. What is meant by the terms excessive bail? Who are to be the judges? What is understood by excessive fines? It lies with the court to determine'. Futilely arguing that 'we ought not to be restrained from making necessary laws by any declaration of this kind', Livermore unsuccessfully opposed the inclusion of the Eighth Amendment's language as follows: 'No cruel and unusual punishment is to be inflicted; it is sometimes necessary to hang a man, villains often deserve whipping, and perhaps having their ears cut off; but are we in the future to be prevented from inflicting these punishments because they are cruel?' (Bessler 2012a). In other words, in the twenty-first century, the text of the US Constitution does not pose any barriers to a judicial declaration that the death penalty is unconstitutional. On the contrary, just as American judges no longer tolerate the cutting off of an offender's ear or limb, the judiciary should no longer allow the state to take an offender's life.

References

Abramson, J.B. 2001. *We, the Jury: The Jury System and the Ideal of Democracy*. Cambridge: Harvard University Press.

Amnesty International ('Amnesty') 2012. *Death Sentences and Executions 2011*. London: Amnesty International Publications.

Banner, S. 2002. *The Death Penalty: An American History*. Cambridge, MA: Harvard University Press.

Barabak, M. 2013. L.A. as Death Penalty Capital Belies California's Political Image. *Los Angeles Times*, 4 October.

Beales, D. 2005. *Enlightenment and Reform in Eighteenth-Century Europe*. New York: I.B. Tauris & Co.

Bessler, J.D. 1997. *Death in the Dark: Midnight Executions in America*. Boston: Northeastern University Press.

Bessler, J.D. 2009. Revisiting Beccaria's Vision: The Enlightenment, America's Death Penalty, and the Abolition Movement. *Northwestern Journal of Law and Social Policy* 4(2), 195–328.

Bessler, J.D. 2012a. *Cruel and Unusual, The American Death Penalty and the Founders' Eighth Amendment*. Boston: Northeastern University Press.

Bessler, J.D. 2012b. Tinkering Around the Edges: The Supreme Court's Death Penalty Jurisprudence. *American Criminal Law Review* 49(4), 1913–43.

Bessler, J.D. 2013. The Anomaly of Executions: The Cruel and Unusual Punishments Clause in the 21st Century. *British Journal of American Legal Studies* 2(2), 297–451.

Bosworth, M. 2002. *The U.S. Federal Prison System*. Thousand Oaks, CA: Sage Publications.

Brundage, W.F. 1997. *Under Sentence of Death: Lynching in the South*. Chapel Hill, NC: University of North Carolina Press.

Bunbury, H. 1874. *The Lee Papers, 1782–1811*. New York: New York Historical Society.

Caso, A. 1995. *We, the People: Formative Documents of America's Democracy*. Boston, MA: Branden Publishing Co.

Davis, A.J. 2007. *Arbitrary Justice: The Power of the American Prosecutor*. Oxford: Oxford University Press.

Death Penalty Information Center ('DPIC') 2007. *A Crisis of Confidence: Americans' Doubts About the Death Penalty*, 9 June.

Death Penalty Information Center ('DPIC') 2011. *Struck by Lightning: The Continuing Arbitrariness of the Death Penalty Thirty-Five Years After Its Reinstatement in 1976*, 22 June.

Death Penalty Information Center ('DPIC') 2013. *Facts about the Death Penalty*, 20 November.

Erastus-Obilo, B. 2009. *Reason Curve, Jury Competence and the English Criminal Justice System: The Case for a 21st Century Approach*. Boca Raton, FL: Universal Publishers.

Evans, K.M. 2010. *Capital Punishment: Cruel and Unusual*? Farmington Hills, MI: Gale.

Garland, D. 2010. *Peculiar Institution: America's Death Penalty in an Age of Abolition*. Cambridge: Belknap Press of Harvard University Press.

Gatrell, V.A.C. 1994. *The Hanging Tree: Execution and the English People 1770–1868*. Oxford: Oxford University Press.

Gilmore, M. 1994. *Shot in the Heart*. New York: Anchor Books.

Goldstein, S. 2013. Dallas DA Craig Watkins to Push for Law Allowing Appeals Based on Racial Factors. *Dallas Morning News*, 21 January.

Gottlieb, G. 2006. Theater of Death: Capital Punishment in Early America, 1750–1800. PhD thesis, University of Pittsburgh.

Gross, S.R. 2012. David Baldus and the Legacy of McCleskey v. Kemp. *Iowa Law Review* 97(6), 1905–24.

Hall, H.V. 2008. *Forensic Psychology and Neuropsychology for Criminal and Civil Cases*. Boca Raton, FL: CRC Press.

Hodgkinson, P. and Schabas, W.A. 2004. *Capital Punishment: Strategies for Abolition*. Cambridge: Cambridge University Press.

Hood, R. and Hoyle, C. 2008. *The Death Penalty: A Worldwide Perspective*. 4th ed. Oxford: Oxford University Press.

Jones, M. and Johnstone, P. 2012. *History of Criminal Justice*. 5th ed. Waltham, MA: Anderson Publishing.

Keve, P.W. 1995. *Prisons and the American Conscience: A History of U.S. Federal Corrections*. Carbondale, IL: Southern Illinois University Press.

Koch, L.W., Wark, C. and Galliher, J.F. 2012. *The Death of the American Death Penalty: States Still Leading the Way*. Boston: Northeastern University Press.

Kronenwetter, M. 2001. *Capital Punishment: A Reference Handbook*. 2nd ed. Santa Barbara, CA: ABC-CLIO.

Lewis, O.F. 1922. *The Development of American Prisons and Prison Customs*. Albany, NY: J.B. Lyon Co.

Lewis, W.D. 1965. *From Newgate to Dannemora: The Rise of the Penitentiary in New York, 1796–1848*. Ithaca, NY: Cornell University Press.

Liebman, J.S., Fagan, J. and West, V. 2000. *A Broken System: Error Rates in Capital Cases, 1973–95*.

Lytle, L. 2008. *Execution's Doorstep: True Stories of the Innocent and Near Damned*. Boston: Northeastern University Press.

McLynn, F. 1989. *Crime and Punishment in Eighteenth-Century England*. New York: Routledge.

Mello, M. 1996. *Against the Death Penalty: The Relentless Dissents of Justices Brennan and Marshall*. Boston: Northeastern University Press.

Miller, W.R. 2012. *The Social History of Crime and Punishment in America: An Encyclopedia*. Thousand Oaks, CA: Sage Publications.

Mintz, H. 2012. Defeat of Proposition 34: California's Death Penalty Battle Will Continue. *Mercury News*, 7 November.

Morris, N. 1995. *The Oxford History of the Prison: The Practice of Punishment in Western Society*. Oxford: Oxford University Press.

Mowbray, A. 2012. *Cases, Materials, and Commentary on the European Convention on Human Rights*. 3rd ed. Oxford: Oxford University Press.

National Research Council of the National Academies ('NRCNA') 2012. Deterrence and the Death Penalty, 18 April.

Oette, L. 2011. *Criminal Law Reform and Transitional Justice: Human Rights Perspectives for Sudan*. Surrey, England: Ashgate Publishing.

Ogletree, C.J. and Sarat, A. 2012. *Life Without Parole: America's New Death Penalty?* New York: New York University Press.

Pace, A. 1983. *Luigi Castiglioni's Viaggio: Travels in the United States of North America, 1785–87*. Syracuse, NY: Syracuse University Press.

Palmer, L.J. 1998. *The Death Penalty: An American Citizen's Guide to Understanding Federal and State Laws*. Jefferson, NC: McFarland & Co.

Protocol No. 6 to the Convention for the Protection of Human Rights and Fundamental Freedoms concerning the abolition of the death penalty (1983).

Protocol No. 13 to the Convention for the Protection of Human Rights and Fundamental Freedoms, concerning the abolition of the death penalty in all circumstances (2002).

Schabas, W.A. 2002. *The Abolition of the Death Penalty in International Law*. 3rd ed. Cambridge: Cambridge University Press.

Sentencing Project 2013. *Life Goes On: The Historic Rise in Life Sentences in America.*

Smith, R.J. 2012. The Geography of the Death Penalty and Its Ramifications. *Boston University Law Review* 92(1), 227–89.

Stratford, M. 2013. Ark. Governor Reverses Course on Death Penalty. *San Francisco Chronicle*, 16 January.

Texas Coalition to Abolish the Death Penalty ('TCADP') 2012. Texas Death Penalty Developments in 2012: The Year in Review.

Tischauser, L.V. 2012. *Jim Crow Laws*. Santa Barbara, CA: Greenwood.

Tonry, M. and Frase, R.S. 2001. *Sentencing and Sanctions in Western Countries*. Oxford: Oxford University Press.

Udoma, E. 2012. Connecticut Abolishes Death Penalty. *Chicago Tribune*, 25 April.

Wagner, J. 2012. National NAACP Leader to Join Md. Death Penalty Opponents. *Washington Post*, 9 January.

Chapter 5
Clear and Ever-Present Dangers? Redefining 'Closure' in a Post 9–11 World

Jody Lyneé Madeira

Introduction: Reconceptualizing Closure

In mass media and popular culture, closure can denote 'a sense of absolute finality', or 'getting over it' – meanings that family members and survivors almost universally despise and denigrate (Madeira 2012: 41). But in their lived experience, some use closure to refer to 'coping with, comprehending, or contextualizing' a murderous incident (Madeira 2012: 41). I have argued elsewhere that closure embraces a host of other coping behaviours, that it is affected by both internal processes (thinking about and narrating a toxic event) and external developments (arrests, trials, executions), that it is a juggling act where victims must tend to numerous priorities of daily life in addition to memorializing and seeking justice for loved ones, and that it is communicative, blending the intrapersonal and interpersonal (Madeira 2012: 48–9). I define closure as memory work – the process of working through and narrating experiences such as the Oklahoma City bombing and 11 September 2001 attacks ('9–11') (Madeira 2012: 49). In America, closure is popularly associated with the death penalty, and prosecutors have asked juries to award death sentences to give closure to victims' families. Yet a death sentence is the most difficult criminal penalty to enforce; less than 1 per cent of all homicides result in a death sentence and execution (Death Penalty Information Center 2012).

As a social process, closure is contingent and perpetually in flux. Across time, space, and culture, individual and collective memories of a toxic or 'culturally traumatic' event morph into different, perhaps unrecognizable forms. We can therefore anticipate closure processes will be very different in the Oklahoma City bombing than in 9–11. But one of the lessons from Oklahoma City is that the perpetrator's identity can also influence closure processes and affect perceived needs. I have documented how several family members and survivors felt trapped in an involuntary relationship with McVeigh during the years between his arrest and execution, largely because of his defiance and high media visibility (Madeira 2012: 19–37). Although both McVeigh and Osama bin Laden could be termed 'terrorists', they were different from one another in just about every possible way, including ethnicity, nationality, collaboration and motivation, just to name a few. It is difficult – but not impossible – to compare Oklahoma City to 9–11, and McVeigh to bin Laden, and doing so yields many provocative parallels.

This chapter explicates how closure from perpetrators' deaths was constructed in the contexts of the Oklahoma City bombing and 9–11 terrorist attacks. Part I describes the Oklahoma City bombing and discusses core closure themes present in family members' and survivors' desire to witness McVeigh's execution, based upon interviews with 33 individuals. Part II relates the events of 11 September 2001, and explores three key patterns in closure rhetoric within media coverage of bin Laden's death in a US special forces raid, and the ensuing debate over whether to release death images.[1] Part III compares and contrasts these closure trends, focusing on three developments: the expansion of 'justice stakeholder' status beyond family members and survivors, the government's commitment to fulfilling closure needs, and how execution method impacts these perceived needs. The chapter concludes by exploring how capital punishment and mass media together can create and intensify closure needs by prolonging victims' involvement with criminal justice processes and perpetrators, and why non-death sentences such as life without parole can more effectively and efficiently fulfil closure needs.

The Oklahoma City Bombing

The damage caused by the Oklahoma City bombing was profound. A total of 842 persons were injured or killed, 168 people were killed (included 19 children), 462 were left homeless and 312 buildings and businesses were damaged (Sitterle and Gurwitch 1999). In subsequent trials, Timothy McVeigh and Terry Nichols were indicted and each was charged with eight counts of first-degree murder for the deaths of federal officials and three other counts, and a third conspirator, Michael Fortier, received a ten-year prison sentence. While McVeigh was convicted in June 1997 on all counts and sentenced to death, the jury in Nichols' federal trial found him guilty of involuntary manslaughter and conspiracy, and failed to reach a unanimous verdict on whether Nichols planned the bombing 'with the intent to kill'. After being sentenced to life in prison without the possibility of parole, Nichols was tried and convicted in 2004 of 162 counts of first-degree murder in the Oklahoma state court, but again escaped the death penalty.

The legal aftermath of the Oklahoma City Bombing culminated in McVeigh's execution. On 12 June 2001, 232 witnesses – ten in the death house at the state penitentiary in Terre Haute, Indiana and 222 at a remote viewing location in Oklahoma City – gathered for McVeigh's last moments. Whereas 'live' witnesses viewed a side profile of McVeigh, 'remote' witnesses observed the closed circuit feed from a camera positioned on the ceiling of the death chamber directly over McVeigh's face.

1 My conclusions here are based upon a content analysis of newspaper and magazine articles; I am currently conducting interviews with family members, survivors, and rescue workers.

McVeigh's Visibility

From the beginning, Timothy McVeigh was a very different type of offender. Shock greeted his arrest; few expected to see a white, 27-year-old decorated American veteran charged with the crime. It did not take long for family members and survivors (hereinafter 'participants') to form impressions of him; most concluded that McVeigh was defiant and remorseless after watching media footage of him being led out of the Noble County courthouse in Perry, Oklahoma. Survivors' and victims' families' lived experiences of McVeigh's execution were heavily influenced by his media visibility. A very outspoken defendant, McVeigh granted numerous media interviews from the time of his arrest to his execution. In 1995 he was the subject of cover stories in *Newsweek* and *Time* and was a runner-up for *Time*'s Man of the Year; in 2000 he was interviewed by *60 Minutes* reporter Ed Bradley, and his authorized biography was released in April 2001. Participants frequently perceived McVeigh was trying to manipulate them through news media, to the point that he became an unwelcome presence in their lives (Madeira 2012: 19–37). McVeigh was so visible that Attorney General John Ashcroft asked the media to exhibit 'self-restraint' prior to his execution to prevent him from inject[ing] more poison into our culture', begging them 'not [to] become Timothy McVeigh's co-conspirators in his assault on America's public safety and upon America itself' (DOJ Press Release 2001).

McVeigh's refusal to remain quiet and therefore invisible behind prison walls was also a constant irritation to many victims' families and survivors. Participants connected McVeigh's continued media presence with a desire to silence him: 'if he wouldn't have been writing people and calling people and giving interviews and making pronouncements and so on, you know, it'd be a lot easier to live with him, being in prison for the rest of his life' (Participant 19). Participants resented the media for their seemingly endless coverage of McVeigh: 'I just wanted the media to quit talking about it [the execution] … I just wanted … as much return to normalcy as I could have' (Participant 3). They were particularly angered when McVeigh termed the deaths of 19 children in the America's Kids daycare facility 'collateral damage'. One participant even remarked that McVeigh needed to be silenced through execution, in contrast to Nichols, whose quiet prison presence meant that he could 'live with' his continued existence:

> McVeigh, even though he knew that he was getting the death sentence, he was defiant all the way up to the point where it actually happened, okay? He would speak out to the media … And everything that he did was doing nothing but hurting the family members here in Oklahoma. So the only way for us to have any kind of peace was to execute this man. (Participant 25)

Thus, for the federal government and for family member and survivor witnesses, McVeigh's execution was not only about the display of disciplinary power but about silencing him.

In one last bid for publicity, McVeigh himself requested the execution be nationally televised, but this request was denied; an internet company too was refused broadcast permission (Entertainment Network, Inc. v. Lappin 2001). Though hundreds wished to witness, only eight were permitted within the Terre Haute, Indiana, death house. Numerous survivors and family members sought to persuade Attorney General Ashcroft to arrange for a closed circuit execution broadcast to Oklahoma City. On 10 April 2001, Ashcroft visited Oklahoma City and met with 100 individuals who explained why they wanted to witness McVeigh's death, and assented two days later, citing closure needs. Stating that the 'Oklahoma City survivors may be the largest group of crime victims in our history', Ashcraft believed they warranted 'special provisions … in accordance with our responsibilities to carry out justice' (DOJ Press Release 2001).

The two months before McVeigh's execution were marked by a flurry of public commentary on whether executions should be publicly broadcast. Much of the debate centred around transparency, scrutinizing the death penalty to better ascertain its moral status: 'every aspect of capital punishment, including the ultimate act, should be subject to as much public scrutiny as possible' (Mauro 2001). A few journalists raised deterrence arguments (Mauro 2001). Others argued that the American public was also victimized; law professor Robert Blecker stressed that the attack targeted the Murrah Building and America as much as the 168 victims, and noted that 'the people' are 'always the victim … [when] the prosecution is commenced in their names' (NewsHour 2001). Victim representative Bonnie Bucqeuroux, however, warned that broadcasting the execution would normalize violence, suggest that all victims were 'monolithically in support' of the execution, and mask political manipulation of victims (NewsHour 2001). Other journalists objected to an execution broadcast either because they judged it in bad taste (Shister 2001) or because McVeigh himself advocated for the broadcast (Phillips 2001).

Constructing Closure after Oklahoma City

Family members' and survivors' descriptions of closure in the context of McVeigh's terroristic attack on the Murrah Federal Building can be described in terms of three themes: the sense of being compelled to witness, a perception of communicative action, and a sense of completion. These concerns were very different than others revealed in the debate over whether or not McVeigh's execution should be publicly televised, which revolved around the relative merits of transparency versus good taste.

A Compulsion to Witness

Many family members and survivors spoke of a compulsion to witness McVeigh's execution because of a need to 'see justice done'; McVeigh's execution was the last legal proceeding, and several had advocated for the closed-circuit broadcast. These individuals felt a strong personal need to see McVeigh's final moments: 'I had watched that man and I needed to complete the process. I needed to see it through' (Participant 22). It was almost as if some felt little choice but to witness: 'I have to do this. That's the least I can do is follow it through. I fought a long, long battle to not face, to not see it to the end' (Participant 28).

Communicative Action

In addition, family members and survivors described McVeigh's execution as a communicative interaction – a specific episode in which someone makes meaning by drawing on enculturated systems of communicative practices, and strategically choosing spoken, written, or gestural behaviours. McVeigh's execution was structured both through his gazing behaviour and his silence. Family members and survivors perceived that McVeigh knew that others were watching and was in turn trying to stare back at them, communicating defiance: '[he] glared into the room, you know, trying to figure out who was who, who was in there and where we were standing at' (Participant 25). Witnesses, in turn, wished that McVeigh had been able to see their reactions, either so that he could know their pain or that 'we were going to survive this thing and we would be better afterwards' (Participant 25). Two live witnesses in fact held small photographs of their loved ones up against the glass during the execution, invoking a dual sense of witness by both victim and family member. Many witnesses believed that it was appropriate to communicate social censure though pain, and were disappointed when McVeigh appeared to die peacefully and quickly, in contrast to the years of suffering he had inflicted on his victims.

Completion

Finally, closure from McVeigh's execution marked completion of legal proceedings, of his death sentence, and consequently of his life. Family members and survivors experienced completion from the execution because it silenced McVeigh and enabled a transition to a different, and perhaps transformative, state of peace and respite from both McVeigh and media sources: 'when those people are executed and you know they're *gone*, there, there is a change for the people that were victims of that crime. It's gotta be better. It was for me' (Participant 1). Importantly, this was not a closure in terms of finality; as one individual remarked, '[a] reporter ... who asked me about closure and why we kept opening up our wounds and my answer to that was I never closed and I never will' (Participant 24). Instead, it was most often experienced as a marked relief: 'Peace. I mean I felt a real peace. Within myself. And again because I'm not carrying him in my head' (Participant 29). Several felt free, as they had not since before the bombing: 'all the media packed up, like you know what, we are free, they will not ever come back in this manner again ever, you know, you will not ever get any more pronouncements from McVeigh on anything' (Participant 19).

Transparency

Prior to McVeigh's execution, legal experts and journalists weighed in on the respective merits of traditional First Amendment transparency concerns – the idea that the American public deserved to see what is done in their names and with their tax dollars – with the (im)morality of showing McVeigh's final moments. Deterrence as a justification for public broadcast was mentioned, but far less often. Broadcast proponents linked the American public's closure interest to McVeigh's intent to attack America and stressed that the government had prosecuted McVeigh and would execute him under public authority. Opponents stressed that the execution would be too graphic, too banal, or too likely to trivialize human life (Campbell 2001, Holston 2001, Kellerman 2001, Porter 2001). Thus, the debate largely opposed public 'rights' – the right to know what is done in the name of 'the people' – to the morality of rendering execution visible, and thus to the fundamental morality of capital punishment.

The 11 September 2001 Attacks

Just months after McVeigh's execution, on 11 September 2001, terrorists hijacked four planes and crashed them into the World Trade Center towers, the Pentagon, and a farm field near Shanksville, Pennsylvania. The attacks killed 2,996 people and spawned a global 'war on terror' fought in Iraq and Afghanistan. Al Qaeda claimed responsibility for the 9–11 attacks; US forces pursued its leader, Osama bin Laden, for nine years and ultimately killed him in a raid on his Abbottabad, Pakistan compound on 2 May 2011. Following his death, bin Laden's body was removed by soldiers and transferred to the USS Carl Vinson, where it was cleaned, photographed, and shrouded. Following a short ceremony, bin Laden's remains were 'buried at sea' somewhere in the North Arabian Sea. His death was witnessed only by special forces soldiers and key Obama administration personnel in real time; the administration debated whether to release photos but decided against it, though members of Congressional intelligence committees were permitted to view certain images.

As previously described, McVeigh perceived himself as a soldier on a mission, and envisioned his bombing as an act of war against the government (Madeira 2012: 184–200). He was held accountable through criminal justice processes – arrested by civilian police, incarcerated in civilian prisons, tried by an Article III court rather than a military tribunal, and executed in a federal civilian prison according to Department of Justice protocols. Media references to closure from the execution were addressed towards family members and survivors. In contrast, major American mass media sources described bin Laden's death in both criminal justice and militaristic terms. Family members and survivors were not at the centre of closure discourse. While President Obama and other officials justified bin Laden's killing by referencing family members' need for closure, the debate over publicizing photos of his corpse focused instead upon the needs of the American public, and the likelihood that others could misuse these images. A content analysis of news articles reveals the true extent of these mixed signals, and the underlying uncertainty over how to regard 9–11 – as a crime, an act of war, both, or neither.

The Discourse Surrounding bin Laden's Demise

Six days after 9–11, President George W. Bush invoked images of tough frontier justice when he stated bin Laden was 'wanted dead or alive' (Zernike and Kaufman 2011). Various parties spoke of wanting 'justice' (Zernike and Kaufman 2011, Carey 2011, Grier 2011, Sherry 2011b) and of conducting a 'manhunt' for bin Laden (Zernike and Kaufman 2011) or 'tracking him down to send the message that crimes would not go unanswered' (Page and Kiely 2011). Bin Laden was deemed a 'mass murderer of Muslims' and 'Public Enemy No. 1' who should receive 'just deserts punishment' out of 'revenge' (Carey 2011). After his death, President Obama remarked that the nation had been united in 'bring[ing] those who committed this vicious attack to justice' (Obama 2011) and that 'justice had been done' (Baker and Mazzetti 2011).

Most references to bin Laden's death used militaristic language. Sources said bin Laden had begun a 'holy war' and 'declared war on Americans' (Zernike and Kaufman 2011), and described the American response as a 'war on terrorism' and a 'campaign against al Qaeda (Baker and Mazzetti 2011, Page and Kiely 2011). The media highlighted the late bin Laden's own martial qualities; he was deemed a 'dictator' (Zernike and Kaufman 2011) and the 'most wanted mujaheddin on Earth' (Wax 2011) who had 'cultivated a warrior image' and 'built a reputation on combat experience in Afghanistan in the 1980s' (Zernike and Kaufman 2011). These terms could be depersonalizing; bin Laden was deemed a 'high-value target' (Baker and Mazzetti 2011) or a 'US target' (LaFranchi 2011a). The highly dramatic circumstances in which bin Laden died were variously described as a 'targeted operation' (Baker and Mazzetti 2011), a 'military action' (Editorial Should the US Release 2011a), a 'mission' (Shear 2011, Sherry 2011a), a 'strike' (Baker and Mazzetti 2011) and a 'US operation' or 'US military operation' (Editorial Make Public 2011c, Grier 2011, Miller 2011, Casteel 2011). These arrangements had only been possible after extensive cooperation between the military and the 'intelligence community' (Shiffman 2011). His death or 'elimination' (Grier 2011) took place at the hands of special forces, variously referred to as a 'helicopter-borne raiding squad' (Burns and Woodward 2011), US or American 'commandos'

(Farhi 2011a, Editorial No Good Reason 2011b, Anonymous 2011), 'Navy Seals' (Farhi 2011b), and 'US forces' or 'US Special Forces [who] rappelled into a sleeping Pakistani compound' (Sonmez 2011, Grier 2011). Some articles referred to his death as an 'assassination' (Memoli and Nicholas 2011, Littwin 2011).

Some language could be interpreted as invoking either criminal justice or militaristic themes. Bin Laden was characterized as 'evil' (Zernike and Kaufman 2011, Page and Kiely 2011) and deemed a 'wanted man' (Farhi 2011a), the 'mastermind of the most devastating attack on American soil in modern times and the most hunted man in the world' (Baker and Mazzetti 2011). The United States had conducted a 'raid' (Stanley 2011, Memoli and Nicholas 2011, Shiffman 2011) or a 'daring, high-stakes raid that worked' (Stanley 2011), an 'attack' or an 'assault' (Grier 2011), Special forces soldiers could be described as an 'assault force' (Miller 2011). Bin Laden had been 'gunned down at his hideout' (Whitlock and Wan 2011), 'killed in a firefight' (Zernike and Kaufman 2011, Baker and Mazzetti 2011, Whitlock and Wan 2011, Editorial Make Public 2011c), 'killed during a raid' (Shear 2011), 'killed in an exchange of gunfire' (Farhi 2011b), or 'killed in a pre-dawn raid' (Miller 2011). Hunting terminology was also rife; bin Laden's death was a 'kill' (Stanley 2011) and President Obama refused to release photographs of his body on the grounds that 'we don't trot this stuff out as trophies' (Shear 2011, Memoli and Nicholas 2011, Editorial Make Public 2011c).

Following bin Laden's death, there were also debates over authority, its absence or abuse – particularly with respect to bin Laden's dubious status as the leader of al Qaeda, and the authority of the United States to penetrate into Pakistan to carry out the operation. News articles noted that American officials deemed bin Laden 'more symbolically important than operationally significant', but acknowledged he 'remained the most potent face of terrorism around the world' (Baker and Mazzetti 2011, Grier 2011). One article termed bin Laden American's 'bearded bogeyman' (Grier 2011). His death was described as 'a symbolic stroke affirming the relentlessness' of American justice (Baker and Mazzetti 2011). Evidence recovered in bin Laden's compound following the raid, however, illustrated that 'bin Laden remained highly active in directing' al Qaeda (Miller 2011). Bin Laden had reportedly dyed his beard black before his death, perhaps indicating that 'he was preparing to film another video' (Bender 2011).

Justifying the Secrecy of bin Laden's Death Images

Interestingly, both officials and mass media made it clear that the two populations most relevant to the decision whether to release the images were the American public (see, e.g., Starr 2011) and individuals who might misuse the photos. Transparency was a paramount concern; officials wanted to 'make sure that not only the American people but the world understand exactly what happened' (Burns and Woodward 2011). President Obama initially considered releasing the photos but decided against it; apparently, however, it had been a close enough call to prompt CIA Director Leon Panetta to predict release (LaFranchi 2011b). The administration later agreed to allow members of the Senate and House Intelligence and Armed Services committees to view some images at CIA headquarters, ostensibly lending 'more credibility' to government accounts (Sherry 2011a). After viewing them, some legislators remarked that the photos could provide a lesson to the 'bad people who want to kill Americans' (Sherry 2011b) and a 'deterrent to other potential terrorists' (Shiffman 2011).

Not releasing the photos would purportedly 'prevent revulsion in the Muslim world' (Marquand 2011), retain 'the moral high ground' (LaFranchi 2011a), prevent 'too gruesome' images from being published (Editorial Should the US Release 2011a), keep bin Laden from becoming a martyr (Editorial Should the US Release 2011a), 'avoid offending Muslim sensibilities over the manner of bin Laden's burial' (Whitlock and Wan 2011), and 'avoid enflaming Muslim emotions' (LaFranchi 2011b). Numerous media sources mentioned that this decision came at a sensitive time for the Obama administration, which had weathered other credibility crises. President Obama decided against release the week after he released his official birth certificate to quell a longstanding 'birther' controversy over whether he had been born a US citizen (LaFranchi 2011a, Wax 2011, Shear 2011, Editorial No Good Reason 2011b, Editorial Make Public 2011c, Littwin 2011). Officials also noted that America had previously been criticized for releasing other images, including 'photos of Saddam Hussein in his underwear when he was apprehended by US soldiers' (LaFranchi 2011a) and 'graphic photos of the corpses of Saddam Hussein's two powerful sons to prove that US forces had killed them' (Burns and Woodward 2011, Wax 2011, Hall 2011). Newspapers had also carried photos of Hussein's body after his impromptu execution in Iraq, and of Iraqi terrorist Abu Musab al-Zarqawi after he was killed in an airstrike (Farhi 2011a).

Invocations of Closure Following bin Laden's Death

Mass media articles on reactions to bin Laden's death accorded many groups besides family members and survivors status as 'justice stakeholders'. Those quoted in news articles ranged from families of military personnel killed overseas in Iraq or Afghanistan (Fairbanks 2011) to victims' family members from the United States or Canada (Karoliszyn and Schapiro 2011, Weichselbaum and Hutchinson 2011, Belluz 2011) to tourists and workers rebuilding the Freedom Tower/1 World Trade Center 1 (Karoliszyn and Schapiro 2011) and residents of New York's 'Muslim enclaves' (Karoliszyn and Schapiro 2011).

Bin Laden's death and the release of death images were both frequently linked to closure and justice. Former President George W. Bush stated that bin Laden's death 'marks a victory ... for all those who lost loved ones on September 11, 2001', and President Obama remarked on the evening of the raid that 'we can say to those families who have lost loved ones to Al Qaeda's terror, justice has been done' (Baker and Mazzetti 2011). One article termed bin Laden's death an 'emotional[ly] important sense of closure for many' – including victims' families, a ballpark crowd chanting 'USA!' and a crowd gathered outside the White House (Page and Kiely 2011). Another article reported that 'interested parties ranging from members of Congress to family members of 9/11 victims' had requested that death photos be released 'to allow for a sense of closure' (LaFranchi 2011a). An expert interviewed in one article stated that bin Laden's burial at sea enabled 'no resting place, no closure' (Whitlock and Wan 2011), and a pundit in another referred to the death as 'allow[ing] many Americans some degree of closure' (Grier 2011). Finally, a legislator who viewed the death images at CIA headquarters remarked that the experience 'gave him a sense of "finality and closure" to the ordeal' (Sherry 2011b).

Several media sources remarked on how bin Laden's death also provided 'closure' for an entirely new group – the generation that had been children when 9–11 occurred, who had grown up with the war against terrorism (Popiolkowski 2011). Accounts described how 'mostly young people celebrated in the streets of New York and Washington', and how this 'historic moment' marked time coming 'full circle for our generation' (Baker and Mazzetti 2011, Carey 2011). Here, bin Laden's death represented 'the end of a tragic chapter in American history and a continuation of the healing process' (Popiolkowski 2011). His visibility apparently sparked this celebratory atmosphere: '[t]he sight of bin Laden's face on television or a smartphone news feed might have been enough to move people from the sidelines into the streets, to cheer for the home team' (Carey 2011).

For their part, victims' family members emphasized that bin Laden's death could 'mean a lot' (Page and Kiely 2011) or 'bring a measure of comfort' that his activities would cease, but that it would never 'ease our pain, or bring back our loved ones' (Baker and Mazzetti 2011). Some acknowledged 'it doesn't change our lives that much' (Simon and Farrell 2011). Soldiers' family members felt 'only relief and joy' and saw the death as 'confirmation that their sons and daughters, husbands and wives died for a reason' (Fairbanks 2011). Articles recounted a wide variety of positive emotions; a rescue worker's father felt there had been 'victory for all the souls of 9–11' (Karoliszyn and Schapiro 2011), a 9–11 victim's headstone bore a note stating 'Justice! Bin Laden is dead' taped to it, and a family member characterized it as 'a good feeling … good finally triumphing over evil' (Simon and Farrell 2011). But not all reactions were uniformly positive; others found 'no sense of justice' or remarked that bin Laden's death 'does little to ease the pain' (Belluz 2011). Significantly, survivors and their reactions were markedly absent in the aftermath of bin Laden's death – a vast contrast to media coverage of the Oklahoma City bombing.

Constructing Closure after 9–11

Whereas McVeigh's death was primarily framed through criminal justice themes, bin Laden's death was discursively constructed primarily as an act of war.

Similarly, while bin Laden's killing was justified by reference to victims' family members, 'justice stakeholders' – those with a recognized interest in *seeing* his demise – included not only family members but legislators; military, intelligence, and national security officials; and the American public. Though a completion theme pervaded narratives of both McVeigh's execution and bin Laden's killing, other trends were very different. In contrast to the themes of compulsion and communication within Oklahoma City family members' and survivors' reactions to McVeigh's execution, the reactions to bin Laden's death yielded themes of confirmation and credibility.

Completion

As in Oklahoma City, completion was a major theme in reactions to bin Laden's death. The sense of completion was made more intense by the vast time period – nearly a decade – between 9–11 and his killing. News articles observed that these years had been punctuated by bin Laden videotapes and audiotapes (Page and Kiely 2011) that reflected bin Laden's lengthy tenure as al Qaeda's actual or symbolic leader (Baker and Mazzetti 2011). Officials eagerly seized this occasion as evidence of progress and finality in the war against terrorism; after viewing images of bin Laden's corpse, Representative Bob Brady remarked '[w]e killed him … he's dead. It's over' (Bender 2011). Significantly, bin Laden's end came incredibly fast; it was 'compacted … done and over, just like that', whereas other 9–11 proceedings, like the Guantanamo military tribunals, have been so protracted that their completion seems illusory (Carey 2011). These characterizations of bin Laden's death, however, are also problematic and overly simplistic. They obscure the fact that bin Laden's death was enabled by years of collaboration among the CIA, National Security Agency, and Department of Defense (Grier 2011). Moreover, the sense of completion may be a false hope; news articles questioned the extent of 'completion' even as they invoked it, reminding readers that bin Laden's death had not ended the war on terrorism (Marquand 2011).

Confirmation and Credibility

Intertwined themes of confirmation and credibility run throughout media coverage of bin Laden's killing and the ensuing debate over the release of his death images. Mere hours after bin Laden's death was announced, scepticism inserted itself into the celebratory public discourse (Wax 2011). The Obama administration was scarcely a stranger to suspicion. Calls for the photos' release were linked to providing closure to the American public – rarely, if ever, were family members or survivors mentioned.

Opponents' objections stressed 'protection' in the dual sense of safeguarding media audiences from gruesome or grisly sights and protecting Americans and

American soldiers against reprisal attacks (Memoli and Nicholas 2011); some legislators, however, observed that the photos could also protect Americans by deterring terrorist activity (Sherry 2011b, Shiffman 2011). Previous instances where American officials had been criticized for releasing controversial images – of Saddam Hussein's sons, of Hussein himself when captured, and of other dead or humiliated terrorists – provided further evidence that releasing bin Laden's death images would be harmful rather than helpful. Against this, proponents cited the need to confirm bin Laden's death, and spoke of a 'crisis of confidence between authorities and citizens' (Marquand 2011), an increasingly cynical public (LaFranchi 2011a), a steep rise in conspiracy theories (Marquand 2011), a need to 'debunk [the] latest myth' (LaFranchi 2011a) and 'to answer public doubts, and to help answer some of the lingering questions' (LaFranchi 2011a). Demands came from sources as varied as the Afghan Taliban (LaFranchi 2011a) and '9–11 truthers' who were sceptical of official accounts of 9–11 (Sherry 2011a).

Ultimately, the Obama administration decided not to release photos for two reasons. First, bin Laden's identity had already been confirmed through facial recognition procedures and DNA identification. Second, officials stressed that sceptics would only have claimed the images were falsified (Whitlock and Wan 2011, LaFranchi 2011b, Memoli and Nicholas 2011). Allowing Senate and House Intelligence and Armed Services committee members to view the bodies further muted the debate, as did al Qaeda's official acknowledgment of bin Laden's death (Sherry 2011a). Reuters news agency released other images of the compound and dead men that it had obtained from a Pakistani security official. Senator Mark Udall of Colorado, who had pressured the White House to allow legislators to view the photos, felt that Americans already had enough evidence: 'Americans trusted the Navy Seals who led the raid and felt comfortable with the already released videos taken from bin Laden's compound showing how the terrorist leader lived' (Sherry 2011a).

Ultimately, the Obama administration was caught between martial and moral credibility. Releasing photos of the raid and of bin Laden's corpse would have demonstrated and perhaps enhanced America's martial credibility, proving its commitment to fighting terrorism and portraying terrorism's consequences (Editorial Make Public 2011c). As Sarah Palin tweeted, 'Show photo as warning to others seeking America's destruction. No pussy-footing around, no politicking, no drama; it's part of the mission' (Shear 2011). But in releasing the photos, the United States might have damaged its moral credibility; as President Obama emphasized, '[t]hat's not who we are' (Shear 2011) and 'we don't need to spike the football' (Memoli and Nicholas 2011). Some went so far as to assert that such actions were more typical of terrorists, who 'show beheadings and assassinations online … to inflict maximum pain and suffering' (Editorial No Good Reason 2011b).

The speed and efficacy of bin Laden's death was, and still is, contrasted to efforts to prosecute Khalid Sheik Mohammed and his four accomplices in Guantanamo, which has undergone credibility-damaging delays. Mohammed was captured in 2003 in Pakistan, interrogated for three years overseas, and sent to Guantanamo for trial in 2006. Proceedings halted in 2009, however, after the President unsuccessfully tried to relocate the trial to Manhattan federal court, which many felt cost precious time. After it was moved back on 7 March 2011, Congressional changes to the Military Commission system forced the prosecution to start over. The trial's end would scarcely be the end; any verdicts would be reviewed automatically by a military appellate court, and then could be appealed through the civilian federal appeals system up to the US Supreme Court (Straw 2012).

Closure and the Perils of Visibility

I suggest that the hermeneutic key to explicating McVeigh's execution and bin Laden's killing is visibility – particularly the visibility of each terrorist's demise. Themes of visibility and invisibility have always been central to theories of discipline and punishment.

These concepts are the cornerstone of the panopticon, a prison structure designed by Jeremy Bentham in 1785 that allowed one prison official to supervise an entire population of prisoners while simultaneously keeping the official invisible and isolating all prisoners from one another. The panopticon consisted of a ring-shaped building with a tower at the centre; in the tower were wide windows into the larger ring beyond. The ring was divided into cells the width of the building, with outside windows providing light (Foucault 1979: 200). The panopticon simultaneously isolated inmates while rendering them perpetually visible; prisoners would experience an 'anxious awareness of being observed' without knowing whether the supervisor was there (Foucault 1979: 202). This design also rendered prisoners invisible to the outside world, and was a 'guarantee of order' as it facilitated disciplinary power (Foucault 1979: 202, 187). For Foucault, visibility is inherent within disciplinary power, which requires the human gaze – of supervisors and others – to achieve its communicative goals. To fulfil his job, the supervisor need not consider inmates' individuality; their bodies are objectified, of interest only because they might rebel or escape.

The objective gaze that observes the inmates has as its antecedent the horrified and curious gazes with which anonymous masses viewed grisly medieval public executions. Most often, crowds attended public executions as a form of entertainment. Power was communicated through pain; executions were public to teach the citizenry certain moral and civic lessons, including the 'truth of the crime', the vindication of the sovereign, and a healthy fear of his justice (Foucault 1979: 35, 47). Condemned bodies were educational objects, bloody communicative mediums upon which penal lessons were inscribed (Foucault 1979: 43). Significantly, these bodies were kept invisible until execution (Foucault 1979: 43).

The advent of 'bloodless' lethal injection changed everything. Contemporary lethal injection executions occur within prison 'death houses' often resembling inverted panopticons; the inmate is restrained upon a gurney in a sterile central chamber encircled by viewing rooms separated from the execution chamber by one-way glass windows. Often, these windows are covered with a curtain that opens after the prisoner is strapped to the gurney and all preparations are complete and closes moments later, after the prisoner is pronounced dead. The lethal injection protocol casts the execution as a humane, quasi-medical procedure in which the prisoner, strapped to a gurney and often shrouded by a linen sheet, receives an intravenous injection of lethal chemicals. Lethal injection's sanitized nature is critical; it is allegedly both more humane and easier to witness. Invisibility and visibility themes are still prevalent in lethal injection. The United States Supreme Court has observed that the paralytic in the lethal cocktail helps to ensure death while preserving decorum and found that the state 'has an interest in preserving the dignity of the procedure, especially where convulsions or seizures could be misperceived as signs of consciousness or distress' (*Baze v. Rees* 2008: 1535). The inmate appears to fall asleep, rendering death itself largely invisible. The state still incarcerates the inmate on death row until execution, where he is made visible only for a very limited time and to a handful of authorized witnesses – prison and governmental officials, media representatives, and family members of the victim(s) and the defendant. Except for the defendant's relatives, most are motivated to witness by his crimes and not by his personal identity, and attend out of duty, civic obligation, public interest, or a need to see how the prisoner will behave in his last moments.

The perpetrator's visibility is closely related to each of the closure themes identified for the Oklahoma City bombing and 9–11 attacks: compulsion to witness, communicative action, completion, transparency, credibility and confirmation. In its most literal sense – the capacity to be seen – visibility plays a significant role in the debates over whether to make McVeigh's execution and bin Laden's death photos available, to whom, and how. Cultural norms govern the propriety of bodies and their visibility in various social contexts – when it is permissible for a body to be visible and to whom, and how. Significantly, visibility in terms of criminal justice or militaristic killing occurs on the state's terms. A body that is made visible has an expanded physical and temporal presence; it can be resurrected through recordings or remembrances, its actions replayed and reconsidered. McVeigh's bodily presence was not just 'in' Terre Haute but extended to Oklahoma City through the closed-circuit broadcast; similarly, bin Laden's corpse does not merely lie beneath the North Arabian sea so long as photographic likenesses exist on dry land.

In both Oklahoma City and 9–11, concerns over visibility were intertwined with noise, in particular McVeigh's and bin Laden's capacity for speech. McVeigh's predilection for media contact motivated Attorney General John Ashcroft to plead with media sources not to increase his visibility in the months leading up to his execution; similarly, bin Laden was deemed the 'face' of al Qaeda and terrorism and often sent videos to al Jazeera (Zernike and Kaufman 2011). His 'obituary' in the New York Times described how he became a 'new national enemy, his face on wanted posters' who 'gloated on videotapes, taunting the United States and Western civilization' (Baker and Mazzetti 2011). One legislator who viewed his death photos observed that his beard was dyed black, opining that 'Maybe it was to get ready to say hello to us … No more, though' (Bender 2011). Conversely, invisibility was correlated with silence – a cessation of media interviews with McVeigh and of videos from bin Laden, together with a sharp reduction in media coverage of both men.

Visibility-as-noise can be harmful for family members and survivors; the remarks of numerous Oklahoma City individuals illustrate that a perpetrator may not lose his potential to wound until he is silenced, and a 'need' for execution may be linked to a perpetrator's expressions as well as his crimes. McVeigh, though in state custody, did not accept visibility on the State's terms and continued to give many media interviews in the period between his trial and execution. As a fugitive, bin Laden had ample opportunities to maintain his visibility through several channels, including continued participation in terrorist activities.

Considering both Oklahoma City and 9–11 – two sequential terrorist attacks that were respectively the most devastating acts of domestic and international terrorism on American soil – yields several compelling parallels that help us to further understand how closure as a concept has changed, and continues to change, in response to these toxic events – and how closure discourse continues to be intertwined with visibility. Here, I will focus on a few: the ever-increasing scope of persons accorded a 'stake' in the justice process, the idea that governmental commitment to closure needs is more discursive than procedural without strong victim advocacy, and the impact of the execution format upon closure needs. Each of these concerns is oriented towards visibility – the visible participation of new groups of people in criminal trials as justice stakeholders, the government's evaluation of the need to render a perpetrator's body visible to justice stakeholders, and the importance that these stakeholders ascribe to viewing the perpetrator's death or dead body.

The Ever-Increasing Scope of Justice Stakeholders

There are two reasons why new groups have been accorded status as 'justice stakeholders' – individuals regarded as intimately connected to a traumatic event and accountability proceedings. One reason stems from crime victims' increasing visibility in American culture and within American criminal proceedings. Since *Payne v. Tennessee* authorized victim impact testimony in state sentencing proceedings, new participative opportunities have been extended to family members, symbolizing a shift in focus from defendants' constitutional rights to victims' therapeutic needs (Bandes 2009). McVeigh's federal trial was in effect a forum for working out the propriety of emotion and emotional testimony in criminal courtrooms (Madeira 2012: 136–9).

The second reason why new groups receive justice stakeholder status comes from the nature of terrorism itself – its potential to hit huge targets with profound loss of life. As devastating as the Oklahoma City bombing was, the events of 11 September 2001 overshadowed it. Not only was 9–11 so much larger in scope and loss of life, but the intended 9–11 targets – New York City and Washington, DC – were nerve centers, at the centre of multiple American and international economic, intellectual, and social cultures. If Oklahoma City was the 'heartland' terrorist target, then New York City and Washington, DC were 'headland' targets. In addition, Americans outside the targeted cities were more impacted by the 9–11 attacks due to extended media coverage, personal connections to targeted cities or to victims, and disrupted personal routines, new travel procedures and threat levels. Moreover, while McVeigh allegedly intended his attack as retaliation for the federal government's actions at Waco and Ruby Ridge and to vindicate American ideals he considered sacred, al Qaeda and bin Laden sought to destroy not only American values but America itself. Finally, the long-term effects of the Oklahoma City bombing were more limited: increased awareness of domestic paramilitary and militia organizations and new preventative measures such as architectural changes to government buildings. The 9–11 attacks, however, spawned a war in two countries and a multinational effort to eradicate an international terrorist network.

The magnitude of 9–11 meant that the 'victim' population included not just family members and survivors but also new groups, some of which were directly connected to 9–11 such as relatives of soldiers killed abroad and others indirectly connected like the 'American public'. Flexibility in defining who has status as a justice stakeholder can be positive, and allows for a more nuanced and appropriate response to a variety of possible terrorism scenarios. But this flexibility comes at a cost. If stakeholder status is expanded too widely – say, to an entire nation's citizenry – then the concept itself becomes meaningless, and is of little or no value to anyone.

Government Commitment to Closure Needs

The closed-circuit broadcast of McVeigh's execution would not have occurred without family members and survivors who advocated for their felt closure needs. A tradition of victim advocacy is part of the legacies of both Oklahoma City and 9–11. After the Oklahoma City bombing, family members and survivors joined groups to build a national memorial and museum, sue providers of the fuel and fertilizer used to make the bomb, reform capital habeas proceedings to ensure quicker executions, and pass laws allowing testifying family members and survivors to view the trial, and mandating closed-circuit trial broadcasts in certain circumstances (Madeira 2012). Thus family members and survivors who wanted to witness McVeigh's execution were not content to merely submit their names for one of eight seats assigned by lottery but confidently challenged these arrangements.

After 9–11, family members and survivors also joined groups, becoming involved in memorial proceedings, efforts to initiate a governmental investigation into the attacks' cause, lawsuits against airlines and security companies responsible, and advocating for closed-circuit trial broadcasts. However, 9–11 survivors do not seem to have been as involved as in Oklahoma City, and were integrated into few 9–11 groups. In addition, neither family members nor survivors made a serious demand for the bin Laden photos' release, nor did any governmental sources take up the cause for them, or solicit their opinions on the matter. While government officials invoked family members as a reason for seeking 'justice' through bin Laden's death, they apparently did not consider or allow for the possibility that this same population would want to see what took place in their names. It was almost as if the precedent of making special provisions to allow family members and survivors to witness McVeigh's execution had never occurred.

It is true that the Department of Justice's determination to expand execution witnessing opportunities and the Obama administration's decision not to release images of bin Laden's corpse are very different situations. There are stronger precedents for execution witnessing; most capital punishment states also allow victims' families to witness. However, setting up a secure location for credentialled individuals to view images of bin Laden does seem to have been impossible, particularly after the government had previously arranged a secure closed-circuit broadcast to a large remote location (although contacting and credentialling thousands rather than hundreds of individuals is a daunting task). These different outcomes – permitting one set of victims to view the perpetrator's death, but not permitting another set to view the perpetrator's corpse – demonstrate that the closure discourses in Oklahoma City and 9–11 shared a similar starting point – helping to justify the perpetrator's death – but had very different end points – seeing or not seeing the body.

There are several possible reasons for these divergent outcomes. It is possible that the government's commitment to closure concerns is more discursive than procedural; no permanent witnessing arrangements were put in place after McVeigh's execution. Another likely explanation is that different governmental agencies were involved – ones not conventionally linked to closure. McVeigh's trial was adjudicated through criminal justice institutions like the Department of Justice and Article III courts, while bin Laden's demise involved the Department of Justice, the Department of Defense, and the Central Intelligence Agency, among others, and was ambiguously constructed, using both criminal justice and militaristic discourses. Finally, it may be that the government's commitment to closure needs is heavily dependent on, or triggered by, victim advocacy; if victims do not voice the need to see the perpetrator's death or body, then they will not be given the opportunity. But no matter the reason(s) behind them, these difference outcomes illustrate closure's responsiveness to an international terrorist incident in a post-9–11 world.

Execution Formats and Closure Needs

Ironically, family members and survivors expended the most effort to witness a perpetrator's lethal injection – the death that was least dramatic, but most highly dramatized. Many Oklahoma City family members and survivors wanted McVeigh to suffer in dying, and were disappointed by lethal injection's efficacy and peace. Nonetheless, most witnesses were satisfied with the execution since it silenced him. Bin Laden's killing was much more dramatic, and produced images deemed grisly and gruesome, yet family members and survivors did not demand to view images of his corpse.

Again, the reasons for this disparity are unclear. Perhaps McVeigh's high media visibility over the four years between his trial and execution prompted a more intense desire to see him silenced, in contrast to bin Laden's infrequent video appearances spread over nearly ten years. It might be that McVeigh's death sentence provided a stronger assurance that he would die in a finite timespan; after all appeals were denied or withdrawn, the execution date would be set and the sentence carried out. In contrast, locating, capturing and killing bin Laden had long been a matter of speculation and 'get tough' rhetoric, with no end in sight. After a certain point, one stopped expecting imminent news of his apprehension or demise. Perchance the absence of a trial and death sentence meant that any family members and survivors hoping to view bin Laden's death had nothing to attach their hopes to; his first accountability proceeding was also his last.

Similarly, the exercise of disciplinary authority – demanding accountability – might be pivotal, in comparison to the mere sight of a perpetrator's body. After death, it is too late for the perpetrator to utter last words, or for family members and survivors to attempt to send a message in turn. Finally, it may be important that bin Laden was not the ultimate or only 'target' as McVeigh was. Only three perpetrators were identified in the Oklahoma City bombing – McVeigh and accomplices Terry Nichols and Michael Fortier – and McVeigh was the one who lit the fuse. In contrast, the 19 hijackers who actually carried out the mission were all dead and beyond reach, and bin Laden, though heavily involved in planning, had been thousands of miles away on the morning of the attacks. Moreover, killing bin Laden did not ensure America's safety. Al Qaeda, like the mythic hydra, has multiple heads; one can heroically chop off the most ferocious only to find that more grow back in its place.

Conclusion: Closure – Always Imperfect, Inherently Incomplete

For Oklahoma City family members and survivors, witnessing McVeigh's execution rendered 'justice' visible, and McVeigh invisible. In 9–11, however, the witnessing opportunity came after bin Laden was dead – after 'justice' had been done, ensuring he would soon fade from sight. Analysing closure in both contexts suggests that ambiguous but attractive terms such as 'justice' do not merely relate to a perpetrator's crime, but also to his personality and behaviour before and after trial and sentencing. Closure is often most complete when a perpetrator is rendered as invisible as possible (a few will always seek contact and answers from the perpetrator). What closure means will continue to change over time, in response to the identities of those who seek it, the characteristics of the traumatic events that create closure needs, and the attributes of the offenders responsible.

In both Oklahoma City and 9–11, closure themes related to silencing perpetrators, reducing their visibility, and seeking completion, were profoundly important. These are very real and important closure needs; however, their intensity is likely aggravated by the possibility of a death penalty, in combination with the mass media's penchant for dramatic stories. Executions make for intriguing subject matter, and especially newsworthy executions such as McVeigh's can create a perfect storm of coverage that sweeps up and subsumes family members and survivors.

Terry Nichols's case provides a sound example of what could have happened if McVeigh had instead been sentenced to life in prison. Following Nichols's federal trial, many family members and survivors – even those favouring the death penalty – did not support a second proceeding because of its great expense and emotional turmoil, especially since Nichols was incarcerated for life. Nichols's second and final life sentence in the Oklahoma state court was profoundly disappointing to many, but they were able to 'let go', accept that proceedings were over, and adjust to the result. As one family member observed, 'that cleared my mind right there and that was the end of it' (Participant 25). Another family member who supported execution recalled, 'I was devastated … it took about a month to recover' (Participant 22). Finally, a survivor explained, 'it was shocking … someone else gets convicted of something lesser than that and gets a death penalty … He is gonna have to meet his maker one day … [I just] walk away and, you know, life goes on' (Participant 21). If completion is the paramount closure need, then life in prison without parole can achieve incapacitation much quicker than death penalty proceedings, with their extended appeals. Existing procedures also inflict additional suffering upon those who oppose execution, who are harmed not only by the perpetrator's unwelcome presence but also the knowledge that he will be killed in their names.

Moreover, efforts to silence perpetrators such as McVeigh can create numerous problems. One cannot expect to silence every convicted offender for all purposes; defendants, particularly those with innocence claims, must be free to exercise their First Amendment rights to publicize problematic aspects of their cases and obtain outside assistance with appeals. Mass media organizations could and should police their own practices, and be very cautious about how they publish information that is sensationalist or intended to wound family members and survivors. One sensitive accommodation would be to select other newsworthy images besides perpetrators' pictures. In addition, defendants like McVeigh are exceptional; most inmates convicted of murder are not responsible for multiple deaths, do not commit politically motivated crimes, do not rely upon the media to engage in posturing, do not seek to abuse media access, and could not command that degree of media attention even if they wanted to. Relatedly, few family members and survivors are victimized by these unique perpetrators, and subject to these same aggravating factors. Uniform policies and regulations must therefore be based on statistically normative cases, not outliers.

As closure and closure needs change, so must research inquiries. Researchers should be striving not only to identify victims' closure needs but also to ascertain how they can be aggravated and eased by social and institutional processes. The death penalty system in the United States yokes crime victims to condemned perpetrators in lengthy and often involuntary relationships. Without the possibility of a death sentence, legal proceedings would not be as protracted, and perpetrators would not be so newsworthy. Ironically, then, the very system that is popularly thought to assuage closure needs is likely the very system that most aggravates them. This analysis of closure following two terrorist attacks incontrovertibly illustrates that closure is inherently imperfect and incomplete. Though some might derive peace or relief from these consequences, a perpetrator's death will not resurrect loved ones or heal damaged bodies and psyches. Closure will forever be an ongoing and aspirational project.

References

Anonymous. 2011. Hit or Miss? US gov't releases behind-the-scenes images as bin Laden killed. *PR Week*, 6 May, 2.

Baker, P., Cooper, H. and Mazzetti, M. 2011. Bin Laden is dead, Obama says. *The New York Times*, 2 May, A1.

Bandes, S. 2009. Victims, 'Closure', and the Sociology of Emotion. *Law and Contemporary Problems*, 72: 1–26.

Baze v. Rees [2008] 128 S.Ct. 1520.

Belluz, J. 2011. Still no justice. *Maclean's*, 16 May, 167.

Bender, W. 2011. Brady sees Osama photo. Verdict: 'It's over.' *The Philadelphia Daily News*, 13 May, 3.

Burns, R. and Woodward, C. Not everyone believes bin Laden really is dead. *Pittsburgh Post Gazette*, 3 May, A-5.

Campbell, K. 2001. Does public have a right to watch? *Christian Science Monitor*, 12 June, 1.

Carey, B. 2011. Celebrating a death: Ugly, maybe, but only human. *The New York Times*, 6 May, A17.

Casteel, C. 2011. Inhofe sees 'grotesque' pictures of bin Laden. *The Oklahoman*, 12 May, 1A.

Death Penalty Information Center 2012. Facts about the death penalty. Available at http://www.deathpenaltyinfo.org/FactSheet.pdf.

Department of Justice. (12 April 2001). Press Release, Attorney General Ashcroft's statement regarding the execution of Timothy McVeigh. United

States Department of Justice. Available at: http://www.justice.gov/opa/pr/2001/April/169ag.htm.

Editorial. 2011a. Should the U.S. release a photo of Osama bin Laden's body? *USNEWS.com* (*U.S. News & World Report*), 3 May.

Editorial. 2011b. No good reason to reveal photos. President Obama was right not to release the photographs of a dead Osama bin Laden, which would do more harm than good. *The Denver Post*, 6 May, B-12.

Editorial. 2011c. Make public photographs of bin Laden. *Tampa Bay Times*, 6 May, 10A.

Entertainment Network, Inc. v. Lappin [2001] 134 F.Supp.2d 1002.

Fairbanks, P. 2011. Killing brings relief to local families of war dead; news confirms their loved ones died for a reason. *Buffalo News*, 3 May, A3.

Farhi, P. 2011a. Showing a wanted man's death. *The Washington Post*, 4 May, C10.

Farhi, P. 2011b. Reuters releases blood raid photos. *The Washington Post*, 5 May, A12.

Foucault, M. 1979. *Discipline & Punish: The Birth of the Prison*. Trans. Alan Sheridan. New York: Vintage.

Grier, P. 2011. The bin Laden effect: How the Al Qaeda leader changed America; In life, Osama bin Laden made a huge impact on the US, all in the name of preventing another 9/11. If he and Al Qaeda fueled antagonism between the US and the Muslim world, they also pushed America toward a better understanding of the Middle East. *The Christian Science Monitor*, 7 May.

Hall, M. 2011. White House still considering whether to release photographs. *USA Today*, 4 May, 5A.

Holston, N. 2001. As McVeigh checks out, should we tune in? *Star Tribune*, 13 May, 1E.

Karoliszyn, H., Cunningham, J.H. and Schapiro, R. 2011. 'Payback' brings relief, joy to so many. *New York Daily News*, 3 May, 9.

Kellerman, J. 2001. Don't – it's bloodlust. *USA Today*, 11 June, 13A.

LaFranchi, H. 2011a. Bin Laden alive? To debunk latest myth, White House near release of photo. The US had reason to bury Osama bin Laden at sea. But now conspiracy theories are cropping up that he is not dead, adding to domestic pressure on the US to release a photo of his body. *The Christian Science Monitor*, 3 May.

LaFranchi, H. 2011b. US won't release bin Laden photo: 'We're not interested in … trophies'; Concerns that release of a 'gruesome' bin Laden photo could spark a backlash in the Muslim world won out over a desire to defuse conspiracy theories that Al Qaeda's leader was still alive. *The Christian Science Monitor*, 4 May.

Littwin, M. 2011. A tale of two photographs. *The Denver Post*, 8 May, D-05.

Madeira, J.L. 2012. *Killing McVeigh: The Death Penalty and the Myth of Closure*. New York: New York University Press.

Marquand, R. Osama bin Laden conspiracy theories race across the world; The quick burial of Osama bin Laden and the decision not to release photos of his body are sparking wild rumors, not just in Pakistan and the Arab world, but also in Europe and the US. *The Christian Science Monitor*, 3 May.

Mauro, T. 2001. Televise – for the public's sake. *USA Today*, 11 June, 13A.

Memoli, M. and Nicholas, P. 2011. No release of death photos Obama cites security in keeping bin Laden pictures from public. *St. Louis Dispatch*, 5 May, A1.

Miller, G. 2011. In videos, bin Laden an 'active' leader. *The Washington Post*, 8 May, A01.

Obama, B. 2011. Remarks by the president on Osama bin Laden. 2 May. Available at: http://www.whitehouse.gov/the-press-office/2011/05/02/remarks-president-osama-bin-laden.

Page, S. and Kiely, K. 2011. Osama's death not an end to terror; 9/11 mastermind no longer center of conflict. *USA Today*, 2 May, 1A.

Payne v. Tennessee [1991] 501 U.S. 808.

PBS NewsHour with Jim Lehrer 2001. Witness to an Execution. 12 April. Available at: http://www.pbs.org/newshour/bb/law/jan-june01/mcveigh_5-12.html.

Phillips, A. 2001. Dead man talking. *Maclean's*, 23 April, 28.

Popiolkowski, J. 2011. Shaping a generation: For many young adults living in Western New York who were not even teenagers on Sept. 11, 2001, bin Laden's death represents a form of closure or the end of a chapter in American history. *Buffalo News*, 5 May, A1.

Porter, J. 2001. Let's see McVeigh execution; but don't make it an excuse for party. *Philadelphia Daily News*, 10 May, 10.

Shear, M.D. 2011. Obama blocks release of graphic photos for second time. *The New York Times Blogs*, 5 May.

Sherry, A. 2011a. The death of Osama bin Laden; Udall pushed for photos; Members of several congressional panels can view the images at the CIA. But some ask what the point is now that al-Qaeda confirmed its leader's demise. *The Denver Post*, 11 May, A-01.

Sherry, A. 2011b. Bin Laden photos; Release urged as warning to 'bad people'; Rep. Doug Lamborn visits the CIA to view images of the slain al-Qaeda leader. *The Denver Post*, 13 May, A-01.

Shiffman, J. 2011. 2 local lawmakers view photos of bin Laden's corpse. *The Philadelphia Inquirer*, 13 May, A16.

Shister, G. 2001. In reversal, '60 Minutes' honcho says he'd air execution. *The Philadelphia Inquirer*, 25 April, D08.

Simon, D. and Farrell, J. 2011. A town that lost many on 9/11 revels in bin Laden's death. *The Philadelphia Inquirer*, 3 May, A10.

Sitterle, K.A. and Gurwitch, R.H. 1999. The terrorist bombing in Oklahoma City, in *When a Community Weeps: Case Studies in Group Survivorship*, edited by E.S. Zimmer and M.B. Williams, 161–90). Philadelphia, PA: Brunner/Maxel.

Sonmez, F. 2011. Panetta says photos of body will probably be released. *The Washington Post*, 4 May, A09.

Stanley, A. 2011. As word spread about bin Laden's death, it became a TV moment. *The New York Times*, 3 May, F8.

Starr, M. 2011. bin Laden kill video? Dream on. *The New York Post*, 3 May, 73.

Straw, J. 2012. Long, difficult road to justice at Guantanamo Bay trials of Khalid Sheikh Mohammed and cohorts. *New York Daily News*, 21 October.

Wax, E. 2011. Already, skeptics question reports of bin Laden's death. *The Washington Post*, 3 May, C07.

Weichselbaum, S. and Hutchinson, B. 2011. Survivors get 'very real' hugs quality time with the prez. *New York Daily News*, 6 May, 11.

Whitlock, C. and Wan, W. 2011. U.S. cautious on releasing visual proof. *The Washington Post*, 3 May, A08.

Zernike K. and Kaufman, M. 2011. An emblem of evil in the U.S., an icon to the cause of terror. *The New York Times*, 2 May, A10.

PART III
Asia

Chapter 6
Why Does Japan Retain the Death Penalty? Nine Hypotheses

David T. Johnson

Over the past half-century there has been a major decline in capital punishment in many parts of the world. As of 1970, only 21 nations had abolished the death penalty for all crimes or for 'ordinary offences' (all crimes except insurrection and offences committed in wartime). As of 2011 the total was 105, and 35 more retained it in law but had not executed anyone for at least 10 years. Conversely, 58 nations retained capital punishment and had executed at least one person in the previous 10 years. At present, therefore, more than 70 per cent (140/198) of all countries in the world have abolished the death penalty in law or practice. Moreover, only 21 nations – less than one in nine – carried out executions in 2011.

The death penalty has also declined in Asia. As of 2011, nine Asian jurisdictions had formally abolished capital punishment, and seven more had gone at least 10 years without an execution, while 13 retained capital statutes and carried out at least one execution in the previous decade.[1] Hence more than half of all Asian jurisdictions have abolished the death penalty in law or practice. In 2011, 23 of these 29 Asian jurisdictions – nearly 80 per cent – did not carry out a single execution. Of the six jurisdictions that did execute in 2011, only two executed more than five people (China and North Korea), and Japan went the whole year without executing for the first time since 1992.

One result of these declines is that Japan and the United States are now the only two developed democracies that retain capital punishment and continue to carry out executions on a regular basis (Japan executed seven people in 2012 while the US executed 43).[2] It has often been observed that Japan's annual per capita

1 Asian countries with abolition of death penalty for all crimes: Australia (abolished in 1985), Bhutan (2004), Cambodia (1989), East Timor (1999), Hong Kong (1993), Macao (n.a.), Nepal (1997), New Zealand (1989) and the Philippines (2006). Countries with 'de facto' abolition (no executions for ten years or more): Brunei Darussalam (last execution in 1957), Laos (1989), Maldives (1952), Myanmar (1989), Papua New Guinea (1950), South Korea (1997) and Sri Lanka (1976). Countries with retention: Bangladesh, China, India, Indonesia, Japan, Malaysia, Mongolia, North Korea, Pakistan, Singapore, Taiwan, Thailand and Vietnam (see Johnson and Zimring 2009a, and Johnson and Zimring 2009b).

2 If Taiwan is also considered a developed democracy, as some analysts argue, then it joins Japan and the United States as nations that retain capital punishment and continue

execution rate (executions per million population) is lower than that for the United States. Though that has been the case for at least 25 years,[3] the per capita rate is not the only measure of execution frequency. Stalinist nightmares aside, persons are not randomly selected for execution, they are, for the most part, condemned and executed from a larger pool of potentially capital cases. In Japan and America, this pool consists entirely of homicide crimes. Because Japan's homicide rate is much lower than that for the United States (about one-tenth as high in 2010) its execution rate per homicide is often higher than the parallel rate for America, and in some years it rivals or surpasses the rates in high-rate American states such as Texas and Virginia (Johnson 2006a, Johnson 2006b).

A large scholarly literature tries to explain why America, alone among Western democracies, maintains capital punishment,[4] but there has been little serious study of the analogous question for Japan. The main aim of this chapter is to stimulate more research about the causes of Japan's continuing commitment to capital punishment – especially by Japan's own fine scholars. The essay presents nine hypotheses organized around three themes: explanations that focus on *history*; explanations that emphasize facts and forces *external* to Japan; and explanations that stress features *inside* the country. These are, of course, overlapping categories. When it comes to the retention of capital punishment in Japan and other countries, the causes are multiple and interactive. I believe that some of the suppositions that follow shed light on Japan's retention conundrum, and all of them are put forward in the hope that they will spur further investigation. My main mission is to raise questions and point to possibilities (and to some dead ends), not to provide conclusive answers. Future engagement with the question of Japan's retention will no doubt be advanced if researchers recognize that this social fact (like many others) is probably 'overdetermined' in the sense that a variety of causes – a variety not an infinity – need to enter into the answer (Garland 1990).

The hypotheses

I. Historical

1. A missed opportunity in the postwar occupation.
2. Long-term rule by the (conservative) Liberal Democratic Party.

---

to carry out executions. Taiwan performed no executions in the four years between 2006 and 2009, before executing four persons in 2010, five in 2011, and six in 2012.

3 Even when Japan's execution total spiked to 15 in 2008, its per capita rate of 0.118 per million population was still slightly lower than the American rate of 0.122 – and this was a year in which the American rate reached a 15-year low.

4 The literature on American retention is vast, but three of the most instructive accounts are Steiker (2002), Zimring (2003) and Garland (2010). For other accounts of American retention, see Garland (2005, 2007a, 2007b), Banner (2003) and Hammel (2010).

3. Japan can afford to be different because of its geopolitical strength, democratic stability, and legal self-sufficiency.

II. External

1. The legitimacy provided by American capital punishment.
2. The company of South Korea.
3. The weakness of regional organizations in Asia.

III. Internal

1. Public support for capital punishment.
2. Japanese beliefs about atonement and human rights.
3. Penal populism, *genbatsuka* (increasing punitivism), and the perceived need to serve victims.

Historical Explanations

Hypothesis 1: A Missed Opportunity in the Postwar Occupation

Most men are married to a certain woman this year because they were married to her last year. More abstractly, an effect created by causes at some previous period can become a cause of that same effect in succeeding periods. On this 'historicist' explanation, Japan has capital punishment in 2013 because it had it in 2012 and in 2011 and so on, back in time (Stinchcombe 1968).

To be satisfying, this kind of explanation needs to describe the conditions under which a practice such as capital punishment tends to be preserved or abolished. On this subject there is evidence from around the world that the death penalty frequently disappears when an authoritarian regime falls. This is what happened in West Germany after the fall of Hitler, in Italy after Mussolini, in Portugal after Salazar, and in Spain after Franco. It is also what happened in a total of 13 nations in Central and Eastern Europe after Soviet hegemony ended in 1989 (Zimring 2003: 23, Puhar 2003). In Asia, similar abolitions occurred in Cambodia after the end of the Khmer Rouge (1989), in the Philippines after Marcos (1987) and in East Timor after it gained independence from Indonesia (1999). In these nations and others, a new regime eliminated capital punishment as one part of the process of distancing itself from the authoritarian excesses of its predecessor. The most memorable illustration of this recurrent pattern is Romania, where dictator Nicolae Ceausescu was overthrown in 1989. The new government then did two things in quick succession: it executed the autocrat, and it abolished the death penalty.

Japan experienced a major regime change after World War Two, but the death penalty endured it. The persistence of capital punishment through a seven-year period of foreign occupation is a puzzle that needs to be researched. The occupation authorities could have abolished the death penalty, and their decision not to was neither natural nor inevitable (Johnson 2006a). The occupation agenda was highly ambitious: land redistribution, equality of the sexes, the downsizing of the emperor from 'god' to mere 'symbol of the state of the unity of the people', the establishment of the Diet as the highest organ of state power, the authority of judicial review and so on. But capital punishment was nowhere on the agenda, and this absence not only distinguishes the occupation of Japan from the parallel occupation of Germany (Evans 1996), it also helps explain why Japan remains retentionist today. One part of the persistence story concerns the desire of American officials to put 'war criminals' to death in the Tokyo War Crimes Trial (seven were executed in December 1948). But to my knowledge, a thorough account of why capital punishment endured through a time when so much else in Japan was changing – and in circumstances that have precipitated abolition in many other nations of the world – has never been constructed. The moment was ripe but the reform never happened. Why not?

Hypothesis 2: Long-term Rule by the (Conservative) Liberal Democratic Party

Another recurrent pattern of death penalty decline is that the ultimate punishment sometimes disappears when a liberal or progressive party takes control of government from a party on the right. In Europe, this was the precipitating circumstance for the abolitions that occurred in Austria (1950), Great Britain (1969), and France (1981), while in Asia executions ceased in South Korea during the presidencies of progressives Kim Dae Jung (1998–2003) and Roh Moo Hyun (2003–2008), and in Taiwan executions plummeted under the left-of-centre leadership of President Chen Shui-bian (from 2000 to 2008) before increasing under conservative President Ma Ying-jeou (Zimring 2003: 23, Johnson and Zimring 2009).

In Japan, the persistence of capital punishment may be partly explained by the long-term rule of the Liberal Democratic Party, which governed the country almost continuously from its inception in 1955 until 2009 – for more than half a century. Prior to the landslide victory of the Democratic Party of Japan in August 2009, the LDP spent only 11 months out of power, in 1993–94. During that brief interregnum – and despite the presence of at least nine opponents of capital punishment in the new coalition government's cabinet – four persons were hanged, yet open criticism of the executions 'could not be heard from among the government', not even from members of the Social Democratic Party who had hoped for abolition and expected that there would be a moratorium on executions (Schmidt 2002, 78–83). Some analysts have argued that the rule of the non-LDP government was too brief and tenuous to enable meaningful movement towards abolition (Johnson and Zimring 2009: 82). That argument was plausible in the past, but the DPJ's control of government from 2009 to 2012 made possible a more meaningful test of this hypothesis, and the results provide little support for it. Under DPJ rule, not only was there no significant move toward abolition, there were two executions in 2010 and seven more in 2012, leading some analysts to conclude that Japan's 'progressive' party returned to the same death penalty position that prevailed when the conservative LDP ruled the country prior to 2009.[5] The DPJ's performance while in power has been panned for many reasons. Most of the promises in its 2009 election manifesto – including assurances that it would proceed cautiously on capital punishment – ended in failure, and its crushing defeat in the national election of December 2012 reflected voters' frustration at its inability to govern effectively. Few people expect the resurgent LDP to pursue significant death penalty reform while it is in power, and fewer still will be inclined to claim that a leftward transition of power is likely to lead to the abolition of capital punishment. Abolition may well be more likely under a liberal party than under a conservative one, and another left-liberal transition of government could be a necessary condition for the death penalty's disappearance in Japan. But the recent past suggests that a leftward transition is not a sufficient cause of capital punishment's demise.

Hypothesis 3: Japan Can Afford to be Different Because of its Geopolitical Strength, Democratic Stability, and Legal Self-sufficiency

Japan and the United States are the only two advanced industrial democracies that retain capital punishment and continue to conduct executions. Their common resistance to complying with a norm of abolition that is rapidly becoming international has been attributed to three shared features of their political and historical circumstances (Bae 2009).

First, both Japan and the United States have sufficient geopolitical and economic strength to make it difficult for external forces (such as the European Union or international law) to impose meaningful sanctions for noncompliance. On this view (which political scientists call 'realism'), powerful states rarely cede to supranational entities; they pick and choose the international norms that serve their own purposes and reject those that do not.

Second, big events such as war, revolution, regime change and economic crisis often trigger major policy changes through the mechanism of elite learning. But as hypothesis two about LDP hegemony made clear, Japan had a stable and conservative democratic system for more than half a century. This stability sharply distinguishes Japan's recent political history from those of South Korea and Taiwan, two East-Asian neighbours that started to accept the norm of abolition before Japan, despite being at earlier stages of economic and democratic development. The key circumstance that made it easier for South Korea and Taiwan to move towards abolition may be the fact that both countries experienced sharp breaks with the political authoritarianism of their pasts.

5 Source: *Asahi Shimbun*, 'Shikei e Shincho Shisei, Itten', 3 August 2012 (evening edition), 15.

Third, Japan, like the United States, has only recently and reluctantly begun to participate in the process that led to the creation of an international human rights regime.[6] Until the early 1990s, Japan was strongly criticized for its refusal to ratify international human rights treaties. Since the end of the Cold War, the country has started to take human rights more seriously, but when it does ratify treaties it often does so with reservations. In many respects, Japan remains committed to a model of law and government that considers self-sufficiency a major virtue. The main exception seems to be Japan's penchant for following the American lead in matters of human rights and foreign policy. Some analysts believe that in these matters Japan's subordination is so extreme that it can be called a 'puppet state' (McCormack 2007).[7] In this way, explanations like this – that Japan can afford to resist international norms because of its strength, stability, and self-sufficiency – blur into hypothesis 4, the first of the externally-oriented possibilities for explaining Japan's retention of capital punishment.

External Forces

Hypothesis 4: The Legitimacy Provided by American Capital Punishment

A 'counterfactual' conditional statement is an if-then proposition indicating what would be the case if the antecedent were true. Consider three examples:

1. If I had eaten more for breakfast, I would not be hungry at 11 a.m.
2. If Lee Harvey Oswald had not shot John F. Kennedy, someone else would have.
3. If the FBI and CIA had been better coordinated, the attacks on 9/11 would not have occurred.

Counterfactual thinking is a staple in novels, history and many forms of social science. Its 'what-if' approach has generated interesting insights in a wide variety of fields (see, for example, Ferguson 2000, and Morgan and Winship 2007). The economic, political, military and cultural power of the United States makes one wonder what would happen if it abolished the death penalty. Here is one

6 In addition to the international norm of abolition, the United States has also resisted or rejected norms related to torture, the Kyoto Protocol on climate change, the International Criminal Court, the Biological Weapons Ban, the Trade in Light Arms Treaty, and the Anti-Ballistic Missile Defence Treaty.

7 With respect to capital punishment, this form of followership enables Japan to continue its death penalty practices, including a secrecy policy that is taken to extremes not seen in other nations. One justification Japanese officials sometimes use to defend the lack of transparency in their own death penalty system is that America's more open execution policies are even worse (Johnson 2006a, 103–9).

possibility: *If America abolished capital punishment, Japan would do the same.* Sceptics may think this 'what-if' is fanciful – a little like wondering what would happen if elephants could fly. But looking back, the failure of the United States to abolish the death penalty in the 1970s or early 1980s might have been 'something of an historical accident – a near miss' (Steiker 2002). On this view, the historical trajectory of American capital punishment looks in many respects 'remarkably similar to that of other western nations' (at least until the 1970s), and the persistence of the institution to the present reflects nothing essential about American culture but rather 'contingencies' that could well have been different than they actually were (Garland 2005: 365). Similarly, looking forward – and not very far – some analysts are optimistic that abolition will occur in the 33 states (and the federal system) that still retain the ultimate punishment (see Ogletree and Sarat 2009).[8] Among the signs that give them hope are declines of more than 60 per cent in the number of American death sentences and executions from their peak levels in the late 1990s, and the exoneration of more than 140 persons from American death rows since 1973, which have had a significant softening effect on public and political support for capital punishment in many parts of the country (Baugartner et al. 2008).

Thus, America came close to abolition in the recent past, and abolition in the American future might not be as distant a dream as some people suppose. If America does abolish – and the most likely mechanism would be a decision by the US Supreme Court – then the attention of the world's transnational abolitionist movement would focus much more on Japan. In that circumstance, Japan might be able to resist pressure to conform to the international norm of abolition (as it has done with respect to whaling since 1982), but perhaps a more likely response would be for the country to do what it has frequently done in its modern history: go with the flow, by adapting to the imperatives of its external environment (Pyle 2007, Flowers 2009).

There is no doubt that America's retention of capital punishment provides 'cover' for nations that want to resist international pressure and retain the ultimate sanction. America is a superpower 'which regards itself as the archetypal liberal democracy and guardian of human rights' while at the same time rejecting human rights arguments about capital punishment except for those expressed by its own Supreme Court (Hood 2001). But if America did abolish, the legitimacy it lends to other retentionist nations would disappear, and countries like Japan would be more exposed. For Japan, the benefits of retention might be deemed too meagre to sustain the institution of capital punishment in the face of external pressure from human rights activists and abolitionist leaders in the rest of the world.

8 Note, however, that in Ogletree and Sarat's edited book *The Road to Abolition?* (2009), Michael W. McCann and David T. Johnson are pessimistic about the prospects for American abolition in the near future. The title of their chapter is 'Rocked but Still Rolling: The Enduring Institution of American Capital Punishment in Historical and Comparative Perspective'.

Hypothesis 5: The Company of South Korea

The legitimating effects of American capital punishment are powerful for Japan and for other retentionist nations. But in the absence of abolition in the United States, the most important foreign influences on Japan during the next decade may come from East Asia – and perhaps from South Korea. Long regarded as a poor, primitive, and dependent relation to Japan, South Korea has in recent years made great progress economically, culturally, and politically. Indeed, over the half generation or so since 1990, it has made up much of the gap in wealth, political status and influence that has separated the two nations for centuries. Some analysts see South Korea as the most dynamic and progressive polity in the region. If the Japanese are looking over their shoulders at any non-China competitors,[9] it is the South Koreans – and the South Koreans seem at least as focused on Japan (Johnson and Zimring 2009: 97–9).

South Korea has not carried out any executions since 19 men and four women were hanged in five different prisons on 30 December 1997. Ten years later, at the end of 2007, the nation became 'abolitionist de facto' because it had gone a decade – the entire terms of Presidents Kim Dae Jung and Roh Moo Hyun – without executing. Two years later, South Korea's government took another step toward formal abolition when it pledged to the Council of Europe that it would not carry out executions.[10] The promise is striking not only because few Asian nations have made similar commitments, but also because the pledge was made by the conservative administration of President Lee Myung-bak at a time when public opinion in the country supported capital punishment by more than 3-to-1 and when there were public and media calls to hang some notorious serial killers who have been condemned to death in recent years – at least one of whom had volunteered to be executed. But at the time of writing in January 2013, South Korea has gone more than 15 years without a single execution.

South Korea's pride in its achievements may provoke it to make comparisons with Japan – and perhaps to try to outpace the Japanese in a competition over human rights. For Japan, falling behind the Koreans in a domain associated with 'civilization and enlightenment' could be uncomfortable. A Catholic priest in Seoul has said that 'if the Korean National Assembly votes to abolish the death penalty, Japan will follow because they hate for Korea to surpass them in anything' (quoted in Bae 2005: 322). If that hunch is true – and many observers believe it is – then continued progress toward abolition in South Korea (and to a lesser extent in Taiwan) could put pressure on Japan. Under those circumstances, the most

9 Of course, China is another major rival of Japan, but it is hard to imagine the PRC generating significant pressure on Japan to improve its human rights record, especially with respect to capital punishment. In recent years China, with an estimated 4000 executions in 2011, has probably carried out more than 90 per cent of all the executions in the world.

10 Source: *Hankyoreh*, 2 September 2009, 'South Korean Government Pledges Non-Application of the Death Penalty'.

effective tactic for abolitionist evangelists might be to emphasize comparisons between East Asian nations, which could generate status insecurity in Japan, a country that has long been concerned with its international reputation (Pyle 2007) and with 'taking its proper station in the world' (Benedict 1946: 43).

Hypothesis 6: The Weakness of Regional Organizations in Asia

In Eastern and Central Europe, nations that did not abolish capital punishment immediately after the Soviet Union imploded became targets of pressure from the nations of Western Europe and the regional organizations – especially the European Union and the Council of Europe – which those nations dominated. One strategy was especially effective: conditioning membership of the Council of Europe and economic integration with Western Europe on the abolition of capital punishment in want-to-join nations. These incentives played a major role in the abolitions that occurred in Albania, Bulgaria, Estonia, Latvia, Lithuania, Poland and Turkey (Zimring 2003: 36).

In Asia, nations and cultures have been interacting for centuries, and there are at present a large variety of regional and sub-regional organizations, including ASEAN, ASEAN Plus Three, East Asia Summit and APEC. For the most part, however, these regional associations remain bodies for dialogue about economic and security matters, not human rights. More fundamentally, they are usually organs of 'much talk and little action', in part because of the widely varying levels of development and political systems that exist in the region. Under these circumstances there appears to be little potential for pressure to develop at the regional level in favour of abolition or other human rights commitments. The movements toward death penalty reform that are occurring in Asia are being pushed mainly by domestic developments within individual nation-states and by external influences that are more international than regional. In this respect, Asia in general and Japan in particular are more difficult environments in which to achieve abolition than were the nations of Central and Eastern Europe after the fall of the Iron Curtain in 1991 (Johnson and Zimring 2009a: 337–44).

Internal Forces

Hypothesis 7: Public Support for Capital Punishment

The Japanese public has long supported capital punishment, and their support has strengthened in recent years. Since the Occupation ended in 1952 there have been nearly 40 major surveys on the subject, and in almost every instance a large majority of citizens said they want to retain the death penalty (the exceptions involve unrepresentative samples and advocacy polls conducted by abolitionists; for an overview, see Sato 2007). Most recently, a Cabinet Office Poll in 2009 found that 86 per cent of Japanese respondents said they favour retaining the death penalty while only 6 per cent said they want it abolished (9 per cent were unsure).[11] This was the highest level of support ever recorded in Japan, and it was substantially higher than the 65 per cent of Americans who said in the same year that they supported capital punishment. As Japanese prosecutors often claim, perhaps Japan retains capital punishment because it is a democracy and because most of its citizens want to keep the ultimate sanction? If so, then does Japan's retention of capital punishment reflect 'democracy at work'?[12]

This hypothesis does seem plausible, for Japan is a democracy, and democracies are generally supposed to deliver what their citizens want. But the public support hypothesis has at least two problems.

First, there is strong support for capital punishment everywhere in Asia, yet death penalty policies and execution rates vary widely across the region. Public support in the Philippines (a democracy) was around 80 per cent at the time it abolished the death penalty in 2006, while in the democracies of South Korea and Taiwan, two-thirds or more of adults say they support capital punishment, yet South Korea has not carried out any executions since 1997, while Taiwan stopped executing for four years from 2006 to 2009. In authoritarian China, the world's most aggressive executing state, a survey by the Max Planck Institute in 2008 found that public support for capital punishment (58 per cent) was considerably *lower* than in the other Asian nations for which decent evidence exists. In Asia more generally, 16 out of 29 jurisdictions have abolished the death penalty in law or in practice, and where evidence is available it indicates that they did so despite the fact of majority support for the institution at the time of its disappearance (Johnson and Zimring 2009a: 302, 368). Under these circumstances, it is hard to see how a constant – public support – could be a primary cause of so much variation in death penalty policy and practice.

Of course, one way of rescuing the 'democracy at work' hypothesis would be to show that Japan's democracy is more inclined or compelled to be responsive to public opinion than are the democracies in other Asian nations – South Korea, Taiwan, the Philippines – where capital punishment has been abolished or significantly reformed. Though that might be the case, it is by no means obvious. In fact, many well-regarded studies of Japan contend that its political

11 Similarly, in a victimization survey conducted by Ryukoku University Professor Koichi Hamai in 2006, 86 per cent of Japanese respondents said they favour retaining the death penalty (Hamai 2009: 13).

12 The claim that punishment policy works best when it reflects 'democracy at work' is most closely associated with James Q. Wilson (1997). Hypothesis 7 is also the Japanese version of what historian Stuart Banner (2003: 301) asserts about America: 'The difference between the United States and other wealthy democracies with respect to capital punishment may simply be that the United States is more democratic, in the sense that elected officials find it more necessary to implement policies supported by a majority of the voters'. Similar arguments about American retention have been made by Posner (2002: 32–4) and Bohm (2003: 27–54).

system is actually quite *non-responsive* to the preferences of its citizens (see van Wolferen 1989: 5, C. Johnson 1995: 115, 212 and Inoguchi and Jain 2011).

The second problem with the public support hypothesis is that while Japanese citizens may favour capital punishment, they do not seem to be well informed about it. In the *Furman v. Georgia* case of 1972, US Supreme Court Justice Thurgood Marshall stated what came to be called 'the Marshall hypothesis', which holds that the more one knows about capital punishment, the less one supports it. On this view, support for the death penalty is a function of lack of knowledge about it and is responsive to efforts at reasoned persuasion. Some scholars have tried to test the Marshall hypothesis, and the evidence is complicated and conflicted. Yet there is some evidence to suggest that when Japanese citizens are provided with information and time to deliberate about the death penalty, they are likely to change their attitudes on the subject – in both directions (see Sato 2009).[13] Moreover, because Japan's system of capital punishment has long been concealed by policies of secrecy and silence that go to extremes not seen in other nations, Japanese citizens may be unusually ignorant about the realities of its administration (see Fuse 2009). When I interviewed Japanese citizens about capital punishment in 2003 and 2004, many respondents mistakenly believed that Japan uses the electric chair (a belief that seems to reflect the influence of Hollywood films) (Johnson 2006a: 111–17, Kaoru 2008: 173–81). In addition to the policies of secrecy and silence, another feature of Japan that helps explain the low level of citizen knowledge about capital punishment is the fact that since the 1980s, when four inmates on Japan's death row were exonerated and released, no more death row exonerations have occurred. By comparison, from 1973 to 2012, the United States has exonerated and released more than 140 condemned persons because of evidence of their innocence. These exonerations and the 'moral potency' of the innocence argument have significantly eroded support for capital punishment in the United States (Clarke and Whitt 2007: 134, Baumgartner et al. 2008). In Japan, by contrast, the innocence argument has gained little traction, though probably not because every inmate on death row deserves to be there (Shikei Haishi Henshu Iinkai 2004).

In sum, the public support hypothesis needs more research, but simple claims that 'Japan has the death penalty because the Japanese want it' are challenged by comparative evidence from other countries and by evidence from Japan which suggests that public opinion is not well informed. In the years to come, Japan's new system of lay judge trials will expose, directly and indirectly, many more citizens to the realities of capital punishment. It remains to be seen whether learning more about the death penalty will undermine support for it, though some analysts have predicted that is one likely result.[14]

---

13 In this study, 40 per cent (of 50 participants) 'changed their attitudes toward the death penalty through the provision of information and deliberation', and attitude changes were seen in both directions, from retentionist to abolitionist and vice-versa.

14 Under the lay judge system that took effect in 2009, a mixed panel of three professional judges and six lay citizens decide guilt and determine sentence in murder

Hypothesis 8: Japanese Beliefs about Atonement and Human Rights

Hypothesis 7 posited a general cultural explanation for the endurance of Japanese capital punishment by pointing to the breadth of public support for the institution. Hypothesis 8 is 'cultural' in a more specific sense, for it stresses not the volume of support in Japanese society but rather the purported presence of two cultural patterns that make it difficult to abolish the death penalty. The first pattern is the belief that death is an appropriate way – and sometimes the only way – of atoning for heinous crimes. On this view, in order for an offender to make amends and in order to satisfy society's sense of justice, the offender must give up his or her life: it is a matter of moral proportion and symbolic purification. As Minister of Justice Kunio Hatoyama explained in October 2008 (quoted in *Japan Focus* 2007):

> This is why 80% of the public support me. As I said before, I think we should think calmly about the death penalty. I recognize the tide of abolitionism that is sweeping the European Union and other places. On the other hand, regarding present day Japan, I do not think that we can consider abolition … *As the Japanese place so much importance on the value of life, it is thought that one should pay with one's own life for taking the life of another.* You see, Europe is a civilization based on force and strife. Conversely, things there are moving against the death penalty. This is an important point to understand. The so-called civilizations of force and strife are the opposite of us. From incipient stages, their conception of the value of life is weaker than that of the Japanese. Therefore, they are moving toward abolition of the death penalty. It is important that this discourse on civilizations be understood … I am criticized for being irresponsible. People say, 'he shouldn't be a justice minister …' But isn't this [capital punishment] very human? Life should not be disposed of haphazardly. As a minister, I cannot escape this point. *As I respect life, I want those who take life as murderers to compensate appropriately* … Despite the rising tide against the death penalty, from the standpoint of public security and the principles of respect for life, we cannot allow those who kill repeatedly to escape the death

---

and other serious cases. For the view that this system would stimulate major death penalty reforms, see Ambler (2007), and for the contrary view that the prospects for change under the lay judge system are 'exceedingly small', see Landsman and Zhang (2008: 220). As of November 2012, lay judge panels in Japan had made 19 life-or-death decisions, resulting in 14 death sentences, four life sentences, and one acquittal. Thus, the new system delivered a death sentence in almost three-quarters of the trials where prosecutors sought the ultimate punishment. This rate is slightly higher than the death sentencing rate that prevailed under Japan's old trial system in which panels of three professional judges made sentencing decisions in murder cases, and it is substantially higher than the death sentencing rates produced by juries in the state and federal systems of America. The evidence at the time of writing is thin, but it does suggest that the proposition posed by Justice Marshall – the more you learn about capital punishment, the less you will like it – is receiving little support from Japan's new trial system.

> penalty. That's why I think the death penalty should be carried out, and the system should not be abolished (emphases added).

In this explanation of Hatoyama's willingness to authorize executions (he signed 13 death warrants during the 13 months he served as Minister in 2007–2008)[15] there are echoes of traditional Japanese sensibilities about *seppuku* (*hara-kiri*), a traditional Japanese method of self-destruction through self-execution that became institutionalized during Japan's feudal period (1190–1867) as one part of the discipline of the *samurai* class. For centuries this form of ritual suicide was imposed on some offenders as 'a form of honorable but necessary punishment' (Seward 1968: 9).[16] While *seppuku* itself has almost completely disappeared, some Japanese still seem to believe in the values that this form of execution was originally meant to express (Ross 2006, Asahi.com 2006). Indeed, one way of making sense of the Ministry of Justice's frequent emphasis on inculcating 'emotional stability' (*shinjo no antei*) in condemned persons on death row before the day of their execution is to interpret this imperative as deriving from historical practices that established what it means for certain culpable persons to make amends and die honourably.[17]

A second cultural pattern that might support capital punishment is what the eminent comparative sociologist S.N. Eisenstadt has called the Japanese penchant for negating 'the universalistic claims of other civilizations' (Eisenstadt 1996, Johnson 2008). On this view, universal assertions – such as the 'right to life' and the belief in the 'inherent dignity' of all humans – are inconsistent with the beliefs of a 'non-axial' Japanese civilization that seldom sees gaps between the transcendental and mundane orders and therefore rarely tries to reform society according to an idealistic vision. As Karel van Wolferen (1989: 9) put it:

> [I]n the final analysis … the most crucial factor determining Japan's socio-political reality, a factor bred into Japanese intellectual life over centuries of political suppression … is the near absence of any idea that there are truths, rules, principles or morals that always apply, no matter what the circumstances.

---

15 Many Japanese reject Hatoyama's claim that the use of capital punishment reflects the sanctity of life in Japanese society. In June 2008, for example, the *Asahi Shimbun*, Japan's newspaper of record, called Hatoyama the 'Grim Reaper' (*shinigami*) because of his apparent enthusiasm for executions.

16 For an historical account of crime and punishment in pre-feudal Japan which stresses 'the essentially political notion of *tsumi*', see Williams (2003).

17 A different way of interpreting the Ministry of Justice emphasis on the condemned's 'emotional stability' is to regard it as rhetoric intended to justify the policies of secrecy and silence that surround executions in Japan – and that sometimes lead to symptoms of insanity among persons on death row (see Johnson 2006a: 73 and Amnesty International, 2009). Sociologist Georg Simmel famously said that 'the purpose of secrecy is, above all, protection' (quoted in Johnson 2006b: 251). Similarly, the purpose of stressing 'emotional stability' may well be to protect the policy of secrecy and other Ministry prerogatives.

> Most Westerners as well as most Asians who have stayed for any length of time in Japan will be struck by this absence; and some Japanese thinkers also have seen it as the ultimate determinant of Japanese public behavior. Concepts of independent, universal truths or immutable religious beliefs, transcending the worldly reality of social dictates and the decrees of power-holders, have of course found their way into Japan, but they have never taken root in any surviving world view.

If the views of Eisenstadt and van Wolferen do describe real features of Japanese culture, then aversion to the absolutism of human rights frames and claims may be a significant obstacle to death penalty reform. More research is needed into this hypothesis, too.[18]

Hypothesis 9: Penal Populism, Genbatsuka, and the Perceived Need to Serve Victims

In recent years much has been written about the growth of *genbatsuka* ('increasing the severity of punishment') and penal populism in Japan (Hamai and Ellis 2008 and Miyazawa 2008a). Similarly, Japanese victims have acquired much more status, salience, and influence in the criminal process than they possessed in the post-war past (Miyazawa 2008b; Johnson and Tagusari 2012: 134–61). These developments help explain the surges in death sentences and executions that have occurred in recent years, but since they are *recent* changes, they cannot explain the persistence of Japanese capital punishment for the five decades or so that preceded their onset. Looking back, these factors only became operative in the last decade or so; looking forward, they may continue to shape punishment policy in the years to come.[19]

For people who would like to see Japan's executioners retire, the good news is that major death penalty reform – outright abolition or an extended moratorium on executions – seldom seems to depend on developments elsewhere in the criminal justice system. The Philippines, Thailand and Taiwan have all experienced abolitions or moratoria despite the presence of moral panics, salacious media coverage of crime and punishment issues, and 'get-tough' posturing and policy creation by politicians and prosecutors. In those countries and contexts (and in South Korea as well, where penal populism has not yet appeared), the key proximate cause of change in death penalty policy has been leadership from the front – and in the face of resistance from citizens and officials who would prefer a more punitive approach.

18 It is not obvious that this 'cultural pattern' even exists, for under some circumstances the Japanese state has adopted international norms and laws that are in direct conflict with its own domestic norms (Flowers 2009).

19 When Professor Setsuo Miyazawa (2008b: 132) asked 'Will penal populism in Japan decline in the foreseeable future?' his answer was an unequivocal 'no'.

With the landslide victory of the Democratic Party of Japan in August 2009 – and the ascent of an abolitionist (Keiko Chiba) to the minister of justice position – the situation seemed ripe with possibility for Japan's new government to steer capital punishment in a markedly different direction than it had been travelling for the past ten years. Some analysts even predicted that Chiba's 20-year record as a staunch opponent of capital punishment made it 'a certainty that hangings will be put on hold' while she is minister (Parry 2009). But as explained above in the section on long-term rule by the (conservative) Liberal Democratic Party (hypothesis 2), that did not happen. In my view, the future of Japan's death penalty might depend on the trajectory that the country's general punishment policy takes, but it will certainly be connected to the fate of party politics in the years to come.

Conclusion

In 1931, the year before he was appointed to the US Supreme Court, Benjamin Cardozo predicted that

> [p]erhaps the whole business of the retention of the death penalty will seem to the next generation, as it seems to many even now, an anachronism too discordant to be suffered, mocking with grim reproach all our clamorous professions of the sanctity of life. (Cardozo 1931 in Steiker 2002: 97)

Six decades later, when Forum 90 – Japan's largest abolitionist organization – was formed, its central aim was to persuade Japan's government to ratify the International Convention on the Abolition of Capital Punishment (Schmidt 2002). But Cardozo, Forum 90, and many other abolitionists have been disappointed. The main aim of this chapter is to stimulate research by Japan's own fine scholars into the causes of their country's continuing commitment to capital punishment. Many articles and books have been written about American retention; by comparison, the Japanese question has been neglected and under-researched. Although the list of explanatory possibilities presented in this chapter is by no means exhaustive, perhaps there is something here that will spur more study of the persistence of an institution whose continued existence is not only an interesting intellectual puzzle but also a practical problem of considerable importance – as one analyst puts it, 'the gravest real-life problem in the law' (Turow 2003: 11).

Of course, the question of the *persistence* of capital punishment in Japan is not the only one that needs research. There are also several puzzles related to the ways in which Japanese capital punishment seems to be *exceptional*. What are the historical origins of the policies of secrecy and silence that still shroud Japan's execution process (Johnson 2006a)? Why did death sentences and executions in Japan increase in recent years (Johnson and Tagusari 2012)? What legal techniques and narrative strategies do Japanese defence lawyers use in their efforts to save defendants' lives and in the face of harsh public and media criticism for representing persons accused of heinous crimes (Johnson 2011)? And what will happen to Japanese capital punishment under the lay judge system for adjudicating capital cases that took effect in 2009 (Fukui 2011)? These questions deserve serious study, and they presuppose the presence of an institution that this chapter has taken as its focus of analysis.

References

Ambler, L. 2007. The People Decide: The Effect of the Introduction of the Quasi-Jury System (*Saiban-in Seido*) on the Death Penalty in Japan. *Northwestern University Journal of International Human Rights*, 6(1), 1–23.

Amnesty International. 2009. Hanging by a Thread: Mental Health and the Death Penalty in Japan. September 10. Available at: http://www.amnesty.org/en/library/info/ASA22/005/2009/en

Asahi.com (2006). Minshuto Veteran Urges 'Death' Before Dishonour. [11 March, 2006].

Bae, S. 2005. Ending State Killing in South Korea: Challenging the Asian Capital Punishment Status Quo, in *The Cultural Lives of Capital Punishment: Comparative Perspectives,* edited by A. Stanford, Sarat and C. Boulanger. CA: Stanford University Press.

Bae, S. 2009. *Self-Sufficiency, Democratic Stability, and Noncompliance: When Advanced Democracies Violate International Human Rights Norms.* [Unpublished paper.]

Banner, S. 2003. *The Death Penalty: An American History.* Cambridge, MA: Harvard University Press.

Baumgartner, F.R., De Boef, S.L. and Boydstun, A.E. 2008. *The Decline of the Death Penalty and the Discovery of Innocence.* New York: Cambridge University Press.

Benedict, R. 1946. *The Chrysanthemum and the Sword: Patterns of Japanese Culture.* Cleveland and New York: Meridian Books.

Bohm, R.M. 2003. American Death Penalty Opinion: Past, Present, and Future, in: *America's Experiment with Capital Punishment,* edited by J.R. Acker, R.M. Bohm and C.S. Lanier. Durham, NC: Carolina Academic Press.

Clarke, A.W. and Whitt, L. 2007. *The Bitter Fruit of American Justice: International and Domestic Resistance to the Death Penalty.* Boston: Northeastern University Press.

Eisenstadt, S.N. 1996. *Japanese Civilization: A Comparative View.* Chicago: The University of Chicago Press.

Evans, R.J. 1996. *Rituals of Retribution: Capital Punishment in Germany, 1600–1987.* London: Penguin Books.

Ferguson, N. 2000. *Virtual History: Alternatives and Counterfactuals.* New York: Basic Books.

Flowers, P. 2009. *Refugees, Women, and Weapons: International Norm Adoption and Compliance in Japan.* Stanford: Stanford University Press.

Fukui, A. 2011. *Shikei to Mukiau Saibanin no tame ni* [Capital Punishment and Japan's Lay Judge System]. Edited by A. Fukui. Tokyo: Gendai Jinbunsha.

Fuse, Y. 2009. *Publicity and Secrecy Concerning Execution: A Contrast between the United States and Japan.* [Paper presented at the annual meeting of the American Society of Criminology, Philadelphia, November 5, 2009.]

Garland, D. 1990. *Punishment and Modern Society: A Study in Social Theory.* Chicago: The University of Chicago Press.

Garland, D. 2005. Capital Punishment and American Culture, in *Punishment & Society*, 7(4), 347–76.

Garland, D. 2007a. The Peculiar Forms of American Capital Punishment. *Social Research*, 74(2), 435–64. Available at: http://www.jstor.org/stable/40971939.

Garland, D. 2007b. Death, Denial, Discourse: On the Forms and Functions of American Capital Punishment, in *Crime, Social Control and Human Rights: From Moral Panics to States of Denial – Essays in Honour of Stanley Cohen,* edited by D. Downes et al. Portland, OR: Willan Publishing.

Garland, D. 2010. *Peculiar Institution: America's Death Penalty in an Age of Abolition.* Cambridge, MA: The Belknap Press of Harvard University Press.

Hamai, K. 2009. *Capital Punishment in Japan.* [Paper presented at the annual meeting of the American Society of Criminology, Philadelphia, 4 November, 2009.]

Hamai, K. and Ellis, T. 2008. Genbatuska: Growing Penal Populism and the Changing Role of Public Prosecutors in Japan? *Japanese Journal of Sociological Criminology*, 33, 67–92.

Hammel, A. 2010. *Ending the Death Penalty: The European Experience in Global Perspective.* New York: Palgrave Macmillan.

Hood, R. 2001. Capital Punishment: A Global Perspective. *Punishment & Society*, 3(3), 331–54.

Inoguchi, T. and Jain, P. 2011. *Japanese Politics Today: From Karaoke to Kabuki Democracy.* Edited by T. Inoguchi and P. Jain. New York: Palgrave Macmillan.

Japan Focus. 2007. Why I Support Executions. [Interview with Justice Minister Hatoyama Kunio, with translation and commentary by Michael H. Fox, December 19, 2007 (originally published in *Shukan Asahi*, October 26, 2007).]

Johnson, C. 1995. *Japan: Who Governs? The Rise of the Developmental State.* New York: W.W. Norton.

Johnson, D. and Zimring, F.E. 2009a. *The Next Frontier: National Development, Political Change, and the Death Penalty in Asia.* New York: Oxford University Press.

Johnson, D. and Zimring, F.E. 2009b. Death Penalty Lessons from Asia. *Asia Pacific Journal*. Available at: http://www.japanfocus.org/-David_T_-Johnson/3228.

Johnson, D.T. 2006a. Japan's Secretive Death Penalty Policy: Contours, Origins, Justifications, and Meanings. *Asian-Pacific Law & Policy Journal*, 7(2), 62–124.

Available at: http://blog.hawaii.edu/aplpj/files/2011/11/APLPJ_07.2_johnson.pdf.

Johnson, D.T. 2006b. Where the State Kills in Secret: Capital Punishment in Japan. *Punishment & Society*, 8(3), 251–85.

Johnson, D.T. 2008. Japanese Punishment in Comparative Perspective. *Japanese Journal of Sociological Criminology*, 33, 60–89.

Johnson, D.T. 2009. Early Returns from Japan's New Criminal Trials. *The Asia-Pacific Journal*, 36-3-09. Available at: http://www.japanfocus.org/-David_T_-Johnson/3212.

Johnson, D.T. 2010. Asia's Declining Death Penalty. *Journal of Asian Studies*, 69(2), 1–10.

Johnson, D.T. 2011. War in a Season of Slow Revolution: Defense Lawyers and Lay Judges in Japanese Criminal Justice. *The Asia-Pacific Journal*, 9, Issue 26(2). Available at: http://japanfocus.org/site/view/3554.

Johnson, D.T. and Tagusari, M. 2012. *Koritsu Suru Nihon no Shikei* [Japan's Isolated Death Penalty]. Tokyo: Gendai Jinbunsha.

Kaoru, S. 2008. Futatsu no 'Shikei' Seido: Nichibei no 'Korosu' Bunka o Kangaenaosu. *Sekai*, 782, 173–81.

Landsman, S. and Zhang, J. 2008. Tale of Two Juries: Lay Participation Comes to Japanese and Chinese Courts. *UCLA Pacific Basin Law Journal*, 25, 179–227.

McCormack, G. 2007. *Client State: Japan in the American Embrace*. London: Verso.

Miyazawa, S. 2008a. The Politics of Increasing Punitiveness and the Rising Populism in Japanese Criminal Justice Policy. *Punishment & Society*, 10(1), 47–77.

Miyazawa, S. 2008b. Will Penal Populism in Japan Decline? A Discussion. *Japanese Journal of Sociological Criminology*, 33, 122–35.

Morgan, S.L. and Winship, C. 2007. *Counterfactuals and Causal Inference: Methods and Principles for Social Research*. Cambridge: Cambridge University Press.

Ogletree, C.J. and Sarat, A. 2009. *The Road to Abolition? The Future of Capital Punishment in the United States*. New York: New York University Press.

Parry, R.L. 2009. Death Penalty Opponent Keiko Chiba Made Japanese Justice Minister. *The Independent*, 17 September 2009.

Posner, R. 2002. Capital Crimes. *The New Republic*, 1 and 8 April 2002.

Puhar, E. 2003. *The Abolition of the Death Penalty in Central and Eastern Europe: A Survey of Abolition Processes in Former Communist Countries*. Master's thesis, National University of Ireland. Available at: http://www.wmin.ac.uk/law/pdf/Eva.pdf.

Pyle, K.B. 2007. *Japan Rising: The Resurgence of Japanese Power and Purpose*. New York: Public Affairs.

Ross, C. 2006. *Mishima's Sword: Travels in Search of a Samurai Legend*. Cambridge, MA: Da Capo Press.

Sato, M. 2007. Public Opinion and the Death Penalty in Japan. [An unpublished paper based on Sato's 2006 LL.M thesis in Criminology at the University of London School of African and Oriental Studies.]

Sato, M. 2009. Deliberative Survey on the Japanese Death Penalty System. Available at: http://www.tuj.ac.jp/icas/pdf/icjs_090616.pdf.

Schmidt, P. 2002. *Capital Punishment in Japan.* Leiden, The Netherlands: Brill.

Seward, J. 1968. *Hara-Kiri: Japanese Ritual Suicide.* Tokyo: Charles E. Tuttle Company.

Shikei Haishi Henshu Iinkai. 2006. *Hikari-shi Saiban: Naze Terebi wa Shikei o Motomeru ka.* Tokyo: Impakuto Press.

Shikei Haishi Henshu Iinkai. 2004. *Mujitsu no Shikeishu-tachi.* Tokyo: Impakuto Press.

Steiker, C.S. 2002. Capital Punishment and American Exceptionalism. *Oregon Law Review*, 81, 97–130.

Stinchcombe, A.L. 1968. *Constructing Social Theories.* Chicago: The University of Chicago Press.

Turow, S. 2003. *Ultimate Punishment: A Lawyer's Reflections on Dealing with the Death Penalty.* New York: Farrar, Straus and Giroux.

van Wolferen, K. 1989. *The Enigma of Japanese Power: People and Politics in a Stateless Nation.* New York: Alfred Knopf.

Williams, Y. 2003. *Tsumi – Offence and Retribution in Early Japan.* New York: Routledge Curzon.

Wilson, J.Q. 1997. Criminal Justice in England and America. *The Public Interest*, 126, 3–14.

Zimring, F.E. 2003. *The Contradictions of American Capital Punishment.* New York: Oxford University Press.

Chapter 7

Death Penalty Moratorium in South Korea: Norms, Institutions and Leadership[1]

Sangmin Bae

South Korea carried out its last executions in December 2007. Since then it has maintained a *de facto* abolitionist status – one that retains the death penalty for ordinary crimes without, however any executions during the past ten years or more. International organizations and human rights advocates applaud South Korea's suspension of the death penalty while expecting and hoping for its subsequent official abolition. South Korea's *de facto* moratorium on executions is indeed highly noticeable because of the frequency and scope of the use of the death penalty in the rest of the Asian region. As David Johnson states, 'if Asia has an abolitionist vanguard it may well be South Korea' (Johnson 2008: 101).

This chapter seeks to explore the driving force behind South Korea's abolitionist developments and its implication for the rest of Asia. Focusing on the political and legal leadership, as well as the role of grassroots actors who have led the abolitionist movement, I discuss the prospects of the death penalty system in Korea. South Korea is neither the first nor the only country in Asia to halt executions. Yet, in the context of the greater debate over capital punishment, South Korea's experience stands out not only because of the announced political intention of the two recent governments to abolish the death penalty, but also because of the normative nature of political and social discussion surrounding the death penalty, which is mostly associated with the discourses of democratic values and human rights (Cho, Chong and Kim 2004). It is important, therefore, to explore Korea's developing social norm regarding the death penalty and its willingness to abide by an international standard of human rights.

I begin the chapter with a brief overview of how capital punishment was, until recently, enforced as a powerful social institution in South Korea. Next I trace the evolution of the death-penalty trend in South Korea, especially during the period of democratic transition. Given the significance of political leadership in championing and leading a variety of activities in opposition to the death penalty, I focus on the three branches of government – executive, legislative and judiciary –

1 An earlier version of the chapter appeared as 'Death Penalty Moratorium in South Korea: Democratic Transition and Political Leadership', in *The Politics of the Death Penalty in Countries in Transition*, edited by M. Futamura and N. Bernaz. 2013. Routledge. New York, pp. 92–106.

and discuss their efforts to put the issue of capital punishment on the human rights agenda. Following this, I move on to an analysis of grassroots activism directed towards the goal of abolition and, finally, I discuss the wider implications of my findings.

The Modern History of the Death Penalty in South Korea

Frequent use of the death penalty in Korea's modern history was often taken for granted. Amid a series of upheavals that characterized the South Korean modern political landscape – associated with Japanese colonial rule, the division of the nation, and the 30 years of military-dominated authoritarian rule, the death penalty system and its practice were rarely questioned or challenged. During the Japanese occupation of Korea in the first half of the twentieth century the death penalty was routinely used to suppress Korean nationalism. The power vacuum left by the Japanese withdrawal after World War II, and the further division of Korea, led to the formation of authoritarian regimes at both ends of the peninsula. The outbreak of the Korean War and the lack of a lasting peace accord between the two Korean states after the war allowed the undemocratic civilian government and, later, the military governments of South Korea to support the frequent use of capital punishment under the guise of national security. For several decades after its liberation from Japanese rule in 1945, South Korea was no exception to other East Asian states in supporting the traditional role of the law and the judiciary in imposing punishments.

Since the establishment of the modern republic in 1948, over 900 people have been executed in South Korea, most of them by hanging (Han 1999: 43–72). This number does not include anonymous executions carried out by the military court. South Korean criminal law broadly recognized the death penalty as a statutory penalty for most crimes against the national interest as well as for murder, robbery and the 'theft of national treasures'. The use of the death penalty was a major social control mechanism employed by authoritarian governments against those who refused to collaborate with the state's political principles and direction. When the United Nations General Assembly adopted the Universal Declaration of Human Rights in 1948 as 'a common standard of achievement for all peoples and all nations', South Korea passed the National Security Law in the very same year. This draconian law banned any acts 'praising' or 'benefiting' communist North Korea, and violators were subject to harsh punishment, including the death penalty. The fear of communist subversion provided the authoritarian regime with an enduring excuse to deploy the government's forces against pro-democracy protests. In contrast to traditional modernization theory, which assumes a positive correlation between economic development and democracy, the success of modernization and economic growth in South Korea did not entail any corresponding political liberalization or respect for human rights. In fact South

Korea was more democratic when it had a per capita income of $200 in 1960 than it was with a per capita income of $1,000 in 1980.

South Korea's industrialization process consistently involved gross violations of human rights, which, in turn, caused social disintegration. The death penalty was frequently imposed on political dissidents, often in the name of social stability, yet it seemed to undermine this stability because the denial of basic civil rights provoked political discontent and opposition among the people. This led to a vicious circle of excessive emphasis on stability, human rights violations, and further political and social instability. Until the transition to democracy in 1987, more than half of those executed were political prisoners who had violated security-related laws such as the National Security Law (1948), the Anti-Communism Law (1961) and the Special Law for Safeguarding the Nation (1971). Given the existence of the various security-related measures, state killings largely occurred within the legal framework.

The prolonged authoritarian regimes could not withstand the increasing tension between the state and civil society. In response to massive urban demonstrations throughout South Korea, stimulated first by student groups, trade unions, religious organizations, and later joined by many middle-class adults, a political liberalization announcement was released in June 1987. From that moment on, a succession of events radically reshaped the political power structure. The civil groups generated publicity and public support for their campaigns for economic justice, environmental integrity, fair elections, consumer rights and gender equality. Despite a wide variety of reform programmes affecting society, however, executions continued for about a decade; from the moment South Korea formally entered a new stage of democratic transition in 1987 until the last executions in 1997, 101 people were put to death. When Kim Young-sam, the country's first truly civilian president since 1961, came into office in 1993, he pledged extensive reform to deepen democracy and improve accountability. A wide range of democratic experiments proceeded under Kim's presidency, from outlawing all anonymous financial transactions to reshaping civil-military relations, and from encouraging the activities of civil society groups to recruiting several high-ranking public officials from citizens' movements. In terms of penal reform, however, President Kim Young-sam endorsed executions even more strongly than his predecessor, Roh Tae-woo. During Roh's tenure from 1988 to 1992, there were 39 legal executions, but under Kim's administration from 1993 to 1997, 57 prisoners were hanged from the gallows, including 23 convicts who were executed in a single day: 30 December, 1997. Table 7.1 shows that the death penalty was routine under the authoritarian military governments and even under the newly democratized, civilian governments until 1997.

Table 7.1 Number of executions in South Korea since 1970

Year	1970	1971	1972	1973	1974	1975	1976	1977	1978	1979
executions	14	9	34	7	58	0	27	28	0	10
Year	**1980**	**1981**	**1982**	**1983**	**1984**	**1985**	**1986**	**1987**	**1988**	**1989**
executions	9	0	23	9	0	11	13	5	0	7
Year	**1990**	**1991**	**1992**	**1993**	**1994**	**1995**	**1996**	**1997**	**1998–present**	
executions	14	9	9	0	15	19	0	23	0	

The Executive Branch in the Leadership of Abolition

President Kim Dae-jung took office in February 1998. His election to the presidency marked the first time in Korean history that the ruling party had peacefully transferred power to a democratically elected opposition party. As part of the affirmation of South Korea's status as a newly democratized nation, President Kim ensured that a human rights agenda became an integral part of his government. The Kim government took measures to institutionalize human rights policies, especially through the creation of the National Human Rights Commission (NHRC). Formed in 2001, the NHRC is an independent, government-mandated body with the stated mission of preserving and promoting human rights. This commission has the authority to conduct education programmes on human rights, report on the level of human rights protection, and investigate human rights violations in the public and private spheres.

Since the start of Kim Dae-jung's administration no one has been executed in South Korea. Kim never signed death warrants and instead commuted the sentences of 18 inmates on death row to life imprisonment during his presidency (Kang 2007). In his public appeal in 2006 in support of Amnesty International's campaign to abolish South Korea's death penalty, the former president wrote, 'The reason [I opposed the death penalty] is [that] capital punishment cannot be the true solution and it also goes against democracy and human rights. I dearly hope that capital punishment can be abolished to [accomplish] the true completion of democracy not only in Korea but in the whole world' (Kim 2006). At a ceremony to mark the fourth World Day against the Death Penalty held in Seoul in 2007, Kim stated that 'human life is a God-given right. Nobody can violate dignity of life', adding 'when I was about to leave presidential office, I tried to commute [the] sentences of all fifty-four death row inmates to life imprisonment. However, due to the obstinate resistance of the authorities involved, I could commute [those] of only thirteen people' (Kim 2007).

Like his predecessor, President Roh Moo-hyun, did not endorse any executions during his entire term. As a human rights lawyer, President Roh had represented political prisoners, and he himself participated in the pro-democracy 'June Struggle' in 1987 against the dictatorship of Chun Doo-hwan. Celebrating South Korea's Independence Day, President Roh considered commuting the sentences of all death row inmates in August 2005, but his plan was not actualized, mainly because of the opposition of his own supporters, who were concerned about his plummeting popularity ratings. Nevertheless, six death row inmates had their sentences commuted to life imprisonment on 31 December 2007, under a special presidential amnesty. As one of the last political decisions at the end of Roh's term, this move made headlines because it occurred just a few days after South Korea marked a ten-year moratorium on executions. In fact, a government official said, 'the international community is watching us as this country has become an abolitionist in practice. As the final act of the government that has emphasized the value of human rights, the President has granted commutations of death sentences for the prisoners who have served at least ten years in prison' (Shin 2007).

Major governmental bodies under the administrations of Kim Dae-jung and Roh Moo-hyun gave significant support to the value of abolition. The National Human Rights Commission (NHRC) first included capital punishment as a human rights agenda item in 2003 and two years later in 2005 it recommended abolition of the death penalty. In early 2006 the NHRC released its recommendations for the National Action Plan for the Promotion and Protection of Human Rights (Human Rights NAP) (The National Human Rights Commission of Korea 2006). This plan was given impetus by greater participation in the United Nations World Conference on Human Rights, and drawn up as part of the Vienna Declaration and Programme of Action. The Human Rights NAP was presented to the UN as required in June 2006, and subsequently implemented in 2007. Among the provisions of the Human Rights NAP is a recommendation that the government review the adequacy, costs and consequences of introducing a term of life imprisonment without parole, and abolishing the death penalty. Ahn Kyung-hwan, then chairman of the National Human Rights Commission appointed by President Roh Moo-hyun, said that South Korea should abolish the death penalty despite public opposition, as was done in most European countries (Kim 2007).

South Korea's abolitionist movement is based primarily on two rationales: the right-to-life principle, on the one hand, and the state's effort to comply with the standards of international human rights, on the other. According to the first of these, all human beings have a fundamental right to life, and capital punishment obviously violates this right. South Korea's decades-long concern about security prevented society from generating and promoting a wider discussion about the death penalty as a human rights issue. Although those in the abolitionist camp would simply argue that Korea's national division and concern for national security should not excuse or justify a denial of the right to life, such reasons have often been cited by supporters of capital punishment. For them, the state's ultimate sanction remains outside the realm of human rights, and the abolitionist movement is considered a challenge to state authority. A contrasting view is that a government's prerogative to execute is a gross violation of human rights, especially if there remains a possibility that the individual is innocent. President Kim Dae-jung, who has stood out in East Asia as a leading defender of universal human rights, argues that 'to end a person's life even in the name of law, clearly runs counter to the basic principle of human rights' (*The Korea Times*, 26 February 2006). The NHRC also cited the right to life as the primary grounds for its recommendation of abolition. The NHRC contends that the death penalty infringes the right to life, violating Article 10 of the Constitution, and also violates other provisions of the Constitution that prohibit disproportionate punishment, and cruel and unusual punishment (The National Human Rights Commission of Korea 2005a, 2005b).

In addition to the right-to-life argument, objections to capital punishment in South Korea may also stem from the government's willingness to comply with international human rights norms. By actively seeking to participate in international human rights campaigns, the governments of Kim Dae-jung and Roh Moo-hyun indicated an interest in becoming part of the trend towards stronger human rights initiatives on a global scale. The two governments were themselves motivated in this way, having voluntarily participated in programmes like the UN World Conference on Human Rights. As political leaders of a relatively recently industrialized nation of increasing global importance, these two presidents, Kim and Roh, may feel that South Korea should support human rights initiatives for purposes of prestige. In his call to abolish the death penalty, President Kim Dae-jung linked Korea's international legitimacy to abolition: 'Korea now comes to join the advanced nations in terms of human rights'. He cited an increasing number of nations that have already abolished capital punishment and commended Europe's leading role in the spread of the anti-death penalty norm (Kim 2007).

The progressive leadership of these two presidents is noteworthy for their central role in pushing South Korea in this new direction of abolishing the death penalty. The logical question then was whether President Lee Myung-bak, a political conservative, and an evangelical Christian, would continue to carry on the human rights leadership, or change course. He was the only presidential candidate in 2007, among liberals and conservatives, who opposed the abolition of the death penalty (No and Ko 2007). But even under the Lee administration, the South Korean government agreed to 'the non-application of the death penalty' requested by the Council of Europe as part of their agreement to adhere to the Protocol to the European Convention on Mutual Assistance in Criminal Matters. Confirming this pledge, the Justice Ministry said, 'Given that most European nations have agreed on the Convention on the Transfer of Sentenced Persons (European Treaty Series No. 112) and support the non-application of the death penalty, our government has followed it' (*The Hankyoreh*, 2 September 2009). Lee's successor, conservative President Park Geun-hye, publicly voiced her support for capital punishment arguing that it should serve as a strong warning to possible criminals. As the death penalty has never been used in South Korea since December 1997, however, controversial moral and political debates will accompany the resuming of the ultimate sanction, if that ever happens.

The Legislative Initiative against the Death Penalty

Many countries abolishing the death penalty found that the National Assembly or the Parliament, as the legislative body, played a key role in the abolition process of adopting laws and making constitutional amendments (Sarat and Boulanger 2005: 9–10). This is especially true among transitional countries that saw abolition as an essential part of the democratic process. By eliminating the death penalty in the early phase of democratic transition, they sought to prove the maturity of their societies. The Central and Eastern European countries all reformed harsh criminal procedures and laws that had prevailed under communist rule. Poland, Estonia, Latvia, Bulgaria, Moldova, Georgia, Azerbaijan, Serbia, Montenegro and Armenia are good examples. For them, reforming the criminal justice system meant terminating their authoritarian pasts and constructing new democratic regimes. Similar cases are also found in Asia and Africa. Cambodia and East Timor abolished the death penalty in 1989 and in 1999 respectively, as an important political symbol signalling the end of governmental abuse of the rights of civilians (Anckar 2004: 20). Rwanda became the first country in Africa's Great Lakes region to abolish the death penalty; a majority of the Rwandan Parliament voted to scrap it in 2007. Political scientists find that it is transitional democracies, not the long-established, most stable ones, that are more willing to accept international human rights enforcement (Checkel 1997: 473–95, Keeler 1993: 433–86, Moravcsik 2005: 171–6).

In South Korea resolutions calling for the abolition of the death penalty had repeatedly been brought forward under the democratic regimes of Kim Dae-jung and Roh Moo-hyun. The Special Bill on Abolishing the Death Penalty (hereafter referred to as the 'Special Bill') was presented three times to the National Assembly – in 1999, 2001 and 2004. The major aim of the Special Bill is to remove the death penalty from the Criminal Code and the Special Act, and to introduce life imprisonment without parole (Ho 2000, 223–36). The first of its kind in Korea, the Special Bill submitted in 1999 to the fifteenth session of the National Assembly received assent from 91 of the 299 members. This first attempt, initiated by Representative Yoo Jae-gun, failed because the bill failed to pass the Legislative and Judiciary Committee (LJC) of the National Assembly. In South Korea, bills are voted on once in the National Assembly and are then passed to the appropriate committee for discussion and approval before being returned to the National Assembly for a second and decisive vote.

In October 2001, Representative Chyung Dai-chul initiated a second bill to abolish the death penalty, which was supported by 155 members of the sixteenth National Assembly, then consisting of 273 members. Despite majority support, the Special Bill again failed to be discussed by the LJC, and the bill lapsed when the National Assembly finished its term. Most politicians involved in the abolitionist cause argued that abolition would enhance South Korean prestige and recognition in the international human rights community. Representative Chyung (2002) argued that state executions should be prohibited not only because they contradict the spirit of the constitution, which declares for a concern for human dignity and respect for life, but because the abolition of capital punishment is also a global trend: a hundred nations have so far sought abolition in their legal systems. According to him, therefore, to abolish capital punishment is to join an international human rights project.

As the same bill has been repeatedly presented, more and more lawmakers have joined the cause and put their names to it. In 2004, 175 members of the Seventeenth National Assembly, consisting of 299 members, again introduced the Special Bill to abolish the death penalty, leading to the reintroduction of the bill to the LJC in 2005. The LJC, which has 16 members and is divided into two subcommittees, discussed the Special Bill for the first time in February 2006, and a public hearing was held at the National Assembly in April 2006. The hearing revealed that only a small majority of the LJC supported the Special Bill, which was not unexpected, given that the committee was mostly composed of former prosecutors who had strongly supported the death penalty.

Many lawmakers support the abolition bill, citing human rights principles laid down in domestic and international law. According to Representative Yoo Ihn-tae, who took the lead in championing the 2004 abolition bill, each step the nation takes in the field of human rights narrows the long-standing gap between the world's leading nations and South Korea, a country seeking to earn respect on the global stage. Yoo argues that the death penalty is a topic that transcends national debate; it entails a significant international dimension (*Chosun Ilbo*, 9 December 2004). It is also 'contrary to the spirit of the constitution that the government possesses the power to take the life of a human being' (quoted in Lee 2005). Other lawmakers who sponsored the Special Bill share the view that it is a contradiction to take the life of a criminal in the name of justice – that doing so is at odds with the idea of human dignity, and the right to life guaranteed by the constitution. The right-to-life argument is a source of controversy, however, as not all see it as an inalienable personal right. At the hearings on the proposed abolition bill, Min Kyung-sik of the Korean Bar Association argued that the protection of lives and property comes before the rights of the individual criminal, even the right to life (*Korea Times*, 4 April 2006). Death-penalty advocates believe that criminals do not deserve the same rights as the rest of the public. They argue that the death penalty does not violate the right to life because convicted criminals have lost this right because of the community's right to safety. A key debate, therefore, centres on whether this is a human rights issue at all: Do we regard the death penalty as a cruel, inhuman or degrading form of punishment? The anti-death penalty norm may prove too morally contestable to be widely embraced. In addition, as seen in other countries' experience, legislators often cannot persuade the majority on the issue of abolition. The members of the National Assembly are often unwilling to risk clashes with public opinion and go against the popular demands for severe treatment of criminals.

No clear political divisions among parties regarding these abolition bills were evident. In the case of the 2004 bill, although it was supported primarily by lawmakers of the Uri Party and the Democratic Labour Party, some lawmakers of the Grand National Party also pledged their support (*Korea Times*, 4 April 2006). On the other hand, when the National Human Rights Commission released the Human Rights National Action Plan in 2006, which included a recommendation for the abolition of capital punishment, the then ruling Uri Party and the minor opposition parties, the Democratic Party and the Democratic Labour Party, supported it, but the chief opposition party, the Grand National Party, opposed it on the grounds that 'the recommendations will destroy the basic order of the democracy and shake the basis of the country' (*Korea Times*, 10 January 2006).

The Role of the Courts in Abolitionist Efforts

While the death penalty was still being used in 1996, the Constitutional Court of South Korea was asked for the first time to vote on the legality of the death penalty in Korea.

In its 7–2 ruling, the Constitutional Court said that the right to life applies only to innocent citizens and does not extend to convicted criminals. Seven of the nine justices claimed that the death penalty violates neither the constitution nor the principle of proportionality, asserting the efficacy of the death penalty in reducing crime (Constitutional Court of South Korea 95 Hun Ba 1). This 1996 decision, however, included a clause that limits the use of the death penalty: 'The death penalty should be applied only in exceptional cases where it is necessary to protect another life, or is in the public interest' (Constitutional Court of South Korea 95 Hun Ba 1: 546). Furthermore, it included a remark on the possibility of change in the future: 'Debates over the death penalty must continue regardless of the decision regarding constitutionality. Once the penalty is no longer needed as a criminal deterrent, it should be abolished' (Constitutional Court of South Korea 95 Hun Ba 1: 548). In addition, the ruling included two important dissenting opinions that have been widely quoted ever since by supporters of abolition. According to Justice Kim Jin-woo, cruel and inhuman punishment that deprives a citizen of life is incompatible with Article 10 of the constitution, which declares, 'All citizens are assured of human worth and dignity and have the right to pursue happiness. It is the duty of the state to confirm and guarantee the fundamental and inviolable human rights of individuals'. He added that capital punishment is inhuman in the sense that it infringes on the freedom of conscience and dignity of the judges who have to pass sentence in capital punishment cases, and of the people in charge of actual executions (Constitutional Court of South Korea 95 Hun Ba 1: 538). The other dissenter, Justice Cho Seung-hyung, stated that the death penalty violates the proviso of Article 37(2) of the constitution, which declares, 'The freedoms and rights of citizens may be restricted by law only when necessary for national security, the maintenance of law and order, or for public welfare. Even when such restriction is imposed, no essential aspect of the freedom or right shall be violated'. According to Justice Cho, the death penalty fails to conform to a central purpose of punishment, which is to make a criminal understand and repent the crime committed and return to society (Constitutional Court of South Korea, 95 Hun Ba 1: 539).

After the collapse of communism much of Eastern Europe abolished the death penalty through the constitutional courts. In 1990, the Constitutional Court of Hungary, the first in Eastern Europe to take this step, declared that the right of the state to kill contravenes the right to life and, as such, is unconstitutional. Soon after that a number of other countries followed suit. Lithuania in 1998, Albania in 1999, and Ukraine in 1999 all abolished the death penalty by decision of their constitutional courts. Some years earlier, in 1995, when the Constitutional Court of South Africa found the death penalty to be unconstitutional, the court made it clear that public opinion alone should not decide government policy, particularly not one that determines life and death. According to the court, states should reject public opinion if it does not accord with standards of humanity and decency. Even if this stance is unpopular, the court stated, it is the inescapable duty of honest politicians to explain to the electorate what stance they would take, especially on significant human rights matters (Constitutional Court of South Africa, *The State v. Makwanyane and Mchunu* 1995). In the face of strong public support for the death penalty, legislators and other elected officials are often reluctant to join the abolitionist movement. They decline to go against public opinion because this might jeopardize their incumbency or candidacy. This may be the main reason why such an important decision on abolition was made by the Constitutional Court, rather than through political decisions and processes.

In 2006 South Korea's Ministry of Justice ordered a review of capital punishment to determine whether abolition was desirable, as part of a larger effort to improve human rights in the criminal justice system. The Ministry conducted a public hearing on the matter, an unusual step reflecting the growing significance of capital punishment as a social issue in South Korea. The results of the hearing were intended to guide the Ministry of Justice in deciding whether or not to endorse the abolition bill, which would help it eventually reach the floor of the National Assembly. Despite its previous support for capital punishment, and in contrast to its previous position that talk of abolition was 'premature', the Ministry signalled its intent to eventually drop the death penalty in favour of life imprisonment without parole.

Changing attitudes towards capital punishment are apparent in the courts. Although judges still sentence some convicted offenders to death, they are reluctant to do so. The judiciary continues to affirm the status of capital punishment as the most extreme punishment, reserved for correspondingly extreme circumstances. An example of the opposition to the overuse of capital punishment occurred in a case in April 2006. A Seoul court rejected the death penalty for a man convicted of sexually assaulting and murdering a schoolgirl, despite the strong objections of the public. The court stated that capital punishment had been ruled out because the crime was not premeditated: 'The death penalty is a very exceptional punishment which takes human life, and it should be handed down only when there is evident and objective reason' (*Korea Times*, 13 April 2006). The court here appears to recognize that capital punishment is a potential violation of the right to life, though it is suitable in exceptional cases. Such reluctance to impose the death penalty provides hope for the movement towards abolition, as people already recognize the severity of the death penalty in contrast to other forms of punishment. Supreme Court Justice Chon Soo-an appointed by President Roh Moo-hyun expressed her support for abolition, strengthening the position of the abolitionist camp in the highest court (*Korea Times*, 29 June 2006).

In 2002 the Constitutional Court ruled as unconstitutional a clause in the National Security Law allowing the death penalty to be imposed on those found guilty of repeatedly praising North Korea or encouraging others to do so. Again, in 2007 the Constitutional Court ruled that the South Korean law that automatically imposes the death penalty on any soldier convicted of killing his or her superior officer is unconstitutional. The Constitutional Court stated that 'without asking the motive behind the killing of the superior officer, the current code simply prescribes the death penalty. That is an excessive punishment'. The court said the clause goes against the nation's judicial system, which respects human life (*Hankyoreh*, 29 November 2007).

While hopes for abolishing the death penalty were growing among human rights advocates, the Constitutional Court upheld the retention of the death penalty in South Korea. The Constitutional Court ruled in February 2010 that the death penalty does not violate the constitution, saying: 'The death penalty is a kind of punishment that the current constitution permits, and cannot be seen as a measure that profoundly infringes upon the dignity of human life'. Lee Kang-kook, president of the Court said executing serious criminals helped 'protect innocent ordinary citizens and significant public interests' adding that 'society needs to change more before it is scrapped' (*Yonhap News*, 25 February 2010). This was the second time after 1996 that the Constitutional Court of South Korea has ruled in favour of the death penalty. One might argue that the court's 5–4 decision in 2010 proves that support for the death penalty has decreased in the Constitutional Court compared to the 7–2 vote in 1996. But most human rights advocates expressed regret over the decision, arguing that it might be influenced by the position of the incumbent administration. In fact the Lee Myong-bak government, the ruling Grand National Party, and the Ministry of Justice under the Lee administration have repeatedly stated that the death penalty is a legitimate form of punishment and that the government may consider re-starting executions. During the open hearing held in June 2009 the representative from the ministry insisted that 'Capital punishment has been proven to have a greater effect than a life sentence in preventing violent crimes … . There is little chance of the system being abused or misused' (*The Korea Herald*, 26 February 2010). Kim Kyung-han, the Minister of Justice said: '[I] am seriously considering resuming executions'. The position of the Ministry of Justice under the Lee administration is in contrast with the ministry's stance on the death penalty in 2006 when it conducted fundamental research into the necessity of the death penalty in order to answer social and political calls for the abolition of the death penalty (*The Korea Herald*, 24 February 2006).

If the ruling of the Constitutional Court in 2010 had been different, South Korea would have participated in the strong worldwide trend to abolition, and dealt a further blow to the Asian *status quo*. Instead, the ruling and the changed position of the Ministry of Justice in recent years demonstrate how easily issues relating to the death penalty can be influenced by the executive. Would the verdict of the Constitutional Court have been the same if Korea had a President who opposes the death penalty? Wouldn't the Ministry of Justice have continued to review the possibility of ending the death penalty if the President supported abolition? South Korea's judiciary has often been criticized for its lack of independent power. As the Constitutional Court asked the National Assembly to take up the issue of the death penalty through legislation, it seems very unlikely that the death penalty will be abolished by the courts independently, without active support and coordination from politicians.

Grassroots Actors in the Abolitionist Process

In its 1988 report Amnesty International stated that only a few defence lawyers and judges in South Korea were able to offer a critical view of the death penalty. The International Human Rights League of Korea, the first organization to campaign openly for the abolition of capital punishment, limited itself to conducting a number of surveys on the death penalty (Amnesty International 1989: 162–3). In most cases, not only was the death penalty taken for granted, but it was ignored as a key human rights issue. Despite the cruel political climate under the authoritarian governments, or because of it, there was no organized voice against these arbitrary executions until the late 1980s. In addition, ongoing public support for the death penalty seemed to present the most difficult obstacle to abolitionist activism.

As the process of democratic transformation continued throughout the 1990s, however, activist groups started the campaign for the abolition of the death penalty. One such group is Lawyers for Democratic Society, or Minbyon, organized by lawyers who used to defend victims of the military government. Religious groups, active in the abolitionist movement for decades, are also using the current state of affairs to attempt to persuade the government. The Pan-Religion Union for Abolition of the Death Penalty was formed in early 2006 to unite members of varied religious groups, from Catholicism, Protestantism and Buddhism to Korean folk religion, in the common cause of abolition. Catholic groups in South Korea have long advocated abolition, especially the Catholic Bishops' Conference of Korea (CBCK), which has conducted an independent campaign against the death penalty. They needed to convince policymakers and the majority of Koreans of the need for and desirability of a new punishment system.

Amnesty International, noting the decade-long moratorium, is urging formal abolition in South Korea. Already engaged in a worldwide campaign to promote abolition, Amnesty International singled out South Korea in 2006 for a pro-abolition campaign – the first time this influential human rights organization focused on a single nation. Its branch organization, Amnesty International Korea, has played a crucial role in placing the death penalty issue at the heart of the human rights agenda, while other South Korean human rights groups have been somewhat indifferent to the abolitionist campaign. Amnesty International Korea has organized the ongoing campaign against capital punishment, and produced detailed accounts of the status of the death penalty both in South Korea and in the rest of world. In 2006 Amnesty International teamed up with individual activists and nongovernmental organizations across Asia to form the Anti-Death Penalty Asia Network (ADPAN), with the objective of pressing the National Assembly of the Republic of Korea to pass the abolition bill. Justice Minister Chun Jung-bae in the Roh Moo-hyun administration singled out the role of Amnesty International when he announced the Ministry's research initiative regarding South Korea's death penalty system in 2006: 'I was keenly aware that Amnesty International has selected Korea as a target country for its campaign to abolish death sentences' (Mun and Baek 2006).

Abolitionists exerting influence from within grassroots activism and the government can cooperate toward forging majority support among legislators and citizens. Many abolitionist countries have done so by demonstrating the inefficacy of the death penalty as a deterrent, and by providing additional support for victims and their survivors (Hood 2002: 208–45). Korea's suspension of executions has largely come about because of grassroots efforts to raise awareness regarding wrongful executions, and, more importantly, because of the leadership of the new democracy that has controlled the past two administrations. Given continuing popular support for the death penalty, the role of the political leadership appears to have become particularly crucial to its formal abolition. Like many other countries that have abolished the death penalty despite public support for it, South Korea must also depend on political leadership for formal abolition.

Discussion and Conclusion

South Korea's current moratorium on executions is important in the following three respects. First, it is voluntary, rather than the result of a 'contagious effect'. Quite often the political decision to abolish the death penalty is influenced by actions taken in neighbouring countries. What happened in Europe, in particular, confirms that regional effects can result from the strategic nature of death-penalty policy. Most European governments halted executions when other countries in their region did so (Bae 2008: 129–45). By contrast, peer-group pressure from neighbouring countries in Asia has never been of decisive significance in advancing the abolitionist agenda. South Korea has suspended executions, although surrounded by countries that practise the death penalty.

Second, South Korea's abolitionist activity has occurred without pressure from international organizations. Asia is the only continent that does not have regional enforcement mechanisms to safeguard human rights. Elsewhere regional interstate human rights organizations or agreements – such as the African Human Rights Convention, the European Convention on Human Rights, or the Inter-American Convention on Human Rights – play a role in promoting human rights principles. In Central and Eastern Europe, in particular, the influence of international organizations in the process of abolition was decisive. Most countries that abolished the death penalty there did so mainly to meet the condition for admission to the Council of Europe and the European Union. Such binding multilateral checks on domestic policies are lacking in Asia, which highlights the significance of South Korea's decision to become a *de facto* abolitionist state without any outside pressure.

Third, the moratorium on execution prevails in the face of public opposition. Public sentiment in South Korea remains strongly supportive of the death penalty. When the National Human Rights Commission under the Roh administration issued an official position statement against the death penalty in 2006, it noted that around 70 per cent of the population favoured the death penalty. In the same year, the Korea Society Opinion Institute found a similar result, reporting that 66 per cent were in favour of it. Associated Press-Ipsos polls conducted in 2007 in nine countries (Britain, Canada, France, Germany, Italy, Mexico, South Korea, Spain and the United States) found that 72 per cent of South Koreans favoured the death penalty for convicted murderers, making this country the strongest of the nine in its support for the death penalty (Associated Press, 26 April 2007). A more recent poll conducted in September 2012 again found that a large majority of the public in South Korea supported the death penalty: 64 per cent of people were in favour of it while 19 per cent were against it (*The Korea Herald*, 4 September 2012).

What this all means is that South Korea's abolitionist stance has been taken in opposition to the opinion of the majority. Some politicians frequently cite public opinion as a major factor in the decision to retain the death penalty, arguing that it is in accordance with democratic rules, but others believe that, in parliamentary democracies, penal policy should not be determined by popular sentiment alone. In fact, the link between public opinion and capital punishment is extremely weak across the nation. Countries that have abolished the death penalty have often done so in spite of public opinion, not in response to it (Marshall 2000: 12–14, Zimring 2003: 23).

South Korea is on the way to formally abolishing the death penalty. If formal abolition happens in South Korea, 'it will become an important test of how quickly abolition gets institutionalized in East Asia' (Johnson and Zimring 2008: 110). The resilience of South Korea's moratorium on executions has been tested under the administration of Lee Myong-bak. President Lee supported the death penalty and once declared that he would consider resuming executions, and yet the moratorium continued even under a pro-death penalty president. President, Park Geun-hye, who took office in February 2013, is also in favour of the death penalty and sees it as deterrent: capital punishment should be retained, she argues, 'because it tells criminals that they too can die if they harm others' (*The Korea Herald*, 4 September 2012). Whether President Park sincerely believes in the death penalty or was simply making a populist statement, it is unlikely that executions will resume in South Korea. The longer the moratorium stays in place the harder it is to reinstate the death penalty. And if and when the death penalty is formally abolished in South Korea, especially under a conservative administration, this will make a great case for the power of the anti-death penalty norm prevailing in many parts of the world today.

References

Amnesty International. 1989. When the State Kills … The Death Penalty: A Human Rights Issue, New York: Amnesty International.

Anckar, C. 2004. *Determinants of the Death Penalty: A Comparative Study of the World.* London: Routledge.

Associated Press, The. 2007. Highlights from Death Penalty Polls in 9 Countries. Available at: http://www.signonsandiego.com/news/nation/terror/20070426-0021-deathpenalty-countries.html.

Bae, S. 2008. Friends Do Not Let Friends Execute: The Council of Europe and the Anti-Death Penalty Movement. *International Politics*, 45(2): 129–45.

Checkel, J.T. 1997. International Norms and Domestic Politics: Bridging the Rationalist-Constructivist Divide. *European Journal of International Relations*, 3(4): 473–95.

Cho, B., Chong, J. and Kim, C. 2004. Suyongjaŭi inkwŏnbohomit chŏwugaesŏnŭl wihah chŏngch'aek yŏn'gu [Policy Research on Human Rights Protection and Promotion for Prisoners]. *Commissioned report for the National Human Rights Commission of Korea,* Seoul: Korean Institute of Criminology.

Chyung, D. 2002. *Capital Punishment Abolition Campaign in Korea and Its Prospects.* Paper presented at the conference 'Justice and Human Rights in Council of Europe Observer States: The Abolition of the Death Penalty', Tokyo, Japan.

Han, I. 1999. *Yŏksajŏk yumulrosŏŭi sahyŏng* [The Death Penalty as an Historical Artefact] *Samok.* Seoul: Catholic Bishops' Conference of Korea.

Hood, R. 2002. *The Death Penalty: A Worldwide Perspective.* Oxford: Oxford University Press.

Johnson, D.T. 2008. The Death Penalty in Asia: Introduction to a Special Issue of Punishment & Society. *Punishment & Society*, 10(2): 99–102.

Johnson, D.T. and Zimring, F.E. 2008, Law, Society, and Capital Punishment in Asia. *Punishment & Society*, 10(2): 103–15.

Kang, Ŭ. 2007. Majimak sahyŏng 10-nyŏn [Last Execution Ten Years Ago]. *Yonhap News* (30 December).

Keeler, J.T.S. 1993. Opening the Window for Reform: Mandates, Crises, and Extraordinary Policy-Making. *Comparative Political Studies*, 25(4): 433–86.

Kim, D. 2006. *A Contribution to the Campaign of Amnesty International for the Abolition of Capital Punishment.* Asia Death Penalty. Available at: http://asiadeathpenalty.blogspot.com/2006/03/south-korea-kim-dae-jungs-call-for.html.

Kim, D. 2007. *In Appreciation of the Announcement of Korea as a De Facto Abolitionist Country.* (10 October). Available at: http://www.kdjlibrary.org/kdj/engweb/presidentkdj/newsView.jsp?pkid=37&currentPage=6&searchField=&searchValue=.

Kim, N. 2007. *Sangkwan salhaenŭn sahyŏng kunhyŏngbŏp wihŏnkyŏljŏng* [Mandatory Death Penalty for Killing of Superior Officer is Unconstitutional]. *Hankyoreh,* 29 November.

Kim, Y. 2007. *Sahyŏngjenŭn inkwŏnmunje ... bosujŏngbudo chiphaenghimdŭlgŏt* [Death Penalty is the Issue of Human Rights … Executions Unlikely Even Under the Conservative Government]. *Hankyoreh*, 20 December The Korea Herald, 2012. Crimes rekindle debate over capital punishment. (4 September). Available at: http://nwww.koreaherald.com/view.php?ud=20120904001309.

Marshall, J.M. 2000. Death in Venice: Europe's Death-Penalty Elitism. *New Republic*, 223(5): 12–14.

Moravcsik, A. 2005. The Paradox of U.S. Human Rights Policy, in *American Exceptionalism and Human Rights.* M. Ignatieff, ed. Princeton: Princeton University Press.

Mun, B. and Baek, I. 2006. Ministry Says It Will Study Abolition of Executions. *JoongAng Daily*, 21 February.

National Human Rights Commission of Korea, The. 2005a. *Inkwŏnwi, sahyŏng pyŏiji ŭikyŏn pyŏmyŏng* [The Human Rights Commission Presenting Its Opinion on the Death Penalty Abolition]. Available at: http://www.humanrights.go.kr/04_sub/body02.jsp?NT_ID=24&flag=VIEW&SEQ_ID=554900.

National Human Rights Commission of Korea, The. 2005b. *Sahyŏngjedoë taehan kungminŭisikjŏsa* [Public Opinion Survey on the Death Penalty]. Available at: http://edu.humanrights.go.kr/know/product/45_T20051115_01.pdf.

National Human Rights Commission of Korea, The. 2006. A Roadmap to a National Human Rights Culture: A Practical Guide to the Recommendation for the 'National Action Plan for the Promotion and Protection of Human Rights' (Human Rights NAP). Available at: http://www.humanrights.go.kr/english/nap_01.jsp.

No, H. and Ko, C. 2007. Sahyŏngje sasilsang p'yeji [Death Penalty Abolished in Practice]. *Hankyoreh*, 30 December.

Sarat, A. and Boulanger, C. 2005. *The Cultural Lives of Capital Punishment: Comparative Perspectives.* Palo Alto: Stanford University Press.

Shin, S. 2007. 31-il majimak t'ŭksa, Kim U-jung ssi poham 70-80 myŏngsŏn [The Last Presidential Amnesties on the Thirty-First]. *Hankyoreh*, 30 December.

Zimring, F.E. 2003. *The Contradictions of American Capital Punishment*. Oxford: Oxford University Press.

Chapter 8
Why Taiwan's *de facto* Moratorium was Established and Lost

Fort Fu-Te Liao

Introduction

After a long period under martial law, Taiwan started in 1986 to move towards democracy. Although democratization did not automatically mean it became an abolitionist state, the number of executions per annum did diminish as it became more democratic, though this was not immediate and the number of executions first increased and then decreased in several stages, with 1990 constituting a peak year with 78 executions, and with executions having ceased by 2006 (Liao 2008).

This, according to one optimistic view, was 'a great step forward' (Hood 2009) leading to the comment that Taiwan appeared to be 'on the road to abolition' (Hood and Hoyle 2009: 91). A more measured position predicted two likely scenarios for Taiwan: 'a lengthening period of non-execution – a low-visibility moratorium that receives little political fanfare – or a resumption of executions under a new president in small volume and episodic regularity' (Johnson and Zimring 2009: 222).

Initially, Taiwan seemed to follow the first scenario, as there were no executions for more than four years between January 2006 and March 2010. Some have suggested that a state could be considered abolitionist *de facto* according to the 'ten year no executions rule' (Hood and Hoyle 2009: 88). While Taiwan did not have an execution for four years, and therefore cannot be considered as abolitionist *de facto*, it at least had a *de facto* moratorium for a period of time. However, Taiwan then changed its approach in April 2010 when it resumed executions.

There have been a series of push-and-pull forces involved, both from above and below. Indeed, one 'can imagine a two-tiered dialogue on the death penalty in Taiwan, with proponents of execution stressing crime control concerns and abolitionists placing a stronger emphasis on human rights' (Johnson and Zimring 2009: 223). It should be noted that movements both to support and oppose the death penalty have not always come from above or below. According to several public opinion surveys between 1990 and 2010, death penalty approval rates ranged from 63 per cent to 83 per cent.[1] These relatively high levels of approval

1 Polls in recent years can be examples. A 2006 poll indicated that 85 per cent of respondents believed that the death penalty was helpful in combating serious crimes;

suggest that most Taiwanese were in favour of maintaining the death penalty and carrying out executions, and that as a consequence the government's *de facto* moratorium did not have widespread public support. How – and indeed why – the various branches of government resisted or responded to such a high degree of support for the death penalty thus becomes an important issue to elucidate.

Taiwan has had several political changes since 2006, with the judicial, legislative and executive branches all having had new members and leaders. Lai In-Jaw became president of the Judicial Yuan[2] (JY) on 1 October 2007 after being nominated by former president Chen Shui-Ban, who was a member of the Democratic Progress Party (DPP).[3] New members of the Legislative Yuan (Parliament, LY) took office on 1 February 2008 when the Kuomintang (Chinese Nationalist Party, KMT) won over 71 per cent of the seats. Between 2000 and 2008 Chen Shui-Ban of the DPP was the LY President. Ma Ying-Jeou, who was the nominee of the KMT, became the new LY President on 20 May 2008, the result of which was that the KMT controlled both the executive and legislative branches after May 2008.

This chapter examines the thinking of these branches of government in Taiwan, to try to shed some light on why there was for a period a *de facto* moratorium – and why it came to an end. Views within the executive, legislative and judicial branches are examined in sections 2, 3 and 4 respectively. In section 5, the focus is on the criminal, execution and amnesty procedures, to highlight the interaction between the executive and judicial branches when they decide whether to carry out a death sentence.

Views within the Administration

This section focuses on three distinct factors: Taiwan's human rights policy, the role of the Minister of Justice and its ratification of the International Covenant on Civil and Political Rights (ICCPR), and attitudes within the administrative branch of the government towards the death penalty.

---

76 per cent opposed abolition. See Chiu (2006). The Centre for Criminology of National Chung-Cheng University held a poll in January 2010. It found 74 per cent of respondents supported the death penalty (see page A 9, *United Daily News*, 29 January 2010). The media too held polls on this issue and their results were also similar. For example the *United Daily News* had a poll in March 2010. 74 per cent of those interviewed opposed abolition; 12 per cent supported it (see *United Daily News*, 11 March 2010). The Ministry of Justice held a public poll in February 2008. Its results were quite similar to previous ones. Death penalty approval rates kept at 80 per cent (see Central News Agency, 1 February 2010).

2 The Judicial Yuan is the highest judicial institution in Taiwan.

3 The DPP was formed in 1986 and was the main opposition party between 1986 and 2000. It won the presidential election in 2000 and ended KMT's 55-year rule from 1945.

Human Rights Policy

Taiwan had a DPP government between May 2000 and May 2008, after which date the KMT gained power. The DPP has had a tendency to support the abolition of the death penalty: when it was in opposition, it drew up an 'Action Plan: Our views on current issues', of which Point 26 stated the aim to 'respect life and search for ways to abolish the death penalty'. On 20 May 2000, former President Chen emphasized in his inaugural speech that his 'government will request the Legislative Yuan to pass and ratify the International Bill of Rights as a domestic law of Taiwan, so that it will formally become the Taiwan 'Bill of Rights'' (Chen 2000). His policy of 'state building on human rights' included the 'gradual abolition of the death penalty'. A major reason why the policy was one of 'gradual' abolition was the lack of public support for abolition itself, as indicated by opinion polls. In 2007 Chen even expressed his hope that 'in the future wording will be added to the Constitution forbidding capital punishment'.[4] However, as the DPP held a minority government in the LY between 2000 and 2008, even supposing they had wished to propose legislation or constitutional amendments to the LY, they would have had little chance of the legislation or amendments being passed.

During the 2008 presidential election campaign, the DPP candidate Frank Hsieh supported abolition and even stated that Taiwan could be the first Asian state to set aside the death penalty,[5] a view consistent with the DPP's approach to abolition. It could be said that while the DPP held a policy of abolition, it was unable to put this policy into effect when it formed the executive, but remained in a minority within the LY. Its loss of the executive branch of government in 2008 meant the DPP also lost any opportunity to move forward on the abolition of the death penalty.

The KMT for its part never formally expressed any firm policy on abolition, emphasizing instead 'pragmatically' that 'when the crime rate is high the time is not right for abolition'. During the 2008 presidential election campaign, the KMT candidate Ma Ying-Jeou presented a softer response to the issue, saying 'when conditions become mature and with public acceptance we hope to move toward this goal'.[6] He also presented a 'Taiwan human rights declaration in the new century'[7] during his campaign, though it omitted any reference to the death penalty.

After Ma became President, the 'Taiwan human rights declaration in the new century' was a major source of guidance for his government. While President Ma himself did not say much on the death penalty, there were references to it in

4 Source: Office of the President. 10 May 2007. News Releases, President Chen Shui-Bian Meets Dutch Human Rights Expert Dr Theodoor C. Van Boven.

5 Source: *Liberty Times*, 6 March 2008.

6 Source: *Liberty Times*, 6 March 2008.

7 Source: *Ma's campaign website* 'Human rights policy – Taiwan human rights declaration in new century' at http://2008.ma19.net/policy4you/humanrights (visited on 8 March 2010).

several of his speeches. He stressed that, while many people have strong beliefs on the abolition of the death penalty, social consensus on the issue is vital: 'It is true that there is not yet a consensus on doing away with the death penalty. Our approach before such a consensus is reached is to gradually reduce the number of death sentences handed down'.[8]

He was also of the view that 'as Taiwan is a state of rule of law, unless there are legal reasons, executions, should not be postponed',[9] referring to his own experience as minister of justice between February 1993 and October 1996, when he signed every execution order except one where there was a possible judicial error. He did, however, refer to a possible gradual reduction in executions. These statements suggest that, in Ma's view, the death penalty should not be abolished unless there is a public consensus on the matter. His response as President was not to lead on this issue, but to follow public opinion.

It also appears from his speeches that Ma believed death sentences should be carried out, since between 1993 and 1996, 18, 17, 16, and finally 22 persons were executed each year while he was the minister of justice. His reference to his own past experience seemed to indicate that such a direction was still possible for Taiwan. As for the one case where Ma did not sign the execution order, it was the notorious 'Hsichih-trio' case[10] where several special appeals were deemed unnecessary in 1996. As Minister of Justice Ma could, or even should, legally have signed off the execution of the three convicted men, his decision not to proceed was subsequently used to demonstrate his respect for the right to life.

Concerning moves towards a reduction in executions, Ma may in fact be missing the more fundamental point. As Taiwan had no executions for several years, the real issue was whether to execute at all rather than to simply reduce the number of executions. Professor Speedy Rice, on behalf of the World Coalition against the Death Penalty, wrote to President Ma, 'to remind your Excellency that you expressly assured the official delegation of the WCADP led by me in 2008 that the moratorium on the death penalty would remain in force' (Rice 2010). However, it appears President Ma never gave such an assurance himself, and the official press release from his Office[11] makes no reference to the moratorium. He did suggest some measures could be taken, including 'replacing mandatory death penalties with a discretionary death penalty; not allowing death or life sentences to be given to persons under the age of 18 or over 80; and not imposing death

---

8 Source: Office of the President, News Release (14 May 2009) 'President Ma's Europe Day Dinner Address'.

9 Source: Office of the President. News Release (11 March 2010) 'Office of the President issues two-point statement on whether ROC will abolish capital punishment'.

10 Source: *Taipei Times*. 29 August 2010, 'Guilt by association?'. Available at: http://www.taipeitimes.com/News/-feat/archives/2010/08/29/2003481562.

11 Source: Office of the President. News Release (18 June 2008). 'President Ma Meets with Delegation from International NGOs Opposed to the Death Penalty'.

sentences on pregnant women'.[12] It should be noted that all of these measures had been carried out by the previous DPP government. He also added that rather than abolishing the death penalty, 'the possible directions for Taiwan in the future could be the lengthening of prison terms and stricter conditions on granting parole to persons sentenced to life imprisonment'.[13] These two measures had however been put forward by the former DPP government which had proposed increasing imprisonment to a maximum of 30 years and stricter conditions on granting parole for serious crimes. The DPP government also proposed using life imprisonment without parole to replace the death penalty for the most serious crimes.

When President Ma became chairperson of the KMT in July 2009 he in fact became the head of both Taiwan's government and the KMT which currently holds 65 per cent of the seats in the LY. If Ma had the political will to abolish the death penalty, he could undoubtedly achieve that goal by rallying his party, government and the LY. However, as noted above, Ma decided to follow public opinion, not to lead it, and thus agreed to allow executions. In these circumstances it seems unreasonable to expect that Ma's government will move toward abolition, as the U-turn in April 2010 came with the resumption of executions.

Role of the Minister of Justice

Having compared cases in which a Justice Minister and a President signs the execution order in Taiwan and South Korea respectively, Bae argued that 'the autonomy and prerogative of the president's political leadership allows Korea to take a stronger stance in favor of the abolitionist cause' (Bae 2008: 241).

Under Taiwan's political structure, the Justice Minister must follow the lead taken by the President. Thus when the DPP formed the government between 2000 and 2008, it was President Chen who drove forward his human rights policy, with his ministers of justice following his lead. After Chen announced his 'State Built on Human Rights' policy, he called for a 'gradual abolition' of the death penalty which was followed by his government's 'Human Rights Policy White Paper' of 2002 promising to 'move in stages towards achievement of total abolition'.

There were two ministers of justice during President Chen's eight-year term: Chen Ding-Nan from May 2000 to February 2005, and Shi Mao-Lin between February 2005 and May 2008. In 2002, Chen Ding-Nan called for abolition to occur by 2004, a deadline that was not met. It was during Shi Mao-Lin's term that Taiwan finally ended all executions. There was a series of exchanges between President Chen and Minister Shi which led to the latter allowing lawyers for death-row inmates to review documents and seek to appeal. These unique, behind-the-scenes political manoeuvres resulted in 2006 becoming Taiwan's first year

12 Source: Office of the President. News Release (18 June 2008). 'President Ma Meets with Delegation from International NGOs Opposed to the Death Penalty'.

13 Source: Office of the President. News Release (18 June 2008). 'President Ma Meets with Delegation from International NGOs Opposed to the Death Penalty'.

without executions. Shi even sent an internal memo in March 2008 [14] requesting that prosecutors consider the gradual abolition policy and avoid requesting the death penalty.

The KMT's practice in Taiwan is different. As President Ma appears to have no intention to maintain a *de facto* moratorium on executions, and since he thinks death sentences should be carried out, it is more than likely that the Minister of Justice during his presidency will not follow the path to abolition, and will therefore sign execution orders. This is in a sense confirmed by the departure of Wang Ching-Feng, whose term as Minister of Justice ran between May 2008 and March 2010. Wang expressed her personal support for the abolition of the death penalty in a newspaper interview after her nomination in April 2008,[15] emphasizing that this was an international trend. However, after expressing that position, she confronted a dilemma.

On the one hand was what she described as political leadership, which she illustrated with the example of French President Mitterrand, who in 1981 abolished the death penalty despite 60 per cent of the public's being opposed to such a move.[16] Her dilemma was that, on the other hand, since she was not the President, the ultimate decision did not belong to her. In France, it was the Justice Minister Robert Badinter who was able to achieve the abolition of the death penalty, since President Mitterand – the political leader – shared the same commitment. Wang could only have been a 'Badinter' in Taiwan if President Ma had been a 'Mitterrand'. President Ma had a fixed four-year term until May 2012, but the Minister did not. It is assumed in Taiwan that a minister, not the President, must resign when a government policy is not accepted by the public. That was indeed what happened when Wang left her position on 11 March 2010 after clashing with the Prime Minister and the President over whether or not to proceed with executions.

There were other tensions between the Minister and the Deputy Minister of Justice: the then Deputy Minister, Huang Shi-Ming, who is now the Attorney-General, said that while he personally supported abolition, he nevertheless believed that executions had to be carried out according to the law.[17] Wang for her part stated that abolition of the death penalty meant the protection of right to life, and that therefore its protection needed to be guaranteed immediately, and not some time in the future (Wang 2010). At the same time she called for a legal moratorium.[18] Prime Minister Wu Den-Yih expressed the view – shared by the Minister of Interior Affairs and Chief Police Officer – that Taiwan had to take a position between abolition and execution, and that the decision not to execute

14 Source: Ministry of Justice, Document No 0970800850, 12 March 2008.

15 Source: *Apple Daily*, 23 April 2008.

16 Source: *China Post*, 2 February 2010.

17 Source: *Central News Agency*, 8 March 2010.

18 Source: Ministry of Justice: Press Release (10 March 2010), available at http://www.moj.gov.tw/public/Attachment/03101461527.pdf [accessed 1 April 2010].

was Minister Wang's personal position. The Control Yuan (Ombudsman) finally stated that it would investigate whether not to execute was against the law. Such events showed that Minister Wang was somewhat isolated within the top echelons of government at the time: being stuck without firm support either from above or below, she had no choice but to resign.

On the other hand, she did affirm that the question of whether to proceed with the abolition of the death penalty raised professional and public support issues, and that the formal move to abolish depended on a consensus being reached. Therefore her strategy was to establish a network to win public support, and to introduce measures such as cracking down on criminals and improving prison administration that were designed shorten the transition period toward abolition. She toned down her rhetoric by saying that the policy of gradual abolition of the death penalty, 'had already been set in motion by the Ministry of Justice before she assumed her position',[19] in other words she was following rather than leading. A cynical observer might suggest these words were a political face-saving device since they suggest that any fault in the matter lies with the former government. The Ministry of Justice (MOJ) also emphasized that there was no time schedule for abolition.[20]

During the time Wang was the Minister, she established a 'Group for research and promotion of the policy of gradual abolition of the death penalty', chaired by a deputy Minister of Justice and composed of 27 members, including representatives from governmental agencies, human rights defenders, scholars and lawyers. Its mission is to work out a set of projects to be the basis for abolishing the death penalty, including a moratorium, alternative penalties to replace the death penalty, prison management after abolition, the parole system after abolition, the protection of victims, the strengthening of social security and analyses of the social and economic costs and benefits of the death penalty and of abolition. Their main goals are to promote acceptance of the abolition of the death penalty and to pave the way for it.[21] The Group started to function on 23 March 2010, after Wang resigned. The title, goals and projects of the Group were not amended. It seems that Wang's legacy continues, but it is still too early to judge how much the Group will contribute to the goal of abolition.

After Wang's resignation, Tseng Yung-Fu, a life-time prosecutor, became the Minister of Justice. Naturally he agreed with the President and the Prime Minister that executions should be carried out according to the law. This meant that the political will to stop executions came to an end. Tseng signed execution orders on 30 April 2010, ending the *de facto* moratorium that had been in place since 2006.

19 Source: *China Post*, 2 February 2010.

20 Source: *Ministry of Justice*, Press Release No. 360 (1 February 2010).

21 Source: *Ministry of Justice*, Press Release No. 360 (1 February 2010).

Ratification of the ICCPR

As former President Chen of the DPP emphasized, the acceptance of the International Bill of Rights after May 2000 meant that the Executive Yuan (EY) would ratify the International Covenant on Civil and Political Rights (ICCPR) without reservation, and refer it to the LY as part of the necessary legislative procedure for ratification in April 2001. On 31 December 2002, the LY passed the ratification; at the insistence of some KMT members however, there was a reservation on Article 6 (right to life). The DPP members were dissatisfied and requested a rehearing. Consequently, the ratification procedure was not completed during the DPP's tenure in government.

During the presidential election in 2008, Ma Ying-Jeou also promised to implement the ICCPR in his 'Taiwan human rights declaration for the new century', though he had yet to persuade his KMT colleagues in the LY to approve the ratification without a reservation to Article 6: for this purpose, Ma summoned a meeting concerning ratification of the ICCPR on 11 February 2009. Some scholars, and the then Minister Wang, noted that Article 6 of the ICCPR did not require a contracting state to abolish the death penalty immediately; therefore, there was no need to enter a reservation to this article. Following this Ma decided to proceed with the ratification of the ICCPR without a reservation to Article 6.[22] As the KMT dominated the LY, the ratification was finalized on 31 March 2009 with the passing of the Act to Implement the International Covenant on Civil and Political Rights and the International Covenant on Economic, Social and Cultural Rights, entering into force according to Article 9[23] on 10 December 2009. Article 8 of the legislation states:

> All levels of governmental institutions and agencies should review laws and regulations within their functions according to the two Covenants. All laws and regulations incompatible with the two Covenants should be amended within two years after the Act enters into force by new laws, law amendments, law abolitions and improved administrative measures.

Article 6(2) of the ICCPR requests 'in countries which have not abolished the death penalty, [the] sentence of death may be imposed only for the most serious crimes'. Article 6(6) also requires that a state party should not invoke this article 'to delay or to prevent the abolition of capital punishment'. Hood has argued that the implications for the government of Taiwan, now the treaty was embedded in domestic law, could not be clearer (Hood 2009: 23). The government therefore

22 Source: Records of the Meeting concerning Ratification of the ICCPR and the ICESCR on 11 February 2009, available at http://www.humanrights.moj.gov.tw/public/Data/98209412937.doc (visited on 23 February 2010).

23 Article 9 rules that the date the Act comes into force shall be decided by the Executive Yuan.

should at least, firstly narrow down the ambit of the death penalty to the most serious crimes and, secondly, regard moving towards abolition as not just a policy but a treaty obligation.

However, concerning the first point, the Ministry of Justice proposed that only Article 261 of the Criminal Code and three provisions of the Drug Control Act be amended. The criterion applied was that these crimes do not lead to a deprivation of life,[24] though the NGOs had asked for changes to those provisions of the Drug Control Act which could lead to the death penalty.[25] It should also be noted that there are still 50 crimes that carry a discretionary death penalty under Taiwan's laws,[26] with new ones even being added after 1999.[27]

Although there is a broad range of laws under which the death sentence can be applied, between 1987 and 2000 the death penalty was only imposed for six categories of crime, including rape with homicide, murder, robbery, kidnapping for ransom, drugs, and banditry. After 2000, it was imposed for only four categories of crime (murder, robbery with homicide, rape with homicide and kidnapping for ransom).[28] If it wishes to implement treaty obligations and substantially reduce death sentences, the Ministry of Justice will have not only to narrow down the ambit of the death penalty, but also to review whether capital punishment should be retained for these six crimes. If it takes seriously the criterion of depriving life, the Ministry of Justice will need to impose the death penalty only for crimes of murder, robbery with homicide and rape with homicide. Such an approach would implement the ICCPR and comply with its own gradual abolition policy. Once the death penalty is applied only for these three crimes, the debate over abolition can

---

24 Source: Ministry of Justice, 9 December 2009: *List of examinations by governmental agencies on whether laws and administrative measures comply with the ICCPR*, p. 10.

25 Source: Taiwan Alliance to End the Death Penalty. 29 June 2009. Press Release, Abolishing provisions of the Drug Control Act that impose the death penalty immediately

26 Those include: (1) Criminal Code, Articles 101, 103, 104, 105, 107, 120, 185-1, 185-2, 226-1, 261, 271, 272, 328, 332, 333, 334, 347, 348; (2) The Anti-Sexual Business Provisions for Children and Teenagers, Article 26; (3) Water Act, Article 91; (4) Civil Aviation Law, Articles 100, 101, 110; (5) Punishment Act for Violation to Military Service Systems, Articles 16, 17; (6) Smuggling Punishment Act, Article 4; (7) Drug Control Act, Articles 4, 6, 15; (8) Law on the Punishment of Genocide, Article 2; (9) Act Governing the Control and Prohibition of Gun, Cannons, Ammunition, and Knives, Article 7; (10) Criminal Law of the Armed Forces, Articles 14, 15, 17, 18, 19, 20, 24, 26, 31, 41, 42, 47, 48, 49, 50, 53, 58, 65, 66.

27 In March 1999, new provisions of Articles 185-1 and 185-2 of the Criminal Code were inserted. They set a discretionary death penalty for crimes of hijacking or threatening aviation safety or facilities. In June 2002, Article 4 of the Smuggling Punishment Act was amended to include a discretionary death penalty for smugglers and those causing death or serious injuries.

28 Please see below for further details.

become much more focused. It would arguably constitute a great step towards it and demonstrate real political leadership.

On another point, it is regrettable that the President and justice ministers have not been able to focus on such possible approaches. Although former Minister Wang emphasized the need to protect the right to life, she did not make a connection between the *de facto* moratorium and compliance with the treaty obligation not to delay or prevent the abolition of capital punishment after Taiwan ratified the ICCPR. Currently, Minister of Justice Tseng is of the view that executions do not violate Article 6(6) of the ICCPR, while President Ma has not expressed a view on this point. It is therefore doubtful whether the current Taiwan government takes this provision seriously, since the previous *de facto* moratorium could have been seen as a step toward abolition – in conformity with Article 6 – whereas a return to executions is a backward step that can be seen as delaying or preventing the eventual abolition of the death penalty.

The Parliament

The DPP expressed its aim to 'respect life and search for ways to abolish the death penalty' in its plan of action, former DPP President Chen's human rights policy included the 'gradual abolition of the death penalty', and no DPP member of the LY expressed support for the death penalty.

While the current KMT government continues the policy of 'gradual' abolition of the death penalty, this attitude can be attributed to the insistence of former Minister of Justice Wang and it is not clear if this stills holds at the KMT in the LY. The KMT has always held the majority in – and thus dominated – the LY. One example of the KMT parliamentarians' attitude toward the death penalty was their refusal to allow capital punishment to be replaced by life imprisonment as part of the general pardon brought in to commemorate the twentieth anniversary of the lifting of the martial law order covering crimes committed before 24 April 2007. Article 1 of the Law Reducing Sentences 2007 provided that life imprisonment would replace capital punishment: in fact, the legislation had so many exceptions that sentences for serious crimes did not qualify.[29] As a result, none of the 24 death-row inmates at that time had their sentences transmuted.

In December 2002 the KMT members of the LY also decided to enter reservations on Article 6 of the ICCPR because of their concern that the provision might involve the abolition of the death penalty. At that time the DPP held executive power: when the KMT gained control of the executive in 2008, the KMT members in the LY agreed not to force the issue of reservations on Article 6 of the ICCPR, thus complying with the initiatives of President Ma (and Chairperson of the KMT). It seemed that the KMT members of the LY were willing to follow President Ma: presumably, they would also have done so if he had adopted a firm

29 Source: Articles 2 and 3 of the Law Reducing Sentences 2007.

position on the abolition of the death penalty. However, as mentioned above, Ma has not done so.

It is noticeable that all support for the death penalty in parliament came from KMT members. For example, Wu Ching-Chih and Lii Ming-Shing, both KMT members, expressed strong opposition to abolishing the death penalty and stated that if the Ministry of Justice were to propose a bill for its abolition, they would vote against it.[30] Another KMT member, Chiu Ie, once proposed draft legislation to impose the death penalty on those who killed their lineal relatives; this proposal was endorsed by several members of the KMT.[31] Wu Yu-Sheng, also a KMT member, questioned the then Minister of Justice saying that the lack of executions for four years had resulted in 'good people wronged and bad people laughing'.[32] Wu then asked the Minister to resume executions or to resign. Minister Wang thus faced tremendous pressure, not only from her colleagues in the executive branch, but also from the legislative branch and the public. Of course, not all KMT members supported the death penalty or asked the Minister to proceed with executions. For example one KMT member in the LY, Hsieh Kuo-Liang, was of the view that 'it would be a massacre if we were to execute all death-row inmates'.[33] In this regard, it should be pointed out that there has been no comprehensive survey of the views of all members of the LY.

It is however clear that KMT members of the LY do not always blindly follow President Ma's policies. One example was the issue of allowing US beef, beef on the bone, and beef mince to be imported into Taiwan. The KMT administration had signed an agreement with the US government to allow all three categories to be imported. Due to public pressure, the KMT members of the LY decided to amend domestic law to prohibit beef mince from being imported. Although domestic law prohibited only one category, this event was regarded as a political storm for President Ma.

Could this also happen with respect to the issue of the abolition of the death penalty? In the case of the 'US beef event', public opinion was the key factor inclining the KMT members of the LY to turn away from President Ma. It seems that, for the KMT members of the LY, two factors can be decisive: how firmly the President supports abolition and how strongly the public supports the death penalty. Since President Ma has not publicly taken a firm political stance in favour of abolishing the death penalty, and as polls indicate that the public support the death penalty, there is in fact no disagreement as far as the positions of the President, the public and the KMT members of the LY are concerned. Therefore, it is unlikely that the KMT members of the LY would adopt a different position from the President and support the abolition of the death penalty.

---

30 Source: *Central News Agency*, 10 December 2009.

31 Source: *United Daily News*, 22 April 2009.

32 Source: *United Daily News*, 24 February 2010, page A 9.

33 Source: *United Daily News*, 11 March 2010.

The Judicial Branch

The judiciary can play a decisive role when a state is moving towards the abolition of the death penalty, but this was not case in Taiwan, even when the administrative branch tried to move in this direction. The first example of this 'resistance' can be seen in the view of the Council of Grand Justices (CGJ, Constitutional Court) in relation to the death penalty. The CGJ has undoubtedly played a crucial role in facilitating political transitions and constitutional reforms, most notably as a guardian of human rights with special emphasis on the rule of law. However, the CGJ, in Interpretations Nos. 194, 263 476, has consistently ruled that the death penalty is constitutionally permissible, whether before or after Taiwan's democratization, and has thus endorsed capital punishment – even the mandatory death penalty – as constitutional. Further, in December 2006 the CGJ declared inadmissible an application which argued that the death penalty violated the right of equality and the right to life as guaranteed by the Constitution. The CGJ asserted that no further explanation was warranted given Interpretations Nos 194, 263 and 476. Following this, a number of death-row inmates brought another application to the CGJ in 2009, arguing that provisions of the Criminal Procedure Law breached the Constitution and the ICCPR: again, in May 2010, the CGJ deemed the application inadmissible.[34] While the CGJ has been a guardian of human rights for several decades, it is not taking the lead as far as the abolition of the death penalty is concerned.

A second example in this regard is the JY's attitude to the policy of abolition of the death penalty. In a meeting with NGOs against the death penalty,[35] the President of the JY, Lai In-jaw, welcomed Taiwan's move towards abolition. Despite also being chairperson of the CGJ, he did not address the issue of whether the death penalty complied with the constitution, but merely indicated that the Ministry of Justice should make every effort to facilitate abolition, emphasizing that judges must rule on that basis of existing laws.[36] It seemed no movement for abolition would come from the JY, and that the issue would be sent back to the Ministry of Justice.

A final example is JY's position on amending provisions of the Criminal Procedure Law. Under the DPP government, former Minister of Justice Shi wished to amend this legislation in order to require compulsory legal representation, oral debate and unanimous consent among judges in cases involving the death sentence at the Supreme Court. The proposed bill was however rejected by the JY. In April 2010, President Ma advanced ideas similar to those of Shih, though he also indicated that these were possibilities designed to reduce rather than abolish

34 Source: Records of the 1358th meeting of the CGJ.

35 They included World Coalition against Death Penalty, Anti-Death Penalty Asian Network and Amnesty International.

36 Source: *Central News Agency*, 18 June 2008.

death sentences, and hence not a radical departure from established policies.[37] The Ministry of Justice however responded at once, indicating it would draft a bill based on these proposals for the JY's consideration. It may be that this initiative had actually originated in the Ministry of Justice several years ago.

Indictment, Judgment, Execution and Amnesty

Under Taiwan's criminal procedure, the criminal process begins with indictments from criminal prosecutors with criminal cases then proceeding to court for judgment. After a death sentence is confirmed, if there is no amnesty, it goes back to the Ministry of Justice for a confirmation of execution. Details of indictment, judgment, execution and amnesty – and of death-row inmates themselves – are examined in this section.

Indictments

Table 8.1 shows the annual number of indictments by prosecutors asking for capital punishment, and the number of final judgments imposing the death penalty and executions in Taiwan between 2000 and 2009.

Table 8.1 Indictments, judgments and executions 2000–2009

	Indictments (Source: Ministry of Justice)	Final Judgments (Source: Yearbooks of the Supreme Court)	Executions (Source: Yearbooks of the Ministry of Justice)
2000	94	22	18
2001	103	11	10
2002	103	7	9
2003	107	6	7
2004	116	7	4
2005	86	8	1
2006	57	11	0
2007	59	5	0
2008	35	3	0
2009	24	13	0

Although a policy of gradual abolition was adopted in 2001, the actual number of indictments by prosecutors asking for capital punishment did not go down

37 Source: *United Daily News*, 7 April 2010.

until 2005. It is possible that it was only after the DPP won a second term in the presidential election of 2004 and started to propose specific amendments replacing compulsory capital punishment with discretionary capital punishment that prosecutors realized the movement towards abolition was seriously being adopted as government policy. Further, as noted above, in 2008 the Minister of Justice requested that prosecutors should not seek the death sentence, and his successors have done likewise. Although not a compulsory request, in practice prosecutors have increasingly avoided asking for capital punishment.

Judgments

Table 8.1 also shows that the number of judgments imposing the death penalty did not steadily decrease, but fluctuated up and down after 2000. Three observations can be offered to explain this phenomenon. First, the number of judgments imposing the death penalty was far fewer than the indictments seeking it. This may be due to concerns for the rule of law and protection of human rights, and the numerous amendments (20 times between 1990 and 2009) to the Criminal Procedure Law. These many changes offered more protection to suspects and accused people, and imposed more responsibilities on prosecutors and stricter rules of evidence on judges. This led to a decrease in the success rates of prosecutors, and in some cases, rejection by judges of the prosecutor's request for the death sentence, even though an accused's guilt was established. Second, the gradual movement towards abolition, and the policy of not proceeding to an execution could have had a psychological effect on judges. Some judges have even said that, since the Minister of Justice did not wish to proceed with executions, there was no point in them imposing the death sentence.[38] Third, some judges assumed they had little option but to decide cases in accordance with current legislation, since the death sentence was still available as a penalty for serious crimes. These factors can explain why the number of judgments imposing the death penalty has gone up and down over the years.

Execution

According to Article 460 of the Criminal Procedure Law, the Minister of Justice receives the file once a death sentence becomes final. Article 461 then stipulates that the execution should be carried out within three days after the Minister of Justice authorizes it. However, if the prosecutor in charge of the file finds there is any reason for retrial or special appeal, he or she may ask the Minister of Justice to review it. While some members of the LY, and some in the media have argued that the Minister of Justice did not have any discretionary power in this regard,

38 Source: *United Daily News*, 9 March 2010.

the legislation clearly requires that both the prosecutor and the Minister of Justice proceed carefully when deciding whether to proceed with an execution. It requires the Minister of Justice and prosecutors to identify a valid reason for retrial or special appeal.

The Minister of Justice did not have any detailed rules on determining whether to grant permission for an execution until 1999 when Guidelines for Reviewing Death Sentence Execution ('Guidelines') were adopted. As Table 8.1 shows, the number of executions dropped steadily after 2000, and it seems one of the main reasons for this was the Guidelines themselves which set out a careful procedure that excludes executions if there is any opportunity for special appeal or retrial, or if there is any doubt regarding their reasonableness.

According to the Guidelines, the Supreme Court Prosecution Office should not submit a case imposing the death penalty to the Minister of Justice if the defendant or his/her relatives have applied for special appeal, retrial or constitutional interpretation to the CGJ, or if the defendant or his/her attorney has not had the final judgment for more than ten days. This rule has become an important legal platform for the Ministers of Justice to continue their support for not proceeding with an execution. While only individuals can raise the ground of constitutional interpretation, prosecutors may apply for retrial and the Attorney General may apply for special appeal. The Minister of Justice can therefore grant special appeals or retrials in most cases imposing death sentence. The reason offered by the two Ministers of Justice for the end of executions in Taiwan after 2006 was that, since all death row inmates had applied for retrial, special appeal or constitutional interpretation, the Guidelines precluded the signing of execution orders.

Several remarks need to be made about these grounds. First, the Criminal Procedure Law does not actually provide for constitutional interpretation by the CGJ: it was subsequently added by the Minister of Justice and could be legally challenged. However, this specific ground can have far-reaching effects: special appeals and retrials only concern individual cases, whereas constitutional interpretation can affect all death-row inmates. Where several inmates have submitted applications, no inmate should be executed before the CGJ delivers its final interpretation. If the Minister of Justice does not accept this argument, executions can resume, as only some of the inmates have applied for constitutional interpretation. Justice Ministers have had different views on this point. Former Minister Wang took this point seriously, saying that before the CGJ decided on issues of constitutional interpretation, she would not sign any execution order. Currently, Justice Minister Tseng is of the view that each application should be considered on its merits: the execution of those who have not applied would not be affected. These different possible interpretations create a degree of uncertainty, and a rejection of the constitutional validity claim can lead to an even worse situation for those making it, since they lose their right to apply for special appeal and retrial, and so could be executed.

Second, not all death-row inmates apply for retrial, special appeal or constitutional interpretation, and this leads to calls for their execution by some in the media or members of the LY. This resulted in the execution of four inmates who did not apply for constitutional interpretation in April 2010, thus ending Taiwan's *de facto* moratorium.

Third, Article 6(4) of the ICCPR reads 'Anyone sentenced to death shall have the right to seek pardon or commutation of the sentence'. The Guidelines, however, have not been updated to include such a possibility after Taiwan ratified the ICCPR. Indeed, several death-row inmates have applied to President Ma for amnesty, so far to no avail. Because the Guidelines do not include this possibility, no Minister of Justice ever has taken this as a ground for not signing an execution order.

Fourth, the Guidelines are still a set of procedural regulations drafted by the Ministry of Justice, and are not enshrined in law. They can therefore be amended at any time on an *ad hoc* basis according to the whims of the Minster of Justice. After Minister Wang's resignation, KMT members of the LY even required the new Minister to promise to proceed with executions.

Fifth, a prosecutor or a Minister of Justice who violates the Guidelines is not legally liable, since only an internal regulation has been breached. It would therefore be better, from a legal point of view, to make the Guidelines part of the Criminal Procedure Law. One difficulty with this is the KMT's majority in the LY. It is doubtful that, when an opportunity arises to amend the legislation, they would adopt stricter procedures for executions.

Amnesty

Once a death sentence is confirmed, only the executive branch of government can release the person from death-row by exercising the power of amnesty, including general pardons and general or individual amnesty. While sentence reductions must be mandated by legislation, Article 40 of the Constitution empowers the President to grant amnesty individually or generally without the need for specific legislation.

After 1987, there were three general pardons in 1988, 1991 and 2007 when the death penalty was reduced to life imprisonment.[39] The 1988 pardon was to honour the death of late President Chiang Ching-Kuo, the 1991 one was to commemorate the eightieth anniversary of the foundation of the Republic of China, and the 2007 pardon was to commemorate the twentieth anniversary of the lifting of martial law. There were 26 and 38 persons, respectively, in 1988 and 1991 whose death sentences were reduced to life imprisonment.[40] There was no death-row inmate who qualified for a reduced sentence in 2007.

39 Source: Article 2 of the Law Reducing Sentences 1988, Article 2 of the Law Reducing Sentences 1991 and Article 1 of the Law Reducing Sentences 2007.

40 Source: Ministry of Justice, 2004, *The Situation of Implementing the Law of Reducing Sentence*, available at http://www.moj.gov.tw/public/Attachment/512231059235.pdf.

As to individual amnesty, in 2009 the Taiwan Alliance to End the Death Penalty (TAEDP),[41] representing all 41 people then on death-row, applied to President Ma for amnesty. Despite the right to seek pardon or a commutation of the death penalty enshrined in Article 6(4) of the ICCPR, no Taiwanese law guarantees that a death-row inmate may seek either. After Taiwan's ratification of the ICCPR in 2009, the TAEDP argued the need for legislation to guarantee this right. There is still no such legislative proposal.

It should be noted that between 1986 and 2008, none of the three persons who served as President of Taiwan, Chiang Ching-kuo, Lee Teng-Hui and Chen Shui-Bian, ever granted amnesty to an individual on death-row. Even former President Chen, who adopted a policy of 'state-building on human rights' which included the 'gradual abolition of the death penalty', did not do so. So far, there is no sign that President Ma will grant amnesty to any death-row inmate.

Death Row Inmates

Although a broad range of Taiwan legislation provide for death sentences, in the past 25 years the death penalty has been imposed for only six categories of crimes: rape with homicide, murder, robbery, kidnapping for ransom, drug dealing and banditry (Liao 2008: 159) (Table 8.2). By March 2010 there were 44 death-row inmates who were sentenced for only four categories of crimes.

Table 8.2 Death row inmates and their crimes[42]

Crime year[43]	Murder	Robbery	Rape with homicide	Kidnapping for ransom	Total
2000	0	0	0	2	2
2003	1	0	0	0	1
2004	0	2	0	0	2
2005	3	1	4	0	8
2006	5	5	0	0	10
2007	2	1	2	0	5
2008	1	0	1	1	3
2009	5	4	3	1	13
Total	17	13	10	4	44

41 It was established in September 2003 by human rights-related NGOs.

42 This table shows information about 44 inmates up to March 2010. After the execution of four in April 2010 there are currently 40 inmates.

43 Year final judgment decided. Sources: TAEDP and Yearbooks of the Supreme Court.

The TAEDP conducted a survey of the 44 inmates on death-row in March 2010 and received 38 replies. All were men; 68 per cent of those who replied had education below junior high school and only 9 per cent had college-level education. When committing their crimes, 78 per cent were blue-collar workers and 6 per cent were unemployed. Thirty per cent committed their crimes when they were under 30 years of age: 32 per cent were in their 30s, 35 per cent in their 40s, and 3 per cent in their 50s or older.[44] These figures suggest that, when committing crimes, the inmates tended to be young, blue-collar men with low levels of education.

By the end of 2006, when Taiwan had had no executions for a year, there were 23 death-row inmates. The number was to grow to 44 by March 2010, leading to calls from the public, victims and their relatives and members of the LY and the media for executions to resume, which they did in April 2010.

Conclusion

When Taiwan had in place a *de facto* moratorium on executions between January 2006 and March 2010, one might have expected it would proceed to a *de jure* moratorium or even the abolition of the death sentence. Obviously, any move toward these two goals needs to have the cessation of executions as a starting point. This also requires political and judicial leadership to move the process forward so that the abolition of capital punishment becomes accepted as a human rights issue (Hood 2009: 11). Sadly, such dedicated political and judicial leadership seems to be lacking in Taiwan.

When it formed the government, the DPP adopted the cessation of executions as a halfway measure towards the final goal of abolition. It took an effort of political will for the DPP government to maintain this approach. After May 2008, the gradual abolition policy was followed by the KMT administration, though this was largely due to former Justice Minister Wang herself, rather than to any consensus among leaders in the KMT government and the LY. President Ma did not have a firm policy on abandoning executions. KMT members in the LY forced Minister Wang's resignation and asked for the resumption of executions. The CGJ, in terms of the judicial branch, endorsed the death penalty. Though the overall numbers of judgments resulting in the death sentence have diminished, the trend remains uncertain since 2009 saw an increase.

Under these circumstances, there are no firm barriers to executions, in the absence of political will and judicial leadership. The situation could even become worse in the near future: the presence of 40 inmates on death-row means that the resumption of executions could give rise to numerous killings in the next few years. With a number of new cases each year where the death sentence has been imposed, executions are likely to become regular rather than episodic. The path to abolition will still be long.

44 The author got this data from the TAEDP's unpublished file.

References

Bae, S. 2008. The Abolitionist Movement in Death Penalty-Friendly Asia: The Cases of South Korea and Taiwan, in *Against the Death Penalty International Initiatives and Implications*, edited by J. Yorke. Burlington: Ashgate.

Chen, Shui-Bian. 2000. Inaugural speech: *Taiwan Stands Up: Towards the Dawn of a Rising Era* (20 May 2000).

Chiu, Hei-Yuan. 2006. *Deterrence, Dignity, and the Death Penalty – Analyzing Taiwanese Attitudes toward the Abolition of Death Penalty.* Paper presented to the Taiwan Alliance to End the Death Penalty, 4 October 2006.

Hood, R. 2009. *Abolition of the Death Penalty: Progress and Prospects Towards World-wide Abolition.* Paper presented to the Taiwan Alliance to End the Death Penalty, Taipei, 16 November 2009.

Hood, R. and Hoyle, C. 2009. *The Death Penalty. A Worldwide Perspective* (4th edn.). Oxford: Oxford University Press.

Johnson, D.T. and Zimring, F.E. 2009. *The Next Frontier National Development, Political Change, and the Death Penalty in Asia.* Oxford: Oxford University Press.

Liao, F.F-T. 2008. From seventy-eight to zero: Why executions declined after Taiwan's democratization. *Punishment & Society*, 10(2): 153–70.

Rice, T.H.S. 2010. Letter to President Ma following the resignation of his justice minister over Taiwan's moratorium on executions. *World Coalition Against the Death Penalty.*

Wang, C-F. 2010. *Rationality and Forgiveness – Calling for Moratorium.* Statement by the Minister of Justice, 9 March 2010.

Chapter 9
The Norms of Death: On Attitudes to Capital Punishment in China

Børge Bakken

Over the last two to three decades the world has seen a virtual revolution in the way in which the death penalty is practised and perceived. In 1977, only 16 countries had abolished the death penalty for all crimes.[1] By the end of 1988 35 countries had eliminated the death penalty altogether (Hood 2009: 1–21). Today more than two-thirds of the countries in the world have abolished the death penalty in law or practice, and among the 58 remaining death-penalty countries, only 18 were known to have carried out executions in 2009.[2] Although the Chinese death penalty numbers are still regarded as 'state secrets', there is no doubt that China alone executes many more individuals than the rest of the world combined. Unofficial Chinese reports counted an average of 15,000 executions per year between 1997 and 2001 (Chen 2006: 13), and an estimated 5,000 executions in 2009, still more than all other countries combined.[3]

In terms of public opinion, there has been a worldwide revolution over the last ten to 20 years. When President Mitterand stood for election in France in 1981 on a manifesto that included abolition of the death penalty, 63 per cent of the population supported its use. Today the figure stands at 45 per cent, with only 14 per cent who 'strongly favour' the death penalty in France, and 31 per cent who are 'somewhat in favour'.[4] The European Union was declared 'death penalty free' in 1998, and the practice is now banned within its borders (Council of the European Union 2006). Only the United Kingdom, with a 50 per cent support rate, defies the trend in Western Europe. It is the only country without a majority of public opinion against the death penalty. In Australia, opinion has swung even more dramatically, from 53 per cent support of capital punishment in 1995, to a mere 23 per cent support in 2009.[5] By contrast, a large death penalty survey done

1 Source: Figures on the Death Penalty. Available at: http://www.amnesty.org/en/death-penalty/abolitionist-and-retentionist-countries [accessed 11.11.2010].

2 Source: Death Penalty Numbers. Available at: http://www.amnesty.org/en/death-penalty/numbers [accessed 11.11.2010].

3 Source: *Dialogue*, 2010(41), 1–6.

4 Source: http://www.ipsos-mori.com/researchpublications/researcharchive/poll.aspx?oItemId=163, Sample from 26.04.2007 [accessed 11.03.2010].

5 Source: http://www.roymorgan.com/news/polls/2009/4411/ [accessed 25.10.2010].

by the Chinese Academy of Social Sciences 15 years ago, in 1995, showed that 99 per cent of the Chinese population supported the death penalty, the highest rate of support in the world.

When we focus on the majority trend in the world today, the recent rapid change in attitudes runs counter to assumptions formerly taken for granted regarding punitive norms in general. Until recently it was argued that people's attitudes towards punishment represent a core element of culture and that people's punitive attitudes are an important cultural point of reference. An explanation often found in textbooks was that, 'we learn to react punitively … just as we learn to speak a language' (Sutherland et al. 1992: 328). In other words, punitive norms are strong markers of culture and stick to us in much the same way as our language does. In what follows I argue that punitive norms fluctuate much more readily and are much less culturally rooted than the learning of a native language.

The Chinese government and many Chinese intellectuals share the assumption that Chinese attitudes towards the death penalty have deep cultural roots. China's Premier Wen Jiabao has claimed that China would not abolish the death penalty due to 'consideration of China's national conditions'.[6] In a recent anthology on the uses of the death penalty in China, Professor Gao Mingxuan argues similarly that execution is based in what he sees as a Chinese retributive culture. Gao goes on to argue that the consequences of such deeply rooted punitive preferences is that 'China will not abolish the death penalty at present or in the near future' (Gao 2004: 15–20, 23–30 (19, 21)). Again and again, in Chinese journals and books we hear the argument that China has a '5000-year-old tradition of the death penalty', and that this accounts for why China still adheres to the practice. One may ask, is there any country that doesn't look back on a heritage of thousands of years of 'death penalty traditions'?

Of course there is a tradition of retributive 'penal populism', in China as elsewhere, where people believe in the alleged effectiveness of harsh punishment (Pratt 2007, Roberts et al. 2003). And yes, there are popular traditions of revenge in China (Madsen 1990: 175–98). Of course, there are always cultural links to violence, as in the occasional uprisings in history by poor peasants seeking vengeance for harm visited upon them. Elizabeth Perry has noted that certain policies of the state under Mao Zedong contributed to the survival and strengthening of traditional patterns of violent activity (Perry 1985: 414–40). The early Communist Party had seen the death penalty as a cruel practice, and on 15 June 1922 formally suggested that the death penalty should be abandoned (Zhao 2004: 11–14, 18–22 (11, 18)). But Mao saw the notion of people's revenge as a political tool. He declared that the death penalty – although it should be 'used with caution' – must be effectively utilized against 'the worst local tyrants and evil gentry' in order to strengthen the

6 Source: Wen Jiabao, http://english.peopledaily.com.cn/200503/14eng20050314176777.html, People's Daily Online, 14.03.2005 [accessed 03.12.2007].

class-consciousness of the masses.[7] Mao advocated that the people should have the right to take revenge against their exploiters. He refuted the argument that peasants had 'gone too far', and supported the killing of landlords, claiming 'it is necessary to create terror for a while in every rural area' to be able to fight the rule of the landlords.[8] Mao saw execution as justified on the grounds of retribution to 'assuage the people's anger' (Mao 1951/1977: 53, 56). The Maoist argument about appeasing the people's anger seems to have developed into a basic legal principle that still persists, legitimizing state violence and capital punishment.

In a survey of legal personnel in China conducted in 2007, 90 per cent of the respondents answered that the principle of *minfen* (vengeance) continued to play a role in the use of the death penalty. Only two per cent thought the aspect of 'people's anger' had no impact at all (Kang 2005: 116). The paradox here is that a society that claims to work to create a 'harmonious society' (*hexie shuhui* 和谐社会) is based on such basic principles of revenge.

Chinese scholars have picked up on this paradox. Professor Lu Jianping opposes the practice of killing in the name of popular opinion and indignation. It is clear, says Lu with characteristic understatement, that 'killing is not the best way to make people live a better life'. Well aware of the practices of (now fading) public executions and public sentencing rallies (*shenpan dahui* 审判大会), Lu addresses the dark sides of collective behaviour, noting that '(people's) rationality could be reduced in a public event', and that in some cases, a 'square effect' (*guangchang xiaoying* 广场效应) – or maybe better and less directly translated – a 'crowd effect' may occur, and people may just become bewitched and follow the lead of others; a fact that can be very well demonstrated by the excesses of the Cultural Revolution' (Lu 2009: 66–79 (76)).

Let us go back to Professor Chen Xingliang's argument about revenge. Although he supports a limited use of the death penalty, he argues against the principle of *minfen* or people's anger. He basically maintains that the anti-crime 'hard strike' (*yanda* 严打) campaigns that started in 1983 brutalized the justice system because 'we believed too much in the deterrence of punishment, and because the emphasis was put on the masses' feelings of retribution' (Chen 2005: 75 (71–85)). These feelings of retribution, or the masses' 'revenge psychology' (*baoying xinli* 报应心理) has had the unfortunate effect, according to Chen, of increasing resentment and hatred (*yuanhen* 怨恨) among victims' families, and potentially vast numbers of people in society. He continues: 'We abused the death penalty, and we accumulated hatred and grievances in society (*shehui jiyuan* 社会积怨)' (Chen 2005). The point about accumulated social hatred is very important. The basic argument he uses, and which he could have made more use of, since it concerns the death penalty as such, and not just the

7 Source: Mao Zedong, 'Report on an investigation of the peasant movement in Hunan': 38.

8 Source: Mao Zedong, 'Report on an investigation of the peasant movement in Hunan': 29.

extent to which it is used, is that the death penalty sends an example of revenge that is disruptive to the very argument and management of a 'harmonious society'. Chen touches on the very important theme of the *escalating character* of revenge-based principles and hatred. Lu's and Chen's warnings are well founded. It has been pointed out by scholars in the field of revenge and retribution that revenge seems always to tend towards excess and 'escalating cycles of violence', where we are 'likely to lose control' rather than stay in control; that the appetite for blood is hard to stop when such principles are set in motion (Govier 2007: 8–9). Without going into such detail here, we have seen clear examples of *minfen* targeting the government in China lately (Yu 2009). Lu's 'square effect' or 'crowd effect' escalating violence is supported by the general literature on revenge. While Lu emphasizes that public opinion is not always reactionary, but can be 'advanced' as well (Lu 2009: 78), Chen Xingliang adds to his 'revenge psychology' argument that the value of human life is not high in China, and that this is a main argument for thinking that the time has not yet come to abolish the death penalty in China (Chen 2003). Qiu Xinglong, the best informed abolitionist in Chinese legal circles, opposes this argument. Agreeing that the value of life has always been low in China, due to a lack of a strong 'humanitarian concern' (*renwen guanhuai* 人文关怀), he turns the argument against the elites when he goes on to say that this is mainly due to a general and persistent lack of respect for human life among Chinese scholars (*xuezhe* 学者) and the elite as such (Qiu 2002: 54 (51–4)). He further claims that his colleagues lack academic independence and professional integrity. If the scholarly community clings to the dogma that the death penalty might be abolished sometime in the future, but is needed for the current socio-political conditions, as claimed by Chen, then the death penalty will never be abolished (Qiu 2001: 13). We will come back to Lu and Qiu's arguments with concrete survey evidence later. Yuan Bin is right when he sees public opinion as extremely changeable and unstable, 'manageable or malleable' (*keyi yindao de* 可以引导的) (Bin 2009: 99–112).

Despite Chen Xingliang's keen observation of the principles of the escalating violent character of revenge, one has to question his very premise of Chinese death penalty core culture based on an all-embracing popular 'revenge psychology'. In particular we have to address this question when it is being used to legitimize the continued use of the death penalty in China.

Is there in China a strong popular tradition of people's revenge by means of executions? Professor Qu Xuewu at the Chinese Academy of Social Sciences in Beijing doubts the cultural argument of a '5000-year-long tradition' (Qu 2005: 6 (6–26)). Qu coins the term Chinese 'multi-culture' (文化的多元性 *wenhua de duoyuan xing*) of alternatives to death penalty practices. He notes that Chinese popular culture was not guided exclusively by the principles of 'a life for a life' (*sharen changming* 杀人偿 命) or 'blood debt' (*xiezhai* 血债).

For example, some Chinese national minorities instead of practising 'blood debt' had the principle of 'life debt' (命债 *mingzhai*), through the practice of monetary 'life compensation', so-called *peimingjia* (赔命价), where the murderer had to compensate the family for the killing of their family member (Qu 2005: 7). The issue was solved without killing the perpetrator. We know of such practices in many pre-industrial societies, not just in China. J.A. Barnes claims that: 'the ethnographic evidence shows that, in general, primitive societies are not characterized by repressive laws' and that '*it is governmental action that is typically repressive*' (Barnes 1966: 168–9). The cultural explanation of 'people's revenge' is secondary, the governmental practices of the dynastic, bureaucratic machine have been primary. The death penalty has always been primarily political, not cultural. Now a culture of popular violence has become a *pretext* enabling the state to explain and justify the use of the death penalty.

What about Imperial Chinese history? When we look at the practices of the imperial state, there is no reason to believe that they were more punitive than those in other parts of the world. Historically, China was influenced by the brutal legal elite philosophy of the ancient Legalist school (*fajia* 法家), but this was tempered by the approach of the Confucian school (*rujia* 儒家). The Legalists forcefully advocated harsh punishment without mercy, whereas Confucian scholars emphasized virtue (*de* 德), benevolence (*ren* 仁) and mercy (*renci* 仁慈). No doubt the Legalist paradigm has left a lasting legacy of a brutalizing state, but on the whole we cannot see that Chinese history has been more brutal than, let us say, European history. We should approach with caution the concept of 'the West' here. In terms of punitive practices and attitudes, Europe and America are strikingly different. James Whitman has argued that these differences between Europe and America are due to fundamentally different traditions in legal institutions and thinking (Whitman 2003).

In short, the state's need for control helps to explain the use of capital punishment, but the state can also show mercy, and that tradition was as strong, or stronger, in China than it was in Europe, where the concept of mercy also played a role.

The presence of systems of mercy, argues James Whitman, made Europe less punitive than America (Whitman 2003). Mercy instead of revenge comes *de haut en bas* – from on high to those below. In some fundamental way, it seems, one has to have the social distinction of high and low to be able to grant mercy to subordinates. Mercy is first and foremost a matter of power, and paradoxically only power seems to be able to grant mercy. Only a strong state could show that mercy. Through the French Revolution the more lenient punishment used for the upper classes was granted to the common man. One of the lasting effects of the revolution was, in other words, a more lenient punishment regime. In America egalitarianism came in another form, in a form we may call 'violent egalitarianism'. Here, it seems, what was granted to the common man was that a lord should be treated in the same way as a horse thief – they were both hanged without mercy. Europe became and stayed far less punitive than America.

Is the lack of legal mercy the reason why China developed such a strong culture of revenge and harshness? China did have a strong state, and status hierarchies like those Whitman described in the case of Germany and France. Did China not develop the institutions of mercy necessary to follow the historical trend of mildness in punishment? The answer is that China historically possessed all the ingredients expected to promote leniency and a milder system of justice. The same status hierarchies were found there as in Europe, lenient punishment for the elite was developed through the *bayi* (八议) system (Jiang 1992: 4), and a system of legal mercy based on an established status-hierarchy was more developed in China than in any other part of the world. Feudal rule was of course always harsh, but China displayed more mercy than Europe. General amnesties and acts of grace or mercy were granted more frequently in China than anywhere else. Brian McKnight has translated the Chinese expression *she* (赦) as 'acts of grace' or 'amnesty' (McKnight 1981: xi). The most extensive forms of mercy were called *dashe* (大赦), 'great acts of grace'. These general amnesties applied to the whole empire and were conducted with much ritual pomp and circumstance. While ordinary amnesties merely reduced penalties, the great acts of mercy forgave the offenders entirely. Here it will be enough to point to the existence of an extremely strong Chinese culture of mercy to argue for a legal history favouring milder punishment rather than harsher sanctions. From the founding of the Jin dynasty in 280 AD to the fall of the Tang dynasty in 907, a great act of mercy was issued on average once every 18 months. The remarkable system of legal mercy reached its peak during the Song dynasty (960–1279). Executions were reduced extensively by it. Even during the last and brutal Qing dynasty executions were often suspended, and the system of legal mercy did not disappear before the empire disappeared in 1911. This is not to say that the imperial order was not extremely harsh, but all the ingredients for a more lenient system existed in China even more than in Europe. China is one of the few civilizations (which include India and Japan) where the death penalty was abolished in feudal times. From 747–759 AD the Tang dynasty abolished the practice because the Legalists' forceful advocacy of harsh punishment without mercy went against the emperor's strong regard for human life (Benn 2002: 209–12). During other dynasties there were decades where no execution was carried out. Klaus Mühlhahn sums up the essence of penal history in imperial China: '(E)xecutions in late imperial China were no match for the ferocious events staged in eighteenth-century Europe'. He concludes that the punishments carried out in imperial China were largely reversible and relatively bloodless, marked by the intention to carefully refine and graduate the use of state violence (Mühlhahn 2009: 40, 54).

Public Opinion Surveys and the Modern Reality of Rapid Change

The idea of an age-old unchangeable revenge culture does not fit the picture of rapid change now occurring in China and the rest of the world. Let us go back to where we started, to the massive change in capital punishment practices and opinions throughout the world over the last few decades. The change in global attitudes to the death penalty and associated policies is one of the most rapid and unlikely norm reversals of our time. The picture is complex, but the most noticeable change has been what is termed the 'innocence frame'. The fact that innocent people had been convicted and executed, the discovery of forensics, the use of DNA evidence; all of this diverted attention away from theoretical and philosophical issues of morality to focus instead on the possibility of errors in the criminal justice system. A 'tipping point' has been reached in the death penalty debate where changes in public opinion has led to further changes in policy, which in turn reinforce those same changes in public opinion (Baumgartner et al. 2008: 10).

In sociology, scholars like Mark Granovetter have explained how norms can change suddenly and in spectacular fashion. Granovetter talks about 'threshold models of collective behaviour', and explains how a critical number of opinion holders can suddenly challenge a 'mainstream' opinion (Granovetter 1978: 1420–43). The informed journalist Malcolm Gladwell explains the potential rapidity of normative change by the use of the term 'tipping point', 'threshold', or 'boiling point' where rapid normative change occurs (Gladwell 2000). Such processes have proved to be self-reinforcing. Policies and practices that have been stable for decades, reinforced by an established way of viewing a problem, can change suddenly and dramatically when new dimensions arise. The mainstream anti-smoking norm burst into what public opinion research calls a 'social cascade' of norm change. Studies on social cascades have recently focused on how information disseminates through social links in online social networks (Ball 2004, Barbasi et al. 2003, Cha et al. 2003 and Watts 2003).

The Internet in China has created a 'blogosphere' of great importance for the spread of information and rapid opinion change. The point to be emphasized here is that sociology contradicts the Chinese allegation of slow cultural change in a range of areas. Penal norms in general and death penalty norms in particular are not necessarily core cultural norms, learnt like a language, and hard to change. The death penalty norm has changed dramatically world-wide in only a decade or so. We have to look at how the death penalty debate is being publicly framed. What is new is what has been called the 'innocence frame'. An 'innocence movement' developed in Europe and America among academics and activists in the late 1980s and has exploded into the main frame of death penalty debates today (Bedeau and Radelet 1987: 21–179). The former 'deterrence frame' has been severely weakened. Gone are the days of 1975 when Isaac Ehrlich, an economics professor, went to congress with 'evidence' that one execution could save at least eight future victims (Ehrlich 1975: 397–417). Such arguments are now thoroughly dead and buried, and the methodology used by Ehrlich has since been condemned as flawed and unscientific by the mainstream scholarly community.[9] Instead, the

9 The controversy over Ehrlich's work was so important that the National Research Council convened a blue ribbon panel of experts to review it. The panel decided that the problem was not just with Ehrlich's model, but with the idea of using econometric methods to resolve controversies over criminal justice policies. See a short presentation of the debate in Goertzel (2002: 19–23).

framing of the debate is now focusing on an issue of system failure that is now even penetrating the closely controlled Chinese blogosphere.

The innocence frame has affected American sentencing practices. The number of executions has gone down substantially over the last ten years. When attitudes are tied to core values, however, new information does not seem to produce substantial attitude change (Alvarez and Brehm 2002). If not challenged, people tap into their core values. The reason change in America is slower than in Europe is historical, but also explained by the fact that most Americans' views on the death penalty are closely linked to their religious sentiments. In China the claim that attitudes to punishment are based on cultural core values seems to lack substantial evidence other than in the form of anecdotal examples. The use of sayings like 'kill the chicken to scare the monkey' (*sha ji jing hou* 杀鸡儆猴) or 'scare one to warn a hundred' (*sha yi jing bai* 杀一儆百) are mere anecdotes of popular retribution, not evidence of a serious core culture of retribution, and definitely not evidence of support for capital punishment. As in any society that is emerging from a rural and authoritarian past, there will be support for such practices, but this does not enable us to understand current attitudes to the death penalty. If we look at the most recent opinion data from China, we find evidence that attitudes to the death penalty are anything but core values. In the recent representative survey done by the Max Planck Institute in cooperation with Wuhan University only 25 per cent of all respondents were concerned with the issue of the death penalty. Many respondents answered: 'don't know' or 'not sure' to the questions asked (Oberwittler and Qi 2010). When the public does not really pay attention to the death penalty question, this may serve to prevent change. At the same time, low salience opens up large possibilities for change; it certainly does not demonstrate the 'strong cultural roots' of punitive attitudes among Chinese people as claimed by the culturalist argument. Instead of reflecting core values, this evidence points in the direction of lack of interest, or confusion, a situation that is highly susceptible to change.

The Survey Evidence

Not until very recently has the degree of support for capital punishment in China been scientifically documented and/or empirically verified by research. This is not to say that we have not had interesting data to work with, but only recently has the survey data based on cooperation between the Max Planck Institute and Chinese researchers been able to present a cutting-edge representative survey on capital punishment in China. The survey was conducted in three provinces (Hubei, Guangdong and Beijing) during 2007 and 2008, and the data was released recently. Parallel to this survey, the University of Wuhan conducted a survey among legal professionals, using a very similar questionnaire (Kang 2005). We also have data from the big survey carried out by the Academy of Social Sciences in Beijing in 1995 (Hu 2000). In addition, a string of other surveys of greater or lesser importance and methodological stringency has been made available to us over the last decade or so (Yuan 2009: 99–112).[10]

We know that survey results can be dramatically affected by the methodology used, the way in which questions are phrased, and even by the questioning sequence used (Bohm 1987: 380–96, Bohm and Vogel 1994: 125–43). The most common question asked in capital punishment surveys is whether respondents favour the death penalty 'in the case of murder'. It can be easy to support the death penalty in the abstract without knowledge of specific circumstances – in response to a survey question – even if one might well be influenced by the possibility of errors in particular cases. The innocence argument is closely related to the shift from thinking of the issue in the abstract to considering a concrete decision about a particular individual. This shift may not be fully reflected in most public opinion surveys, but becomes evident when a specific case involving execution is brought to the attention of the respondent (Baumgartner et al. 2008: 170).

Let us then look at the survey data, and start with that particular question. Normally public opinion surveys have a lower percentage answering in favour of capital punishment in the case of murder than for capital punishment in general. In America 58 per cent still supported the death penalty in general in 2012 (the lowest support in 40 years), while only 49 per cent supported the death penalty for murder.[11] We find this pattern in other societies as well. The strange result found in China is that 78 per cent voiced support for the death penalty in cases of murder, but in answer to the general question of support for the death penalty only 59 per cent were in favour of it, much lower support than in the United States. Whatever the explanation for this finding, in comparison with the 99.2 per cent support found in 1995, this is a very dramatic development. Those in the 'death penalty for murder' group may answer 'don't know' or 'not sure' to the general question, but there has nonetheless been an increase in those in favour of abolition – from 0.8 per cent in 1995 to 14 per cent in a recent survey. The debate on reducing the number of executions, however, seems to have led to a massive change in opinion. In a Public Security survey in 1992 as many as 60 per cent thought punishments were 'too lenient' and only two per cent thought the draconian death penalty regime was 'too strict' (Zhonghua 1992: 42, 60, 250 ff). In the 1995 survey this number had increased marginally to just over three per cent who thought the death penalty 'too strict', including the 0.8 per cent who wanted the death penalty abolished.

In a 2008–2009 survey many groups in China had majority opinions against or favouring restrictions to the death penalty (Yan 2009: 22–112). Among the 1131 students in the survey, nearly 85 per cent wanted to reduce or abolish capital punishment. There was also majority support for abolition among jobless people. Most notably, 726 inmates in prisons or reform-through-labour institutions were

10 Yuan did his survey in Beijing, Guangdong, Hebei, Gansu, and Jiangxi provinces.

11 Source: http://www.gallup.com/poll/1606/Death-Penalty.aspx [accessed 07.01. 2013].

surveyed, and 91 per cent of them favoured abolition or reduction of the use of the death penalty. In short, the particular situation a respondent happens to be in explains their attitude towards the death penalty, not an alleged popular 'core culture'. One third of the inmates wanted the death penalty abolished, not because they were on death row, but because they had seen the injustices in the system at close range. This is what is called situational as against cultural core norms.

Another piece of evidence that the moralist core argument does not work well is the growing awareness of the class bias of capital punishment. Asked the question: 'If a poor person and a rich person in China committed the same serious crime, for which the death sentence could be imposed, is one of them more likely to be actually sentenced to death than the other?', nearly 70 per cent of the respondents answered 'the poor person' (Oberwittler and Qi 2010: 22). The significance here is that the common man in China has begun to see the flaws in the judicial system. We know from various data that the jobless and the poor are victims of capital punishment in China, like anywhere else. Jeffrey Reiman's famous line: 'The rich get richer and the poor get prison' also applies to China, even if we replace 'prison' with 'the death penalty' (Reiman 1979). In a survey of executions where the offenders' occupations were known, it was found that 62 per cent were either unemployed or peasants. Nearly 70 per cent had a low status job. The vast number of Chinese executed for common street crimes had low status occupations or none at all (Hong and Miethe 2007: 80). The sudden growth in doubt as to the justice provided by the system, questions about fallibility and unjust treatment, the accurate perception of the class bias of capital punishment, despite the secrecy shrouding numbers, are all central to the 'innocence frame' that has changed public opinion in so many countries recently. Through the media, and in particular through the Internet, the Chinese public has become aware of the fact that innocent people are sentenced to death because of sloppy procedures, unjust treatment, and a corrupt, uncaring justice system. Let us look at a few recent cases that have caught the public's eye.

In 2005 the Ministry of Public Security ordered that a rape-murder case should be reopened, when a new suspect was caught ten years after 21-year-old Nie Shubin was executed for the crime. Nie Shubin was convicted of murder and rape in Shijiazhuang in 1994 and was executed after Hebei's Higher People's Court upheld a lower court's sentence of death in April 1995.[12] Similarly, a butcher in Mayang County in Central China's Hunan Province, was wrongfully convicted and executed for a crime he did not commit. A local woman's dismembered body was found floating in a river. The authorities investigating the crime claimed at the trial that the murderer must have been someone experienced with a knife – someone like a butcher – because the techniques used to dissect the body were 'very professional'.[13] But after the execution the woman he was supposed to have murdered suddenly reappeared alive. In another well-publicized case, a man was

12 Source: *Shanghai Daily*, 18.03.2005, 1.

13 Source: *China Daily*, 23.06.2005, 4.

sentenced to death with a two-year suspension in 2000, but his alleged victim, presumed dead for 11 years, turned up at his home earlier this year.[14] Such cases have begun to appear on Internet blogs fairly regularly. In another recent example netizens took an interest in the case in which a Henan citizen named Zhao was released from prison thanks to the reappearance of the neighbour he supposedly murdered more than a decade previously.[15]

The Max Planck survey addresses the issue of innocence for the first time in China. The findings amply confirm the potential for change in this country. Asked the theoretical question whether innocent people might be wrongly executed, 60 per cent agreed, while only 26 per cent of the respondents disagreed (Oberwittler and Qi 2010: 18). Of even greater interest is the answer to the concrete question 'Would you still support the death penalty if there were evidence of executions of innocent persons within the judicial system?' As many as 44 per cent of the undecided and pro-death penalty respondents would oppose the death penalty if proof was found that innocent people had been executed. Thirty-one per cent were still undecided, and only 25 per cent would still support the death penalty (Oberwittler and Qi 2010: 16). This is a level of support lower than that in the United Kingdom today. Since the innocence debate has yet not been a central issue in the Chinese media, this is remarkable. Flexibility and change is the picture here, not that of a retributive core culture. We find similar evidence of the potential for rapid change in non-representative surveys. In a survey of 2000 people in China in 2002, 82 per cent supported the death penalty, while 14 per cent said they wanted it abolished (Zhao 2004: 221–36, 226). When the question was changed, and rephrased on the hypothesis that the death penalty had already been abolished, only 60 per cent wanted to retain the death penalty, while the number of abolitionists increased to 33 per cent. This reflects what we already know from death penalty opinion research in other countries: if the state passes legislation banning the use of the death penalty, as a rule public opinion will follow suit. For our purposes here it is enough to conclude that there are no fixed and culturally strong drivers that force Chinese opinion to routinely support the death penalty (Liang 2003: 47).

At this point more has to been said about opinion change. In many ways, public opinion surveys give a fairly conservative view since they tend to focus on individuals. When we study individuals, we often see constancy, but when we study aggregates, a new picture of orderly change appears. Some people are fairly constant in their opinions. These are people with strong core values: political, often religious, and in particular fundamentalist values. America and Poland are countries where core values relating to capital punishment are linked to a literalist religious belief. Let us put such respondents in the *core value group*. Opinion follows a flat line of stability in groups like this. A small proportion of the public, however, moves systematically in response to changing circumstances and new

14 Source: *Shanghai Daily*, 08.05.2010, A08.

15 Source: *South China Morning Post*, 14.05.2010, A5.

information. In the death penalty debate in America and Europe these people were the ones who turned to the innocence frame. In the literature such groups represent systematic change – *the signal* – that will appear clearer only over time. This *signal group* can influence the climate of opinions in a remarkably short period of time. Another group, that can be called the *ambivalent group*, fluctuates between the core value group and the signal group. This group is caught between the two other groups, but we can see the trend of change in how this group leans towards one or the other end of the spectrum. The signal group is the important one to focus on to see change in the making, and this includes noting its impact on the ambivalent group. If the signal group is the instigator of change, the ambivalent group are their immediate followers: they indicate the direction of general opinion change (Baumgartner et al. 2008: 168).

In the Max Planck survey, this group – who often answered 'don't know' and 'not sure' – tended to be fairly large. On the main question: 'In general, do you favour or oppose the use of the death penalty?' 58 per cent were 'in favour' of the death penalty, 14 per cent were 'opposed', and 28 per cent were 'not sure' (Oberwittler and Qi 2010: 10). Some people might argue that these people have no clue at all, but this is untrue.

It is important to look at where the ambivalent group is moving. In the Chinese death penalty debate we see this group moving towards the signal group, the abolitionist minority. The undecided group may not say yes or no to the use of the death penalty in general, but we still have a clear profile of them. When asked whether the death penalty is an effective way to prevent crime, the ambivalent group of 'undecided' respondents have the same profile as the signal group opposing the death penalty. More people in both these groups tend to be sceptical about the effectiveness of the death penalty in preventing crime. They simply regard the deterrence effect as 'very low' (Oberwittler and Qi 2010: 17–18).

This is vividly illustrated in the graph showing attitudes towards the perceived efficiency of the death penalty in terms of deterrence shown in the Max Planck survey in Figure 9.1.

The undecided respondents lean towards the signal group, the abolitionists. We can find this trend in a lot of the survey questions. The profile of the ambivalent group of 'don't knows' suggests the future for opinion trends in China. The 'don't knows' in China, as in Europe in recent decades, are leaning towards the signal group of abolitionists. Even those not open to change at present will be affected by this trend in the long run if we believe aggregate opinion theory. The survey shows the flexibility and changeability of public opinion on the death penalty, contradicting the assumptions of hard-to-change penal norms and strong core culture of 'revenge psychology'.

Let us focus again on the latter assumption, that the common man – the *laobaixing* (老百姓) – is to blame for China's use of the death penalty, and that the people's 'anger' is preventing its abolition. It seems that the so-called Chinese masses are not the conservative 'deeply rooted retributive' element holding back reforms. The survey data points, rather, in quite the opposite direction. Public

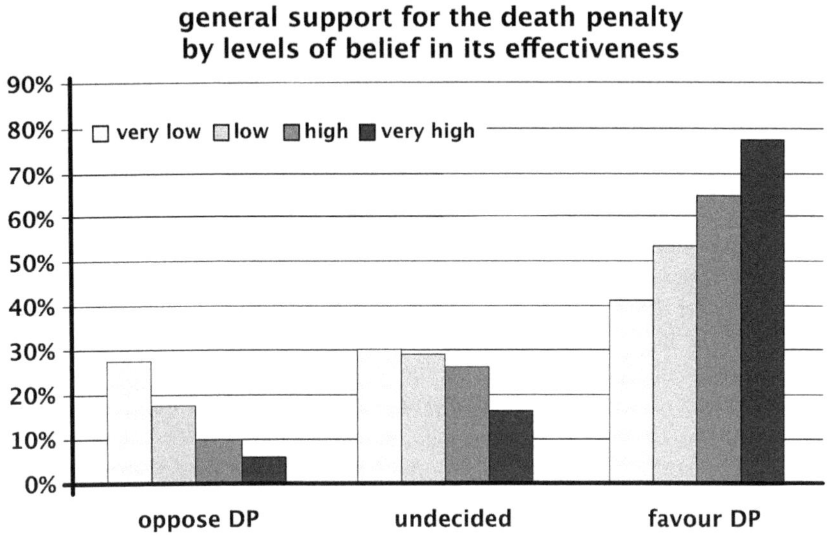

N=4472 (weighted data), missing values 13.3%

Figure 9.1 Public opinion on the death penalty in China
Source: Oberwittler and Qi 2010: 17–18.

opinion seems to have changed faster than legal institutions and the slogans of the government and the Communist Party. Let us look again at these data. A 1995 survey conducted by the Academy of Social Sciences using rather confusing categories of 'high class' and 'low class' found that 'high class' respondents were less likely to support the death penalty than 'low class' respondents. There were very few in either category in 1995 who chose abolition or reduction of the death penalty, but the highest and the lowest class categories chose this option more often than the middle class categories (Hu 2002: 342). If we look at the different job categories, however, we find the highest support for capital punishment among military personnel, where 43 per cent responded that there was 'too little' of it in 1995. There was a long jump down to the second most punitive group, retired officials, where 28 per cent were of this opinion. Personnel in the legal sector were the most liberal among the elites in the 1995 survey. Only nine per cent believed there was 'too little' use of the death penalty. Young people under 25 were the most likely group to support abolition, and those over 61 were the most conservative of the age cohorts, with the fewest number of abolitionists (Hu 2002: 344). Women were slightly less punitive than men (Hu 2002: 342), and the allegedly vengeful people, the category called 'the masses' (*qunzhong* 群众), saw twice as many ticking the boxes for abolition or reduction of capital punishment as compared to 'central Party cadres' (*zhonggong dangyuan* 中共党员). While only 20 per cent of the 'masses' wanted more capital punishment in 1995, 30 per cent of central

Party cadres wanted more of it (Hu 2002: 345). As far as leading by example to overcome the things of the past goes, the Party cadres are certainly not standing in the front line to educate the masses. The same can be said about intellectuals. The survey showed that illiterates and those with only primary school education were twice as likely to support abolition or reduction than respondents with 'university' education. The higher the education, the higher too was the percentage giving the most pro-death answers. Close to 30 per cent of those with the highest education wanted more capital punishment, while only 20 per cent of illiterates and those with only primary school education were that punitive. In sum, the strongest support for the death penalty was found among military personnel, party cadres, those with the highest education, and the elderly. The lowest support was found among those with the least education, the category called the 'masses', and those under 25 years of age. The only elite groups going against the trend towards elite support for the death penalty were legal elites and the richest. Among the legal elites there were few abolitionists, but much more support for reducing the use of execution and limiting the scope of the death penalty. High income respondents feared capital punishment for corruption or economic crime and this made them liberal, in the face of a poorly regulated financial market where the distinction between entrepreneurialism and corruption is not always clear. These facts somewhat muddle the categories 'high class' and 'low class' in the survey, and leave the findings somewhat irrelevant.

In two representative surveys from Wuhan we have a lot of evidence that the elite group of people working within the legal system are much more punitive than the general population. In a 2005 survey, the support from the death penalty among this group was 88.4 per cent. Although 48 per cent of the supporters of the death penalty wanted to 'limit the use' of it in the future, over 10 per cent even wanted to use it more frequently than before.[16] A more recent, but smaller survey showed that the support among this elite group had increased to 91.2 per cent.[17] The abolitionists constituted only 7.5 per cent among the legal elite group, but was nearly twice as large among the general population at 14 per cent.[18]

The conclusion we can draw from this table comparing the general population and the most liberal elite, the legal elite, is that the supposedly 'backward' group of common people is actually more liberal on the death penalty question than any of the elite groups. The argument here is not that of 'deeply rooted revenge

16 Kang, Junxin, *Lixiang yu xianshi. Zhongguo sixing zhidu baogao* (Ideals and reality. Report on the Chinese death penalty), Beijing, Zhongguo renmin gongan daxue chubanshe, 2005: 143.

17 Information supplied by Roger Hood, consultant to the more recent survey. See: Death Penalty, reform, 13 January 2013, http://www.gbcc.org.uk/death-penalty-reform.aspx [accessed 19.02.2013].

18 Kang, Junxin, 28, 143, and Oberwittler, D. and Qi, S, 'Public Opinion on the Death Penalty in China. Results from a General Population Survey Conducted in Three Provinces in 2007 (2009)', 10.

psychology' of the masses or a general 'penal populism' in China. We rather see clear survey evidence of '*penal elitism*'. The death penalty is a political instrument upheld not by a 5000-year-old 'culture', but by the state and its elites. This is a political, not a cultural issue, and involves a conservative, excessively slow-moving state and party bureaucracy. As regards the secrecy shrouding the numbers executed in China, the general public is also more advanced than the party and state elite. Asked whether the Chinese government should publish the annual number of executions, 64 per cent answered yes, and less than 16 per cent said no (Oberwittler and Qi 2010: 21).

In conclusion, we can say that public opinion in China is moving faster than the system itself. The only thing that seems 'deeply rooted' in the Chinese death penalty debate is the deeply rooted myth of a general retributive and vengeful attitude standing in the way of reducing or abolishing the death penalty. The penal norm, as we have seen, is far from the old mainstream assumption that 'we learn to react punitively … just as we learn to speak a language', a matter of hard-to-change core culture. On the contrary, the penal norm in China is not part of a never changing, deeply rooted core-culture. It is changing rapidly and substantially. The new innocence frame is one of the driving forces in the change we have already seen for some years across the world. This frame is beginning to establish itself in China too. John Kingdon has quoted Victor Hugo in trying to understand the power of framing. Hugo once said: 'Greater than the tread of mighty armies is an idea whose time has come' (Kingdon 1984: 1).[19] The innocence frame is clearly an idea whose time has come, and attitudes to the death penalty in China is in the process of radical change.

References

Alvarez, R.M. and Brehm, J. *Hard Choices, Easy Answers: Values, Information, and American Public Opinion.* Princeton, NJ: Princeton University Press.

Ball, P. 2004. *Critical Mass: How One Thing Leads to Another.* New York: Farrar, Straus and Giroux.

Barbasi, A.-L. 2003. *Linked: How Everything is Connected to Everything Else and What It Means.* New York: Plume.

Barnes, J.A. 1966. Durkheim's Division of Labour in Society. *Man*, 1(2), 158–75.

Baumgartner, F.R., De Boeuf, S.L. and Boydstun, A.E. 2008. *The Decline of the Death Penalty and the Discovery of Innocence.* Cambridge, NY: Cambridge University Press.

Bedeau, H.A. and Radelet, M.L. 1987. Miscarriages of Justice in Potentially Capital Cases. *Stanford Law Review*, 40(1), 21–179.

19 The Hugo quote has various translations, and in the original French the quote is: '*On résiste à l'invasion des armées; on ne résiste pas à l'invasion des idées*'; (Hugo 1852/1877).

Benn, C. 2002. *Daily Life in Traditional China – The Tang Dynasty.* Westport. CT: Greenwood Press.

Bohm, R.M. 1987. American Death Penalty Attitudes: A Critical Examination of Recent Research. *Criminal Justice and Behaviour*, 14(3), 380–96.

Bohm, R.M. and Vogel, R.E. 1994. A Comparison of Factors Associated with Uninformed and Informed Death Penalty Opinions. *Journal of Criminal Justice*, 22, 125–43.

Cha, M., Mislove, A., Adams, B. and Gummadi, K.P. 2010. Characterizing Social Cascades in Flickr. Available at: http://www.mpi-sws.org/~gummadi/papers/Cascades-WOSN.pdf [accessed 05.11.2010].

Chen, Xingliang. 2003. Xingfa linian daodu. Beijing: Falü chubanshe.

Chen, Xingliang. 2005. Cong 'qiangxia liuren' dao 'faxia liuren' [From saving life from the gun to saving life from the law], in: *Sixing – Zhongwai meizhu de jiaodian [Death penalty – The global focus]*, edited by Chen Zexian. Beijing: Zhongguo gong'an daxue chubanshe.

Chen, Xingliang. 2006. Kuanyan xiangji xingshi zhengci yanjiu (shang) [Severity and leniency of mutual benefit to criminal policy research (1)]. *Xingshi faxue* [Criminal Law], 7.

Council of the European Union. 2004. Death is not Justice: The Council of Europe and the Death Penalty, Strasbourg: Council of the European Union.

Death Penalty, reform, 13 January 2013. Available at: http://www.gbcc.org.uk/death-penalty-reform.aspx [accessed 19.02.2013].

Ehrlich, I. 1975. The Deterrent Effect of Capital Punishment – A Question of Life and Death. *American Economic Review*, June 1975, 397–417.

Gao Mingxuan. 2004. Lüetan wo guo de sixing lifa jiqi fazhi qushi (On Chinese Legislation Concerning the Death Penalty), in *Zhongguo feizhi sixing zhi lu tansuo* [The Road of the Abolition of the Death Penalty in China], edited by Zhao Bingzhi. Beijing: Zhongguo remnin gong'an daxue.

Gladwell, M. 2000. *The Tipping Point: How Little Things Can Make a Big Difference.* Boston: Little Brown.

Goertzel, T. 2002. Myths of Murder and Multiple Regression. *The Skeptical Inquirer*, 26(1), 19–23.

Govier, T. 2007. *Forgiveness and revenge.* London, New York: Routledge.

Granovetter, M.S. 1978. Threshold Models of Collective Behavior. *American Journal of Sociology*, 83(6), 1420–43.

Hong, Lu and Miethe, T.C. 2007. *China's Death Penalty. History, Law, and Contemporary Practices.* New York, London: Routledge.

Hood, R. 2009. Abolition of the Death Penalty: China in World Perspective. *City University of Hong Kong Law Review*, 1, 1–20.

Hu, Yunteng 2000. *Cun yu fei- sixing jiben lilun yanjiu* [Retain or abolish – Basic theoretical research on the death penalty]. Beijing: Zhongguo jianchu chubanshe.

Hu, Yunteng 2002. Application of Death Penalty in Chinese Judicial Practice, in *Implementation of Law in the People's Republic of China,* edited by Jianfu et al. The Hague: Kluwer Law International.

Hugo, V. 1852/1877. *Histoire d'un Crime* [The History of a Crime] [Trans. T.H. Joyce and A. Locker].

Jiang, Chunfang 1992. Zhongguo da baike quanshu: Faxue [Chinese Encyclopedia: Law]. Beijing: Beijing da baike quanshu chubanshe.

Kang, Junxin 2005. *Lixiang yu xianshi. Zhongguo sixing zhidu baogao* [Ideals and reality. Report on the Chinese death penalty]. Beijing: Zhongguo renmin gongan daxue chubanshe.

Kingdon, J.W. 1984. *Agendas, Alternatives, and Public Policies.* Boston: Little Brown & Co.

Liang, Genling 2003, *Zhongguo sixing jiantao yi 'qiangxia liuren an' wei shijiao* [Review of the death penalty in China from the perspective or 'save the life from the gun case'], in Chen Xingliang, ed. (2005).

Lu, Jianping. 2009. Sixing shiyong yu minyi [The use of the death penalty and public opinion], in *Sixing zhidu zhi xianshi kaocha yu wanshan jianyan* [Observing the realities of the death penalty system and suggestions for its improvement], edited by Zhao Bingzhi. Beijing, Zhongguo remnin gong'an daxue chubanshe. [In English in *Chinese Sociology and Anthropology*, Summer 2009, 66–79(76)].

McKnight, B.E. 1981. *The Quality of Mercy. Amnesties and Traditional Chinese Justice.* Honolulu: The University Press of Hawaii.

Madsen, R. 1990. The Politics of Revenge in Rural China during the Cultural Revolution, in *Violence in China. Essays in Culture and Counterculture*, edited by J.N. Lipman and S. Harrell. New York: State University of New York Press.

Mao, Zedong. 1951/1977. Strike surely, accurately and relentlessly in suppressing counter-revolutionaries. *Selected Works of Mao Zedong* 5.

Mühlhahn, K. 2009. *Criminal Justice in China. A History.* Cambridge, MA, London: Harvard University Press.

Oberwittler, D. and Qi, S. 2010. *Public Opinion on the Death Penalty in China. Results from a General Population Survey Conducted in Three Provinces in 2007/08*. Max Planck Institute for Foreign and International Criminal Law. April 2010, http://www.mpice.de/shared/data/pdf/forschung_aktuell.41.pdf.

Perry, E.J. 1985. Rural Violence in Socialist China. *The China Quarterly*, 103, 414–40.

Pratt, J. 2007. *Penal Populism.* London, New York: Routledge.

Qiu Xinglong. 2001. *Bijiao xingfa* [Comparative criminal law] 1. Beijing: Zhongguo jiancha chubanshe.

Qiu, Xinglong. 2002. Sixing de daoxing [The moral character of death penalty]. *Zhengce yu falü*, 2, 51–4.

Qu, Xuewu. 2005. Zhongguo sixing wenhua de duoyuan xing yu yibenhua [The multi-culture of Chinese death penalty and], in *Sixing – Zhongwai meizhu de jiaodian* [Death penalty – The global focus], edited by Chen Zexian. Beijing: Zhongguo gong'an daxue chubanshe.

Reiman, J.F. 1979. *The Rich get Richer and the Poor get Prison: Ideology, Class and Criminal Justice.* New York: Wiley.

Roberts, J.V., Stalans, L.J., Indermaur, D. and Hough, M. 2003. *Penal Populism and Public Opinion. Lessons from Five Countries.* Oxford: Oxford University Press.

Sutherland, E.D., Cressey, D.R. and Luckenbill, D.F. 1992. *Principles of Criminology* (11th edn.). New York, Boulder: General Hall, Rowman & Littlefield.

Watts, D.J. 2003. *Six Degrees: The Science of a Connected Age.* New York: Norton.

Whitman, J.Q. 2003. *Harsh Justice. Criminal Punishment and the Widening Divide between America and Europe.* Oxford and New York: Oxford University Press.

Yu, Jianrong. 2009. *Rigid Stability: an Explanatory Framework for China's Social Situation.* Available at: http://chinadigitaltimes.net/2009/05/yu-jianrong-rigid-stability-an-explanatory-framework-for-china%E2%80%99s-social-situation-1/.

Yuan, Bin 2009. Sixing minyi jiqi neibu chongtu de diaocha yu fenli [Survey and analysis of the internal conflicts of popular opinion on the death penalty]. *Faxue*, 1, 99–112.

Zhengfa daxue (China University of Administration and Law). Available at: http://203.208.39.132/search?q=cache:iZoY4Vi9l5wJ:chinadigitaltimes.net/2009/05/yu-jianrong-rigid-stability-an-explanatory-framework-for-china%E2%80%99s-social-situation-1/+yu+jianrong&cd=2&hl=zh-CN&ct=clnk&gl=cn&st_usg=ALhdy2-USOAKOnQ3Oza3bPO_EXRx6RD6yw.

Zhao, Bingzhi. 2004. Cong Zhongguo sixing chengce kan fei moli fanzui sixing de zhubu feizhi wenti [On the Chinese policy of gradual abolition of the death penalty for non-violent crimes], in *Zhongguo feizhi sixing zhi lu tansuo* [The Road to the Abolition of the Death Penalty in China], edited by Zhao Bingzhi. Beijing: Zhongguo remnin gong'an daxue.

Zhonghua renmin gongheguo gonganbu, editor [The PRC Ministry of Public Security, editor]. 1992. Nin ganjue anquan ma? [Do you feel safe?]. Beijing: Qunzhong chubanshe.

Chapter 10

A Knotty Tale: Understanding the Death Penalty in India

Bikramjeet Batra[1]

With two executions in three months – from November 2012 to February 2013 – India appears to have shown that rumours of the early demise of capital punishment in the country were greatly exaggerated.[2] Yet, although Indian courts sentence over a hundred persons to death every year, there have been few executions actually carried out. Only one had been carried out from mid 1997 to late 2012.[3] This chapter seeks to unravel the knots in the tale of India's lack of executions in the recent past by examining the legal and institutional framework within which capital punishment operates in the Indian judicial and political system, and charting the dramatic decline in capital sentences in India over the decades. In an attempt to understand how the current situation has come about, it also interrogates the gaps and cracks within the clemency process – in particular the role played by some holding the office of the President of India. Given India's return to executions, the chapter concludes by asking whether we are witnessing another twist in the tale of the death penalty in India.

Introduction

The 'modern' era of the death penalty in India began with its inclusion in the Indian Penal Code (IPC) drafted in the mid-nineteenth century and enacted in 1860 by the British colonial government. It was retained in the law-books after Indian independence in 1947 and the new constitution of 1950.[4] Since then, the number

1 The author is a Policy Adviser at Amnesty International. The views in this chapter are personal.

2 Ajmal Kasab was executed in Pune on 21 November 2012 and Afzal Guru was hanged in Delhi on 9 February 2013.

3 Dhananjoy Chatterjee was executed in Kolkata on 14 August 2004.

4 The Constitution of India makes an indirect reference to the death penalty in Article 21, which recognizes the right to liberty and life *except* according to 'procedures established by law'. In addition, there are also direct references to the death penalty where reference is made to the powers of the President and Governor to commute death sentences (Articles 72 and 141 respectively).

of offences punishable by death in the IPC has steadily increased, including most recently in February 2013 in the context of sexual assaults.[5] In addition there are a number of special legislations (including anti-terrorist laws) and state-specific legislations that allow for capital punishment.[6]

In terms of procedure, the death sentence is ordinarily awarded by a single judge of the trial court.[7] The death sentence must however be confirmed by the High Court.[8] At this stage, the prisoner is deemed to be 'sentenced to death', but can appeal to the Supreme Court and/or apply for executive clemency/mercy to the

---

5 The death penalty can be imposed for the following offences in the current Indian Penal Code, or for criminal conspiracy to commit any of them (section 120-B):

Treason, for waging war against the Government of India (s.121)
Abetment of mutiny actually committed (s.132)
Perjury resulting in the conviction and death of an innocent person (s.194)
Threatening or inducing any person to give false evidence resulting in the conviction and death of an innocent person (s.195A)
Murder (s.302)
Murder committed by a life convict (s. 303)
Abetment of a suicide by a minor, insane person or intoxicated person (s.305)
Attempted murder by a serving life convict (s.307(2))
Kidnapping for ransom (s.364A)
Inflicting injury during sexual assault that leads to death or causes the person to be in a persistent vegetative state (s.376A)
Repeat conviction for sexual assault (s.376E)
Dacoity with murder (s.396).

6 Laws relating to the Armed Forces, for example the Air Force Act 1950, the Army Act 1950 and the Navy Act 1950 and the Indo-Tibetan Border Police Force Act 1992; Defence and Internal Security of India Act 1971; Defence of India Act 1971 (s.5); Commission of Sati (Prevention) Act 1987 (s.4(1)); Narcotic Drugs and Psychotropic Substances (Prevention) Act, 1985, 1988 amendment (s.31A); Terrorist and Disruptive Activities (Prevention) Act 1987 (TADA) (s.3(2)(i)); Prevention of Terrorism Act 2002 (POTA) (s.3(2)(a); Scheduled Castes and Scheduled Tribes (Prevention of Atrocities) Act 1989 (s.3(2)(i)); Explosive Substances Act 1908, 2001 amendment (s.3(b)); Arms Act 1959, 1988 amendment (struck down by the Supreme Court), (s.27); Unlawful Activities Prevention Act 1967, 2004 amendment (s.16(1)).

7 There are no distinct capital trials such as there are in many countries. Instead the death sentence can be awarded in any conviction for murder in a hearing on sentencing which takes place after the conviction of the accused for the offence. Prosecutors invariably seek the maximum punishment. All persons accused of murder and other serious crimes can avail themselves of free legal assistance but the quality and adequacy of this legal aid raises serious concern.

8 The state authorities refer the matter to the High Court, irrespective of whether the accused/convict appeals the decision or not. At least two judges of the High Court hear the case and re-examine the evidence that was placed before the trial court. After determining whether the decision to award the death sentence made by the lower court was correct or not, they may confirm the death sentence, commute it to life imprisonment, alter the conviction and punishment to some other lower charge or even acquit the person.

Governor of the State. Once the Supreme Court has refused to admit the appeal, or dismisses the appeal and upholds the death sentence, the prison authorities forward a mercy petition to the Governor of the state. If dismissed or rejected, a second petition is sent to the President of India for a final decision.[9] No execution can take place until the mercy petition is rejected by the President.[10]

The debate on the death penalty in India generally takes place in fits and starts – invariably against the backdrop of a well reported crime or when an execution takes place. The retention of the death penalty and increase in capital-eligible offences in India can be attributed to the death penalty being used as a rhetorical and symbolic device by politicians across party divides and ideologies, as well as by the Government and judges of the Supreme Court.

In the current context of terrorism, regular bomb blasts and constant fear of sexual violence and other violent crime, proposals for increased death sentences as a central pillar of a broader hard-line stance on crime appear to have broad public support. Importantly, this support comes not only from the elites and the growing middle class, but also from the poorest in society, who often bear the brunt of violent crime. With 34,305 murders in 2011, India's murder-rate of 2.8 per 100,000 persons remains a significant concern (NCRB 2011, 55).[11]

On the other hand, despite many attempts, a death penalty abolitionist movement barely exists in India. Although most civil liberties groups and many human rights organizations oppose the death penalty, the opposition 'in principle' has rarely transformed itself into active mobilization or campaigns against the death penalty. Few political leaders have consistently taken strong positions against capital punishment and institutions such as the National Human Rights Commission have also remained largely ambivalent.

The above suggests why capital punishment in India survives. It begins to explain why various Governments have constantly sought to expand the number of crimes punishable by the death penalty, and why judges continue to award death sentences. What it cannot explain is why, despite all of the above, only three executions have been carried out in India between mid-1997 and early 2013, and why there have been significant spells without any executions.

---

9 As per Indian law, the Governor and President are bound to follow the 'advice' of the cabinet of ministers in the exercise of most powers, including as regards mercy petitions. This means that, although the petitions are sent to the Governor and President, the decision is made effectively by the state and central governments respectively. See judgment of the Indian Supreme Court in *Samsher Singh v. Union of India* 1974.

10 Once all the judicial and executive processes are complete and the mercy petitions have been rejected, the state authorities can approach the trial court which passed the sentence of death to pass a warrant of death giving the date, place and time of execution.

11 In practice, almost all death sentences in India are awarded for murder, albeit combined with other offences (kidnapping and murder, sexual assault and murder). For the purposes of this chapter, all references to death sentences are those for murder, unless specifically mentioned otherwise.

The Incremental Move Away from the Death Penalty

Executions were common in colonial India, particularly in the decades before independence. From 1926 to 1940 the British Indian government executed over 8,240 persons – an average of 550 executions a year (NAI 1946). This increased to 700 per year in the war years from 1941 to 1944 (NAI 1946). From the peak of nearly two executions a day in the early 1940s, the present situation, with hardly any executions since 1997 has not been a sudden phenomenon, but a gradual journey. Table 10.1 illustrates the incremental reduction in executions in independent India.

Table 10.1 Mercy petitions commuted and rejected by the President, 1948–Feb. 2013[12]

Period	Mercy petitions disposed	Number of petitions		Executions per year[13]
		Commuted	Rejected	
1948–54	1410	341	1069	152.7
1955–64	2083	601	1482	148.2
1965–74	1034	543	491	49.1
1975–84	173	52	121	12.1
1985–94	45	4	41	4.1
1995–2004	8	1	7	0.7
2005–Feb. 2013	31[14]	24	7	0.3[15]

12 Data from 1965–2004 is from the annexe in the reply by S. Regupathy, Minister of State in the Ministry of Home Affairs on 29 November 2006 to Rajya Sabha Unstarred Question No. 815 by S.S. Ahluwalia. Information from 1948–64 was collated by the author from files of the Ministry of Home Affairs available at the National Archives of India and is available on file. Information from 2005–13 is based on replies from the Ministry of Home Affairs to various petitions under the Right to Information Act – on file with author.

13 The information in this column is a minimum figure – the actual number of persons executed is likely to be much higher, as many mercy petitions rejected would have included more than one person. Also note that although most rejected petitions led to executions being carried out, there are very rare instances where rejection by the President has not led to execution.

14 Note that the actual number of persons affected by these petitions was much higher – as many individuals were covered by a single mercy petition, for example, although seven petitions were rejected in this period, they covered the cases of 12 persons.

15 Although seven mercy petitions (involving 12 persons) have been rejected, only two executions have been carried out as of the time of writing. The remaining ten condemned prisoners have been successful in challenging the rejection of their petition in the Supreme Court. Executions can only be carried out after their legal claims are rejected.

To appreciate the causes of the decline in executions, it is essential to briefly study the various legislative and judicial factors that have influenced the capital punishment discourse in India.

The first major reform of the death penalty laws came as part of a series of amendments to criminal law in 1955–56. Since it was first enacted in 1861, until 1956, the Criminal Procedure Code (CrPC) provided the death penalty as the ordinary punishment for murder. Special reasons, in writing, were required where the lesser punishment of life imprisonment (or transportation for life, as was then possible) was imposed. This requirement was removed from the code in 1955–56 and either the death sentence or life imprisonment could now be imposed without any requirement to give reasons.[16] The impact of this change in the law appears to have been slow to be felt in the courts, as there does not appear to have been a dramatic decrease in death sentences from 1955 to 1964.[17] A study of mercy petitions of the period indicates that the removal of the 'default' death sentence in law did influence the executive's approach to clemency. This is also supported by a marginal increase in commuted petitions in this decade, resulting in a marginal decrease in annual executions from 1955–64 as compared to the previous post-independence years.

The late 1950s also saw attempts by a few parliamentarians to abolish the death penalty through the introduction of private members bills in both houses of Parliament. Four attempts were made from 1956 to 1962 and under pressure, the government agreed to seek the opinion of the Law Commission of India (an autonomous legal research body which makes recommendations on law reform, and is headed by a former Chief Justice of India).[18] Although the Law Commission's 1967 report rejected calls for abolition of the death penalty, the debate around the issue of abolition, along with the 1955–56 amendments, appears to have impacted the judiciary significantly and the number of death sentences imposed appears to have reduced dramatically in the decade from 1965 to 1974.[19]

---

16 Amending Act XXVI of 1955, which came into effect from 1 January 1956, deleted Section 367(5) of the CrPC. The number of death sentences can be inferred from the number of mercy petitions disposed, since almost all death sentences lead automatically to a mercy petition being filed.

17 This can be inferred from the average number of mercy petitions disposed in the year – 201 from 1948–54 and 208 from 1955–64. A study of Supreme Court judgments of this period found that 'courts appear to have continued to award and uphold the death sentence without applying their mind to the change in law' (AI and PUCL 2008).

18 These included a bill introduced in 1956 by Mukund Lal Agrawal in the Lok Sabha, and another in 1958 by the actor-parliamentarian, Prithvi Raj Kapur in the Rajya Sabha. A couple more followed in 1961 and 1962, introduced by Savitry Devi Nigam (Rajya Sabha) and Raghunath Singh (Lok Sabha) respectively.

19 At an average, 103.4 mercy petitions were disposed every year by the Government, less than half in the previous decade.

In addition to the halving of death sentences imposed, this decade also saw a reversal in the approach of the executive to mercy petitions.[20] Of the mercy petitions disposed, a majority (52.51 per cent) led to commutations – this was much higher than the previous 28.85 per cent (1955–64) and 23.85 per cent (1948–54). The cumulative impact of reduced death sentences and increased commutations was the significant two-thirds reduction in the average execution rate in this decade. The average executions per year in 1965–74 had dropped to 49.1 from 148.2 executions in 1955–64.

The abolitionist-parliamentarians may not have realized it, but their failed efforts to abolish the death penalty had set in motion a series of circumstances that ensured that the debate on the death penalty had completely changed.[21] Although the Law Commission recommended that the death penalty be retained in India, it did however concede that improvements were required, including making the death penalty an exceptional punishment (Law Commission of India 1967). As a result, the new CrPC of 1973 included a provision requiring 'special reasons' to be noted when a death sentence was imposed (Section 354(3)). This was a 180-degree change from the law that existed before 1956 – from being the default and ordinary punishment for murder, the death penalty had become an exceptional and extraordinary punishment in the code itself. In addition to the changes in the code, the Government had also introduced the Indian Penal Code (Amendment) Bill seeking to limit the imposition of the death penalty to a fixed category of cases.

On the other hand, the Law Commission's report had also effectively ended any possibility of an early legislative end to the death penalty. The focus of the abolitionists thus moved to the Supreme Court where they found support from a few judges who had their own concerns about capital punishment (AI and PUCL 2008). Although the initial challenge to the constitutionality of the death penalty failed in 1973, the Supreme Court, in a series of judgments, restricted the scope of the application of the death penalty and often intervened to commute death sentences (AI and PUCL 2008). However, with the judges of the Supreme Court divided, eventually a special bench of five judges heard the challenge to the constitutionality of the death penalty.

The 1980 landmark judgment in *Bachan Singh v. State of Punjab* determined (by a 4–1 majority) that the death penalty in India was constitutional. It however concluded: 'A real and abiding concern for the dignity of human life postulates resistance to taking a life through law's instrumentality. That ought not to be done save in the rarest of rare cases when the alternative option is unquestionably

20 That the Government was taking mercy petitions more seriously is evident from the fact that after 1966, the final decision was made by the Minister of Home Affairs whereas before that, the decision used to be made by the much more junior equivalent to the present Minister of State in the MHA (Batra 2009: 66).

21 To put it in perspective, of the (at least) 3,211 persons who appear to have been executed in Independent India, over 79 per cent (2,551) were executed between 1948 and 1964.

foreclosed'. Rejecting the argument that the death penalty was arbitrarily applied and influenced by the jurisprudence of the US courts, the Supreme Court suggested examples of aggravating and mitigating circumstances that should be taken into account in determining whether a case was 'the rarest of rare' and merited the death sentence.

The new CrPC making the death penalty a truly exceptional punishment, and the various judgments of the Supreme Court restricting the imposition of the death penalty had already diminished the application of the death penalty in the 1970s. With *Bachan Singh* having a great impact in the early 1980s, the number of death sentences imposed unsurprisingly dropped significantly for a second successive decade. Yet it is the scale of the decrease that is astonishing – the number of mercy petitions that were disposed in 1975–84 was a remarkable 83 per cent fewer than in the previous decade suggesting a huge reduction in death sentences imposed (average of 17.3 per year compared to 103.4 in the decade before). Inevitably executions too reduced by three-fourths: averaging 12.1 in 1975–84 as compared with 49.1 the decade before.

The Trickle Post-*Bachan Singh*

The anti-death penalty lobby in the Supreme Court followed up *Bachan Singh* with the ruling in *Mithu v. State of Punjab* (1983) where the mandatory death penalty for murder by a life convict was struck down as unconstitutional. However, with many judges of the Supreme Court supporting the death penalty, there was an attempt to backtrack with the decision in *Machhi Singh v. State of Punjab* (1983). Disguised as a detailed interpretation of the aggravating and mitigating circumstances in *Bachan Singh*, this judgment effectively sought to enlarge the scope for the imposition of the death penalty.

It is arguable that the momentum of *Bachan Singh* could even have led to abolition, but political events, particularly the armed separatist violence in Punjab, ensured that support for capital punishment resurfaced in Parliament. As it was, both *Bachan Singh* and *Mithu* were ignored in 1985 by the enactment of the *Terrorist and Disruptive Activities (Prevention) Act* (TADA) which included a mandatory death penalty for certain terrorist offences. Although the mandatory death sentence was removed in the amended TADA of 1987, a series of other 'social' laws passed in the late 1980s provided for a mandatory death sentence.[22]

The approach taken by Parliament may also have sent a message to the Supreme Court as the backlash beginning with *Machhi Singh* continued through the 1980s in a series of judgments in which judges of the Supreme Court advocated the death penalty to 'protect citizens from barbaric and brutal crime' in response to

22 E.g. Commission of Sati (Prevention) Act 1987 (s.4(1)); Narcotic Drugs and Psychotropic Substances (Prevention) Act, 1985, 1988 amendment (s.31A); Scheduled Castes and Scheduled Tribes (Prevention of Atrocities) Act 1989 (s.3(2)(i)).

'society's cry for justice' (see for instance, the judgment of the Court in *Mahesh s/o Ram Narain and ors. v. State of Madhya Pradesh* 1987). Notwithstanding all these attempts, the impact of *Bachan Singh* limiting the number of persons sentenced to death remains significant. The number of mercy petitions disposed from 1985 to 1994 fell to an average of 4.5 per year – another 75 per cent reduction from the previous decade – indicating that the number of persons sentenced to death by the judiciary was now very small. Although the percentage of commuted petitions fell, in sheer numbers the administration of the death penalty was now reduced to a very small number of cases. Executions had further reduced to an average of only four per year in the decade 1985–94.

Parliament's interest in increasing the scope of the death penalty continued well into the 1990s, albeit not at the same rate as in the mid 1980s.[23] Yet executions continued to remain rarities, reducing even further. Only seven executions were carried out in the decade from 1995 to 2004, six of them in the three-year period 1995–1997, before they virtually came to a halt in mid 1997.

One change from past decades to note in the periods 1985–94 and 1995–2004 was the trend of non-disposal of mercy petitions. Thus, unlike in the past, when the lower number of mercy petitions disposed (column 1 of Table 10.1) was reflective of the number of death sentences awarded by the judiciary, this is certainly not the case in 1995–2004. The number of persons sentenced to death in this decade is likely to have been similar to that in the previous decade (1985–94), however post-1997 there was a growing backlog of mercy petitions at the central level as no mercy petitions were finally disposed from 1998 to 2003, and only a few from then to 2009.

What caused the non-disposal of mercy petitions which in effect stalled executions in India post-mid-1997, or capital gridlock, as Johnson and Zimring (2009) put it? There was no government-declared moratorium on executions or even a policy decision to move away from the death penalty. What makes the situation more curious is that when the trickle of executions stopped completely, it was the largely pro-death penalty Hindu nationalist party (*Bharatiya Janata Party*) that was leading the coalition government. There was no execution in their five years of power. The execution in 2004 took place when the centrist Congress party was leading the government, and in a state ruled by the Communist Party of India (Marxist) which had in the past opposed the death penalty. The capital gridlock occurring in these years appears to be a freak occurrence resulting from a series of unconnected individual actions.

---

23 E.g. a new offence of kidnapping for ransom was made punishable by death (s 364A) in 1993. Some attempts at creating more capital-eligible offences – including for rape and production of spurious drugs etc. – did not succeed.

'Capital Gridlock': The Role of the Presidents

To understand the Indian death penalty in contemporary times, particular attention needs to be paid to the role played by the incumbent President (Pranab Mukherjee) as well as his predecessors – Pratibha Patil, APJ Abdul Kalam and KR Narayanan.

The power of the President with respect to mercy petitions is limited. Mercy petitions, although addressed to the President, are first examined in the Ministry of Home Affairs. The Home Minister makes a recommendation on the mercy petition file and sends it to the President for signing. The President must either accept the recommendation, or return the file once for reconsideration. If it is re-sent with the same recommendation, the President must approve the decision for the cabinet of ministers.

Although limited by the law, many holding the highest office have used their moral standing effectively to persuade the decision-making Government to reconsider the particular decision made. The first President of India, Rajendra Prasad (1950–62) used his legal training to great effect and created a strong foundation for the President being more than just a formal signatory in the rejection of the mercy petition (Batra 2009). His successor Radhakrishnan (1962–67) was an avowed abolitionist and also asserted his position regularly in decision-making on mercy petitions (Batra 2009).

Much like Prasad, Radhakrishnan and others after him, President Narayanan (1997–2002) took his role in the mercy petition process extremely seriously and exercised his prerogative to seek reconsideration of mercy petitions. After the BJP-led government was formed in March 1998, Home Minister Advani submitted nine mercy petitions (including one resubmitted) with advice to reject. Probably unwilling to sign off on executions he was not convinced about, President Narayan took the unprecedented step of keeping eight petitions pending.[24] He was able to do this as there was no time limit laid down within which he was required to accept the recommendation. This effectively allowed President Narayanan some room for manoeuvre and ensured that no executions took place.

Despite this however, the virtual end to executions post-1997 cannot be attributed to President Narayanan, who did reject one mercy petition (Govindasami from Tamil Nadu).[25] Curiously, however, the execution did not take place as the Home Minister granted a stay of execution.

---

24 While he could not return the file of the petition that was resubmitted to him, it is unclear why President Narayanan did not return the other petitions to the MHA to seek reconsideration, instead of keeping them pending.

25 Given his own personal views on the death penalty, President Narayanan would certainly have been glad to see a hiatus in executions but according to Gopalkrishna Gandhi (the former Governor of West Bengal who was Secretary to President Narayanan throughout the presidential tenure), although President Narayanan was personally opposed to the death penalty, he did not believe in making blanket decisions and foisting his personal opinion on official policy. The rejection of Govindasami's petition supports this view. See Batra 2009.

This raises an obvious question: Why did the pro-death penalty BJP-led government choose to stay the execution of Govindasami soon after recommending rejection of the petition? Undoubtedly this was an unusual case where the trial court had acquitted the accused, who was sentenced to death by the High Court on appeal. A civil liberties group stressed the fact that in the eight years between the trial court judgment and the high court death sentence, the accused had lived peacefully, remarried, created a family and was therefore not a threat to society. Active lobbying in Delhi was able to convince four ministers of the government to appeal to their colleague in the MHA. Although Home Minister Advani refused to commute the sentence, he granted a stay of execution and Govindasami remained on death row.[26]

APJ Abdul Kalam was the next President of India (2002–2007) and he inherited the eight mercy petitions kept pending by President Narayanan. He received five more petitions with recommendations to reject, four of which were sent during the last days of the Government's term, in April and May 2004. President Kalam however appears to have continued where Narayanan left off. No action was taken on the 13 files pending with him till the Government's term was complete. Unwilling to execute Govindasami, and unable to execute in the other cases (kept pending by Narayanan and Kalam); the BJP-led coalition ended their stint in Government in May 2004 without having carried out a single execution. It is ironic that the first ruling party that completed a full tenure in government without executions was one that was pro-death penalty and that had rejected all the mercy petitions.

When the Congress-led coalition formed the government in May 2004, nearly seven years had passed without an execution. Yet, almost immediately they were faced with the case of Dhananjoy Chatterjee, which had created a stir in the MHA when the prisoner had been on death row for over ten years due to official negligence. A mercy petition in this case had been rejected in 1994, but the state government had not executed Chatterjee and another round of litigation and mercy petitions took place in 2004. Home Minister Shivraj Patil rejected the petition on 1 July 2004 and President Kalam also eventually rejected the mercy petitions on 3 August 2004.

It was widely reported that President Kalam in principle opposed the death penalty, and that he also consulted the Attorney General to discuss the Chatterjee case to see if there was a way out. An inspection of the Chatterjee mercy petition file in the MHA however did not reveal any reference to President Kalam having returned the file to the MHA for reconsideration. Dhananjoy Chatterjee was hanged on 14 August 2004.[27]

For seven years, including five during the pro-death penalty BJP-led government, there had been no execution, but they appeared to resume almost immediately after

---

26 Govindasami's death sentence was eventually commuted by President Patil on 18 November 2009.

27 Why Chatterjee was chosen to hang remains a mystery. Some have speculated that it was the nature of the case – a rape-murder of a minor – that led to President Kalam allowing the execution despite his opposition to capital punishment. His crime, while brutal, was not particularly unique compared to those of many others on death row.

the centrist Congress party came to power in 2004. In a further irony, the left parties' coalition led by the Communist Party of India-Marxist (CPI-M) that formed the West Bengal government strongly supported the execution, despite the CPI-M being one of the few parties that claimed to oppose the death penalty.

While the impact of the anti-death penalty initiatives around this case on later mercy petitions is unclear, Chatterjee's execution was not followed by others as had initially been feared. Following the norm of a new government providing fresh advice on pending appointments and other matters, the UPA Government resubmitted all the 13 petitions to President Kalam. The MHA also sent the fresh mercy petition of Govindasami and the petition in the Rajiv Gandhi assassination case, along with five more mercy petition files. By end September 2005 there were 20 files pending with the President, all of which reportedly carried the recommendation for rejection.

Instead of signing the petitions, Kalam publicly voiced his dissatisfaction with the existing system of death sentences and clemency on three occasions in October 2005.[28] His views do not appear to have had much influence in the MHA or the Government, as more rejected petitions continued to be sent to him (two in 2006 and one in 2007, taking the total to 23). All remained pending when President Kalam ended his tenure in July 2007. Apart from Chatterjee, the only petition signed by Kalam was a rare one where the government recommended commutation.[29]

Like his predecessor, Kalam rejected only one petition during his tenure. Unlike the case of President Narayanan however, this led to an execution. But like his predecessor, he too left a legacy of pending petitions for the next President. Only now, the list of pending petitions had grown from eight to 23 – the backlog had grown. President Pratibha Patil's load was increased when the MHA forwarded four mercy petitions to reject in 2007–2008.

President Patil initially appeared to be following in the footsteps of Narayanan and Kalam in being unwilling to sign rejections of petitions as a matter of course. In November 2007 she returned one of the mercy petitions to the MHA for reconsideration.[30] After 2009, when a new Home Minister announced that the

---

28 The first was Kalam's deviation from the official text during a lecture at the National Police Academy in Hyderabad on 15 October 2005 where he rhetorically asked why there were only poor people on death row. On 18 October 2005, President Kalam addressed a letter to the MHA asking for a review of the 20 pending mercy files on the basis of new yardsticks prepared by him. The last of President Kalam's public statements on the death penalty was on 26 October 2005 when in response to a question about his letter to the MHA, he is reported to have called for a 'comprehensive policy on the death penalty after all aspects relating to it and mercy petitions were discussed in Parliament'.

29 Kheraj Ram on 29 September 2006. This was also the first commutation since March 1998.

30 Mercy petition of Om Prakash. Ministry of Home Affairs, Reply to application under the Right to Information Act 11 September 2008 notes that the case is being examined in consultation with the Government of Uttaranchal. Om Prakash alias Israel Lakra is believed to be a juvenile. See AI and PUCL 2008, 105.

government would re-submit all the pending files – one case a month – in an attempt to clear the backlog, the President disposed of nine more mercy petitions between November 2009 and March 2011 (involving 20 people) – all with directions to commute sentence. A further 15 persons had their death sentences commuted after President Patil accepted another ten mercy petitions between July 2011 and June 2012. Pratibha Patil's commutations were subject to intense media scrutiny and criticism, forcing the President's Secretariat to officially clarify the limited role played by the President in the clemency process (Presidents Secretariat 2012).

Although President Patil also accepted the recommendation of the Ministry of Home Affairs to reject two mercy petitions in May 2011, and a further third petition in August 2011, no executions took place during her presidency. The five prisoners facing execution challenged the rejection of their petition in the Supreme Court, on the grounds that the delay in deciding amounted to a violation of their constitutional rights – final judgments are awaited at the time of writing.

Three Presidents – Narayanan, Kalam and Patil – effectively ensured that there was only one execution in India for a period of 15 years from mid-1997 to mid-2012. The particular reasons for their decisions are not known, it is unclear whether they were imposing their personal views on the issue or following the diktats of the ruling party. Although some would disagree with their methods, the three Presidents have stretched, but not overstepped, the boundaries of their limited powers with respect to mercy petitions. Their acts, along with the role of the BJP Government in the freakish case of Govindasami ensured that capital gridlock was a dominant feature in the debate on capital punishment in India in the recent past.

Conclusion: The Paths Ahead

The virtual end of executions between 1997 and 2012 led to some optimism that the Indian death penalty may be on its way out. In 2009, Johnson and Zimring stated, 'the most probable future of the death penalty in India is a long but informal continuation of few or zero executions without formal abolition'. According to Johnson and Zimring (2009): 'Indian leaders have little to gain and much to lose by trying to break through the gridlock that prevents almost all executions, especially in a political context in which multiparty coalitions have become the norm and a fragmented political culture makes it difficult for government to take decisive steps'. They (Johnson and Zimring 2009) had referred to the previous BJP-led government's lack of executions and the absence of public pressure for executions to suggest that even the return of the BJP would be unlikely to lead to a resurgence of executions. Similarly, Hood (2009) also asserted, 'India could easily abolish the death penalty without any serious internal political consequence'.

The manner in which the Home Ministry has disposed mercy petitions since late 2009 indicated that the Government was looking to end the capital gridlock, but it was the rejection of three petitions by President Patil between May and

August 2011 that was the first unambiguous indication that such views of abolition may have been optimistic. The rejections and speedy executions of two other men in late 2012 and early 2013 leave little doubt of the political will in the Congress-led government to allow resumption of executions. A significant part in such a situation was played by the incumbent President – Pranab Mukherjee – who appears to have shown a willingness to reject petitions and therefore allow executions to continue. In his first seven months as President he rejected four mercy petitions. In addition to the two executed, another five prisoners remain under the shadow of imminent execution. It is a moot question whether the executions would have taken place had his predecessors been in office.

Even if Mukherjee did allow the executions to proceed, what led the Government to proceed with them after many years without the need for any? It is likely that, with growing domestic political pressure and the possibility of an electoral defeat in the general elections in 2014, the Congress party could not afford to be seen to be soft on terrorism. This was a weakness that the main opposition party (BJP) would almost certainly exploit. The execution of Ajmal Kasab and Afzal Guru – convicted for their role in terrorist attacks, and seen as 'poster boys' for the retention of the death penalty in India by much of the population – may well be the Congress's way of showing its resolve to be seen to be tough on terrorism in particular, and on violent crime in general. The repeated rejection of the United Nations General Assembly resolution against moratorium in 2007, 2008 and 2010 must be seen in this light, as should the introduction of the death penalty for repeat convictions for sexual assault and in the Anti-Hijack Act.

A complete analysis of this twist in the tale of the death penalty in India may require more distance from recent events. The peculiar circumstances around the two executed men and their link with terrorist attacks leaves some hope that further executions may not continue. However, the rejection of petitions affecting ten other death row prisoners suggests the opposite. Even if the Supreme Court – currently hearing most of these cases – was to commute their death sentences on the grounds of the delayed decision on the mercy petitions, the end of the backlog and of capital gridlock means that other petitions may be rejected without similar concerns about delay.

All is not yet lost however. The manner in which the executions of Ajmal Kasab and Afzal Guru took place – carried out in secrecy with even the rejection of the mercy petitions not publicly announced till the hanging had already taken place, and with families unable to meet the prisoners – suggests that there is a certain discomfort with the death penalty even within the Government.

There is also growing discomfort with India's capital-sentencing system. The 'rarest of the rare' formulation has been criticized as arbitrary by analysts including Amnesty International and the People's Union for Civil Liberties (2008) which, after analysing judgments of the Supreme Court over five decades, termed the arbitrary capital-sentencing system a 'lethal lottery'. More importantly, some judges of the Indian Supreme Court too have recognized similar flaws – a series of judgments have acknowledged the failure of the capital-sentencing system in the country.

Although the Supreme Court judges are unlikely to go as far as to grapple with the question of the constitutionality of the death penalty *per se*, it is possible that the Court might be more willing to examine the constitutionality of the administration of capital sentencing. Indian Courts, in the recent past, have been willing to take on the mandatory death penalty – both the Supreme Court and the Bombay High Court have struck it down in the Arms Act and Narcotic Drugs and Psychotropic Substances Act respectively (*State of Punjab v. Dalbir Singh* 2012, *Indian Harm Reduction Network v. Union of India and ors* 2011).

The executions of 2012–13 and the threat of many more have led to the return of the death penalty debate in India with anti-death penalty activists in India mobilized, at least for the time being. They might also draw upon the past decade and a half of 'capital gridlock' to show what a criminal justice system without executions and the death penalty might look like. A glance at government crime figures shows that, while high, the murder rate in India did not increase in the decade from 1998 to 2008, when virtually no executions took place – if anything, it decreased from 4.0 in 1998 to 2.8 in 2008 (see Table 10.2). While the decrease is unlikely to have any relation to the death penalty, the absence of an increase should put an end to the argument that India needs the death sentence or executions as a crime-control measure. The murder rate in India has by and large remained in same range from 1953 (2.7) to the present day (2.8): irrespective of the hundred persons executed every year in the 1950s, the gridlock of the 2000s or the current resumption of executions.[31]

Table 10.2 Murder – crime and punishment 1998–2008[32]

Year	Murder rate (per 100,000 persons)	No. of murders in the year	No. of persons convicted (% of completed trials)	No. of death sentences in the year	No. of death sentences by supreme court	No. of executions
2008	2.8	32,766	20,834 (37.6)	126	4	0
2007	2.8	32,318	20,597 (34.5)	186	4	0

31 NCRB 1953, Appendix II

32 Compiled from data in the NCRB annual reports 'Crime in India' and 'Prison Statistics' from 1998 to 2008. Information on number of death sentences by the Supreme Court is based on the author's analysis of Supreme Court judgments in the period – information on file.

2006	2.9	32,481	22,457 (34.3)	129	3	0
2005	3.0	32,719	20,998 (30.8)	164	7	0
2004	3.1	33,608	22,243 (32.9)	125	4	1
2003	3.1	32,716	21,948 (32.2)	142	6	0
2002	3.4	35,290	22,849 (31.3)	126	6	0
2001	3.5	36,202	20,348 (33.0)	106	2	0
2000	3.7	37,399	Not Available	87	3	0
1999	3.8	37,170	21,348 (35.2)	46	12	0
1998	4.0	38,653	20,396 (31.9)	81	4	0

What then does the future hold for the death penalty in India? At worst, the next few years may see a flurry of executions but it is unlikely that the death penalty in India will remain anything but a symbolic punishment. Conversely, there is a possibility that, with their electoral future secure, the Congress may allow executions to fall into abeyance, as in former years. A formal moratorium on executions appears unlikely, and any abolition (even for ordinary offences) appears out of the question. A further complication is the introduction of life sentences – for the remainder of the prisoner's natural life – without any possibility of review or release.[33] Although dubious when examined from a human rights point of view, the whole-life sentence until the end of a prisoner's natural life, without possibility of release, has the twin 'advantage' of addressing the concerns of those seeking a strong response to violent crime without upsetting those who are squeamish about executions and the death penalty.

Such sentences however raise further questions for those against the death penalty in India. While they might be acceptable to some activists if they lead eventually to the abolition of the death penalty, or even a reduction in executions, those concerned with broader questions of punishment and human rights may find that, given the scale of the problem, allowing whole-life sentences in place of death sentences may be a pyrrhic victory.[34]

33 This began with petitions commuted by the President after 2006 where the MHA directed that there would be no possibility of release. Such sentences also have support from the Supreme Court, which has passed such sentences in a series of judgments since 2001.

34 While over 100 persons are sentenced to death every year, more than 20,000 are sentenced to life imprisonment for the offence of murder. In terms of current population,

References

Amnesty International India and People's Union for Civil Liberties. 2008. *Lethal Lottery – The death penalty in India: A study of Supreme Court judgments in death penalty cases 1950–2006*. New Delhi: Amnesty International.

Bachan Singh v. State of Punjab [1980] AIR 1980 SC 898.

Batra, B. 2009. *'Court' of Last Resort: A Study of Constitutional Clemency for Capital Crimes in India.* Jawaharlal Nehru University New Delhi: Centre for the Study of Law and Governance working paper series.

Hood, R. 2009. Abolition of the Death Penalty: China in World Perspective. *City University of Hong Kong Law Review*, 1, 1–21.

Indian Harm Reduction Network v. Union of India and others 2011, CWP no. 1784 of 2010 (Bombay High Court).

Johnson, D.T. and Zimring, F.E. 2009. *The Next Frontier: National Development, Political Change, and the Death Penalty in Asia.* Oxford: Oxford University Press.

Law Commission of India. 1967. *35th Report on Capital Punishment*. New Delhi: Government of India.

Machhi Singh v. State of Punjab [1983] 3 SCC 470.

Mahesh s/o Ram Narain v. State of Madhya Pradesh [1987] 3 SCC 80.

Mithu v. State of Punjab [1983] AIR 1983 SC 473.

National Archives of India. 1946. *File no. Home (Public)* 1/22/46, New Delhi.

National Crime Records Bureau. 1953. *Crime in India* 1953. New Delhi: Ministry of Home Affairs, Government of India.

National Crime Records Bureau. 2011. *Crime in India* 2011. New Delhi: Ministry of Home Affairs, Government of India.

National Crime Records Bureau. 2011a. *Prison Statistics* 2011. New Delhi: Ministry of Home Affairs, Government of India.

Presidents Secretariat 2012, *Press Release: Clarification Regarding Recent Media Reports on Disposal of Clemency Petitions by the President of India – 25 June 2012*, Government of India.

Samsher Singh v. Union of India 1974, AIR 1974 SC 2192.

State of Punjab v. Singh 2012, CA no. 117 of 2006 (Supreme Court).

---

while India has 477 persons on death row it has 68,935 persons serving life terms (as of 31 Dec. 2011: see National Crime Records Bureau 2011a). A sentence of life imprisonment without possibility of release, unless controlled as strictly as the death penalty now has to be, risks thousands of sentences every year.

PART IV
Countries with Majority Muslim Populations

Chapter 11

Islamic Visions for the Abolition of the Death Penalty

Mohammad Habash

For the sake of bringing humanity to the wells of peace and compassion, and stopping all forms of abuse of human physical integrity and dignity, it is important to eradicate laws that give the judiciary the power to kill people because of their political affiliations and/or criminal activities.

We know that many Islamic scholars reject this view, because they see it as changing the rule of Allah, which in their view ordains the death penalty. Moreover, these scholars consider abolitionism as a departure from the opinions of most Islamic scholars throughout history.

Even if China is still the country with the highest rate of death sentences and executions, and other non-Muslim countries are also still carrying out executions, there is the constant claim that Islam is responsible for the survival of particularly harsh sentences, and corporal punishment, in countries with a Muslim majority. It is in this context, and to address this question, that I offer this chapter, which I hope will add something useful to guide humanity towards a shift from retaliatory punishment to punishment reform. Let us pray that it will contribute to ending torture in all its forms, especially the torture implemented by states which justify its use as necessary to achieve justice.

I will argue in this chapter that Islamic law has a plethora of safeguards against using the death penalty that are found in the Holy Quran.

Islam and the Death Penalty

Islamic law has become a particular focus of attention worldwide when the death penalty is addressed. Most scholars of Islamic law refer to the purposes of Shariah, which aims to safeguard five essentials. These are: *religion*, *life*, *honour (family)*, *intellect* and *property*. The objectives of Islamic law are all encompassed by, and categorized in accordance with, the above-mentioned five essentials.

The Holy Quran states the following as regards sending prophets and laws to administer balanced and merciful justice: ‘We sent aforetime Our apostles with Clear Signs And sent down with them The Book and the Balance (of Right and Wrong), that men may stand forth in justice’ (The Holy Quran 1946: 1505). As

Allah states with utmost clarity: 'We sent thee not [O Muhammad], but as a Mercy for all creatures' (The Holy Quran 1946: 846).

The jurists have written the rules of this noble law, in order to achieve the aforementioned objectives based on evidence from the Quran and the Sunnah (the tradition of the Prophet Mohammad). They have also established other provisions, such as codes of unanimity, analogy, approval, free interest, custom, traditional laws and other provisions mentioned in the books of *Fiqh*[1] scholars.

Throughout the history of Islam Muslims have applied these legal provisions which have formed the basis of legal systems. Today, with the development of criminal law, and the accompanying development of jurisprudence and legislation in a number of Muslim countries, there is a need to review this jurisprudence, and the selection of laws, in the light of how honoured scholars judge that the goals of Sharia are achieved as regards suppressing crime and administering justice.

There is also a need to discuss Sharia in relation to international human rights and humanitarian law. A series of charters and human rights initiatives have been signed by most of the Islamic countries, and it is important that there is discourse among scientists and scholars in all Muslim countries, to clarify how these may harmonize with the objectives of the noble Sharia, and what may constitute necessary reservations.

Despite the fact that many Muslim countries have adopted modern, civilized and flexible laws to deal with criminals and felonies, through cooperation with scholars and local imams, the accusation persists that Islamic legislation generally involves harsh sentences in the fight against crime, and still falls short of international standards. For instance, the impression is that Islam sees the offender as an enemy to get rid of rather than someone who mainly needs treatment and rehabilitation.

This view has been strengthened, and the idea of the brutality of Islamic legislation has been promoted by a particular focus on cases like Somalia and Afghanistan, and on incidents in Algeria during the last decade. In these instances one found the application of bloody reprisals and sanctions against 'sinners' without these 'sinners' being given access to a fair trial. The ruthless and reckless application of 'Sharia' by private parties has contributed to create a bleak picture of Islam in the field of crime and punishment. This image highlights important questions facing Islamic law:

- Is Islamic law incapable of keeping up with the times while maintaining its basic essentials and *Fiqh*?
- Is the focus on corporal punishment in Sharia such that it excludes the logic of the qualification, and thus diminishs the possibility of correct merciful interpretation, training and penal reform to provide the capabilities for a humanitarian, nuanced and just legal system?

1 Editor's note: *Fiqh* is Islamic jurisprudence. *Fiqh* is an expansion of the code of conduct (Sharia) expounded in the Quran, sometimes supplemented by tradition (Sunnah) and implemented by the rulings and interpretations of Islamic jurists.

- Can Islam be considered responsible for the applications of Islamic law made by revolutionary armed militias in the Islamic world under the rallying cry: 'Governorship of God'?

I will argue that Islamic law is capable of keeping up with the times while still maintaining its basic essentials and *Fiqh* through a correct merciful interpretation that is contrary to the way Islamic law is applied by revolutionary armed militias and by Islamic states which kill. So what is the correct and merciful interpretation which shows the human face of an Islamic justice which does not impose capital punishment?

Islam and the Greatest Sin of All – Murder

In Islam, murder is the greatest of all sins. The Quran has many verses on the prohibition of blood and the prohibition of killing the human soul. The Quran states: '… if one slew a person – [unjustly] … it would be as if he slew the whole people and if anyone saved a life it would be as if he saved the life of the whole people' (The Holy Quran 1946: 252). God says: 'If a man kills a Believer Intentionally, his recompense is Hell, to abide therein (For Ever): and the wrath And the curse of God Are upon him, and A dreadful penalty Is prepared for him' (The Holy Quran 1946: 210).

There is no doubt that there are texts comprehensively prohibiting all kinds of killing, and a discourse has evolved to extend the prohibition to all people, regardless of their religion, beliefs and sex. Furthermore, it includes killing murderers, commanding such killings, as well as assisting the ending of a life.

Islam sets strict prohibitions on the killing of animals for no reason. The Prophet, peace be upon him, forbade killing the ant in the wild as well as the bee, the Hoopoe,[2] shrikes and vermin that does not cause any harm. If Islam has such dire warnings for those who cause the killing of birds or cats, obviously the same applies to whoever kills a man or woman just on a suspicion, without evidence or proof of harm!

Islam does make retribution the penalty for killers. As the Holy Quran says:

> O ye who believe! The law of equality Is prescribed to you In cases of murder: The free for the free, the slave for the slave, The woman for the woman. But if any remission Is made by the brother Of the slain, then grant Any reasonable demand And compensate him With handsome gratitude. This is a concession And a Mercy From your Lord. (The Holy Quran 1946: 70)

Furthermore, the Holy Quran says regarding retribution: 'There is (saving of) Life To you, O ye men of understanding; That ye may Restrain yourself. you in retaliation' (The Holy Quran 1946: 71).

2 Editor's note: a bird found across Afro-Eurasia.

But this retribution, which is spoken of in the Holy Quran, is linked with many conditions and constraints. Thus, retribution should be implemented rarely and sparingly. It should also be limited to the most heinous of crimes. However, even in such cases, Islamic jurisprudence states that one should try, by 14 different methods to avoid the death penalty as a sanction and instead take the route of pardon and compensation (*Diyya*).

Some scholars have created a list of crimes which they claim to be punishable by death. These are:

- adultery by a married man or woman
- the crime of Haraba[3]
- change of religion
- heresy
- failure to pray
- sorcery
- homosexuality

However, according to the Holy Quran, these crimes are not necessarily punishable by death. Thus, the interpretation is not grounded in the Holy Quran, and there are doubts in the subsequent appraisal of the *hadith*, *sanad* (the citations or backings used to verify the legitimacy of the hadith in question) and the *matn* (the actual wording of the hadith) justifying the death penalty. Moreover, 95 per cent of Islamic countries do not impose capital punishment for the crimes listed. For example, in the case of Yemen a relatively conservative Islamic state, there are 81 crimes punishable by death, but for only one of these the Holy Quran allows death (Figure 11.1).

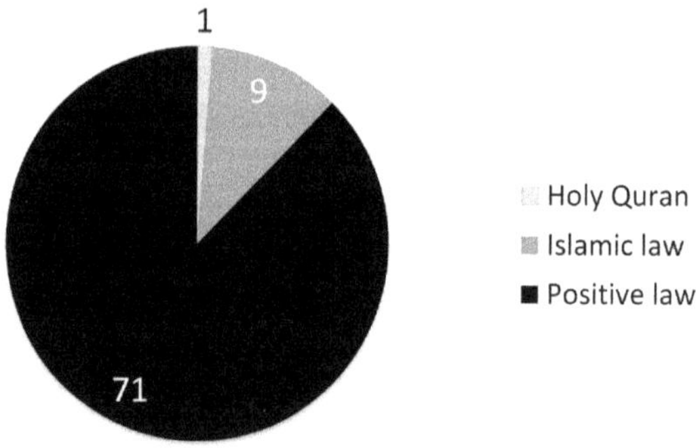

Figure 11.1 Eighty-one crimes in Yemen punishable by death. Holy Quran allows only one

3 Editor's note: a Qur'anic term defined as sowing corruption and chaos on earth.

There are 14 ways in Islam to avoid imposing the death penalty (Figure 11.2). They can be shown as follows:

Figure 11.2 Ways in Islam to avoid the death penalty

First of all: the term retribution does not equal execution. The Holy Quran does not mention the word execution, but the word retribution, and there is a huge difference between the two. Execution is the abolition of life, but retribution means to seeking justice and clarification, equality and compensation. Thus, while execution means murder, retribution means to achieve justice in a way where the seriousness of the punishment fits the seriousness of the crime. Depending on the offence, the punishment may be a fine or restitution.

Second: decisions on life and death belong to God alone. Since the word execution is not mentioned in the texts of the Quran or in the tradition of Prophet Mohammad, peace be upon him, or even in Islamic jurisprudence, capital punishment constitutes an act against the faith.

Third: there is the duty to invite the parents and/or relatives of the victim to pardon the murderer. The retribution verses in the Holy Quran always carry a stern warning and rebuke against participating in killings, and always urge parents and/or relatives to forgive. According to the Holy Quran: 'But if any remission Is made by the brother Of the slain, then grant Any reasonable demand' (The Holy Quran 1946: 178). Another verse states: 'And if Anyone is slain wrongfully, We have given his heir Authority (to demand Qisas Or to forgive): but let him Not exceed bounds in the matter Of taking life: for he is helped (by the Law)' (The Holy Quran 1946: 703). There are many commandments by the Prophet, peace be upon him, advocating amnesty in cases of retribution, for example: 'he would not respond to an evil deed with an evil deed, but rather he would pardon and overlook'.[4]

Fourth: retribution is an essential requirement, as is the necessity of dropping retribution if amnesty is given by any (correct) blood relative. If ten brothers have the right blood relationship to the victim, they must all give the pardon, if one does so. In other words, full consensus is necessary for retribution to be applied.

Fifth: the state has no right to impose the rule of retribution on a killer except in the presence of a true individual claim, and in the absence of a claim, should use alternative sanctions. There is no doubt that preventing the state from exacting retribution, if there is no guardian or relative of the person whose blood has been shed prevents any justification for the state to kill.

Sixth: there is the principle of avoiding punishments if there is any doubt. Islam has stopped the practice of killing the killer if no intent or will to kill has been established. This also applies to accidental deaths. As the Prophet Mohammad, peace be upon him, ordered the judges: 'You must avoid punishment as much as you can and if you find a way. The Imam who mistakenly pardons is better than one who mistakenly punishes'.[5]

Seventh: there is *Diyya* (also known as blood money) which is financial compensation which can be paid to the heirs of a (murder) victim. It is often a huge amount – like 100 camels. *Diyya* legislation is a strong incentive to encourage the heirs of the slain to grant amnesty to the murderer. If *Diyya* were practised in accordance with the Holy Quran, courts would be required to consider *Diyya* as the principal debt, with higher priority than all others. Whether this is possible to achieve in practice or not it nonetheless shows how the Holy Quran creates limits on retribution. As it is practised at present the avoidance of capital punishment through *Diyya* is predominantly a privilege for wealthier groups.

Eighth: the practice of clan payment diverges from one of the main tenets of the Holy Quran that: 'Every soul draws the meed Of its acts on none But itself: no bearer Of burdens can bear The burden of another. Your goal in the end Is towards God: He will tell You the truth of the things Wherein ye disputed' (The Holy

4 See: http://www.ummah.com/forum/showthread.php?351782-The-Messenger-of-Allah-peace-and-blessings-be-upon-him-did-not-strike-a-woman&p=5062340.

5 See: http://dailyhadith.adaptivesolutionsinc.com/hadith/Innocent-Till-Proven-Guilty.htm.

Quran 1946: 339). Islam calls on all clans to contribute, so that the death penalty can be avoided, to collect *Diyya.*

Ninth: according to the Holy Quran, the debtors (*garemoon*), which includes those who pay money to avoid the death penalty, have the right to get a reward from the state in the form of alms equalling their payment. 'Alms are for the poor And the needy, and those Employed to administer the (funds); For those whose hearts Have been (recently) reconciled (To truth); for those in bondage And in debt; in the cause Of God; and for the wayfarer: (Thus is it) ordained by God And God is full of knowledge And wisdom' (The Holy Quran 1946: 458).

Tenth: intercession is permissible in the context of retribution where the death penalty may be applied, but is not necessarily permissible for other crimes. Intercession (Shafa'ah) literally means the pairing of two things. It is for instance used when a highly esteemed person intercedes for a person who has committed a crime, and asks for forgiveness. Maybe the reason this word has been used for such an act is because the actual criminal in no way deserves to be forgiven, and that is why she or he has to be paired with the request and intercession of the highly esteemed person in order to be forgiven.

Eleventh: according to Islam it is forbidden for a Muslim to take revenge on a criminal. Islam clearly prohibits revenge, and individuals killing a murderer – whatever the justification – are committing a predicate or serious offence. Scholar are in agreement on two fundamental conditions: i) the correct implementation of the laws is under the executive authority of the state, and ii) it is important to prevent acts of personal vendetta or revenge. It is the state which is responsible for the implementation and enforcement of punishment through the criminal justice system.

Twelfth: for a retribution to be implemented there needs to be a full consensus among Islamic scholars. If there is not a full consensus, the death penalty as retribution cannot be lawfully carried out. It could be argued that, since the ratification of international treaties, even when lawyers from other nations have important reservations against the use of the death penalty as retribution – this could be interpreted to imply that the necessary consensus is absent.

Thirteenth: there should be a consensus among the judiciary on the necessary retribution in a criminal case. If any of them choose to rule for a pardon or blood money as retribution, the others should make the same ruling. One judge who does not want to pass the death sentence is enough to break the consensus and thus open the way for alternative sanctions.

Fourteenth: the state has a responsibility to stop executions. Sharia emphasizes the responsibility of the state in the implementation of retribution. The state is responsible for halting the implement of such provisions if there is lack of consensus in law or judgment, or doubt concerning guilt.

To conclude: These 14 main points, I would argue, provide evidence that in Islam, execution is not the goal in cases of retribution. The intention is to deter the offender, not to kill her or him.

Even though retribution is mentioned in the verses of the Holy Quran, the Court has the right to avoid using the death penalty and even stop the use of this form of punishment.

This is because the actual use of the death penalty requires these minimum two conditions in Islam: first, the absolute consensus of scholars that the crime necessitates punishment by death, and secondly, a full judicial consensus that there is no way to avoid the death penalty for the criminal in question.

These conditions have prompted some Islamic countries to abolish the death penalty, which hopefully will lead to its abolition altogether.

Islamic Visions for the Abolition of Corporal Punishments and the Death Penalty

I have argued that a correct, merciful interpretation of Islamic law is contrary to how it is applied by revolutionary armed militias and Islamist states which send Muslims to be killed in hundreds. My article has provided an introduction to a merciful and just interpretation showing the human face of Islamic justice – one without capital punishment. It is one of many Islamic visions for the abolition of corporal punishments and the death penalty.

I argue that Islamic law is quite capable of keeping up with the times, and of adhering to international law and human rights conventions while still retaining its basic elements of Islamic jurisprudence – *Fiqh*. It is not by circumventing Islamic jurisprudence that one can abolish the death penalty, but *through* the logic of *Fiqh* and the Islamic tradition.

There are 14 ways in Islam to avoid imposing the death penalty. These are important in and of themselves. They show that in Islam retribution does not necessarily mean execution. They are also manifestations of an overriding intent to create a form of justice which limits the harshness of sanctions and strives towards finding openings for leniency and mercy.

References:

Hadith Explanation: *Innocent Till Proven Guilty.* Available at: http://dailyhadith.adaptivesolutionsinc.com/hadith/Innocent-Till-Proven-Guilty.htm.

The Holy Qur'an (1946) Text, Translation and Commentary by Abdullah Yusuf Ali. McGregor & Werner, Inc.: United States of America.

Umah Forum: Available at: http://www.ummah.com/forum/showthread.php?351782-The-Messenger-of-Allah-peace-and-blessings-be-upon-him-did-not-strike-a-woman&p=5062340.

Chapter 12

An Overview of the Ongoing Debate on the Death Penalty in Morocco[1]

Mohammed Ayatt

As a Moroccan citizen and a practising lawyer, I am very much interested in the debate on the death penalty that is ongoing in my country. I will not dwell here on the arguments for or against the abolition of the death penalty. They all belong to an old and probably interminable debate. That the question of abolishing the death penalty is also a question of principle is very cogently argued by Roger Hood and Carolyn Hoyle (2008: 350). I would like to state upfront that I oppose the death penalty. Like most abolitionists I oppose it because of its uselessness, its cruelty, its irreversible and irremediable character (especially when it is enforced on innocent people following a miscarriage of justice), its very often discriminatory enforcement on the poor and on minorities and last, but not least, because of the frequent misuse of the death penalty by dictators.

The current Moroccan penal code was adopted in 1962; eight years after the independence of Morocco. It was inspired by the penal code of our colonizer: France. The code retained the death penalty.[2] Recently a new Moroccan penal code has been drafted. The draft was finalized in 2007, but it has not been adopted yet. This draft still retains the death penalty.[3] In fact, following the events of the 'Arab Spring', several provisions of this draft penal code will have to be reviewed. These provisions should further echo the demand of the Moroccan people for less discrimination, notably against women, and for more respect for human rights.[4]

On 1 July 2011 a new constitution was voted in by the Moroccan people. The new constitution provides that 'the right to life is the primary right of every human being'. It also provides that the right to life 'is protected by the law'.[5] Such legal protection of the right to life opens a wide door for debate on the legitimacy

---

1 This chapter is an edited version of the oral contribution of the author to the Second Symposium on the Death Penalty held on 8–9 December 2012 at the University of Oslo, Department of Criminology and Sociology of Law.

2 Source: Article 16.

3 Source: Draft of the Moroccan penal code dated 10 July 2007, article 16.

4 A memorandum on this subject was drafted by the National Council on Human Rights to be presented to the Moroccan Ministry of Justice and other interested departments. I was co-drafter of this memorandum.

5 Source: *Constitution*, 1 July 2011, article 20.

(if not on the constitutionality) of the death penalty. The new constitution provides for the establishment of a Constitutional Court. When this Court is established, its judges will certainly have to decide on the constitutionality of death penalty versus the constitutional protection of life. This will not be an easy task. The possibility of a decision in favour of abolition can not be excluded, but it will take a lot of circumspection and courage for the judges to espouse such an approach. Yet it remains clear that no provision in the new constitution explicitly prohibits the death penalty; which makes the debate more challenging. Meanwhile there are currently 111 individuals on death row in Morocco, amongst them two women.[6]

All this considered, there are still some important indications suggesting a favourable trend towards the abolition of the death penalty in Morocco. However this trend sometimes does not seem to be very dynamic. It seems that it is following a slow, step-by-step approach. Thus, the road to abolition is filled with obstacles. These, sometimes, are unpredictable and not easy to overcome and might throw the quest off its course. As Arthur Koestler (1966) quotes Ferdinand Lasalle:

> Show us not the aim without the way.
> For ends and means on earth are so entangled
> That changing one, you change the other too;
> Each different path brings other ends in view

Landmarks on the Path to Abolition

Among significant indications of a definite trend towards abolition of the death penalty in Morocco we could mention the following:

- the readiness of a large segment of Moroccan civil society
- the fact that Morocco is *de facto* abolitionist, meaning there has not been an execution for the last two decades
- the recommendation of the Equity and Reconciliation Commission and their follow up
- the very promising statements made by some Moroccan officials.

The Readiness of a Large Segment of Moroccan Civil Society

Special tribute should be paid to a wide section of Moroccan civil society, in which there has been a very serious debate on the abolition of the death penalty, particularly during the last ten years. In 2003 the Moroccan Coalition against the

6 Sentences to death and their execution (Amnesty International 2011), coupled with a very recent statement made in the media by the General Director of the Prison and rehabilitation department in Morocco.

Death Penalty (CMCPM) was established. It included seven NGOs, mostly human rights associations, together with the Moroccan Bar Association, the Supervisory of Prisons and the Moroccan branch of Amnesty International. Their activities, performed individually or jointly, included appeals for the abolition of the death penalty and the sensitization of both the legal community and the public to the issues involved. They also organized colloquiums and spearheaded demonstrations and sit-ins.[7]

This important work was fully acknowledged by the Moroccan National Advisory Council on Human Rights, especially when the Council was chaired by the late Driss Benzekri, who was a fervent opponent of the death penalty. The National Council on Human Rights is the new body that took over the National Advisory Council in mid-2011. It still strongly supports the calls of Moroccan NGOs for abolition. For about two decades this maturity in Moroccan civil society has been associated with another very important landmark in the path leading to the abolition of the death penalty, the fact that Morocco is a *de facto* abolitionist country.

Morocco is a *de facto* Abolitionist Country

Death penalty sentences are indeed still periodically handed down. For example, M. Othmani, who was the perpetrator of the 28 April 2011 bombing in Marrakech, which killed 17 people, most of them tourists, was sentenced to death in October 2011. Prior to this atrocity, there was a tendency amongst Moroccan judges to avoid imposing the death penalty. Unfortunately this trend slowed down by this terrorist incident. However, since 1993, death sentences have never been enforced (Zamparutti 2011: 76).[8] This practice started during the reign of King Hassan II and was sustained by his successor, King Mohammed VI. It is very significant that since his accession to the throne, the current monarch has never signed an execution decree (Zamparutti 2011: 75). Amnesty International reported that in April 2011 His Majesty commuted five death penalty sentences to imprisonment, within a wider royal amnesty. The King periodically grants Royal Amnesties, particularly on national and religious holidays. On 18 November 2005 the King granted amnesty to 10,000 inmates, 5,000 being released while the rest had their sentences reduced. In the process 25 death sentences were commuted to life imprisonment. When his daughter Lalla Khadija was born, the King granted amnesty to 8,836 prisoners, including 14 sentenced to death. On 30 July 2009,

7 Source: http://cntcpm.unblog.fr/files/2008/07/wcadprapmondarabfr.pdf. [Accessed 5 October 2012.]

8 Source: Cf. la Coalition mondiale contre la peine de mort. http://cntcpm.unblog.fr/files/2008/07/wcadprapmondarabfr.pdf. [Accessed 6 October 2012.]

the tenth anniversary of his accession to the throne, the King also granted several amnesties, including some to inmates on death row (Zamparutti 2011: 75).[9]

Therefore, even though the Moroccan penal code retains the death penalty, Morocco has been a *de facto* abolitionist country for the last two decades. This step should be acknowledged as important progress towards abolition. Nevertheless, it is not sufficient, because as long as the death penalty is retained in the penal code it will be a Damoclean sword. That is why certain other indicators are often scrutinized in order to assess the steadiness of the trend toward abolition. Amongst these we can single out:

- the recommendations of the Equity and Reconciliation Commission and their follow up
- the position of the Moroccan authorities *vis-à-vis* the death penalty.

The Recommendations of the Equity and Reconciliation Body and Their Follow Up

The Equity and Reconciliation Commission (Known as the IER which stands for its French title 'Instance équité et réconciliation') is an institution that oversaw transitional justice in Morocco during the late nineties and the beginning of the second millennium). The Equity and Reconciliation Commission has explicitly recommended to the Kingdom of Morocco the ratification of *the Second Protocol* of *the International Covenant on Civil and Political Rights*.[10] This is undoubtedly another considerable milestone on the way to death penalty abolition. In view of the fact that the recommendations of the Equity and Reconciliation Commission were all ratified by the king, they are strongly indicative of our country's political commitment to the promotion of human rights. A colloquium on the death penalty organized in 2008 by the National Advisory Council on Human Rights firmly underlined their substantial authority.[11] This colloquium took place as a follow up of the implementation of the Equity and Reconciliation Commission's recommendations.

Indeed, the mere organization in Morocco of such forum is very significant on many levels. First of all, it took place with the collaboration of 'Tous contre la peine de mort', an NGO which is very reputable, and internationally

9 Amnesty granted on 11 April 2011. Source: Final Report of the IER, paragraph 2/1, 114 (Arabic version).

10 Same source as footnote number 9.

11 Source: Proceedings of the colloquium on the death penalty organized in Rabat by the National Advisory Council on Human Rights from in 2008 in collaboration with the French NGO 'Ensemble contre la peine de mort, Published by the National Advisory Council, Rabat, 2008, notably page 9 and (of the Arabic version).

renowned.[12] Secondly, it had approached the issues relating to the death penalty from several different angles: philosophical, sociological, criminological and religious. A contribution concerning the religious foundations of the death penalty was presented and discussed by a recognized Moroccan theologian. It was very pertinent in revealing various points that were little known even by the Moroccan intellectual elite, finer religious points and subtleties which could help the Kingdom of Morocco to opt for a more assertive abolitionist perspective. A similar flexibility is apparent periodically in promising statements made by high-profile Moroccan officials. In the same vein it should be underlined that Morocco has hosted in Rabat from 18 to 20 October 2012 the regional congress on the abolition of death penalty organized by the very dynamic NGO 'Ensemble contre la peine de mort'.

Promising Statements made by Moroccan Officials

The latest annual report released by Amnesty International (2011) highlighted a declaration made by the Chairman of the Commission for the Amendment of the Constitution just before the referendum on the draft constitution. The Chairman of the Commission pointed out that article 20 of the constitution, which protects the right to life, was meant to bring to an end the executions of death sentences (see Amnesty International 2011: 3). The same report quoted the statement of the Director of Penal Affairs at the Ministry of Justice. The Director said that the new constitution protects the right to life, and therefore it should speed up the move towards abolition.

This high-ranking magistrate further disclosed that an amendment to the criminal code that is under consideration aims at limiting the number of crimes punishable by death to nine, instead of 30. This amendment will respect the principle that only the most serious crimes could be punished by the death penalty (Amnesty International 2011: 39). It is worth noting that Morocco has hosted a press conference in preparation for the third International Congress against the Death Penalty. During this press conference the president of the National Advisory Council on Human Rights stated that 'there is a consensus in parliament on the necessity for abolishing the death penalty when favourable conditions for such a move exist' (*Maghreb Arab Press*, January 2007, quoted in Hood and Hoyle (2008: 67). Moreover, the Minister of Justice himself has stated 'we would like to

12 More recently a Regional Congress on Death Penalty was held, for the first time in Morocco, on 20–22 October 2012 by 'Ensemble contre la peine de mort' together with the Moroccan Organization on Human Rights and the Moroccan Bar Association. This Regional Congress was organized in preparation for the World Congress to be held in Madrid in June 2013. The author of this chapter contributed to the Congress with a paper on the 'Impact of the Exlusion of the Death Penalty from the Statutes of the International Criminal Tribunals on its Upcoming Universal Abolition'.

abolish death penalty in Morocco by *ad hoc* legislation. A wide range of legislative procedures are being considered in order to amend the penal code that will solve this issue' (quoted in Zamparutti 2011: 76).[13] This undertaking is similar to the one made in parliament by his predecessor, who recommended further progress being made towards abolition.[14]

All these statements and undertakings compel us to ask an important question: Is Morocco really engaged in a progressive move towards the abolition of the death penalty and to what extent?

A Progression towards Abolition?

As mentioned above, the idea of a possible step-by-step road to abolition has been reiterated several times in official talks. It is also important to highlight that such a move is backed by few Moroccan criminal lawyers.

During a legal forum organized by the Tangier Regional Commission on Human Rights a well-regarded Moroccan criminal law professor and former Minister of Justice recommended such a gradual approach. The speaker emphasized the cultural characteristics of Moroccan society including its conservatism. He advised that those cultural limitations should neither be ignored nor affronted. He recalled that reforms in Morocco were very often adopted by consensus in order to avoid radical options.

Some countries, like France, abolished the death penalty at one go, although often after a lengthy national debate. Other countries adopted a more gradual approach more in keeping with their tradition. The British experience is a good illustration of the latter option. In 1965 the United Kingdom initially tested abolition of the death penalty for a five-year period. This was renewable by the vote of the two chambers of parliament. The UK later totally abolished the death penalty in 1969 and ratified Protocol 6 of the European Convention on Human Rights prohibiting the death penalty in time of peace and, and later Protocol 13 prohibiting the death penalty in all circumstances.[15]

Another international example of a step-by-step progression characterized by compromise might be to consider the case of the International Criminal Tribunals.

I believe that the exclusion of the death penalty from the statutes of the International Criminal Tribunals (ICTs) was a very important landmark on the road to universal abolition. Yet this view remains controversial, at least in as much as the abolition of the death penalty is still hotly debated. When the first international penal tribunals were created their charters did not exclude the death

13 The Minister, the late Mohammed Ennaciri was replying to a question addressed to him in parliament on 11 November 2010.

14 Source: International Coalition against the Death Penalty: http://cntcpm.unblog.fr/files/2008/07/wcadprapmondarabfr.pdf, p. 20 [accessed on 4 October 2012].

15 Respectively 9 November 1998 and 10 October 2003.

penalty. Subsequently international standards were developed that prohibited mass crimes, in particular genocide and war crimes. Then, from the mid nineties onwards remarkable progress in international criminal justice ensued. The Genocide convention and the Geneva conventions established the principle of criminalizing serious violations, without specifying the sanctions for them.[16] Instead these conventions gave authority to member states to provide adequate sanctions in their legislations.[17] Therefore, if the death penalty is retained by the penal code of the state where an accused is tried, its imposition for those serious violations is not excluded.[18] Numerous factors have weighed heavily in the debate on the retention or exclusion of the death penalty in the ICTs' statutes. The initial factor relates to those who were involved in the debate. The participants in the debate on the retention or exclusion of the death penalty in the ICTs' statutes were the states. The arguments adduced in the debate on the death penalty nationally were extrapolated to the debate on the international level. The opponents of the death penalty invoked its uselessness, its cruelty and its irreversible consequences in case of miscarriage of justice. Conversely, its proponents based their arguments on the seriousness of the crimes under the jurisdiction of the ICTs, and the deterrent effect of the death penalty. Clinging to a rigid conception of national sovereignty, they defended the right of each state to determine the content of its penal law. Proponents, eager to retain total control of the penal law governing their territories, abstained from backing any international norm they feared might compromise this prerogative.[19] Eventually negotiations did lead to a compromise. On the one hand, the death penalty was excluded from the ICC statute. On the other hand, a special provision was included in the statute. It underlined that nothing on the statute prevented states from applying the sanctions provided by their national law when trying crimes under the jurisdiction of the ICC.[20] Thus, the ICC statute is abolitionist. However, this special provision constitutes an important concession

16 Art. 4 of the Convention on the Prevention and Punishment of Genocide, art. 49 of the first Geneva convention protecting the wounded and sick in armed forces in the field, art. 50 and 51 of the second Geneva convention protecting the wounded, sick and shipwrecked members of armed forces at sea, art. 129 and 130 of the third Geneva convention protecting prisoners of war and art. 146 and 147 of the fourth Geneva convention protecting civilians who find themselves under the rule of a foreign power in the event of international conflict.

17 Art. 7. In fact, few countries have harmonized their law with the provisions of the genocide convention and there were no genocide trials before the Akeyezu judgment by the ICTR in 1998.

18 States have rarely honoured their commitment to try those responsible for mass crimes. There are very few examples of such trials before the establishment of the ICTY and the ICTR. We could cite Adolf Eichmann's trial in Israel in 1961, and those of Klaus Barbie and Paul Touvier, who were tried in France in 1987 and 1994 respectively.

19 This argument was used by the states that on 2 February 2008 sent to the Secretary General of the UN a memorandum against Resolution 62/149 on the Moratorium on the Death Penalty.

20 Art. 77 of the ICC Statute.

in favour of states opposed to abolition of the death penalty. Although this is as such not a clear parallel to the situation in Morocco, nonetheless, it shows that a progression towards abolition also on an international level do not exclude a step by step approach and necessary compromise.

The wise, gradual approach on a national level as exemplified above by the UK example seems to be preferred by some Moroccan authorities and lawyers.[21] However, we should note that the Equity and Reconciliation Commission (IER) explicitly recommends abolition without going into details; which could support any scheme of abolition whether gradual or prompt and immediate. Naturally, gradual abolition has the advantage of being cautious and vigilant. However, obstacles that are not easy to overcome might obstruct the path of such a measured approach.

Are There Obstructions on the Road to Abolition?

The trend towards abolition was obvious in the words of some members of the former governments, and in the explicit recommendation from the Equity and Reconciliation Commission. So what is then the case with the current Moroccan government?

Without prejudging the case we could raise the following concern: to what extent could the current government led by an Islamist party delay or even stop the trend towards abolition?

The current Minister of Justice belongs to a moderate Islamist political wing. He voiced his opinion on the issue while he was first secretary of his party (PJD, Party for Justice and Development) and not yet a member of the government. He stated that 'we are neither in favour of total abolition of the death penalty nor of the status-quo … we would prefer a fresh review of the crimes punishable by the death penalty … and [the death penalty should be] limited exclusively to serious crimes'. It is also important to note that, for the fourth time, Morocco has abstained from voting the moratorium on death penalty adopted by the UN's General Assembly. The last time was in December 2012 under the mandate of the current Moroccan Government led by moderate Islamists. The Government opted once again for abstention, despite the fact that the President of the Moroccan National Human Rights Council publically urged the government to vote in favour of the resolution (declaration made by the President during the Regional Congress on the Abolition of Death Penalty held in Rabat in October 2012). This vote could either be perceived as a regression in the Moroccan progress towards the abolition of death penalty or just a mere confirmation of the *status quo*.[22]

21 The proceedings of the colloquium held in Tangier on 20 September 2012 will be published soon. I was a speaker at the colloquium and used my personal notes to report on the contribution of Professor Mohammed Alami Machichi.

22 Source: http://cntcpm.unblog.fr/files/2008/07/wcadprapmondarabfr.pdf [accessed on 4 October 2012].

When you ask about the foundations for such a stance, Islamists very often argue that death penalty is part of Sharia. Therefore, its abolition is forbidden. Fortunately, this point of view is not universal amongst all Islamic scholars. Some of them have developed other interpretations of Islamic thought and Sharia that could support an abolitionist perspective.[23]

In the specific situation of Morocco there is a compelling argument against the view that seeks to present Islamic precepts as an impediment to the abolition of the death penalty. The Moroccan penal code is neither based on Islamic Law nor significantly influenced by it. This does not exclude Islam from being a point of reference for some provisions of the Moroccan penal code, without being its main source.[24] To put it very simply, the Moroccan penal code is not a religious code. To illustrate this statement let us note for instance that:

- the Moroccan penal code does not punish adultery by stoning, theft by mutilation or drinking of alcohol by flagellation
- the few acts prohibited by direct relation to Islamic religion are not criminalized as such. They are prohibited because of the social nuisance they actually cause, or might cause.

That is, for example, the case for publically breaking the fast during the holy month of Ramadan by a person who is well known to be a Muslim.[25] The same could be said about public and manifest drunkenness. Drunkenness is prohibited and punished (by a Royal Decree) only if it is manifest and happening in a public area or any area that is accessible to the public (for instance in the street, in cafes and restaurants).[26] The acts mentioned above are not forbidden as such. They are prohibited and punished because of the trouble they cause, or might cause, when committed in public. Otherwise, the fact that a Muslim does not fast during Ramadan without a valid reason, or drinks alcohol, does not constitute a crime *per se* in Morocco, as long as such behaviour does not occur in public.[27]

In brief, the fact that the death penalty exists in the Moroccan penal code is not historically linked to religion. It is rather a sanction that was borrowed from

23 Reference could particularly be made to the brilliant contribution of Dr Mohammad Habash at the Second International Symposium on the Death Penalty held at the University of Oslo on 8–9 December 2012.

24 'l'Islam demeure un des référents du système politique et juridique' (in Amzazi 1987: 127).

25 Source: Article 222 of the Moroccan penal code.

26 Source: Décret royal n° 724–66 du 11 Chaabane 1387 (14 novembre 1967) portant loi, relatif à la répression de l'ivresse publique du 22/11/1967 page 1346 Bulletin officiel n° 2873.

27 Yet article 220 of the Moroccan penal code has a noticeable protectionist approach in favour of the Islamic Religion (which is, by the way, pursuant to the Constitution the Religion of the Moroccan State). Its provision punishes those who try to convert Muslims to another religion.

the laws of modern nation states, as was the case for other provisions of the penal code. There is no need to dwell on the fact that this borrowing was done at a time where the debate on the abolition of the death penalty had yet to gain momentum. Nowadays, the landscape has changed dramatically.

Conclusion

Indeed, since the eve of independence for our country, the Moroccan legislature has chosen to adopt a modern penal code, not a religious one. Furthermore, Morocco has chosen to ratify almost all the international covenants on human rights. Thus, without minimizing the importance of the most open debate possible, the Moroccan Kingdom cannot afford not to take seriously recent developments in human rights. These developments have seriously questioned both the usefulness and legitimacy of the death penalty. The death penalty is judged as a cruel, inhumane and degrading treatment to be banished from the criminal codes of civilized nations. Morocco will hopefully not stop half way down the road.[28] The giant steps it has already made, in the field of human rights, could predispose it to be yet again a leader in the Arab world in this field. It could do this by opting for the immediate abolition of the death penalty, or at least for its abolition as soon as possible.

I would like to end this chapter by quoting an important statement made by Kofi Annan when expressing his confidence in a future leading to universal abolition of the death penalty:

> Can the state, which represents the whole of society and has the duty of protecting society, fulfill that duty by lowering itself to the level of the murderer, and treating him as he treated others? The forfeiture of life is too absolute, too irreversible, for one human being to inflict it on another, even when backed by legal process. And I believe that future generations, throughout the world, will come to agree.

References

Amnesty International. 2011. [Online]. Report. Available at: http://www.amnestyinternational.be/doc/agir-2099/nos-campagnes/peine-de-mort-315/article/peine-de-mort-2011-le-rapport [accessed: 7 October 2012].

Amzazi, M. 1987. Islam et droit pénal au Maroc, in *Archives de politique criminelle*, 9, Paris: Pedone Editions.

28 Morocco was urged by several countries during the Universal Periodical Review in June 2012 to abolish the death penalty (Human Rights Council, 26th session 2012, A/HRC/21/3).

Hood, R. and Hoyle, C. 2008. *Death Penalty, A Worldwide Perspective.* Oxford, New York.

Koestler, A. 1966. *Darkness at Noon.* New York: Bantam.

Zamparutti, E. 2011. *Ne touchez pas à Caïn 'La peine de mort dans le monde'* [Report], edited by E. Zamparutti. Rome: Reality Book.

PART V
Reflection and Outlook

Chapter 13
Criminal Justice, Sustainability and the Death Penalty

Vidar Halvorsen

'In the long run we are all dead': the frequently quoted passage from John Maynard Keynes's *A Tract on Monetary Reform* (1923/2000) applies to societies no less than to individuals, although obviously in a different sense to the former than to the latter. Methodological individualism is right to insist on the need to establish micro-foundations for collective entities like societies, states and nations. On the other hand, the histories of individuals are essentially embedded within the histories of states and societies, which transcend the lifespan of individuals in terms of basic functions like reproduction and socialization.

Sustainability

In such a context, *sustainability* might plausibly be taken to refer to a variety of physical and social pre-conditions for stable and orderly development. In 1987 the Brundtland Commission famously and influentially defined sustainability as development that 'meets the needs of the present without compromising the ability of future generations to meet their own needs' (WCED 1987: 8). One of the virtues of this conception of sustainability is that it situates environmental problems within a normative framework of *distributive* justice. When physical preconditions of humans as biological organisms – like the availability of food, non-renewable energy resources and climate stability – are progressively being undermined by on-going economical, political and technological processes, questions of the proper allocation of burdens and benefits become all the more urgent, across social groups, societies and generations.

Retributive Justice

It is not equally obvious, however, that this conception of sustainability is applicable to problems of *retributive* justice. By retributive justice I do not refer to *retributivism*, a philosophical theory of the justifiability of punishment. Rather, by retributive justice I refer to two basic ingredients, which, explicitly or implicitly, are endorsed by all of the five main rationales for punishment: retribution, deterrence, incapacitation, rehabilitation and (collective) self-defence.[1]

These ingredients, shared not only by different theories of the justifiability of punishment, but by abolitionism as well, are the notions of *guilt* and *responsibility*. The concept of punishment is internally connected to the concept of guilt, in the sense that the intentional infliction of harm on a person or group of persons by the state must essentially presuppose the ascription of responsibility for past wrongdoing to that person or group of persons. In other words, because guilt implies the ascription of responsibility for past wrongdoing, they are both inherent in the concept of punishment. Just desert, on the other hand, is a particular *conception* of guilt, invoked by retributivism and other versions of non-consequentialist theories of punishment to *justify* the punishment of wrongdoers.

On this conception of punishment, punishing the innocent is, as Antony Duff (1986: 158–64) has maintained, conceptually flawed: for a judge to declare, 'You are innocent, but I must punish you', is to generate a pragmatic contradiction analogous to the absurdity generated by saying 'It's raining outside, but I'm lying'. Hence, the well-known argument that consequentialist theories of punishment are committed to punishing the innocent whenever the consequences of miscarriages of justice are – all things considered – beneficial, must be rephrased as an argument to the effect that those theories are committed to punitive *deception*, pretending to punish the guilty while actually and knowingly punishing the innocent.

Punitive Practices and Everyday Beliefs

Institutional deception, however, is notoriously unstable and therefore unlikely to succeed. Consequently, a stable punitive practice must accommodate non-consequentialist as well as consequentialist beliefs of citizens. A criminal justice system draws not only on widely shared intuitions on everyday morality about the importance of guilt and responsibility for sanctions against criminal wrongdoing, but also on widely shared intuitions about the importance of proportionate sentencing practices and the effects of such practices on the level of crime.[2] The

---

1 The fifth rationale, (collective) self-defence, is usually ignored in general introductions to the philosophy of punishment. The two most sophisticated attempts to derive the right to punish from the right to threaten in self-defence are probably provided by Warren Quinn, 'The Right to Threaten and the Right to Punish' (1985/93), and Victor Tadros, *The Ends of Harm* (2012).

2 In this chapter I will take for granted that 'everyday morality' is an empirical reality and that it makes sense to contrast it with philosophical positions (consequentialism, deontology etc) in ethics. Although a mixture of consequentialist and deontological reasoning characterizes 'everyday morality', I will by no means assume that 'ordinary people' necessarily must agree on the *applications* of moral principles, norms and values to concrete cases or that they will always succeed in their attempts to reconcile their various intuitions in a coherent way.

stability of the system is crucially dependent on the fact that these intuitions are either reconcilable within an overall justificatory theory of punishment or at least able to function as coherent normative elements within *an overlapping consensus*.

Sustainability as Overlapping Consensus

In *A Theory of Justice* (1971) John Rawls follows David Hume in his analysis of *the circumstances of justice*, and, like Hume, interprets justice as a response to the challenges that these conditions pose for political theories of justice.

Among the circumstances of justice is the fact that although cooperation among the citizens of a political community is objectively possible and necessary, they

> … nevertheless have their own plans of life. These plans, or conceptions of the good, lead them to have different ends and purposes, and to make conflicting claims on the natural and social resources available. As a consequence individuals not only have different plans of life but there exists a diversity of philosophical and religious belief, and of political and social doctrines. (Rawls 1971: 127)

The fact of pluralism is, in other words, inherent in the circumstances of justice. Thus, a normative theory of criminal justice is doomed to fail unless it can reconstruct and build upon normative facts shared by different conceptions of the right and the good. Rawls makes a distinction between two different ways a liberal tradition might meet this challenge, namely, a distinction between political liberalism as a *modus vivendi* and liberalism as an overlapping consensus.

In subsequent elaborations of his theory of *justice as fairness* Rawls has described in greater detail what he takes to be the essential features of liberalism as a *modus vivendi*. In 'Justice as Fairness: Political Not Metaphysical' he claims that

> It may appear that, so understood, the public acceptance of justice as fairness is no more than prudential; that is, that those who affirm this conception do so simply as a modus vivendi which allows the groups in the overlapping consensus to pursue their own good subject to certain constraints which each thinks to be for its advantage given existing circumstances. The idea of an overlapping consensus may seem essentially Hobbesian. (Rawls 1985: 247)

Rawls makes it perfectly clear that *his* idea of an overlapping consensus is a *moral*, not a Hobbesian one. In contrast, in liberalism conceived of as a *modus vivendi* the norms of justice are accepted not because they are *valid* as norms, but rather because it is *rational* to accept them, given one`s preferences. The theory of justice as a *modus vivendi*, then, is reduced to a theory of instrumental rationality.

In 'The Idea of an Overlapping Consensus', these points are elaborated further in a theory of stability:

> We might say: each view supports the political conception for its own sake, or on its own merits; and the test for this is whether the consensus is stable with respect to changes in the distribution of power among views. This feature of stability highlights a basic contrast between an overlapping consensus and a modus vivendi, the stability of which does depend on happenstance and a balance of relative forces. (Rawls 1987: 11)

Justice as fairness is intended as a political theory in three different senses: it applies exclusively to the basic structure of society, including the criminal justice system; it does not presuppose any comprehensive religious, philosophical or moral doctrines; and it intends to capture certain fundamental ideas embedded in the political culture of society, namely, the conception of persons as free and equal citizens within a political community. The capacity of citizens to revise and change their fundamental conceptions of the good is an essential part of their status as moral and political agents.

Nevertheless, Rawls presupposes that an overlapping consensus is indeed possible, despite the fact of pluralism. An overlapping consensus consists in the sharing of certain basic norms and values, but not necessarily in a sharing of their justifications. Thus, agreement on justifications is less likely, in a Rawlsian conception, because justifications tend to be more comprehensive and therefore more likely to generate controversy. Consequently, the starting-point of Rawls's overlapping consensus – the conception of society as a fair scheme of cooperation between free and equal citizens – is something we hardly can argue *for* without ending up in a metaphysical quagmire; rather, it is something we should argue *from* to conclusions that would be acceptable within different conceptions of the good.

Why must a political theory of justice be impartial towards differing conceptions of the good? The answer to this question reveals an essential aspect of Rawls's theory:

> Now one reason for focusing directly on a political conception for the basic structure is that, as a practical political matter, no general and comprehensive view can provide a publicly acceptable basis for a political conception of justice. (Rawls 1987: 4)

Why should a political theory of justice be publicly acceptable to its citizens? Clearly, if the principles regulating the basic structure of a society were based on a particular comprehensive doctrine, adherents of differing doctrines would be prevented from providing normative support for the basic structure or constitution of that society. Use of force and punishment by the state is sometimes necessary to resolve conflicts between comprehensive conceptions of the good. To exercise power, force and punishment to resolve such conflicts is one of the essential characteristics of increasingly multi-national states, and it is precisely for that reason that the basic principles regulating such uses of political authority must be grounded in an overlapping consensus. Clearly, a mere *modus vivendi* between different comprehensive conceptions of justice can hardly fulfil this function in a sustainable manner.

Deterrence and Culpability

Deterrence by threat of punishment relies on a widely shared assumption that the practice of punishment has an *absolute* deterrent value, in the sense that crime and disorder would substantially increase were the practice *per se* to be abolished. Yet, this counter-factual assumption does not provide a justification for punishment on consequentialist grounds. For a consequentialist justification to succeed, the practice of making threats of punishment and inflicting harm when the threats fail to produce the desired behaviour, must be shown to have *marginal* deterrent value as well, generating a greater net gain in utility (or whatever standard of moral assessment we endorse) than alternative methods of social control. Of course, these estimates are notoriously hard to calculate, but most people nevertheless take it for granted that the very existence of a punitive system is justifiable by consequentialist arguments.

Furthermore, granted that we accept the force of these consequentialist arguments, we need to reconcile them with our basic intuitions concerning the culpability of wrongdoers. In terms of everyday morality, punishment is not reducible to social engineering, which treats persons merely as objects of quasi-technological manipulation. Essentially, punishment articulates moral criticism of wrongdoing and hence addresses the wrongdoer as a moral agent. Moral criticism is constrained by two fundamental requirements of fairness: addressees of criticism are properly held accountable and thus justifiably criticized for their wrongdoing only to the extent that they had the freedom to act otherwise, and the severity of the criticism must be proportionate to the seriousness of the wrongdoing.

Because deterrence theories of punishment are theories of rational choice, they recognize the offender as an autonomous actor, but fail to explain why the proportionality requirement must be respected even when disproportionate sentencing would generate greater utility. Traditional retributive theories of just deserts, on the other hand, plausibly explain the proportionality requirement in terms of the censuring and blaming character of punishment, but fail to explain why proportionate moral criticism of conduct ought to be articulated through the infliction of punitive *harm* on offenders. Is it possible to reconcile these partially deficient accounts within an overlapping and sufficiently robust consensus concerning the grounds of punishment and sentencing?

Legal Excuses

Because standard legal excuses are essential ingredients of any penal system, irrespective of its ultimate justification, they are for the same reason essential ingredients of an overlapping consensus concerning the justifiability of punishment. The logic of legal excuses reflects the fundamental conditions of moral resentment embedded in everyday morality. In terms of our everyday moral practices, the infliction of punishment embodies a particularly strong form of moral criticism. When we accept insanity as a legal excuse, we implicitly presuppose that the punishment of an insane person would violate the basic moral principle that 'ought implies can'. According to this principle, to punish people presupposes that their conduct was voluntary in the sense that they were free to act otherwise.

A consequentialist is able, to some extent, to make sense of this principle by arguing, as Bentham did, that an insane person is incapable of reacting rationally to threats of punishment and that threats of punishment would therefore not be a deterrent. Moreover, as Herbert Hart convincingly argues in *Punishment and Responsibility* (1968), the elimination of *mens rea* requirements and legal excuses would radically undermine 'the individual's considered and informed choices' (p. 45), because the capacity to predict and co-ordinate the outcome of such choices would be 'immeasurably diminished' (p. 47) to the extent that the agent's intentions, beliefs, motives and desires were discounted as proper grounds for penal sanctions. In short, the individual's status as a *choosing being* would be jeopardized.

Therefore, Antony Duff is right to observe, in *Trials and Punishments* (1986), that deterrent theories of punishment do not fall prey to the well-known Kantian objection that by punishing the citizen the state treats him merely as a means for purposes of general prevention, ignoring the respect that is due to him as an end:

> What justifies having a system of punishment at all is that it will, consistently with a proper respect for the citizen, effectively reduce crime; but what justifies imposing *this* punishment on *this* person is that she has committed an offence for which this is the prescribed or permitted punishment. (Duff 1986: 172)

Because deterrence theories of punishment are theories of rational choice, they recognize offenders as utility maximizers, capable of selecting appropriate means for the realization of given ends. In other words, the notion of rationality underlying this recognition is the minimalist conception of *instrumental* rationality. Consequently, on the instrumental conception of rationality, punishing offenders who are for various reasons incapable of assessing the *moral* demands of the criminal law is nevertheless justifiable, to the extent that they are capable of assessing and responding to the *prudential* incentives inherent in the formula of punishment: abide by the law, or else suffer the infliction of punishment. Therefore, because 'psychopaths', in this restricted and limited sense, can plausibly be said to act rationally in the instrumental sense, it would hardly be unfair, on the minimalist conception of retributive guilt underlying deterrent theories of punishment, to punish 'psychopathic' offenders, despite the fact that they would not be proper addressees of the criminal law's *moral* demand.

Punishment as Communication: Duff and von Hirsch

However, as Hart has pointed out (1968: 19), even if it were the case that punishing the insane would deter *normal* people from exploiting the insanity defence, we still would hesitate to rest our rejection or acceptance of legal excuses on a consequentialist calculus of costs and benefits. Rather, the moral foundations of legal excuses – and, by implication, the conditions for the distribution of punishment – are based on a non-instrumentalist notion of fairness inherent in everyday morality. It is not self-evident, therefore, that such retributive beliefs and intuitions are easily reconcilable within an overlapping consensus about the justifiability of punishment.

Thus, Antony Duff objects that deterrent theories fail to recognize a person's autonomy in a proper way, providing the citizen with the *wrong kind* of reasons for compliance with the law's moral demands. On Duff's conception of criminal law, (moral) culpability is a necessary, but insufficient, condition for criminal liability and punishment. Criminal law consists essentially of institutionalized prohibitions of those public harms and wrongs that would undermine the mutual respect and recognition characterizing interactions between free and equal citizens in a liberal community. Criminal law includes two mechanisms which are crucial for this purpose: first, it *communicates* to wrongdoers the importance of those moral standards which have been transgressed and to which citizens properly hold one another accountable; and second, it provides a *vehicle* by means of which wrongdoers can express their repentance, remorse and regret to their fellow citizens, namely, the public ritual of punishment.

On this conception, punishment is not merely a prudential device for influencing the decisions and subsequent behaviour of rational maximizers; the practice of punishment must necessarily, in order to fulfil its basic purpose, presuppose the capacity of citizens to reflect on, and respond to, the moral reasons for compliance provided by the law. Given these normative assumptions, it follows that we cannot justifiably punish offenders who are for whatever reason incapable of assessing the moral demands of the criminal law. We cannot, in other words, justifiably punish 'psychopaths'.

In contrast to Duff's position, Andrew von Hirsch (1993) maintains that it is possible to reconcile consequentialism with our basic intuitions concerning the culpability of wrongdoers. He agrees with Duff that in terms of everyday morality, punishment is not reducible to social engineering, treating persons merely as objects of quasi-technological manipulation. Essentially, von Hirsch accepts Duff's premise that punishment articulates moral criticism of wrongdoing and hence addresses the wrongdoer as a moral agent. Indeed, as Peter Strawson has pointed out in his justly celebrated essay 'Freedom and Resentment', a social-technological or 'objective' conception of moral criticism and punishment would, if globalized, radically transform and pervert our everyday moral practices:

> If your attitude towards someone is wholly objective, then though you might fight him, you cannot quarrel with him, and though you may talk to him, even negotiate with him, you cannot reason with him. You can at most pretend to quarrel, or to reason with him. (Strawson 1962/82: 66)

Censure and Sanctions

Although a communicative theory like Antony Duff's plausibly explains the proportionality requirement in terms of the censuring and blaming character of punishment, it fails to explain in an equally plausibly manner why proportionate moral criticism of conduct ought to be institutionalized by way of punitive, intentional harm-inflicting state practices. So the basic problem re-emerges: how can the partially deficient accounts of deterrent and communicative theories be properly reconciled within the framework of an overlapping consensus?

Andrew von Hirsch provides a very interesting and promising attempt in *Censure and Sanctions* (1993). In agreement with Duff, von Hirsch maintains that criminal law first and foremost provides citizens with moral reasons for compliance, and secondly, with grounds for criticism whenever they fail to act on those reasons. However, to recognize oneself (and others) as a moral agent is to recognize oneself as a fallible moral being, exposed to temptation and ignorance in a variety of situations. Hence, citizens with a self-reflective knowledge of their own moral fallibility would rationally choose to impose on themselves a punitive system of external constraints, 'supplying a prudential reason that is tied to, and supplements, the normative reason conveyed by penal censure' (p. 13). In this way, citizens, as the addressees of criminal law, are simultaneously able to recognize themselves as the authors of its prudential incentives as well as its moral demands. Thus, on von Hirsch's interpretation, a system of punishment is not to be understood as a technical device for social control, enabling 'us', the law-abiding citizens, to manipulatively coerce 'them', the wanton non-citizens outside the domain of moral discourse, to act in accordance with the law's moral demands:

> Rather, it should be one which free citizens could devise to regulate their *own* conduct … A sanctioning system, in a democratic society, should be of the kind which such persons could accept, as a way of assisting them to resist their own temptations, in a manner that respects their capacity for choice. (von Hirsch 1993: 5, author's italics)

It is an empirical fact, however, that a minority among those who violate the rights of their fellow citizens find themselves excluded from the domain of moral discourse, in virtue of the fact that they are incapable of grasping the moral demands of the criminal law. It would seem that punishing such wrongdoers is tantamount to treating them in a way that von Hirsch explicitly rejects:

> Penologists are drawn too easily to viewing offenders and potential offenders as a species apart from law-abiding citizens, as persons who largely are impervious to moral appeals, and who need to be intimidated or restrained into compliance with the law. I do not accept this view. (von Hirsch 1993: 5)

Does it follow from the fact that there are some citizens who 'need to be intimated or restrained into compliance with the law', that they, in virtue of their deficient capacity of moral reasoning, are entitled to invoke the traditional repertoire of legal and moral excuses? That, I think, would be too hasty; there are aspects of von Hirsch's hybrid theory of punishment which might nevertheless serve to explain why citizens capable of prudential, but not moral, rationality, nevertheless can justifiably be punished.

Von Hirsch does not explicitly refer to Rawls. However, his requirement that a system of punishment 'should be one which free citizens could devise to regulate their *own* conduct' might be taken to refer to a kind of Rawlsian overlapping consensus. In Rawls's famous thought-experiment, involving the device of the veil of ignorance, citizens behind the veil are denied the knowledge of their roles, positions and, as in this version, their capacity for moral reasoning. Under such counter-factual circumstances, there are good reasons to assume that they will choose principles of criminal law that closely reflect the basic moral assumptions underlying the device of the veil of ignorance in the first place, namely, the ideas of persons as free and equal citizens. Because the parties' deliberations behind the veil of ignorance are exclusively prudential, they will be able to recognize the deterrent, crime-reducing relevance of punishment, as long as their own status as choosing beings are not jeopardized. A system of punishment that allows for punishing citizens endowed with only instrumental rationality, would arguably satisfy this requirement, while an alternative system of preventive detention would not.

Ulysses and the Virtue of Self-Binding

Von Hirsch's description of free and rational, yet morally fallible, persons, exposed to the temptation of crime and other forms of harmful conduct, is artistically visualized by Herbert James Draper's painting (1909) *Ulysses and the Sirens*, inspired by Homer's epic poem *The Odyssey*.[3]

In Homer's poem, Ulysses and his crew are faced with the challenge of navigating their ship through some very dangerous sea territory. What makes their voyage particularly dangerous is the seductive song of the sirens, mermaids who sing so beautifully that sailors ignore the importance of navigation and sail right into disaster.

3 The name of Draper's painting was adopted by Jon Elster in his brilliant book on theories of imperfect rationality and pre-commitment, *Ulysses and the Sirens* (1979).

As a self-reflective being, however, Ulysses is aware of his crew's and his own weakness of will. Furthermore, as a rational agent, he is capable of acting on that self-knowledge, by designing a compensating device, the device of pre-commitment. He puts wax in the ears of his crew, orders them to bind him to the ship's mast and instructs them to ignore him should he beg them to release him. In this way Ulysses is able to resist the temptation of the sirens and safely bring himself and his crew to his ultimate destination.

It is easy to understand why this poetic story of Homer, and its visualization by Draper, has become an effective illustration of the main idea of *constitutionalism*. Like Ulysses, citizens of states hope to be able to navigate their societies through political temptations by binding themselves to a constitution, a set of legal pre-commitments that can only be changed by more demanding procedures. Ulysses` story illustrates, moreover, a basic virtue of constitutional self-binding: by *restricting* their power by self-imposed constraints, citizens are able to *expand* it in the sense that they can now achieve by indirect means objectives they would be unable to achieve in a direct manner.

Constitutionalism

Constitutionalism is an umbrella term for a variety of normative-political theories addressing questions regarding what kind of relations ought to hold between citizens and governmental agencies in (modern) nation states. Although it might be misleading to identify constitutionalism with a focus on *limited* government, a common theme in constitutional theories is nevertheless the importance of *constraints* in governmental politics. Among the institutional mechanisms of constraints are legalized (human) rights, stipulating the conditions under which state power might legitimately interfere in the activities of free and equal citizens.

One central issue in debates about constitutionalism`s preoccupation with the importance of constraints on politics is the proper relation between such constraints and democracy. The idea of democracy is essentially the idea of popular self-determination – the idea that the citizens of a political community must understand themselves as the authors of the laws that they are supposed to obey as addressees. For self-determination to become possible, however, the rights and organizational mechanisms defended by constitutionalism – the rights to free speech, freedom of assembly, the free exercise of religion, the independence of the judiciary and judicial review, to name a few – must be institutionalized as effective constraints on popular sovereignty.

Far from being non-democratic, constitutional restrictions on the exercise of democratic power are enabling conditions that make democratic opinion- and will-formation possible in the first place. Hence, political freedom and constitutional constraints are conceptually interdependent. On this theory, decision-making by independent judges, for example, increases rather than diminishes the legitimacy of the legal system.

Constitutional Criminal Justice

From a *descriptive* and explanatory point of view, constitutionalism is compatible with a huge variation in the scope, content and practice of criminal law and criminal procedure. There are crucial differences, for example, between the presidential, federal and bicameral form of constitutional arrangements in the USA and the parliamentary, national and unicameral form in Norway. Such differences might to some extent help to answer empirical questions as to why, for example, the American system still has the death penalty and a current (2011) prison population index of 743 (2.3 million) and the Norwegian system a maximum punishment of 21 years of imprisonment (except for war crimes) and a prison population index of 73 (3,600).

Despite these crucial differences between the two constitutional systems, it is a historical fact that the US Declaration of Independence (1776), with its 'self-evident truths' that … all Men are created equal, that they are endowed by their Creator with certain unalienable Rights, that among these are Life, Liberty, and the pursuit of Happiness. That to secure these rights, Governments are instituted among Men, deriving their just Powers from the Consent of the Governed … .[4] served as one of the moral and political rationales for 'the founding fathers' creating the Norwegian constitution of 1814. Moreover, although the two oldest living constitutions in the world are significantly different in many respects, they have both to some extent succeeded in institutionalizing an overlapping, sustainable consensus about which pre-political moral principles should be 'constitutionalized' as internal, normative standards for criminal justice practices in the two countries.

Article 96 of the Norwegian constitution, for example, states 'No one may be convicted except according to law, or be punished except after a court judgment. Interrogation by torture must not take place'. Closely connected to article 96 is article 97, which articulates the essential prospectivity of law: 'No law must be given retroactive effect'. Moreover, these articles were further reinforced by the 'semi-constitutionalization' of the European Convention on Human Rights in 1999, which made article 6 (the right to a fair trial) and article 7 (prohibition of retroactivity) directly applicable to Norwegian legal cases.[5] Taken together, these

4 Interestingly, this justly famous passage from the Declaration includes two comprehensive moral doctrines in Rawls's sense. First, *moral realism*, the meta-ethical claim that moral propositions can be true or false; indeed, *self-evidently* true or false. Second, a *religious natural law* perspective, the claim that pre-political natural rights are grounded in the authority of God. Crucially, however, these comprehensive doctrines are absent from the *constitution* itself, enabling an overlapping consensus on constitutional legitimacy between different positions in meta-ethics and between religious and secular beliefs.

5 The term 'semi-constitutionalization' refers to the fact that article 110c (adopted in 1994) in the Norwegian constitution merely states: 'It is the responsibility of the

articles constitute the Norwegian version of the *principle of legality* (*nulla poena sine lege*), which is widely and quite plausibly believed to be the essence of the *rule of law*: any legal system that fails to incorporate a version of the principle of legality would be seriously defective. Not surprisingly, then, the principle of legality was promptly incorporated in the US Constitution's Bill of Rights ratified by the states in 1791, first and foremost in the Fifth Amendment's due process clause.

Constitutional Fallibility

Ulysses was morally fallible, and as a self-reflective creature he was able to appreciate the fact and significance of his own fallibility. Nevertheless, the predicament of fallibility generalizes and applies to the meta-level of constitutional constraints as well. In other words, constitutions, as devices of Ulyssean pre-commitments, might include provisions that eventually fail to redeem their moral ambitions. Or, alternatively, courts might interpret and apply constitutional provisions in a way that likewise fail to do so.

Consider, for example, the case of Dred Scott. Scott was a slave in Missouri who in 1833 travelled with his master, a US Army doctor (John Emerson), to the Free State of Illinois and later to the Wisconsin Territory and the upper part of the Louisiana Territory, where slavery was also illegal. Missouri court decisions had established that slaves who had been living in states or territories in which slavery was prohibited, could claim the legal standing of free citizens. So, having returned with their owner to Missouri, Scott and his wife (who was also a slave) started proceedings in the Missouri courts in 1846 to obtain legal recognition of the fact that they and their children had been emancipated from slavery.

However, in 1852, the Missouri Supreme Court, in clear violation of its own precedents, reversed a prior trial court decision in favour of the Scott family. Eventually, the case ended up in the federal US Supreme Court, which in 1857 made one of the most controversial decisions in American legal history, in the case known as *Dred Scott v. Sanford* (Sanford referring to the slave owner at that time, the brother of Dr Emerson's widow, John Sanford). Basically the Court declared that Congress did not have the authority to prohibit slavery in federal territories;

authorities of the State to respect and ensure human rights. Specific provisions for the implementation of treaties thereon shall be determined by law'. In other words, the constitution *per se* does *not* specify *which* human rights are worthy of constitutional protection – except for some rights which had been already included in the text in the period between 1814 and 1994. In 1999, The Human Rights Law (HRL) was adopted by Parliament, in accordance with the procedure of simple majority, which regulates ordinary legislation. HRL explicitly incorporates the European Convention on Human Rights, the International Covenant on Civil and Political Rights and the International Covenant on Economic, Social and Cultural Rights in the Norwegian legal corpus.

in other words, that the prohibition against slavery in these jurisdictions was unconstitutional. Moreover, it did not matter whether persons of Afro-American origin were free or enslaved, because, in the eyes of the Constitution's founding fathers, they 'had no rights which the white man was bound to respect'. In short, Afro-Americans were property, and owners could not be deprived of their property without what has later been regularly referred to as 'due process'.

Or, consider the equally infamous Thomas Sims case of 1851. According to the Fugitive Slave Law passed by Congress in 1850, authorities in abolitionist states in the North had a legal obligation to return fugitive slaves to their masters in the slaveholding states in the South. So, after Thomas Sims escaped from slavery in Georgia to freedom in Boston (Massachusetts) as a 17-year-old boy, he was arrested in 1851. Enforcing a court order in accordance with the Fugitive Slave Law, US soldiers put him on a warship, which transferred him back to continued slavery in Georgia. Although the Sims case was not a constitutional case, it serves to illustrate the fact that the insistence in the Declaration of Independence on the freedom and equality of 'all men' were taken by courts to be compatible with the institution of slavery.

Evidently, *Scott* and *Sims* are paradigm examples of wicked cases, generated by manifestly unjust laws or unjust interpretations. A less dramatic and much more recent example of constitutional tension is provided by the Norwegian debate on the legitimacy of the jury in criminal trials. While the jury system in the USA has been thoroughly constitutionalized since the ratification of the federal constitution in 1789, the Norwegian jury system was established in 1887 as part of an extensive democratic reform of ordinary criminal procedure.

Participants in public debates about the legitimacy of the jury system have, in addition to articulating traditional doubts about jurors' epistemic reliability, focused on the problem of how to reconcile a crucial fact about jury verdicts with political accountability, namely, the fact that juries do not *justify* their decisions. Thus, a potential challenge to the legitimacy of the Norwegian jury system stems from the 'semi-constitutionalization' of the European Convention on Human Rights, in particular article 6 on the right to a fair trail. Essentially, jury verdicts, resolving issues of guilt and innocence, are performative assertions. In virtue of being performative assertions jury verdicts must presuppose that there is, in principle, evidence available indicating the truth of what is asserted, namely, that a citizen is guilty or innocent of the charge raised against him by the prosecution. There is, in other words, an internal or conceptual connection between asserted beliefs, truth and justification. This conceptual web explains why it might be *unfair* for a jury, whenever it raises validity claims through the assertion of beliefs about the guilt or innocence of persons in a criminal trial, *not* to redeem an implicit and communicatively generated obligation to provide *reasons* or evidence for its verdict in public.

'Cruel and Unusual Punishment'

Despite the unavoidable predicament of fallibility, the aim of constitutions is to ensure societal sustainability, articulating citizens' shared conception of the legal pre-conditions for a just, stable and orderly development. Does, then, the death penalty properly belong in the catalogue of stabilizing devices endorsed by constitutionalism?

There is a straightforward, historical sense in which this question has been answered affirmatively in at least one political system plausibly classified as a constitutional democracy – the USA, the nation-state with the oldest constitution in the world. The Eighth Amendment's prohibition against 'cruel and unusual punishment' has consistently been interpreted by the Supreme Court as compatible with the death penalty, albeit with some significant modifications that might indicate a trend towards an alternative, more sustainable 'overlapping consensus'.

In *Coker v. Georgia* (1977) the Court held that

> ... a punishment is 'excessive' and unconstitutional if it (1) makes no *measurable* contribution to acceptable *goals of punishment* and hence is nothing more than the purposeless and needless imposition of pain and suffering; or (2) is grossly out of *proportion* to the *severity* of the crime. (italics added)

This statement provides two different and potentially conflicting constitutional rationales for meting out specific punishments for particular offenses. The requirement under (1) articulates a consequentialist conception of instrumental rationality, which might be fleshed out in two different directions. On a *comprehensive* conception of instrumental rationality, judges (and legislators) should adopt punishments that will produce the greatest net sum of crime reduction when available punitive alternatives and their likely consequences are compared. On a more *restricted* interpretation, the costs of punishments should at least be outweighed by their benefits, taken in isolation. If, for example, it is the case that the execution of one murderer will save the lives of 18 innocent persons, the death penalty should be the favoured option.[6] In contrast, on the more comprehensive conception, executions are unjustifiable to the extent that the same net effect could be achieved by the less severe alternative of life imprisonment. Clearly, the

6 This was the conclusion in Dezhbakhsh`s, Rubin`s and Shepherd's study, 'Does Capital Punishment Have a Deterrent Effect? New Evidence from Post-Moratorium Panel Data' (2003). Their results have been thoroughly criticized, first and foremost by John Donohue and Justin Wolfers in 'Uses and Abuses of Empirical Evidence in the Death Penalty Debate' (2005), who find that the 'evidence for deterrence is surprisingly fragile' (p. 794). This is so, they maintain, mainly because the death penalty 'is applied so rarely that the number of homicides it can plausibly have caused or deterred cannot be reliably disentangled from the large year-to-year changes in the homicide rate caused by other factors' (p. 794).

identification of the least restrictive alternative among available punishments is essentially a moralized enterprise, crucially hinging on a normative comparison of possible harmful and beneficial effects likely to be generated by the decision-maker's choice of punitive reactions.

The *Coker* case was not, however, decided on the basis of instrumentalist reasoning at all. On the contrary, the Court applied the retributive understanding of 'excessive' and 'unconstitutional' punishment, the requirement that punishments must not be 'grossly out of proportion to the severity of the crime'. In *Coker*, the petitioner, a convicted murderer, had escaped from a Georgia prison and raped an adult woman. For this, and other instances of very serious violence, he was sentenced to death, a sentence that was eventually affirmed by the Georgia Supreme Court. The federal Supreme Court, however, reversed the judgment, ruling that 'the sentence of death for the crime of rape is grossly disproportionate and excessive punishment and is therefore forbidden by the Eighth Amendment as cruel and unusual punishment'. Thirty-one years later, this interpretation was reinforced and extended by the Court to cover the rape of an eight-year-old girl in *Kennedy v. Louisiana* (2008). Two other decisions, *Atkins v. Virginia* (2002) and *Roper v. Simmons* (2005) applied the *Coker* formula to prohibit the execution of mentally retarded offenders and juveniles under the age of 18, respectively. Unlike the *Coker* case, the Court's decisions in the *Kennedy*, *Atkins* and *Roper* cases were partially informed by the officially endorsed consequentialist rationale for capital punishment as well. There are no convincing reasons to believe, the Court argued in *Atkins*, that to exempt mentally retarded persons from the death penalty would have any bearing on 'the cold calculus that precedes the decision of other potential murderers'.

True, to some extent, this argument is compatible with the concerns of retributivism, as the Court aptly observes in both *Roper* and *Atkins*. The same facts that make, for example, juveniles harder to deter by the threat of capital punishment, also serve to make them less culpable and thus not worthy of the harshest punishment on retributive grounds, according to the Court in *Roper*.[7] Generally, the seriousness of an offender's wrongdoing is a function of the harm he or she has inflicted on the victim and the extent of the culpability in inflicting it: whether he or she intentionally, knowingly, recklessly or negligently brought about the death of the victim. Because juvenile offenders are 'overrepresented statistically in virtually every category of reckless behaviour', they are much less likely to exhibit the aggravating elements that juries and courts must rely on in their sentencing practices.

---

7 The generalized version of this argument explains why both consequentialism and retributivism converge on the conclusion that we cannot justifiably punish insane offenders. The same conclusion is also endorsed by the (collective) self-defence justification of punishment: it is *unfair*, Warren Quinn argues (1985/93), to threaten those among us who cannot grasp the implications of our threats; *therefore*, it is unjust to punish them when they ignore our threats.

Nevertheless, there is a potential conflict between consequentialist and retributive considerations in the *Coker* formula, and courts might be tempted to resolve it in ways that undermine its proportionality requirement. Perhaps the most striking illustration is provided by the non-capital case of *Harmelin v. Michigan* (1991). Here, the Supreme Court upheld, in a 5–4 decision, a mandatory life sentence (without parole) for 45-year-old Ronald Harmelin, who had been convicted under Michigan law of possessing 672 grams of cocaine. Harmelin argued that the punishment was 'cruel and unusual' within the meaning of the eighth amendment because it was grossly disproportionate to the crime of cocaine possession.

The court's majority differed with respect to the reasons given for its rejection of Harmelin's appeal. Justices Scalia and Rehnquist concluded that because the eighth amendment did not contain a proportionality guarantee, a mandatory life sentence could not be considered unconstitutionally disproportional. Justices Kennedy, O'Connor, and Souter, on the other hand, insisted that the Eighth Amendment did contain a proportionality requirement, but that the seriousness of Harmelin´s crime of cocaine possession implied that a mandatory life sentence did not cross an alleged constitutional threshold level of gross disproportionality.

Clearly, the proportionality requirement in the *Coker* formula is radically jeopardized to the extent that courts (or the legislator) for any given category of crime decides to move up on the severity scale for the sake of general or individual deterrence – a practice which was endorsed by the Supreme Court in *Harmelin*. So far, it has refused to do so in cases involving murder or manslaughter. Thus, for example, although thousands of people are killed annually by drunken drivers in the USA, it is very hard to imagine any case in which the Court would fail to recognize that the proportionality principle prohibits absolutely the execution of drunken drivers, despite the fact that, in the words of Thomas Pogge (1995: 260), 'a practice pursuant to which some 200 of the worst offenders are executed annually would presumably have a tremendous deterrent effect and thus would greatly reduce the frequency of the offence'.

'National' versus 'Overlapping' Consensus in the Death Penalty Debate

The abolition of the death penalty for specific categories of crime (rape) and offenders (the mentally retarded, juveniles) during the last three decades points in the direction of a total abolition of capital punishment for all crimes and all offenders – a final step the US Supreme Court so far has refused to take and is probably unlikely to take in the next decade. The closest it has ever come to total abolition was in 1972, when five of the nine justices in *Furman v. Georgia* declared capital punishment unconstitutional on grounds of *procedural* injustice. Moreover, two of the justices (Brennan and Marshall) in the majority forcefully argued that the death penalty was 'cruel and unusual' punishment *per se*; that is, constitutionally untenable independently of the fact that it was unjustly biased against the lower socio-economic and non-white segments of the prison population.

The Court re-established, however, the procedural constitutionality of capital punishment four years later in *Gregg v. Georgia* (1976). Interestingly, in the 'jurisprudence of death' after the *Gregg* decision, the notions of 'national consensus' and 'evolving standards of decency' re-emerged as constraining elements in the court's attempts to qualify its re-endorsement of the death penalty in *Gregg*.

There are some similarities, but also some crucial differences, between a 'national' and a Rawlsian 'overlapping' consensus. A 'national' consensus can be empirically identified from a morally and legally detached, external point of view, as when the Court in *Coker* (1977) relied on 'objective evidence of present public judgment, as represented by the attitude of state legislatures and sentencing juries'. Georgia was the only state, the Court observed, that authorized the execution of an offender for the rape of an adult woman. Likewise, although a 5-to-4 court ruled in *Stanford v. Kentucky* (1989) that a majority of states did not proscribe the execution of juveniles between 16 and 18, standards of decency had evolved since 1989, justifying the subsequent prohibition in *Roper* (2005) 16 years later.

The court`s reliance on empirical indicators of 'national' consensus and 'evolving standards of decency' might be understood in two different senses. Consider, for example, the following statement in *Roper* (2005):

> Three Terms ago [in 2002] the subject [death eligibility for juveniles] was reconsidered in Atkins. We held that standards of decency have evolved since Penry [upholding capital punishment for the mentally retarded in 1989] *and now demonstrate that the execution of the mentally retarded is cruel and unusual punishment.* (italics added)

On a radical interpretation, moral beliefs of citizens and legislators do not track the wrong-making properties of state actions; on the contrary, wrong-making properties cannot exist prior to, or independently of, moral beliefs, but are *constituted* by them. Moral constructivism, however, conflicts with the moral realism implicit in the 'self-evident truths' endorsed by the Founding Fathers and generates untenable results even on an empirical, less metaphysical understanding. Although a constitution is ultimately grounded in the moral and political pre-commitments of a political community, it makes, as John Ely Hart aptly observed in *Democracy and Distrust* (1980: 69), 'no sense to employ the value judgments of the majority as the vehicle for protecting minorities from the value judgments of the majority'.

A more promising interpretation of the majority's position in *Roper* is available, however. Rejecting the assumption in *Stanford* that the Court's own, independent judgment has no bearing on issues of constitutionality under the Eighth Amendment, the *Roper* court repeated its statement in *Coker*, that 'the Constitution contemplates that in the end *our own judgment* will be brought to bear on the question of the acceptability of the death penalty …' (italics added). The same point was made three years earlier in *Atkins* (2002), when the Court recognized its obligation, 'in cases involving a consensus', to examine 'whether there is reason to disagree with the judgment reached by the citizenry and its legislators'.

There is a distinction to be made, then, between two different ways of regarding, or of being committed to, beliefs about 'cruel and unusual punishment', which closely corresponds to Herbert Hart's distinction between the external and internal point of view in *The Concept of Law* (1961/94). On the internal conception, a convergence of beliefs might *constitute* a 'national' consensus in the sense that communities of citizens, legislators and judges agree on the *soundness* of adhering to a particular interpretation. The crucial difference, which the Court's empirical reliance on 'national' consensus and 'evolving standards of decency' obscures, is that with 'national' consensus, the empirical fact of agreement is referred to or presupposed as the ultimate basis for the Court's judgment. In contrast, a Rawlsian overlapping consensus on the soundness of constitutional interpretations is generated in terms of what Stephen Guest (1992: 207) has called a consensus of *conviction.*

However, a Rawlsian conception of an 'overlapping' consensus must face the following challenge of indeterminacy: granted that Supreme Court judges act on their obligation to interpret and apply the Eighth Amendment in order to reach decisions in capital cases, on what basis can they legitimately prefer their own judgment when 'there is reason to disagree with the judgment reached by the citizenry and its legislators'? Legal indeterminacy implies that there might be reasonable disagreements between interpreters, and in such cases, the Court's majority in *Roper* seems to think that individual judges ought to act on their own conception of what would constitute the morally and legally best choice. Hence, this approach must confront and adequately handle the objection raised by Andrew Altman in *Arguing about Law* (1996: 49): why defer to the judge's own moral beliefs and not to beliefs that are widely shared in a political-legal community?

Democratic principles, Altman argues (p. 88), favour the latter alternative. Moreover, as Georgia Warnke (1993: 72–82) has perceptively observed, the latter alternative seems, surprisingly, to be the interpretive strategy the legal philosopher Ronald Dworkin ultimately relies on in *Law's Empire* (1986) in his concrete analysis of the case of *McLoughlin v. O'Brian* (1982), an English tort law case dealing with the issue of compensation after emotional injury, and the case of *Brown v. Board of Education* (1954), the landmark US Supreme Court case dealing with the implications of the Fourteenth Amendment for questions of racial discrimination. However, the claim that deference to popular political morality is required on democratic grounds hinges implicitly on an alleged tension between constitutionalism or the rule of law on the one hand and democracy or popular sovereignty on the other.

This issue might be raised at two different levels: at the level of the political-legal system as such and at the sub-systemic level of adjudication. At the first level, constitutionalism rejects the alleged contradiction between judicial review and democracy by arguing that constitutional constraints are *enabling* conditions, making democratic opinion- and will-formation possible in the first place. At the level of adjudication, constitutionalists are likely to endorse what Steven Burton (1992) has called the *permissible discretion thesis*, which holds that when judges must exercise discretion in the sense that they have to choose among two or more courses of action neither of which is conclusively determined by law, their discretionary judgments violate the values of constitutional democracy only to the extent that they act on reasons excluded by the law. This is not the case, however, when they, among the interpretive candidates warranted by the law, make their choices on the basis of principles that would, according to their own conception, vindicate law's claims to do justice.

Moreover, there is an ambiguity implicit in the expression 'the judge's own moral beliefs' that has been effectively pointed out by Joel Feinberg (1992: 253–5): from the tautology that when judges act on their moral beliefs they act on their *own* moral beliefs and not on somebody else's, there is a tendency to draw the subjectivist conclusion that they merely act on their own preferences, beyond the reach of rational arguments and assessment. However, it is an essential fact about courts and court cases that legal reasoning takes place in public and that decisions reached in the courtroom demand justifications that, in principle, can be scrutinized by anyone. Hence, when judges select one of the interpretive candidates warranted by the law on the basis of their own moral beliefs, they act on the assumption that those beliefs can be established as valid in public discourse.

Conclusion: Ulysses and the Death Penalty

Ulysses bound himself to the mast, enabling himself and his crew to resist the lethal temptations of the sirens. In the eighteenth and nineteenth centuries, citizens in North America and in Europe adopted the Ulyssean strategy of pre-commitment, institutionalizing their shared vision of pre-political natural rights by designing a constitutional framework for their societies. Gradually, the citizens of Europe came to realize that the intentional infliction of death by the state on its fellow-citizens, was neither necessary as a stabilizing device for sustainable development, nor appropriate as a communicative device for retributive justice.

Alas, their American brethren, although sharing much of the underlying philosophy of constitutionalism, have so far resisted the conclusion that they should abolish the death penalty, despite the fact that their constitution's prohibition of 'cruel and unusual punishment' provides them with the legal and moral resources to do so. Politically, they came close to abolition in 1968, when Attorney General Ramsay Clark in the Johnson administration forcefully argued before the Senate Judiciary Committee that 'the abolition of the death penalty is a major milestone in the long road up from barbarism'. Legally, the Supreme Court came close in 1972 in its *Furman* decision. Given the undisputable international momentum towards abolition, the time will surely come again.

References

Altman, A. 1996. *Arguing about the Law*. Belmont: Wadsworth.
Burton, S. 1992. *Judging in Good Faith*. Cambridge: Cambridge University Press.
Dezhbakhsh, H., Rubin, P. and Shepherd, J. 2003. Does Capital Punishment Have a Deterrent Effect? New Evidence from Post-Moratorium Panel Data, in *American Law and Economics Review*, 5(2): 344–76.
Donohue, J. and Wolfers, J. 2005. Uses and Abuses of Empirical Evidence in the Death Penalty Debate, in *Stanford Law Review*, 58: 791–846.
Duff, R.A. 1986. *Trials and Punishments*. Cambridge: Cambridge University Press.
Dworkin, R. 1986. *Law's Empire*. London: Fontana Press.
Elster, J. 1979. *Ulysses and the Sirens*. Cambridge: Cambridge University Press.
Ely, J.H. 1980. *Democracy and Distrust*. Cambridge, MA: Harvard University Press.
Feinberg, J. 1992. *Freedom and Fulfillment*. Princeton: Princeton University Press.
Guest, S. 1992. *Ronald Dworkin*. Edinburgh: Edinburgh University Press.
Hart, H.L.A. 1961/94. *The Concept of Law*. Oxford: Clarendon Press.
Hart, H.L.A. 1968. *Punishment and Responsibility*. Oxford: Oxford University Press.
Hirsch, A. 1993. *Censure and Sanctions*. Oxford: Oxford University Press.
Keynes, J.M. 1923/2000. *A Tract on Monetary Reform*. New York: Prometheus Books.
Pogge, T. 1995. Three Problems with Contractarian-Consequentialist Ways of Assessing Social Institutions, in *The Just Society*, edited by E. Frankel Paul. Cambridge: Cambridge University Press.
Quinn, W. 1985/93. The Right to Threaten and the Right to Punish, in *Philosophy and Public Affairs*, reprinted in Quinn (1993). *Morality and Action*. Cambridge: Cambridge University Press.
Rawls, J. 1971. *A Theory of Justice*. Oxford: Oxford University Press.
Rawls, J. 1985. 'Justice as Fairness: Political Not Metaphysical', in *Philosophy & Public Affairs*, 14(3): 223–51.
Rawls, J. 1997. The Idea of an Overlapping Consensus, in *Oxford Journal of Legal Studies*, 7(1): 1–25.
Strawson, P. 1962/82. Freedom and Resentment, reprinted in 1982 *Free Will*, edited by G. Watson. Oxford: Oxford University Press.
Tadros, V. 2012. *The Ends of Harm*. Oxford: Oxford University Press.
Warnke, G. 1993. *Justice and Interpretation*. Cambridge, MA: The MIT Press.
World Commission on Environment and Development (WCED) (1987). *Our Common Future*. Oxford: Oxford University Press.

Chapter 14
Staying Optimistic[1]

Roger Hood

Dangerous as predictions can be in the social and political sphere, is it now reasonable to conclude that so much progress has been made towards the desirable goal first set more than 40 years ago by the United Nations in 1971 of 'abolishing capital punishment in all countries' that it will be achieved within the foreseeable future? Or should we again be concerned that the movement has achieved as much as it can and faces such strong opposition from several powerful countries that it is unlikely, if ever, to reach this goal?

Limits to Success?

As I have pointed out on previous occasions, at the end of 1980s the prospects were not encouraging and many abolitionists were pessimistic. I concluded my first report for the United Nations in 1988 with the words 'In many regions of the world there is little sign that abolition will occur soon' (Hood 1989: 159). Just a few years earlier, in 1986, United Nations staff had concluded a special issue of their *Crime Prevention and Criminal Justice Newsletter* devoted to Capital Punishment with the words: 'it would appear that the goal of the abolition of capital punishment throughout the world remains remote'. They were reflecting the assessment of the late Professor Günter Kaiser, the eminent head of the Max Planck Institute for Foreign and International Criminal Law in Freiburg, Germany, in the same issue that:

> Today there appears to be little hope that international bodies, whether private or official, will be able to achieve unanimity [among] the majority of countries concerning the restriction or abolition of capital punishment. (Kaiser 1986: 16)

How wrong we were. Shortly afterwards, beginning in 1989 – the year the Berlin Wall came down – the number of countries embracing abolition expanded at an

---

1 This contribution draws on my work over a number of years and more recently with my colleague and co-author of the 4th edition of *The Death Penalty: a World-wide Perspective*, Professor Carolyn Hoyle. We have now begun to prepare a 5th edition together. I am most grateful to her but take responsibility for the views expressed here. I have tried to bring the factual material as up-to-date as possible in September 2013.

unprecedented rate, such that those that had abolished it completely for all crimes in all circumstances doubled from 35 at the end of 1988 to 72 by the end of 1998.[2] Furthermore, 15 retentionist countries ceased executions between these dates and since then have been recognized by Amnesty International as 'Abolitionist in Practice'. In the international sphere such was support for a further impetus that the UN General Assembly adopted the Second Optional Protocol to the International Covenant on Civil and Political Rights (ICCPR) in 1989, article 1 of which states 'No one within the jurisdiction of a State Party … shall be executed'.

Yet the question was raised whether this dramatic change was the result of the particular political circumstances of the time, such as the break-up of the former Soviet Union, the strengthening influence of the Council of Europe and the European Union, and freedom from post-colonial repression in Africa and elsewhere. Had the impetus for change run its course? Sir Leon Radzinowicz, in his academic memoire *Adventures in Criminology*, published in 1999 shortly before his death aged 92, in a chapter entitled 'An issue which refuses to go away', wrote:

> Capital punishment has displayed throughout its chequered and frequently repellent history a truly exceptional degree of durability. This is a fact of deeply rooted and exceptional complexity which cannot be ignored or disposed of by hazy dialectics or confusing generalisations.

He pointed to 'The deadly weight of the United States' and

> a recalcitrant group of states which, for a combination of reasons – religious, political or social – proclaim their right to keep the death penalty and they are unlikely to change. They are particularly unlikely to be sympathetic to the argument that capital punishment is 'cruel and unusual' or that it should be rejected on the grounds that it violates the right to life of every individual.

It was for this reason that he concluded: 'I am inclined to state that I do not expect any substantial further decrease in the appointment and use of capital punishment in the foreseeable future' (Radzinowicz 1999: 291–3).

Grounds for Optimism

Again his pessimism went too far. True there were and remain 'recalcitrant states' but, since he penned this in 1998, 23 countries have abolished the death penalty completely and one has abolished it for 'ordinary crimes'. Another two (Mongolia and Benin) have committed themselves to do so, having ratified Protocol No. 2

2 Only seven of the 37 countries that abolished the death penalty completely in this period had previously abolished it for ordinary crimes.

to the ICCPR abolishing the death penalty as a prelude to abolishing it in their criminal codes. In the United States the death penalty has been abolished in New Jersey, New York, New Mexico, Illinois, Connecticut, and most recently in Maryland, bringing the total number of abolitionist states to 18. At the beginning of September 2013 just over half (106 including Mongolia and Benin) of the 197 independent states in the world have abolished the death penalty. Ninety-nine of them[3] have rejected it completely, an enormous increase from the 12 that had done so by 1966, the year that the ICCPR was adopted by the UN General Assembly. There are now only 39 countries that have carried out an execution since 2003. The remaining 52, which maintain capital punishment in law and have not ratified the Second Optional Protocol to the ICCPR, are classified by the United Nations as 'abolitionist *de facto*', and 33 of them are accepted as 'abolitionist in practice' by Amnesty International, meaning that there appears to be a settled policy not to carry out any executions.

At the international level, the number of countries that voted in favour of the UN resolution for a moratorium on death sentences and executions has increased over the five-year-period since it was instigated in 2007. It has risen from 104 (54 per cent) of those voting in December 2007 to 111 (60 per cent) of those voting in December 2012, while the number voting definitely against the resolution has fallen between the same dates from 54 (28 per cent) to 41 (22 per cent) of those voting. The proportion that abstained rose from 15 to 18 per cent. In 2005 when an attempt had been made at the Commission on Human Rights to secure sufficient support to bring such a resolution before the United Nations it had been opposed by 66 countries on the grounds that there was no international consensus that capital punishment was a violation of human rights and should be abolished. Once a majority of countries had been able to secure introduction of such a resolution at the general assembly in 2007, countries that objected to it in principle, led by Singapore and Egypt, have sent a *Note Verbale* to the UN Secretary-General after each resolution has been passed by a majority, dissenting from it on the same grounds, emphasizing that 'Every State has an inalienable right to choose its … legal and criminal justice systems, without interference in any form by another State' and that there was nothing in the UN Charter that authorized the UN 'to intervene in matters which are essentially within the domestic jurisdiction of any State'.[4] However, the number of countries that signed the *Notes Verbale* fell from 58 following the 2007 vote, to 53 following the vote in 2010 and to 47 following the vote in December 2012. Thus, since 2005, 19 countries have withdrawn their opposition to the international movement on these national sovereignty grounds.

3 Again including Mongolia and Benin; although it should be noted that Amnesty International still classifies them as abolitionist in practice pending abolition in their domestic law.

4 See *Note Verbale* dated 16 April 2013 from the Permanent Mission of Egypt to the United Nations addressed to the Secretary-General. A/67/841, Annex paragraph (e).

Nevertheless the fact is that there were 41 countries that felt strongly enough about the issue to vote against the resolution for a moratorium at the UN in December 2012 and, as mentioned above, there are still 39 countries[5] that have carried out at least one execution within the past ten years and another 52 that maintain the death penalty on their statute books (even if 33 of them appear committed not to resume executions). This may appear a formidable number to convince that they should abolish capital punishment entirely. Naturally, there will be those who wonder whether I and others have gone too far in declaring that the progress made so far has produced such a strong movement that it is bound to succeed. What if there were setbacks, such as dissolution of the European Union, as Nils Christie suggests could happen? Would any or all of the countries of Eastern Europe refrain from re-introducing capital punishment and instead join with Belarus, the only state still carrying out executions in Europe? 'In my evaluation', writes Nils Christie in this book, 'the European ban against death by killing is far from safely established. I do not quite share the optimism expressed in several recent articles by Roger Hood, but hope his views will be the right ones'.

Unlike my colleague William Schabas I have not tried to estimate how many years it will take before all nations outlaw execution of criminals for whatever reason, for whatever crime and under whatever circumstances. In Professor Schabas's opinion one can extrapolate the trend and pace of abolition and arrive at around 2030 as the year when the last country abolishes the death penalty. Bill Schabas has kindly set his reasoning out for me:

> For many years now, States have become abolitionist at a rate of about 2 to 3 per year. There only remain about 40 states that are still practising capital punishment actively. Do the math. Divide 40 by 2.5: that gives 16. So based on consistent patterns and trends the death penalty should effectively disappear within 16 years, or by about 2029. When I say this, people answer that some countries are so intransigent that it is impossible to think they could abandon capital punishment. To that, I recall participating in a panel at the UN headquarters in Geneva in about 1994, along with experts from South Africa and Russia. At the time, there was probably still a majority of states in the world that were considered retentionist. After I gave a little abolitionist presentation, the South African said that his country would never abolish capital punishment. He said that public opinion was deeply in favour, and that there was an extraordinary rate of violent crime. He was followed by the Russian, who said that things were even more extreme in his country, and that public opinion adored capital punishment and that the crime rate was over the top. South Africa abolished the death penalty [in 1995] and Russia [ceased executions] soon after that [in 1997]. Things change very quickly.[6]

5 Not all the same countries as voted negatively, as will be shown below.

6 Personal communication.

I have not been so bold, but I share the view that the balance in what has become a worldwide debate has tipped decisively in favour of the abolitionist camp and that abolition can occur in countries where it might be least expected, especially when there is political change in the direction of democracy. Who would have predicted that in January 2010 President Elbegdorj of Mongolia would call on the Parliament to follow the path of the majority of the world's countries and abolish the death penalty, declaring that 'The road a democratic Mongolia has to take ought to be clean and bloodless'. The Mongolian Parliament responded to his leadership and voted to ratify the Second Optional Protocol to the ICCPR abolishing the death penalty, which came into effect in mid-2012.[7]

Several aspects of the movement to achieve worldwide abolition provide support for those who believe that a 'new dynamic' has been added to the debate on capital punishment over the past quarter of a century. This has sought to move that debate beyond the view that each nation has, if it wishes, the sovereign right to retain the death penalty as a repressive tool of its domestic criminal justice system on the grounds of its purported deterrent utility or the cultural preferences and expectations of its citizens for condign retribution. It aims to persuade countries that retain the death penalty that it inevitably, and however administered, violates human rights that should be *universally* recognized and accepted. These are the rights embodied in the ICCPR, as developed by International Human Rights Institutions and in domestic constitutional courts and legislation: namely, the right not to be arbitrarily deprived of life and the right not to be subjected to a cruel, inhuman or degrading treatment or punishment. Although Article 6 of the ICCPR does not specifically ban the death penalty, allowing it in article 6(2) for countries that had not done so at the time the treaty was established, but only for the 'most serious offences', article 6(6) makes it clear what the objective was, with the words: 'Nothing in this article shall be invoked to delay or to prevent the abolition of capital punishment by any State party to the present Covenant'. Of great importance too has been the protocols aimed at worldwide abolition of the death penalty (notably Protocol No. 2 to the ICCPR (1989) and the regional Protocols Nos. 6 (1983) and 13 (2002) to the European Convention on Human Rights and the Protocol to the American Convention on Human Rights (1990). Thus the movement has been attempting to generate a global *moral* force among the nations of the world, not unlike that which swept away slavery in the nineteenth century. Over half the countries that have joined the abolitionist camp since the end of 1988 have specifically banned the death penalty in their democratically inspired constitutions, thus making it almost impossible to re-introduce it. Altogether, 87 countries have now ratified or signed one or other of the protocols to regional or international convenants which bar the imposition and reintroduction of capital

7 Available at: http://www.amnesty.org/en/news/mongolia-takes-vital-step-forward-abolishing-death-penalty-2012-01-05.

punishment.[8] Even if the countries of Eastern Europe were to leave the EU and Council of Europe, almost all would be bound by their international obligations under Protocol No 2 to the ICCPR not to return to capital punishment. It is notable how commitment to abolition as a universal goal has been galvanized by ratification of these treaties. For example, since the UK ratified Protocols Nos. 6 and 13 to the European Convention on Human Rights abolishing the death penalty and the Second Optional Protocol to the ICCPR in 1999, capital punishment is not only absent from the domestic political agenda but all parties in government have since been strongly committed to promoting abolition worldwide.

There are several other signals than the number of converts to complete abolition that illustrate the powerful influence of the new dynamic on states that cling on to the death penalty. I have discussed them elsewhere so I shall only refer to them briefly here:

- The enforcement of capital punishment in retentionist countries has also been declining. Whereas in 1998 37 countries carried out a judicial execution and 78 imposed at least one death sentence the numbers doing so in 2012 were 21 and 58.[9] With very few exceptions, such as Iran and Saudi Arabia (where public executions are still regularly and brutally carried out in both), the number of executions annually recorded appears to be falling almost everywhere. Singapore which in 2002 was revealed to have executed 112 people between 1996 and 2000 – the world's highest execution rate per head of population[10] – has reduced the number drastically: only five persons in 2009, none in 2010, four in 2011 (two for murder and two for drug trafficking), and none since then. Meanwhile the number of reported murders in Singapore has not risen but fallen – to only 16 in 2011 among a population of over five million. Malaysia, which executed between 13 and 15 persons a year between 1970 and 2000, has carried out very few executions since 2002 and none between 2010 and March 2013, despite the fact that the death penalty remains the mandatory punishment for murder, drug trafficking, and certain firearms offences committed during criminal activity. Thus, Malaysia is now a sporadic or occasional executioner as is Thailand, where there have been no executions since 2009, and Indonesia where there had been none since 2008 until a Nigerian drug trafficker was executed in March 2013. Pakistan which had executed at least 135 people in 2007 and 36 in 2008 has since then adopted a policy not to

8 Eighty-two countries are party to one or more of these treaties and a further five abolitionist countries that have not signed any of them are also barred from reintroducing capital punishment by their ratification of the American Convention on Human Rights: Article 4(3).

9 Executions were not necessarily carried out in the same year that the death sentences were imposed.

10 See Hood 2002: 92

carry out executions (although one did occur under military jurisdiction in November 2012). India also had a lengthy period with no executions between 2004 and November 2012, since when two persons accused of murders committed during terrorist attacks were executed. These examples do not demonstrate that executions are coming to an end in these countries, but they do demonstrate a hesitation to execute and an admission that they can only be justified for the most egregious cases.

- In general this reluctance to execute has meant that very few countries now enforce capital punishment on a scale which can be said to indicate a belief and commitment to it as a crime control measure. Only seven countries have regularly executed ten or more citizens every year for the past decade (2003 to 2012) and not all of them because they believe that it is a necessary deterrent to crime: China, Iran, Iraq, Saudi Arabia, North Korea (probably), Yemen and the USA.
- The majority of countries that have rejected the death penalty since the end of the 1980s have done so as a matter of principle – even though diplomatic and economic considerations have also played their part – after accepting that it cannot be enforced without an abuse of human rights embodied in the ICCPR. This has meant that many countries that appeared to be wedded to capital punishment moved quickly to remove it *completely*, especially when political change embodying democratic liberal values became accepted. For example, Turkmenistan abolished capital punishment in 1999, just two years after the last execution; South Africa in 1995 just four years after. Indeed, the majority (85 per cent) of those who abolished the death penalty for the first time since 1989 did so completely in 'one go', so to speak.[11] This is very different from the pattern in most of those countries that began to abolish the death penalty before the 1980s. Then the doctrine of Beccaria largely held sway, namely that while the death penalty should be abolished for 'ordinary' crimes it could be justified for crimes that would undermine the very existence of the state and civil society. For example, in the Netherlands there was a 112-year-gap between abolition for murder in 1870 and for all crimes in 1982.
- It is notable also that only five of the nations which abolished capital punishment since 1961, reintroduced it; Nepal, Philippines, Gambia, Papua New Guinea and Liberia. Only two of them resumed executions, the Philippines and Gambia (in 2012). Nepal and the Philippines soon abolished capital punishment again. As William Schabas has remarked, the point appears to have been reached where the death penalty once abolished is abolished forever.

11 One of the few countries not to do so, Latvia, first abolished it for ordinary offences in 1999 and then for all crimes in peacetime or wartime, under civil and military law, in 2012.

- Countries that have retained the death penalty and still carry out executions have been encouraged to restrict the types of crimes for which it may be imposed and to implement fair trial standards as required by the ICCPR and the *Safeguards Guaranteeing Protection of the Rights of those Facing the Death Penalty* promulgated by the UN beginning in 1984. Although the death penalty is still retained in law for drugs offences in 33 countries, despite this being declared a breach of article 6(2) of the ICCPR by the UN Human Rights Committee, only six of them, according to the research of Harm Reduction International, have regularly carried out executions for drug offences in the past few years on a substantial scale (Harm Reduction International 2012). It appears that the number of states that regularly carry out executions for crimes other than murder is now quite small, most notably China, Iran, Saudi Arabia, Vietnam, and probably North Korea. Furthermore, great strides have been made in banning, or evading, the imposition of the death penalty as the *mandatory* punishment for murder, drugs offences, robbery or other crimes. It appears that more and more retentionist countries are coming to accept that executions, prior to complete abolition, can only be justified on a discretionary basis for the 'worst of the worst' cases of murder.
- Although this has been pointed out many times, it remains highly significant that the death penalty was excluded as a punishment by the UN Security Council when it established the International Criminal Tribunals to deal with atrocities in the former Yugoslavia in 1993 and Rwanda in 1994, and later in Sierra Leone and Lebanon. Nor is it available as a sanction for genocide, other grave crimes against humanity and war crimes in the Statute of the International Criminal Court established in 1998. This has provided a powerful argument: If it is not available for these atrocious crimes why should it be inflicted as a disproportionate punishment for lesser crimes?

A Universal Right?

Whether the movement is successful will depend, of course, on the extent to which it is able to persuade retentionist countries that protection of citizens from being put to death by the State is a *universal right*, and not merely a question of national criminal justice policy determined by culture or history, or in the belief that it is a necessary deterrent penal measure that lies entirely within a state's jurisdictional competence to enforce or not. This will entail persuading them to reject one of the most persistent justifications for capital punishment: namely, retribution and the need to denounce, expiate and eliminate through execution those whose crimes shock society by their brutality; to accept the view that all human beings have a right to be able to redeem themselves; and that a state has no necessity and no right to take the life of a *captive* citizen. They will also have to reject the utilitarian justification that nothing less severe can act as a sufficient deterrent to those who contemplate committing capital crimes. This is not only because the social science evidence does not support the claims either that executions do or do not have a deterrent impact on the rate of homicide – a finding endorsed by the American National Academy of Sciences in 1978 after a thorough study of all the evidence and again in 2012 after reviewing a further spate of research – but because even if it could have a marginal deterrent effect, this could only be achieved by high rates of execution, mandatorily and speedily enforced. This, abolitionists assert, would increase the probability of innocent or wrongfully convicted persons being executed and also lead to the execution of people for whom, because of the mitigating circumstances in which their crimes were committed, death would be a disproportionate punishment.

Of course, many retentionist countries seek to justify the retention of capital punishment on the grounds that it is a democratically demanded criminal sanction by a large majority of the population which can only be ignored by politicians at their peril, or that without its enforcement there would be a breakdown of order and the criminal justice system and government would lose legitimacy (see Sato 2013).

Abolitionists accept that public opinion cannot be entirely ignored but argue that a country concerned for human rights should not merely accept popular opinion as a reason for retaining the death penalty – especially when it may be based on misconceptions about the assumed deterrent effect of capital punishment, the fairness rather than the arbitrariness of its application, absence of error rather than evidence of mistakes, and other human rights considerations. Evidence that the death penalty may have been erroneously applied to the innocent has a very strong effect on the extent to which members of the public will support the death penalty. Public opinion polls in China,[12] Trinidad[13] and Malaysia,[14] have all shown that when respondents have been asked whether they would be in favour of the death penalty if it were proven to their satisfaction that an innocent person had been executed, the proportion supporting capital punishment has fallen from between 75 to 90 per cent to between a quarter and a third of the respondents. It needs to be remembered that no countries have abolished the death penalty because of popular demand as reflected in opinion polls. The evidence suggests therefore that public opinion is not a bar to abolition. Indeed abolition has been subsequently endorsed at a later date by public opinion, as for example in Ireland. Furthermore, it needs to be recognized that public opinion may be swayed by the emotions aroused by terrible crimes but revert to much lower levels of support in normal times. Nor do the views of angry crowds or of 'netizens' necessarily reflect basic public attitudes on an issue such as capital punishment.

The abolitionist stance is that a government committed to human rights should instead regard its task as informing and leading the general public to appreciate

12 See Oberwittler and Qi 2009, Hood 2009, Zimring and Johnson 2012.

13 See Hood and Seemungal 2011: 18.

14 See Hood 2013.

and then to accept the human rights case for abolition, namely in the words of the EU Guidelines on the Death Penalty that it 'contributes to the enhancement of human dignity and the progressive development of human rights'. The plain fact is that experience of administering capital punishment throughout the world has shown that no perfect system has been devised that can avoid arbitrariness, error and cruelty in its administration. It was of great significance that in post-apartheid South Africa, the newly created Constitutional Court abolished the death penalty in 1995, in face of public opinion in its favour. The Court declared that it was incompatible with the prohibition against cruel, inhuman or degrading punishment and with 'a human rights culture' which would 'protect the rights of minorities and others who cannot protect their rights adequately through the democratic process' (see Hood and Hoyle 2008: 381–2). In other words the abolitionist position is that the law should protect the rights of prisoners in the face of outbursts of vengeful emotions – not satisfy and reinforce such emotions.

Experience shows that a generation that has grown up with the *expectation* that death will be the punishment for murder is relatively slow to abandon this idea, but after abolition the next generation, growing to maturity with no such experience and therefore any expectation, is far more likely to regard capital punishment as a barbaric relic of the past, abandoned as civilization has progressed. In the United Kingdom, for example, demands for the death penalty are now very rare compared to the time when death was the mandatory penalty for murder. The issue is no longer on the political agenda of any party or political faction. Nor is it in France or Germany. The response of the Norwegian people to the mass killing of young people by a racist fanatic in July 2011, described in this book, provides a vivid testimony. The government led the way in rejecting any calls for revenge and imposition of the death penalty and the people responded with a great show of solidarity.

The influence exerted by the weight of numbers as more and more countries have embraced the human rights case for abolition has itself strengthened the *normative* legitimacy of the case against capital punishment. This is well illustrated by the change in the decisions reached regarding extradition of prisoners from Canada to the USA. In 1991 in the case of *Kindler v. Canada*, both the Canadian Supreme Court and the United Nations Human Rights Committee held that there was no bar to extradition because there was no international consensus on the issue of capital punishment. Yet ten years later in *United States v. Burns* (2001) and *Judge v. Canada* (2003) both bodies held that it would be a violation of the defendants' right to life to extradite them without assurances that they would not be executed. They did so because, as the Canadian Supreme Court put it, of the 'significant movement towards acceptance internationally of a principle of fundamental justice … namely the abolition of capital punishment'.[15] In similar vein, in the case of *Öcalan v. Turkey* in March 2003, the European Court of

15 *Kindler v. Canada [1991] 2SCR, 779*; *United States v. Burns* [2001] 1SCR 283; *Judge v. Canada*, HRC Communication No. 829/1998, UN Doc. CCPR/C/79/D/ 1998 (2003).

Human Rights endorsed the view that capital punishment amounts to a form of inhuman treatment which can 'no longer be seen as having any legitimate place in a democratic society'.[16] In 2010, in the case of *Al-Saadoon and Mufdhi v. United Kingdom*[17] the Court was able to proclaim that the death penalty was now contrary to Article 3 of the European Convention on Human Rights (protecting citizens from inhuman or degrading treatment or punishment), despite the fact that article 2(1) had made an exception to the right to life in the case of lawful executions, because over the 60 years since the Convention was adopted, law and practice had evolved to the position where almost all member states of the Council of Europe had abolished the death penalty completely by ratifying Protocol No. 13 to the ECHR (Lehrfreund 2013: 28).[18]

Which Countries Remain to be 'Converted'?

It is helpful to review the countries that voted against the resolution at the UN General Assembly in December 2012 calling for a worldwide moratorium, as well as those which did not, but nevertheless retain the death penalty in law. Table 14.1 shows the countries that voted against the resolution by region and according to when they carried out the last execution.

Several facts stand out:

- Of the 41 countries that voted against the 2012 moratorium resolution, more than a third (16 or 39 per cent) have not executed any person for at least ten years (ADF, the last in Qatar was in March 2003), and five of them are regarded by Amnesty International as 'abolitionist in practice' (AP). These five countries (Burma, Brunei, Grenada, Swaziland and Tonga) presumably voted against on the grounds that the resolution was an attack on their sovereignty, rather than they were against a moratorium as such.
- Of the 25 that can be called 'active retentionists' only one was in the western world: the USA which carried out executions in 2012 and so far in 2013. Nine countries were in the Middle East and North Africa, all with Muslim majority populations, six of which carried out an execution in 2012 and/or 2013. Nine were in Asia and eight of them executed in 2012 and/or 2013. Six were in Africa south of the Sahara, two of which executed in 2012 and/or 2013.

16 Öcalan v. *Turkey*, Application No. 46221/99, ECHR, Judgment 12 March 2003 and 12 May 2005.

17 *Al-Saadoon and Mufdhi v. United Kingdom*, Council of Europe, European Court of Human Rights, Application No. 61498/08, 2 March 2010.

18 As of 3 October 2010, 43 of the 47 member states had ratified protocol 13, two have signed but not yet ratified it (Armenia and Poland) and two have yet to sign or ratify it (Azerbaijan and the Russian Federation).

Table 14.1 Countries that voted against the resolution for a worldwide moratorium on the death penalty in December 2012

Western	Last execution	North Africa and Middle East	Last execution	Asia	Last execution	Africa South of the Sahara	Last execution
Bahamas*	2000 ADF	Bahrain	2008	Afghanistan	2012	Botswana	2012
Barbados	1984 ADF	Egypt	2011	Bangladesh	2012	Ethiopia	2007
Belize*	1985 ADF	Iran	2013	Brunei	1957 AP	Sudan	2013
Dominica*	1986 ADF	Iraq	2013	China	2013	Swaziland	1983 AP
Grenada	1978 AP	Kuwait	2013	N. Korea	2013	Uganda	1999 (Civil) 2006 (Military)
Guyana	1996 ADF	Libya	2010	India	2013	Zimbabwe	2004
Jamaica	1988 ADF	Oman	2001 ADF	Japan*	2013		
St Kitts and Nevis	2008	Qatar	2003 ADF	Malaysia	2013		
St Lucia	1995 ADF	Saudi Arabia	2013	Myanmar/ Burma	1989 AP		
St Vincent and Grenadines	1995 ADF	Syria	2012	Pakistan	2012 (Military)		
Trinidad and Tobago	1999 ADF	Yemen	2013	Singapore	2011		
USA*	2013			Tonga	1982 AP		

* These five countries (Bahamas, Belize, Dominica, and notably Japan and the USA) did NOT sign the *Note Verbale* of Dissent sent to the UN in April 2013 following the 2012 moratorium vote (see page 295 above). ADF = Abolitionist *de facto*, AP signifies those ADF countries that Amnesty International regards as truly 'abolitionist in practice'.

- Thus, only 25, less than two-thirds (64 per cent) of the 39 active retentionists countries that have executed anyone within the past ten years and not yet established a moratorium, voted against the resolution. They account for only 13 per cent of all 197 countries.
- All but five of the 41 countries opposed to the moratorium resolution also signed the *Note Verbale* of dissent (see note to Table 14.1) but it is significant that neither Japan nor the USA were signatories.
- In addition to the 25 actively retentionist countries that had voted against the resolution for a moratorium in December 2012, there were ten countries that had also executed within the past ten years (date in brackets) but which did ***not*** *vote against the resolution.*[19]
- Two voted in favour: Somalia (2013) and South Sudan (2013), and
- Eight abstained: Belarus (2012), Indonesia (2013), Jordan (2006), Lebanon (2004), Nigeria (2007/2013), Thailand (2009), United Arab Emirates (2013), Vietnam (2013).
- Thus seven of these ten countries executed in 2012 or so far in 2013 but only three of the ten (Nigeria, Somalia and United Arab Emirates) signed the *Note Verbale* of dissent in 2013 following the 2012 moratorium resolution.

Before moving to a brief consideration of the depth of opposition to abolition and the significance of particular countries, something must be said about the substantial number of jurisdictions that retain the death penalty in law but are classified as abolitionist *de facto*, or 'in practice'. Abolitionist organizations have been tempted to lump these countries together with those who have abolished it in law so as to marginalize further those who continue to execute. For example, the recently established International Commission against the Death Penalty has stated that 'according to the UN, over 150 countries have abolished the death penalty in law and practice' (*Herald Tribune* article, 21 Feb 2013) and that 'These nations have accepted that state killing is wrong and fails to deter crime'. Three things need to be said about this. First, a policy of non-execution by 'abolitionist in practice' countries does not mean that death sentences are not imposed, nor that they are immediately commuted to a term of (usually life) imprisonment. In fact, Amnesty International reports death sentences imposed in 16 of the 35 'abolitionist in practice' countries that were on its list in 2012. Second, the assumption that executions will never be carried out can sometimes be negated, such as happened in Gambia in August 2012 when nine prisoners were executed after 27 years had passed without a single execution. Third, as Table 14.1 illustrates, some of these countries might not ally themselves with those who bring forward resolutions at the United Nations calling for a moratorium on death sentences and executions in all countries. For instance, at the United Nations General Assembly

19 Not including Chad (which voted in favour) nor Cuba and The Democratic Republic of the Congo (which both abstained). All three countries last executed a person in 2003.

in December 2012, 21 of the 34 'abolitionist in practice' countries which voted either abstained (16) or voted against the resolution (5): only 13 supported it. The number abstaining was higher than in 2008 when 14 did so. It is clearly important that those who lead the campaigns for worldwide abolition should not assume, as sometimes they seem to do, that those who maintain the death penalty in law but do not execute, can be counted 'in the bag'. If most of them could be persuaded to reform their laws, the total of *completely abolitionist* nations would have an even greater impact on the minority who continue to execute, even if only sporadically.

Depth of the Opposition to Worldwide Abolition

Nevertheless, the evidence reviewed above from these voting patterns does not reveal an overwhelming hostility to abolition, or put another way, a large number of nations committed to capital punishment as a crime control measure. Let me briefly discuss the depth of opposition likely to be found. As can be seen in Table 14.1, 11 of the 41 countries that opposed the resolution for a moratorium in December 2012 are small island states in the Commonwealth Caribbean. They grimly maintain the death penalty in law but successful challenges by dedicated human rights lawyers have made it evident that they cannot execute without breaching international human rights law.[20] There has only been one execution within the past ten years. In time they may well accept that they cannot continue to flout international opinion and pressure.

In the Middle East and North Africa, where the population is overwhelmingly Muslim, the number of countries that execute regularly on a substantial scale has now been reduced to Iran, Saudi Arabia, Yemen and Iraq, where it is being used in a war against insurgents. Three Arab countries – Tunisia (1991), Algeria (1993) and Morocco (1993) – have not carried out any judicial executions for almost 20 years and at the end of 2011 Tunisia indicted that it would ratify the Protocol to the ICCPR abolishing the death penalty. Abolition has also been under consideration in Jordan, Morocco (as discussed by Mohammed Ayatt in this book) and Lebanon, and executions have sharply declined in Egypt. Many human rights activists in the area maintain hopes that the so-called 'Arab spring' will further boost the abolitionist movement. In fact several secular states with large Muslim majorities have already joined the abolitionist movement: such as Albania, Azerbaijan, Bosnia-Herzegovina, Kyrgyzstan, Turkey, Turkmenistan and Senegal. Execution rates in Muslim Asia are now at a low level. According to Arab human rights scholars, whether and at what speed retentionist Islamic states will move towards abolition will depend on whether their political and legal systems remain dominated by clerics who support a fundamentalist interpretation of Islam, or whether these states move towards secular democratic government, which will allow for a more modern, 'scientific', less authoritarian and more merciful

20 For an analysis of the position in the Commonwealth see Hood 2008.

interpretation of the Sharia. The fascinating progressive views of Mohammed Habash in this book, based on a humanistic understanding of Islamic teaching, deserve wide attention. They will surely be grasped when political change comes to Iran, Saudi Arabia, and Yemen, and when peace comes to Iraq and Syria.

At the end of 1988, when I published my first report to the UN, the only countries in the African region that had abolished the death penalty were Seychelles and Cape Verde, whereas 16 countries are now completely abolitionist (the most recent being Burundi, Togo and Gabon, soon to be followed by Benin and perhaps by Ghana where the Constitutional Review Commission has recommended that the new Constitution should prohibit the death penalty). Another 21 have not executed anyone for at least ten years. Judicial executions were carried out in 2012 south of the Sahara only in Botswana, Gambia, South Sudan and Somalia, and in Nigeria in 2013. I mentioned above the recent executions in Gambia. It is notable that such was the intensity of international condemnation, notably from the African Union (whose Commission on Human and People's Rights favours an Optional Protocol to the African Charter),[21] that the threat to execute all the other 36 prisoners on death row was quickly suspended by the President of Gambia.

In Asia, voices are now being raised against the death penalty in Indonesia, Malaysia and Thailand. Vietnam, Pakistan and Bangladesh have greatly moderated their stance and their practice. As Bikramjeet Batra explains in this book, India is embroiled in confronting terrorist outrages otherwise it may well have been in line to become at least 'abolitionist *de facto*' by 2014.[22] There is not space to discuss Japan and Taiwan in detail, but suffice it to say that a return to executions (after short moratoria connected with the appointment of Justice Ministers who were opposed to the death penalty had given hope that abolition would follow), has brought the subject more acutely into political debate and highlighted the issue as one that affects adversely the international reputations of both countries. The President of Taiwan in April 2012, when introducing his country's first human rights report stated that he would 'seek public consensus on the issue to move towards the abolition of capital punishment'.[23] Abolition in Taiwan could not fail to have a positive influence on attitudes in the People's Republic of China.

The attitude of the Communist Party of China is changing. China has defended its use of the death penalty on the grounds that Chinese society is still in a state of social transformation, in which public security and stability cannot be guaranteed without the general deterrent impact of the death penalty, and that retributivism, especially the demand for 'a life-for a life', is so deeply rooted in Chinese culture

---

21 'Study on the issue of the death penalty in Africa', May 2012. Available at http://www.fiacat.org/study-on-the-issue-of-the-death-penalty-in-africa.

22 See also Roger Hood 2012: 20–22.

23 'Taiwan: death penalty policy remains unchanged – Justice Minister', 27 October 2011, Central News Agency report, 27 October 2011. And 'Taiwan President vows to work towards ending Death Penalty', Taipei Times.com, 21 April 2012. Available at www.handsoffcain.info/news/index.php?iddocumento=16304931.

that without a change in public opinion the legitimacy of the legal system would be undermined by abolition. This is a claim on which the EU-sponsored public opinion survey carried out in China in 2007, has cast considerable doubt. For example, when asked whether China should speed up the process to abolish the death penalty, only 53 per cent of respondents were opposed to doing so and a further 33 per cent were 'unsure'. This can hardly be said to indicate a fervent desire for capital punishment of a kind that would make abolition politically impossible to achieve. As Susan Trevaskes, a scholar of Chinese criminal justice, has put it, abolition is 'a political choice' arising from a political culture, 'rather than merely the reflection of an immutable cultural norm' (Trevaskes 2012). Borge Bakken argues convincingly in this book that the opinion of elite groups is holding back abolition more than the opinions of the common people.

Nevertheless, the worldwide trends have not been ignored or the United Nations goal rejected. In 2007 the Chinese delegate at the UN Human Rights Council declared: 'The death penalty's scope of application was to be reviewed shortly … with the final aim of abolishment'.[24] Thus the debate in China is no longer stuck on the question of whether or not the death penalty should be abolished: it is about how abolition might be achieved and at what pace reforms should be introduced. The programme adopted is one of gradualism, aimed at making step-by-step reforms in criminal procedure to reach international standards for fair trials, to reduce the scope of the death penalty in the criminal code, and to regulate and moderate sentencing practices to reduce disparities and the total number of executions. Although no one expects complete abolition to be reached for some time, the path appears to have been set. That process began in 2007 with the return of the review of all death penalty sentences to immediate execution from the Provincial High Courts (to which it had been delegated during the 'strike hard' campaigns that began in the 1980s) to the Supreme People's Court (SPC). According to former Chief Justice Xiao Yang, the aim was to impose the death penalty 'strictly, cautiously and fairly … on a tiny number of serious criminal offenders'. This was seen as part of the project of President Hu Jintao for 'Constructing a Socialist Harmonious Society', the criminal policy of which was henceforth no longer to emphasize 'striking hard' but to 'Combine Punishment with Leniency'. Furthermore, China has begun to reduce the number of offences subject to capital punishment. On 25 February 2011 the Chinese legislature adopted Amendment VIII to the Criminal Law which abolished the death penalty for 13 non-violent crimes, thus reducing the total number from 68 to 55 (see Liu Renwen 2013).

It is most regrettable that the Chinese government still refuses to publish any statistics on the number of its citizens sentenced to death annually and the number of them executed and for what crimes. Professor Philip Alston, when he was UN Special Rapporteur for Extrajudicial, Summary or Arbitrary Executions, stigmatized secrecy over the use of the death penalty as 'a violation of human

24 Human Rights Committee, 'Human Rights Council Opens Fourth Session', HRC/07/3, 12 March 2007, p. 9.

rights standards' (Hood and Hoyle 2008: 154). Chinese Criminal Law Professors have also openly joined the call for publication of the statistics on the ground, as one put it at a workshop held in 2009:

> [I]t was a 'moral obligation [on China] as a member of the UN' and would have two advantages: '1) so as to correctly understand the function and role of the death penalty to provide objective, scientific basis, 2) to put the community under the supervision of the whole world, is conducive to strictly limit and reduce the death penalty'. (Hood 2012: 44)

Nevertheless, it is claimed that the influence exercised by the SPC, directly by its own decisions in overturning immediate death sentences and substituting suspended death sentences, and indirectly by changing the sentencing culture of the lower courts, has reduced the annual number of persons executed by at least a half of what the number had been in 2005: possibly from around 8,000 per annum to around 4,000. The UN Secretary-General's Eighth Quinquennial Report on Capital Punishment concluded: 'That there is an important decline in the use of the death penalty within China ... does not seem to be in much doubt'.[25] Nor can it be doubted that the international movement has had a strong influence (see Miao 2013). As Professor Zhao Bingzhi of Beijing Normal University put it at an international meeting I attended in 2009: 'Abolition is an *inevitable international tide and trend* as well as a signal showing the broad-mindedness of civilized countries ... *[abolition] is now an international obligation*' (Bingzhi and Shuiming 2009: 37, my italics). I could not have imagined that anyone would have said this publicly in 2000 when I first went to China to discuss the death penalty.

Further progress in China will depend on the extent to which the academic and judicial elite can influence the political policy makers to accept that the question of whether a modern state should employ the death penalty has advanced to the point when it ought no longer to be conceived narrowly as an acceptable form of crime control governed largely, even if no longer entirely, by national sovereignty. Ratification of the ICCPR by China would be a great step forward in raising the consciousness of Chinese citizens and criminal justice institutions to respect their country's human rights obligations. Watch this space!

The position taken by the United States, to be specific by the retentionist states and the United States Supreme Court, is in my opinion crucial to achieving the goal of worldwide abolition, because many countries that retain the death penalty point to the USA in support of their position that it is *not* a human rights issue. How could it be if the great democratic champion of human rights still retains it? The Federal government has yet to embrace the aspiration, embodied in Article 6 of the ICCPR and UN Resolutions, to abolish the death penalty in due course. Indeed, the official position of the US government communicated to the UN is that:

25 UN doc. E/2010/10, para. 37.

> … in democratic societies the criminal justice system – including the punishment prescribed for the most serious and aggravated crimes – should reflect the will of the people freely expressed and appropriately implemented through their elected representatives. (Hood and Hoyle 2008: 35)

As David Garland has so elegantly expressed it, capital punishment in the United States is a 'peculiar institution' in many respects. Most pertinent is that it is almost wholly under the control of the individual states, subject only to the interpretation of the constitutions of those states by their Supreme Courts and of the US Constitution by the US Supreme Court. The states that retain the death penalty are largely shielded from the international discourse and pressures that have so obviously influenced many other countries.

So what, briefly, are the prospects that the USA as a whole will abandon capital punishment? As in most of the rest of the world the death penalty in the US is in decline and distributed unevenly in frequency of use. Six states have recently abolished it – New Jersey, New York, New Mexico, Illinois, Connecticut and Maryland. There are now 18 non-death penalty states, and 32 that retain it. Others appear to be moving in the same direction, Oregon among them where the Governor has announced a moratorium on executions.

Only nine of the 51 US state jurisdictions actually executed anyone in 2012. Texas alone accounted for 15 of the 43 executions, and along with three other states – Arizona, Mississippi and Oklahoma – accounted for 77 per cent of all executions in the USA. Indeed only ten states have on average executed at least one person a year since executions were permitted to resume in 1976, eight of them in the old south plus Oklahoma and Ohio. The political scientist, Frank Baumgartner, has shown that in only 14 per cent of over 3,000 counties in the USA had there been an execution between 1976 and 2010 (Baumgartner 2010). The number of death sentences imposed annually in the US has fallen from 315 in 1996, when there were about 20,000 murders recorded in the USA, to only 78 in 2012, when recorded murders had declined to around 13,000 a year.

In 2009 the influential American Law Institute decided that it would withdraw its support for the death penalty 'in light of the current intractable institutional and structural obstacles to ensuring a minimally adequate system for administering capital punishment' (C.S. Steiker and J.M. Steiker 2009). Indeed, the growing acceptance of the fact that no 'perfect, no fault or error' system can be devised; that in practice the death penalty cannot be administered fairly, evenly and without discrimination; that attempts to create a 'super due process' system entails very high costs to the state as cases wind for years through state and federal appeals processes with a very low probability that an execution will eventually occur; the revelation that even lethal injection cannot be guaranteed to result in a non-tortuous death; the terrible plight of prisoners on death row for many years and the heartless cruelty of executing them sometimes decades after their conviction; and the incontrovertible evidence that 143 innocent people sentenced to death in 26 states have been exonerated since 1973, may combine to persuade yet more states to follow those that have already banned capital punishment. The impression often given, that in America there is enthusiasm everywhere for executions is now wide of the mark. According to opinion polls, public support has fallen from 80 per cent in 1994 to 60 per cent in October 2013. In November 2012 California held a referendum (Proposition 34) to decide whether the death penalty should be abolished and replaced by life imprisonment without parole. It was defeated by a margin of only six percentage points (53 to 47 per cent).

In recent years the US Supreme Court has begun to recognize human rights norms that have been established elsewhere in the world. The decisions to ban the execution of the so-called mentally retarded (*Atkins v. Virginia*, 2002) and of juveniles convicted of murders committed before the age of 18 (*Roper v. Simmons*, 2005), cited worldwide condemnation of these practices (although not admitting that they were determinative) in support of the evidence that the trend towards abolition of capital punishment for these categories of persons in US States had revealed an 'emerging standard of decency'. The same is emerging for capital punishment as a whole. The 18 abolitionist states will not be the only ones that will reject the death penalty. Quite soon there may come a 'tipping point', a trend that the Supreme Court could not ignore. So those who campaign for abolition worldwide can hope that it will not be many years before the US Supreme Court will be able to find that the majority of States, in line with a majority of countries worldwide, do not support the death penalty for anyone, and therefore rule that 'emerging standards of decency' – in other words that capital punishment *per se* infringes constitutional protection of human rights – will no longer tolerate the use of this cruel and unusual punishment for any crime in any part of the USA, a prospect that both David Garland and John Bessler look forward to in their chapters in this book. The impact will be profound in many parts of the world.

Conclusion

Although a sizeable number of countries remain resistant to the abolition of capital punishment, that number is steadily diminishing. Countries that have opposed the attempt by abolitionist nations to bring about a universal end to capital punishment have stigmatized their efforts as a form of cultural imperialism, as an attack on national sovereignty and an attempt to turn a 'domestic criminal justice issue' into a 'human rights issue'. This implies that if it is one it cannot also be the other. In my opinion this is a false antithesis. Abolition has been embraced across the globe by many different political systems, peoples, religious creeds and cultures. So there can be no doubt that the emphasis on universal 'human rights' has added greatly to the normative, moral, force propelling the abolitionist movement.

There are international treaties that limit the powers of all governments in relation to how they treat their citizens. For instance it is now agreed that no country should enforce or permit slavery. The same case can be made as regards the weight and brutality of punishments inflicted on captive convicted citizens. In other words there should be limits to the power that the state can be permitted to exercise over persons accused of and convicted of crimes, however serious: limits defined by universal human rights principles which should apply to all citizens of the world. So although the choice of a system of punishments *is* a matter for national sovereignty they should not be punishments that are inflicted arbitrarily and inhumanely such that they breach the human rights of the convicted. In almost all the countries that retain and enforce capital punishment, the human rights dynamic has at least produced great restraint. However much they might complain of international pressure, they appear to have accepted that reform is essential.

To sum up: The key to the argument of whether abolition of the death penalty should now be regarded as a goal that *all* countries committed to human rights should pursue lies in the interpretation of Articles 6 and 7 of the ICCPR which all but a few states that retain capital punishment, such as Saudi Arabia, Malaysia and Singapore, have signed or ratified. As mentioned already in this article, it is absolutely clear what the aspiration of this treaty is, as spelled out in Article 6(6) – 'Nothing in [article 6] shall be invoked to delay or to prevent the abolition of capital punishment by any State Party to the present Covenant'. Those countries that still favour capital punishment 'in principle' or believe that it is a necessary weapon in their penal armoury are being faced with convincing evidence of the abuses, discrimination, mistakes, and inhumanity which inevitably accompany it in practice, as has been revealed by death penalty scholars and human rights lawyers. So it clearly breaches Article 7, which protects all citizens from cruel, inhuman or degrading treatment or punishment.

In my view, it is right to press all states party to the ICCPR that still retain the death penalty to recognize that they should feel morally bound by the universalistic goals of the International Covenant to do nothing to delay or prevent the final abolition of capital punishment.

The road is still rocky and the end not yet clearly in sight, but the normative pressure of the abolitionist movement is undoubtedly putting pressure on states that aspire to world recognition as defenders of human rights to abandon the practice. The more that do, the more isolated those who resist will become. When a critical mass is reached and especially when influential powers – such as the USA, China, Japan, India and Egypt – abandon the death penalty, those who still maintain it will come under international pressure to conform to international standards for human rights in the enforcement of punishment. Abolition of capital punishment and its replacement by a humane system of imprisonment is clearly becoming the litmus test for the respect for human rights.

References

Al-Saadoon and Mufdhi v. United Kingdom, Council of Europe, European Court of Human Rights, Application No 61498/08, 2 March 2010.

Baumgartner, F. 2010. *The Geography of the Death Penalty.* Cited on the website of The Death Penalty Information Center. Available at http://www.unc.edu/~fbaum/Innocence/NC/Baumgartner-geography-of-capital-punishment-oct-17-2010.pdf.

Bingzhi, Zhao and Shuiming, Wang 2009. *Development Trend in Death Penalty in Contemporary Era and its Inspiration for China.* Guangzhou China, June 2009.

Harm Reduction International 2012. *The Death Penalty for Drugs Offences: Global Overview 2012. Tipping the Scales for Abolition.* London: Harm Reduction International.

Hood, R. 1989. *The Death Penalty. A World-wide Perspective,* Oxford: Oxford University Press, 1989, at p. 159.

Hood, R. 2002. *The Death Penalty. A World-wide Perspective.* [3rd edition]. Oxford: Oxford University Press, at p. 92.

Hood, R. 2008. Capital Punishment: The Commonwealth in World Perspective. *The Commonwealth Lawyer*, 17(3), 30–35.

Hood, R. 2009. Abolition of the Death Penalty: China in World Perspective. *City University of Hong Kong Law Review*, I(1), 1–22 at 18–21.

Hood, R. 2012. *Enhancing EU Action on the Death Penalty in Asia.* Briefing Paper for the European Parliament, EXPO/B/DROI/2011/22/October/2012.

Hood, R. 2013. *The Death Penalty in Malaysia: Public Opinion on the Mandatory Death Penalty for Drug Trafficking, Firearms Act Offences, and Murder.* London: The Death Penalty Project.

Hood, R. and Hoyle, C. 2008. *The Death Penalty: A Worldwide Perspective.* [4th edition]. Oxford: Oxford University Press.

Hood, R. and Seemungal, F. 2011. *Public Opinion on the Mandatory Death Penalty in Trinidad.* London: The Death Penalty Project.

Kaiser, G. 1986. Capital Punishment in a Criminological Perspective. *United Nations Crime Prevention and Criminal Justice Newsletter*, 12 and 13, 10–18. See also the Introduction.

Kindler v. Canada [1991] 2SCR, 779; United States v. Burns [2001] 1SCR 283; *Judge v. Canada,* HRC Communication No. 829/1998, UN Doc. CCPR/C/79/D/ 1998 (2003).

Lehrfreund, S. 2013. 'The Impact and Importance of International Human Rights Standards: Asia in World Perspective' in Roger Hood and Surya Deva (eds), *Confronting Capital Punishment in Asia: Human Rights, Politics and Public Opinion.* Oxford: Oxford University Press, 23–45.

Liu, Renwen 2013 'Recent Reforms and Prospects in China' in Roger Hood and Surya Deva (eds), *Confronting Capital Punishment in Asia: Human Rights, Politics and Public Opinion.* Oxford: Oxford University Press, 107–22.

Miao, M. 2013. 'Examining China's Response to the Global Campaign Against the Death Penalty' in Roger Hood and Surya Deva (eds), *Confronting Capital Punishment in Asia: Human Rights, Politics and Public Opinion.* Oxford: Oxford University Press, 46–67.

Oberwittler, D. and Qi, S. 2009. *Public Opinion on the Death Penalty in China. Results from a General Population Survey Conducted in Three Provinces in 2007/08.* Max Planck Institute for Foreign and International Criminal Law [Online] Available at http://www.mpicc.de/ww/en/prs/forschung/forschung sarbeit/kriminologie/death_penalty.htm.

Öcalan v. Turkey, Application No. 46221/99, ECHR, Judgement 12 March 2003 and 12 May 2005.

Radzinowicz, L. 1999. *Adventures in Criminology.* London: Routledge.

Sato, Mai 2013 'Challenging the Japanese Government's Approach to the Death Penalty' in Roger Hood and Surya Deva (eds), *Confronting Capital Punishment in Asia: Human Rights, Politics and Public Opinion.* Oxford: Oxford University Press, 205–18.

Steiker, C.S. and Steiker, J.M. 2009. *Report to the ALI Concerning Capital Punishment*, Annex to *Report of the Council to the Membership of The American Law Institute On the Matter of the Death Penalty*, New York: ALI, April 15, 2009.

'Taiwan: death penalty policy remains unchanged – Justice Minister', 27 October 2011, Central News Agency report 27 October 2011. And 'Taiwan President vows to work towards ending Death Penalty', Taipei Times.com 21 April 2012. Available at www.handsoffcain.info/news/index.php?iddocumento=16304931.

Trevaskes, S. 2012. *The Death Penalty in Contemporary China.* New York: Palgrave Macmillan.

Zimring, F. and Johnson, D. 2012. Public Opinion and Death Penalty Reform in the People's Republic of China. *City University of Hong Kong Law Review*, 3(2), 189–96.

Index

www.ingramcontent.com/pod-product-compliance
Ingram Content Group UK Ltd.
Pitfield, Milton Keynes, MK11 3LW, UK
UKHW022011180926
475701UK00003B/306
9780367600839